PRICING

AND

REVENUE OPTIMIZATION

PRICING

AND

REVENUE OPTIMIZATION

ROBERT L. PHILLIPS

STANFORD BUSINESS BOOKS
An imprint of Stanford University Press
Stanford, California

Stanford University Press
Stanford, California

Printed in the United States of America on acid-free, archival-quality paper

Library of Congress Cataloging-in-Publication Data

Phillips, Robert L. (Robert Lewis), 1955–
   Pricing and revenue optimization / Robert L. Phillips.
     p.   cm.
   Includes bibliographical references and index.
   ISBN 0-8047-4698-2 (cloth : alk. paper)
   1. Pricing.   2. Revenue management.   I. Title.
   HF5416.5.P457 2005
   658.15′54—dc22

                       2005009126

Typeset by G&S Book Services in 10/13.5 Minion

Original Printing 2005
Reprinted with corrections 2011

To Doria with love and gratitude

CONTENTS

PREFACE

This book grew out of courses in pricing and revenue optimization developed at Columbia University and Stanford University.[1] At the time there were few other comparable courses.[2] Since then, it has become clear that there is growing interest in pricing and revenue optimization (a.k.a. *revenue management* and *dynamic pricing*) as a topic of study within both business schools and management science/operations research departments. This interest is quite understandable: Not only is pricing and revenue optimization an important applications arena for quantitative analysis, it has achieved widely publicized successes in many industries, and there is growing interest in the techniques of pricing and revenue optimization across many different industries. Some of the issues involved in developing and teaching an MBA course in pricing and revenue optimization have been treated in articles by Peter Bell (2004) and myself (Phillips 2004).

The primary audience for this book is students at the MBA, masters, or undergraduate level. The book assumes some familiarity with probabilistic modeling and optimization theory and comfort with basic calculus. Sections that require somewhat more quantitative sophistication (or at least more patience) have been marked with an asterisk (*) and can be skipped without loss of continuity. In pricing and revenue optimization, as in other applications of management science, what is theoretically elegant is often not practical and what is practical is usually not theoretically elegant. When in doubt, I have erred on the side of presenting the practical. For those who would like to dive deeper into the theory, I would recommend Talluri and van Ryzin's *The Theory and Practice of Revenue Management* (2004).

Among those who read drafts of this book and generously provided comments and suggestions, pride of place belongs to Michael Harrison, who cotaught the pricing and revenue optimization course with me at the Stanford Business School. Not only did Mike read the first draft and provide many helpful comments, but our discussions helped me focus my own thinking. I am also thankful to Brenda Barnes, whose careful reading and thoughtful comments on several chapters resulted in substantial improvements. The late Ken McLeod of Stanford University Press provided encouragement and inspiration in the early days of writing the book. He is very much missed. I would also like to thank Dean Boyd, Bill Carroll, Yosun Denizeri, Michael Eldredge, Mehran Farahmand, Scott Friend, Steve Haas, Jake

Krakauer, Ahmet Kuyumcu, Bob Oliver, Rama Ramakrishnan, Carol Redfield, Alex Roma-nenko, and Nicola Secomandi, who all contributed comments and suggestions that improved the book. Thanks also to my students at Columbia and Stanford, who caught many typos. Finally, thanks to the Columbia University Business School, the Stanford University Business School, Manugistics, and Nomis Solutions, all of whom provided office space and support at various times through the writing of the book.

The book has also benefited from my extensive interactions and discussions with colleagues over the years, including Bill Brunger, Simon Caufield, Glenn Colville, Guillermo Gallego, Tom Grossman, Lloyd Hansen, Peter Grønlund, Garud Iyengar, Anton Kleywegt, Steve Kou, Warren Lieberman, Ray Lyons, Costis Maglaras, Özalp Özer, Özgur Özluk, Jörn Peter Petersen, Özge Şahin, Kalyan Talluri, Van Veen, Loren Williams, Garrett van Ryzin, Graham Young, and Jon Zimmerman, among many others. Special thanks to Christian Albright, Serhan Duran, Jihong Kong, Warren Lieberman, Joern Meissner, and Nicola Secomandi for catching errors in previous printings.

Very special thanks to my parents for their love and support.

Needless to say, any errors in the book are neither the author's fault nor the fault of any of the others mentioned here; they are due to malign outside influences.

NOTES

1. The course at Stanford was developed jointly with Michael Harrison.

2. Notable exceptions were Ioana Popescu's course on dynamic pricing and revenue management at INSEAD, Peter Bell's course on revenue management at the University of Western Ontario, and courses in hotel and restaurant revenue management developed by Sheryl Kimes at Cornell.

1 | BACKGROUND AND INTRODUCTION

What is a cynic? . . . A man who knows the price of everything and the value of nothing

Oscar Wilde (1892)

This is a book about pricing—specifically, how companies should set and adjust their prices in order to maximize profitability. It takes the view that pricing decisions are commonplace, that they can be complex, and that they are usually critical determinants of profitability. Despite this, pricing decisions are often badly managed (or even unmanaged). While most companies have pretty good prices in place most of the time, very few have the processes and capabilities needed to ensure that they have the right prices in place for all their products, to all their customers, through all their channels, all the time. This is the goal of pricing and revenue optimization.

Pricing and revenue optimization is a tactical function. It recognizes that prices need to change rapidly and often and provides guidance on how they should change. This makes it distinct from *strategic pricing*, where the goal is usually to establish a general position within a marketplace. While strategic pricing worries about how a product should in general be priced relative to the market, pricing and revenue optimization is concerned with determining the prices that will be in place tomorrow and next week. Strategic pricing sets the constraints within which pricing and revenue optimization operates.

One of the distinguishing characteristics of pricing and revenue optimization is its use of analytical techniques derived from management science. The use of these techniques to set prices in a complex, dynamic environment is relatively new. One of the first applications of the approach was the development of revenue management systems by the passenger airlines in the 1980s. Since then, the rapid development of e-commerce and the availability of customer data through customer relationship management (CRM) systems has led to the adoption of similar techniques in many other industries, including automotive, retail, telecommunications, financial services, and manufacturing. A number of software vendors provide "price optimization" or "demand management" or "revenue management" solutions focused on one or more industries. In this context, pricing and revenue optimization is increasingly becoming a core competency within many different companies. The purpose of this book is to provide an introduction to this relatively new and rapidly changing field.

In this chapter, we begin by giving some historical context for pricing and revenue optimization. In particular, we give some perspective on why pricing has gone from being a largely ignored and obscure "black art" within many companies to become the subject of intense scrutiny and analysis. We argue that the "pricing problem" has become increasingly difficult and is likely to become even more difficult in the future. We argue further that improving pricing is often one of the highest-return investments available to a company. Hopefully this will whet the reader's appetite for the more quantitative material to come in the following chapters.

1.1 HISTORICAL BACKGROUND AND CONTEXT

For most of history, philosophers took it for granted that goods had an intrinsic value in the same sense that they had an intrinsic color or weight. A fair price reflected that intrinsic value. Charging a price too much in excess of the intrinsic value was condemned as a sign of "avarice" and often prohibited by law. Prices were set by custom, by law, or by imperial fiat. Sermons were preached inveighing against the sin of charging unfair prices in order to receive excessive profits.[1] The problem of pricing did not really exist until modern market economies began to emerge in the West in the 17th and 18th centuries. With the emergence of these economies, prices were allowed to move more freely—untied to the traditional concept of value. Speculative bubbles such as "tulipomania" in the Dutch republic in the 1630s—in which the price of some varieties of tulips rose more than a hundredfold in 18 months before collapsing in 1637—and the "South Sea bubble" in England in 1720— in which the prices of shares in the South Sea Company soared before the company collapsed amid general scandal—fed a sense of anxiety and the belief that prices could somehow lose touch with reality.[2] Furthermore, for the first time, large numbers of people could amass fortunes—and lose them—by buying and selling goods on the market. The question naturally arose—what were prices, exactly? Where did they come from? What determined the right price? When was a price fair? When should the government intervene in pricing? The modern field of economics arose, at least in part, in response to these questions.

Possibly the greatest insight of classical economics was that the price of a good at any time in an ideal capitalist economy is not based on any intrinsic "value" but rather on the interplay of supply and demand. This was a major intellectual breakthrough—on par in its way with the Newtonian view of the clockwork universe and Darwin's theory of evolution. In essence, the price of a good or service was determined by the interaction of people willing to sell the good with the willingness of others to buy the good. That's all there is to it—neither intrinsic "value" nor cost nor labor content enters directly into the equation. Of course, these and other factors enter *indirectly* into pricing—sellers would not last long selling goods below cost, and the prices buyers accept are based on the "value" they placed on the item—but these were not primary. There are many reasons why sellers sell below cost when they are in possession of a cartload of vegetables that are on the verge of going rotten—the classic "sell it or smell it" situation—or to attract a desirable new customer. Just so, the "value" that buyers placed on different goods changed with their changing situation and the dictates of fashion. According to modern economics there is no normative "right price" for a good or service against which the price can be compared—rather, there are only the actual prices out in the marketplace, floating freely without an anchor, based only on the willingness of sellers to sell and buyers to buy.

While classical economics solved the problem of the origin of price, it raised as many questions as it answered. In particular, if prices were not tied to fundamental values—if they had no anchor—why did they show any stability at all? Under normal circumstances, prices for most goods are pretty stable most of the time. If prices are based only on the whims of buyers and sellers, why is the price of bread not subject to wild swings like the Dutch tulip market in 1689? Why doesn't milk cost five times as much in Chicago as it does in New York? How can manufacturers and merchants plan at all and make reasonable profits in order to stay in business? How can an economy based on free-floating prices work at all? And, assuming that such an economy could work, how could it possibly work better than a centralized economy where planners carefully sought to allocate resources across the entire economy?

One of the great achievements of 20th century economics was to show mathematically how a largely unregulated economy could work: that an economy consisting of individuals who supply their labor in return for wages and use their earnings to buy goods to maximize their "utility" combined with firms who seek to maximize profitability can be remarkably stable and efficient.[3] Under certain assumptions, this type of capitalist economy can be shown to be at least as efficient as any centrally planned economy. Furthermore, prices in such an economy would generally be stable and reasonably predictable. The price for a product would equal the long-run marginal production cost of that product plus the return on invested capital necessary to produce the product. If someone were selling the product for less, he or she would go out of business because his or her costs would not be covered. If someone tried selling for more, other sellers would undercut his price, consumers would flee to the lower-priced sellers, and the high-price seller would be forced to lower his price or go bankrupt for lack of business. As this happens simultaneously, economy-wide, prices equilibrate and change only due to exogenous shocks, changes in resource availability, taxation or monetary policy, or changes in consumer tastes.

This view of the world is based primarily on the assumption that most markets are perfectly competitive, where the idea of perfect competition can be summarized as follows.

> A market structure is perfectly competitive if the following conditions hold: There are many firms, each with an insubstantial share of the market. These firms produce a homogenous product using identical production processes and possess perfect information. It is also the case that there is free entry to the industry; that is, new firms can and will enter the industry if they observe that greater-than-normal profits are being earned. The effect of this free entry is to push the demand curve facing each firm downwards until each firm earns only normal profits, at which point there is no further incentive for new entrants to come into the industry. Moreover, since each firm produces a homogenous product, it cannot raise its price without losing all of its market to its competitors . . . . Thus firms are price takers and can sell as much as they are capable of producing at the prevailing market price.[4]

There are no pricing decisions in perfectly competitive markets—prices are determined by the iron law of the market. If one merchant were offering a good for a lower price than another, neoclassical economics assumes that either customers would entirely abandon the higher-price merchant and swamp the lower-price merchant or an arbitrageur would arise who would buy all the goods from the lower-price merchant and sell them at the higher price. In either case, a single market price would prevail. Furthermore, if prices were so high that merchants enjoyed higher profits than the rest of the economy, more sellers would enter, lowering the average price until the return on capital dropped to the market level. In this situation, there are no pricing decisions at all: Prices are set "by the market"—as stock prices are set by the New York Stock Exchange or NASDAQ. The price of Microsoft stock is not set by any "pricer" but by the interplay of supply and demand for the stock. Many financial instruments, such as stocks and bonds, satisfy the economic definition of a commodity. Certain other highly fungible goods—grain, crude oil, and some bulk chemicals—also come very close to being commodities. In these markets, there is simply no need for pricing and revenue optimization—the market truly sets the price.

As any shopper can tell you, much of the real world is messier—prices vary all over the place, sometimes in ways that seem irrational. Buyers often behave erratically, sellers do not always seek to maximize short-run profit, neither buyers nor sellers are possessed of perfect information, and opportunities for arbitrage are not immediately seized. Table 1.1 shows prices for a half gallon of whole milk at different markets in a 16-block area of the upper west side of Manhattan on a single day in May 2002. Prices range from a low of $1.39 to a high of $2.00—a variation of $0.61, or 44%. Furthermore, the price varied by more than $0.40 even for two stores on the same block. How could this be? Why would anybody buy milk at a high price when they could walk a block and save 40 cents? Why don't arbitrageurs buy all the milk at the lower price and sell it at the higher?

TABLE 1.1
*Retail prices for a half gallon of whole milk on
the Upper West Side of Manhattan, May 2002*

Location	Price
74th and Broadway	$1.39
79th and Amsterdam	1.59
77th and Broadway	1.59
74th and Columbus	1.69
73rd and Columbus	1.79
74th and Amsterdam	1.79
75th and Broadway	1.89
71st and Columbus	1.99
78th and Amsterdam	2.00
AVERAGE	$1.75
STANDARD DEVIATION	0.20

The price variation shown in Table 1.1 will hardly come as a shock to most people—after all, both businesses and consumers know that it pays to shop around—suppliers of the same (or similar) products will often charge different prices. Furthermore, there are other ways to pay a lower price for exactly the same product: Wait until it goes on sale, travel to a retail outlet, clip a coupon, buy in bulk, buy it online, try to negotiate a lower price. In fact, it is hardly a secret not only that prices vary between sellers but that a single seller will often sell the same product to different customers for different prices!

The tools that pricers use day to day are far more likely to be drawn from the fields of statistics or operations research than from economics. Marketing science, which deals with the quantitative analysis of marketing initiatives, including pricing, is usually considered part of the broader field of operations research and management science.[5] Application of these techniques to problems of marketing began to emerge in a significant fashion in the 1960s.[6] Since then, marketing scientists have developed, applied, validated, and refined important mathematical models to a broad range of issues, such as forecasting sales, product planning, predicting market response, product positioning, pricing, promotions, sales force compensation, and marketing strategy.[7] True to its name, marketing science has brought some science to what was previously viewed as a "black art."

Despite these achievements, there remains a gap between marketing science models and their use in practice. The reasons for this gap are numerous. Many marketing models have been built on unrealistically stylized views of consumer behavior. Other models have been built to "determine if what we see in practice can happen in theory." Other models seem limited by unrealistically simplistic assumptions. In any case, a leading text on marketing science admitted:

> With an area of such importance and with so much at stake, it might be assumed that a great deal of continuing research and planning would by now underlie the formulation of pricing strategy and the setting of prices. One might also expect that a well-developed body of theory would have resulted in principles to guide pricing decisions. But this does not appear to be the case.[8]

One of the possible reasons for the gap between marketing science theory and its application to real pricing decisions is that pricing decisions are becoming increasingly tactical and operational in nature. Companies increasingly need to make pricing decisions more and more rapidly in order to respond to competitive actions, market changes, or their own inventory situation. They no longer have the luxury to perform market analyses or extended spreadsheet studies every time a pricing change needs to be considered. The premium is on speed. While there has been a general acceleration of business in all fields, the impact on pricing and revenue optimization has been particularly notable. This acceleration—and the corresponding interest in developing tools to enable better pricing and revenue optimization (PRO) decisions—has been driven by four trends.

- The success of revenue management in the airline industry provided an example of how pricing and revenue optimization could increase profitability in a real-time pricing environment.
- The widespread adoption of enterprise resource planning (ERP) and customer relationship management (CRM) software systems provided a new wealth of corporate information that can be utilized to improve pricing and revenue optimization decisions.
- The rise of e-commerce necessitated the ability to manage and update prices in a fast-moving, highly transparent, online environment for many companies that had not previously faced such a challenge.

- The success of supply chain management proved that analytic software systems could drive real business improvements.

Because of their importance to the development of pricing and revenue optimization, we will spend a little time to discuss each of these trends.

1.1.1 The Success of Revenue Management

In 1985, American Airlines was threatened on its core routes by the low-fare carrier PeopleExpress. In response, American developed a revenue management program based on differentiating prices between leisure and business travelers. A key element of this program was a "yield management" system that used optimization algorithms to determine the right number of seats to protect for later-booking full-fare passengers on each flight while still accepting early-booking low-fare passengers. This approach was a resounding success for American, resulting ultimately in the demise of PeopleExpress.

We delve more deeply into the American Airlines/PeopleExpress story in Chapter 6. For now, the importance of the story is in the publicity it garnered. American Airlines featured its revenue management capabilities in its annual report. The team that developed the system won the 1991 Edelman Prize for best application of management science. American Airlines' revenue management has been widely touted as an important strategic application of management science (C. K. Anderson, Bell, and Kaiser 2003), and the tale of American using its superior capabilities to defeat PeopleExpress was the centerpiece of a popular business book (Cross 1997).

Not surprisingly this publicity resulted in widespread interest. Companies began to investigate the prospects of improving the profitability of their pricing decisions. Ford Motor Company was inspired by the success of revenue management at the airlines to institute its own very successful program (Leibs 2000). Vendors arose selling revenue management software systems, and consultants appeared offering to help companies set up their own programs. Revenue management spread well beyond the passenger airlines.

Under its strictest definition, revenue management has a fairly narrow field of application. In particular, the techniques of revenue management are applicable when the following conditions are met.

- Capacity is limited and immediately perishable. Most obviously, an empty seat on a departing aircraft or an empty hotel room cannot be stored to satisfy future demand.
- Customers book capacity ahead of time. Advance bookings are common in industries with constrained and perishable capacity, since customers need a way to ensure ahead of time that capacity will be available when they need to consume it. This gives airlines the opportunity to track demand for future flights and adjust prices accordingly to balance supply and demand.
- Prices are changed by opening and closing predefined booking classes. This is a by-product of the design of the computerized distribution systems, such as SABRE and Galileo, that the airlines developed. These systems allow airlines to establish

a set of prices (fare classes) for each flight and then open or close those fare classes as they wish. This is somewhat different from the pricing issue in most industries, which is not "What fares should we open and close?" but "What prices should we be offering now for each of our products to each market segment through each channel?" The difference is subtle, but it leads to major differences in system design and implementation.

Many companies are understandably wary about adopting "revenue management" programs, protesting that "we are not an airline." In general, this is the right view—the algorithms behind airline revenue management do not transfer directly to most other industries. However, the experience of the airlines contains several important lessons.

- Pricing and revenue optimization can deliver more than short-term profitability benefits. Revenue management enabled American Airlines to meet the challenge posed by PeopleExpress. It also meant the difference between survival and bankruptcy for National Rent-a-Car. In 1992, National was losing $1 million per month and was on the verge of being liquidated by its then-owner, General Motors.[9] At this point, National had been through two rounds of downsizing, and corporate management felt there were no more significant savings that could be achieved on the cost side. As a last-ditch effort, National decided to work on the revenue side. They worked with the revenue management company Aeronomics to develop a system that forecast supply and demand for each car type/rental length at all 170 corporate locations and adjusted fares to balance supply and demand. The results were immediate.

  > National initiated a comprehensive revenue management program whose core is a suite of analytic models developed to manage capacity, pricing, and reservation. As it improved management of these functions, National dramatically increased its revenue. The initial implementation in July 1993 produced immediate results and returned National Car Rental to profitability. (Geraghty and Johnson 1997)

- E-commerce both necessitates and enables pricing and revenue optimization. The airlines pioneered electronic distribution—their computerized distribution systems, SABRE and Galileo, were the "Internet before the Internet." These systems allowed immediate receipt and processing of customer booking requests. They also enabled airlines to change prices and availability and have the updated information instantaneously transmitted worldwide. In effect, the airlines were wrestling with the complexities of e-commerce well before the arrival of the Internet. The necessity to continually monitor demand and update prices accordingly will be felt by more and more industries as electronic distribution channels such as the Internet become more pervasive.

- Effective segmentation is critical. The key to the success of revenue management in the airline industry was the ability of the airlines to segment customers between early-booking leisure passengers and late-booking business passengers. Note that this segmentation was achieved not by direct discrimination—that is, trying to charge a different fare based on demographics, age, or other customer characteristics—but via product differentiation, creating different products that appealed to different segments. Segmenting customers based on their willingness to pay and finding ways to charge different prices to different segments is a critical piece of pricing and revenue optimization—one that we address in detail in Chapter 4.

At heart, airline yield management systems are highly sophisticated opportunity cost calculators. They forecast the future opportunities to sell a seat and seek to ensure that the seat is not sold for less than the expected value of those future opportunities. Most industries do not face capacity constraints as stark as those faced by the airlines. Manufacturers typically have the opportunity to adjust production levels or store either finished or partially finished goods. Retailers can adjust their stocks in response to changes in demand. However, this does not mean that calculating opportunity cost is not relevant to these industries. On the contrary, in many industries facing inventory or capacity constraints, opportunity cost can be the critical link between supply chain management and pricing and revenue optimization. We explore this link in greater detail in Chapter 5.

1.1.2 The New Wealth of Information

As airlines began to develop more sophisticated revenue management systems in the 1990s, other businesses were adopting a new generation of corporate software. Historically, most business software had been homegrown, highly specialized, and oriented toward a single corporate function, such as payroll or invoicing. Such "legacy systems" had often been developed in isolation, were not integrated, and used independent and often-conflicting data sources and definitions. As a result, many companies were reaching the point of diminishing returns on their information technology (IT) investments, with an increasing amount of each IT dollar spent on integrating existing systems rather than building new functionality. Furthermore, the lack of consistent information among departments was often leading to inefficiency and frustration, with identical data entered several times and data items with the same name often having different meanings or interpretation.

This set the stage for enterprise resource planning (ERP) systems. Vendors such as Oracle, SAP, PeopleSoft and Baan began offering integrated client-server ERP systems that enabled corporations to obtain a unified view of all their data. These systems enabled different parts of a company to have access to a consistent, definitive view of corporate data. This in turn enabled efficient and consistent cross-functional business processes without the need for different groups to rekey data or access disparate software systems. The ERP vision is to provide a corporate "information backbone" that supports all business users with consistent and timely data from a single source. Information will then flow freely among business processes. Analytical applications such as supply chain management or staffing systems sit on top of the ERP system and draw the needed inputs from the ERP database. Information "islands" and "fiefdoms" are eliminated, as is the tedious task of shuttling between different software systems and data sources. Corporations will be more efficient, more nimble, and more customer responsive, and IT development can focus on improving functionality rather than integration.

The ERP vision is compelling, but the history of ERP systems has hardly been one of unqualified triumph—many companies have found that replacing their legacy systems with an ERP system can be expensive, disruptive, and painful. Nonetheless, it is clear that the last decade has seen a much-needed consolidation of corporate information. This makes it much easier to implement analytical systems such as pricing and revenue optimization. Such PRO systems require both timely information about product costs and availabilities and the results of recent transactions. By automating and standardizing data consolidation and reconciliation, ERP systems enable much more rapid implementation of pricing and revenue optimization.

Another source of improved data storage and availability came from the increasing adoption of *customer relationship management* (CRM) systems. These involve gathering and storing customer and transaction information and using the results to improve marketing, sales, and customer service. Customer relationship management systems from such vendors as Siebel and e-piphany collect customer and transaction data from different channels and make it available in a data warehouse to various business intelligence, data-mining, and analytic systems.

Pricing and revenue optimization systems are a natural extension of CRM. In essence, CRM systems provide the rich customer and transaction history that pricing and revenue optimization systems need to evaluate customer response and update pricing recommendations. Harrah's Entertainment, which operates 24 casinos and 16 hotels under the Harrah's, Harvey's, Rio, and Showboat brands, provides an example of the successful use of a CRM system with pricing optimization. Harrah's has linked a homegrown CRM system with its reservation and revenue management systems. Based on historical information about customer behavior and preferences, customers are classified into 64 segments based not only on their current value but on their expected lifetime value to Harrah's. The revenue management system forecasts daily hotel room demand for each of these segments and calculates the minimum room price necessary to optimize the room inventory. When customers call for reservations, call-center representatives can see on their screens the customer segment and the approved pricing offers.

The Harrah's system provides an excellent example of a CRM system closely linked with a price optimization system. The CRM system tracks customer behavior and demographics information, such as zip codes, which enables segmentation of customers into such groupings as "avid experienced player" and the calculation of expected profitability and gaming revenue from each segment. The revenue management system balances the need to ensure that rooms will be available for high-revenue customers while not holding back so many rooms that occupancy suffers. The information needed to manage customers at this level of detail simply would not have been available before the advent of customer relationship management technology.[10] Harrah's is an excellent example of how the new wealth of customer information available through CRM systems can enable pricing and revenue optimization.

1.1.3 The Rise of e-Commerce

By the late 1990s, the Internet was widely predicted to be a "revolutionary" and transformative technology that would "change everything." The fact that the Internet will drive a greater need for pricing and revenue optimization is contrary to some early expectations. A number of analysts predicted that Internet commerce would inevitably drive prices down to the lowest common denominator. Many analysts argued, in effect, that the Internet would bring about the world of perfect competition, in which sellers would lose control of prices. This was part of the vision behind Bill Gates' concept of the "frictionless economy." [11] However, the reality has been quite different. Studies consistently show that most online buyers actually do little shopping—for example, a McKinsey study showed that 89% of online book purchasers buy from the first site they visit, as do 81% of music buyers.[12] As a result, online prices often vary considerably, even for identical items. Table 1.2 shows the base price and shipped price for 10 online vendors compared to the list price for Stephen King's book *Bag of Bones*, gathered on April 30, 2002, by an online shopping agent.[13] Note that the delivered price varies by more than $8.00 across the vendors, with none of the 10 vendors offering the book at the same price. Note also that the two most successful online booksellers—Amazon and Barnes and Noble—have neither the highest nor the lowest price, and their prices differ substantially from each other. At least in this case, the Internet seems to support rather than eliminate price variability!

TABLE 1.2
Online book prices for the hardback edition of Bag of Bones
by Stephen King, April 30, 2002

Vendor	Price	Shipping cost	Total
1Book Street	$23.09	$0.00	$23.09
buy.com	19.88	3.25	23.13
Alphacraze	19.41	3.88	23.29
A1 Books	19.50	3.95	23.45
ecampus.com	21.00	2.98	23.98
Amazon	19.60	4.48	24.08
TextbookX.com	21.00	3.48	24.48
BooksaMillion	20.86	3.98	24.84
BarnesandNoble.com	22.40	3.99	26.39
List Price	28.00	—	28.00
Powell's	28.00	3.50	31.50
AVERAGE	$21.47	$3.35	$24.82

The resemblance between the distribution of online book prices in Table 1.2 and Table 1.1 is not totally coincidental. It shows that the Internet supports price differentials in the same way as other distribution channels, such as direct and indirect sales and retail outlets. For any seller offering a large catalog of products (such as an online bookseller), the price of each item needs to be set intelligently based on cost, inventory, current competitive prices, and other information. The pricing problems facing an online bookseller are similar to those facing retailers: Could I increase my profitability by raising my price? by lowering my price? How should my price be updated as inventory changes—as competitive prices change? as demand changes? What is the right relationship between my base price and the total delivered price? Multiply these questions by a catalog of hundreds of thousands of items and a need to update daily, and the full magnitude of the pricing problem faced by online merchants becomes clear.

While one group of analysts was predicting that the Internet would eliminate price differentials and drive prices inevitably toward the lowest common denominator, another group of analysts was predicting exactly the opposite—that the Internet would enable "one-to-one" pricing crafted to the individual propensities of each buyer. According to this school of thought, e-commerce would become a "market-of-one" environment, in which prices would be calculated on the fly to maximize the profitability of each transaction. A customer entering a Web site would immediately be identified, and, based on his past buying patterns, a pricing engine would calculate personalized prices reflecting his willingness to pay. Needless to say, the one-to-one e-commerce pricing world has not yet arrived. And there are powerful reasons to believe it will never fully arrive. For one thing, there is strong buyer resistance to attempts at pricing discrimination that are perceived as unfair or arbitrary. People are no more inclined to accept online price discrimination than they would be willing to accept variable pricing at the time of checkout based on the clerk's estimate of their "willingness to pay." In addition, the transparency of the Internet means that whatever online pricing system a company adopts, the details will be widely known across the buying community within a very short period of time. As a result, price differentiation on the Internet will occur, but it will require careful analysis and execution to be successful.

Given that the Internet will neither drive prices to their lowest common denominator nor lead to real-time personalized pricing, can we conclude that it will have no impact on pricing? Not at all. On the contrary, e-commerce will be a major motivator for companies to improve their pricing capabilities. Four specific characteristics of Internet commerce increase the urgency of pricing and revenue optimization.

- The Internet increases the velocity of pricing decisions. Many companies that changed list prices once a quarter or less now find they face the daily challenge of determining what prices to display on their Web site or to transmit to e-commerce intermediaries. Many companies are beginning to struggle with this increased price velocity now—and things will only get worse. As a possible harbinger of things to come, a typical major domestic airline needs to evaluate more than 500,000 price changes a week. The magnitude and complexity of the pricing decisions faced by the airlines are a direct (if unintentional) result of their widespread adoption of electronic distribution systems more than 20 years ago. Over time, companies selling on the Internet may see 10-fold or even 100-fold increases in pricing velocity.

- The Internet makes available an immediate wealth of information about customer behavior that was formerly unavailable or only available after a considerable time lag. This includes not just information on who bought what, but also who clicked on what, and who looked at what and for how long. This information is being increasingly captured and analyzed by companies both to support cross-selling and up-selling and also to understand customer behavior and segmentation.

- The Internet provides a unique laboratory for experimenting with pricing alternatives and alternative pricing models. eBay and Priceline are two Internet success stories, each with a business model based on variations of auction pricing. The Internet also has the potential to be an ideal laboratory for pricing experiments.

As Michael Marn and his colleagues point out, "Traditional price-sensitivity research can cost up to $300,000 for each product category and take anywhere from six to ten weeks to complete. . . . On the Internet, however, prices can be tested continually in real time, and customers' responses can be instantly received." [14]

- Even in cases where a customer does not buy online, the Internet may provide deeper information about costs and competitive prices. This has been particularly true in "big ticket" consumer purchases, such as home mortgages and automobiles. According to J. D. Power and Associates, in 2001, 62% of new-car buyers consulted the Internet to find information on invoice prices, sticker prices, and trade-in values (Fahey 2002). In this environment, merchants need to be able to use intelligent targeted pricing in order to maintain profitability.

It is too early to predict the ultimate role of the Internet in the world of commerce. However, it is certainly safe to say that it will be an increasingly vital distribution channel in many, if not most, industries. Furthermore, it is only going to increase the pressure for more rapid price updates and transaction responses. And it will deliver ever richer views of customer response and behavior. As a result, the need for pricing and revenue optimization systems to support online pricing and sales will become ever more urgent.

1.1.4 The Success of Supply Chain Management Systems

Supply chain management was another success story of the 1990s. Supply chain software developed and sold by companies such as i2, Manugistics, and SAP enabled companies to improve efficiencies, slash inventories, cut costs, and improve customer service. By 2000, even Alan Greenspan was crediting automated supply chain systems with "driving substantial economy-wide improvements in efficiency and productivity."

The success of supply chain management systems proved that sophisticated quantitative analysis applied to complex corporate problems could lead to real improvements. Pricing and revenue optimization is based on the same basic idea of using analytical techniques to improve corporate decision making—in this case on the marketing and sales side of the organization. The successes of SCM has given corporate management greater confidence that sophisticated analytical software can lead to real improvements in profitability, thereby paving the way for PRO.

Supply chain management has opened the door for pricing and revenue optimization in another way. Most of the major corporate initiatives of the 1990s were focused on improving efficiency and reducing cost. This includes the fad for corporate reengineering that followed the 1993 publication of Hammer and Champy's book *Reengineering the Corporation*, the controversial wave of downsizing and "right-sizing" in the 1990s, and the growing adoption of enterprise resource planning and supply chain management software. What this diverse set of initiatives had in common was a focus on improving corporate efficiency: the "cost" side of the income statement. A 1999 Deloitte and Touche survey of more than 200 companies that had either implemented ERP systems or were in the process of doing so revealed that only 7% of those companies named "increased revenue or profits" as an anticipated benefit from their implementation.[15] While the opportunities to improve efficiency and reduce costs have hardly disappeared, it is fair to say that most companies are beginning to see reduced marginal returns from cost-focused initiatives. This means that the major area remaining for corporate profitability improvement will be on the marketing and sales side. And, among opportunities for improvement in marketing and sales, PRO usually has the most immediate impact and the highest return.

Finally, supply chain management has a natural synergy with pricing and revenue optimization. Supply chain management systems have generally assumed that demand, while uncertain, was exogenous. The job of the supply chain management system was to find a way to fill current and anticipated orders at lowest cost while meeting customer service constraints. Pricing and revenue optimization assumes that variable costs and capacity availabilities are fixed, and it looks to find the set of prices and customer allocations that maximizes profitability, subject to these constraints. While individually critical, each of these capabilities is looking at only a limited subset of the decisions faced by the overall organization. A company that has achieved both supply chain management excellence and pricing and revenue optimization excellence may still have the opportunity to increase profitability further by explicitly linking the operations and the customer-facing sides of the company.

All four of these factors—revenue management, the rise of the Internet, the new wealth of information, the success of supply chain management—point in the same direction, toward a future in which pricing will increasingly become a tactical and operational function, supported by a wealth of customer and supply information and requiring quantitative decision support technology. Both the time available to set prices and the allowable margin of error will continue to decrease while the complexity of pricing decisions will increase. Time-consuming "offline" analyses will become increasingly irrelevant—their results will be obsolete before they can be completed because the world moves too quickly. Automated pricing and revenue optimization systems will be required to respond rapidly and effectively in the new world. However, automated systems are only part of the answer—effective pricing will also require the right supporting business processes, metrics, and supporing organization.

1.2 THE FINANCIAL IMPACT OF PRICING AND REVENUE OPTIMIZATION

Of course, the most compelling reason for a company to improve its pricing and revenue optimization capabilities is to make more money. "For most companies, better management of pricing is the fastest and most cost-effective way to increase profits." So concluded a pioneering study by McKinsey and Associates.[16] Based on the "average economics of 2,463 companies in Compustat aggregate," the McKinsey researchers concluded that a 1% improvement in profit would, on average, result in an improvement in operating profit of 11.1%. By contrast, 1% improvements in variable cost, volume, and fixed cost would produce operating improvements of 7.8%, 3.3%, and 2.3%, respectively. Similar results were obtained from a 1999 A. T. Kearney analysis of 500 companies in the S & P 500. The A. T. Kearney leverage numbers were different, but, as shown in Table 1.3, price improvement had still, by far, the largest impact of the three categories.

TABLE 1.3
Results of two studies on the average impact of a 1%
improvement in different variables on operating profit

	McKinsey (1992)	A. T. Kearney (2000)
Price management	11.1%	8.2%
Variable cost	7.8%	5.1%
Sales volume	3.3%	3.0%
Fixed cost	2.3%	2.0%

The passenger airlines typically claim between 8% and 11% benefit from the use of their revenue management systems (Smith et al. 1992)—a figure remarkably consistent with the numbers shown in Table 1.3. A *Harvard Business Review* article noted that some retailers are achieving "gains in gross margins in the range of 5–15%" from the use of optimization-based assortment and pricing optimization systems. Early adopters include J. C. Penney and Gymboree (Friend and Walker 2001). ShopKo Stores has seen a 24% increase in gross margin from the pilot use of a markdown management system (Levison 2002). Ford Motor Company has used a promotions management system to significantly improve the use of its $9 billion annual North American promotions budget (Leibs 2000) and expects to realize an additional $5 billion in profits over 5 years from effective market segmentation.[17]

Putting it all together, we can see there is a strong case for many companies to consider pricing and revenue optimization. Not only is improving pricing already the "fastest and most cost-effective way to increase profits," but it is likely to gain in importance as the velocity and complexity of pricing decisions inexorably increase. Furthermore, a new generation of information technology provides the information and algorithmic power needed to analyze and exploit market opportunities. Finally, not only does pricing have extremely high leverage in improving profitability, as shown in Table 1.3; it is often the area that can be improved the most with the least investment. The focus on cost improvement throughout the 1990s means that incremental improvements in variable costs and fixed costs will be more expensive and difficult than incremental improvements in pricing and price management.

1.3 ORGANIZATION OF THE BOOK

The structure and dependencies of the remaining chapters are illustrated in Figure 1.1. The topic of each chapter is outlined briefly next.

Chapter 2 discusses pricing and revenue optimization as a corporate process and contrasts it with other approaches to pricing. It stresses that PRO is a highly dynamic process, dependent on continual feedback to ensure that pricing decisions are kept in line with changing market realities. It also discusses the concept that the core of pricing and revenue optimization lies in the formulation of pricing and availability decisions as constrained optimization problems.

Chapter 3 reviews the basic economics behind price optimization. It introduces the idea of a price-response curve and presents several common forms of price-response curve. It shows how the price-response curve can incorporate competitive pricing. It argues that *incremental cost* is also a critical input to pricing a customer commitment. Finally it shows

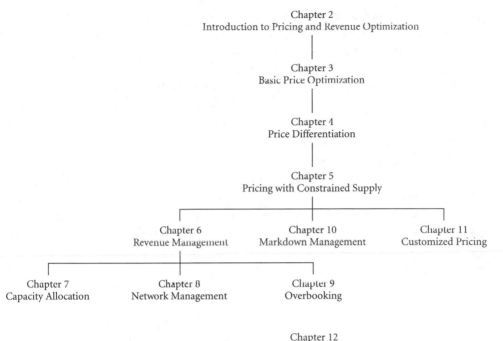

Chapter 2
Introduction to Pricing and Revenue Optimization

Chapter 3
Basic Price Optimization

Chapter 4
Price Differentiation

Chapter 5
Pricing with Constrained Supply

Chapter 6
Revenue Management

Chapter 10
Markdown Management

Chapter 11
Customized Pricing

Chapter 7
Capacity Allocation

Chapter 8
Network Management

Chapter 9
Overbooking

Chapter 12
PRO and Customer Acceptance

Figure 1.1   Relationships among the remaining chapters.

several ways that prices can be optimized in the simplest case of a supplier selling a single product with a known price-response curve.

Price differentiation is at the core of pricing and revenue optimization. Chapter 4 discusses how markets can be divided into different market segments such that a different price can be charged to each segment. Tactics for price differentiation include virtual products, product lines, group pricing, channel pricing, and regional pricing. The idea of *multipricing* is the source of both the benefits of PRO and the challenges involved in managing a large portfolio of prices. This chapter discusses how to optimize differentiated prices in the face of potential cannibalization.

Chapter 5 introduces another major theme in pricing and revenue optimization—pricing when supply (or inventory) is constrained. Supply constraints are ubiquitous. They may arise from the intrinsically constrained capacity of a service provider, such as a hotel, restaurant, barbershop, or trucking company; they may be due to limited inventory on hand; or they may be due to "bottlenecks" in a supply chain that restrict the rate at which a good can be produced or transported. In any case, constrained supply significantly complicates optimal pricing. This chapter also introduces the key concept of an *opportunity cost*—the incremental contribution lost due to a supply constraint.

Revenue management has been one of the most important and publicized applications of pricing and revenue optimization over the past two decades. While it has its origin in the airline industry, it has spread beyond the airlines and is in widespread use at hotels, rental car firms, cruise lines, freight transportation companies, and event ticketing agents. Some of the core techniques are gaining acceptance and use well beyond these industries. We devote four chapters to revenue management. The first—Chapter 6—describes the background, history, and business setting of revenue management. Chapter 7 is devoted to capacity allocation, the techniques used to determine which fare classes should be open and which closed at any time for a product consisting of a constrained resource. Chapter 8 extends this analysis to the case of a network, in which an individual product may use many different resources. Chapter 9 discusses overbooking—the question of how many units of a constrained product should be sold when customers may not show or may cancel.

Markdown management—the topic of Chapter 10—is an increasingly popular application of pricing and revenue optimization. In a markdown industry, a merchant has a stock of inventory whose value decreases over time. His problem is to determine the schedule of price reductions to take in order to maximize the return from inventory. Applications are widespread, from fashion goods, through consumer electronics and durables, to theater tickets. This chapter describes basic markdown optimization models and some of the challenges in implementing markdown management in the real world.

Chapter 11 treats customized prices. Customized pricing is common in business-to-business settings where goods and services are sold based either on long-term contracts or as part of large individual transactions. In these settings, list prices may not exist or may serve only as "guidelines" off of which discounts are set. The pricing and revenue optimization challenge is to determine the discount levels to provide to each customer in order to maximize the *expected profitability* of the deal. This requires estimating the tradeoff between the probability of winning the deal and the margin contribution if the deal is won.

Chapter 12 treats the issue of customer perception and acceptance of pricing tactics. Much of the classical theory of pricing is based on the idea that consumers are rational "utility maximizers." Prices are emotionally neutral signals that guide purchasing decisions. However, both common sense and recent research has shown that this view is incomplete at best and misguided at worst. Consumers can care deeply about prices and the way they are presented. In particular, pricing that is perceived as "unfair" can trigger an emotional rejection. Chapter 12 discusses the implication of consumer "irrationality" for PRO.

1. Robert Heilbroner (1999), in his classic history of economics, *The Worldly Philosophers*, cites a 1639 sermon in which the minister of Boston inveighed against such false principles of trade as "that a man might sell as dear as he can and buy as cheap as he can" and "that he may sell as he bought, though he paid too dear."

2. The classic account of early economic manias is *Extraordinary Popular Delusions and the Madness of Crowds* by Charles Mackay, originally published in 1841 and reprinted many times since. Mike Dash's book *Tulipomania* (1999) is a very readable account of the incredible boom and bust in tulip prices in the 17th century Dutch Republic. John Carswell's *The South Sea Bubble* (2001) is the definitive account of the 18th century British stock scandal. *A Conspiracy of Paper* (2000) by David Liss is an entertaining fictional treatment of the bubble.

3. The most compact summary of this work is Gerard Debreu's *Theory of Value* (1963).

4. This is from the entry on "perfect competition" in the *MIT Dictionary of Modern Economics* (Pearce 1992).

5. As evidence, the journal *Marketing Science* is published by INFORMS, the International Forum for Operations Research and Management Science.

6. See Eliashberg and Lilien (1993, Ch. 1). The journal *Marketing Science* published its first issue in 1964.

7. A good overview of the scope of marketing science can be found in Eliashberg and Lilien (1993).

8. From Lilien, Kotlar, and Murthy (1992).

9. Cross (1997, Ch. 7).

10. See Phillips and Krakauer (2002) and Margulis (2002) for more discussion of Harrah's system.

11. See Gates (1996).

12. This McKinsey study is cited in Baker, Marn, and Zawada (2000). Similar results were reported in a 1999 Jupiter Communications study.

13. Prices do not include state tax. Delivery times and availability vary among vendors.

14. From W. Baker, Marn, and Zawada (1996).

15. Cited in O'Leary (2000).

16. Marn and Rosiello (1992).

17. Cited in Richardson (2002).

2 | INTRODUCTION TO PRICING AND REVENUE OPTIMIZATION

In this chapter, we introduce the basic concepts behind pricing and revenue optimization. We first look at some of the common pricing challenges faced by organizations. These include a lack of consistent management, discipline, and analysis across pricing decisions. We describe three traditional approaches to pricing—cost-plus, market based, and value based—and discuss some of their shortcomings. We then introduce pricing and revenue optimization. At the highest level, pricing and revenue optimization is a process for managing and updating pricing decisions in a consistent and effective fashion. At the core of this process is an approach to finding the set of prices that will maximize total expected contribution, subject to a set of constraints. The constraints reflect either business goals set by the organization or physical limitations, such as limited capacity and inventory. While the use of constrained optimization is common to all pricing and revenue optimization applications, the type of problem to be solved depends on the specific characteristics of the market. Markets vary in terms of timing or cadence of pricing decisions, the nature of the goods and services being sold, and the type of customer commitment being priced.

2.1 THE CHALLENGES OF PRICING

For many organizations, *pricing* includes a remarkably complex set of decisions. While most companies have a good idea of the list prices they have established for their products, they are often unclear on the prices that customers are actually paying. A multitude of different discounts, adjustments, and rebates are often applied to each sale. For this reason it is critical to distinguish between the *list price* of a good and its *pocket price*—that is, what a particular customer ends up actually paying. The list price is generic, while the pocket price may be different for each customer. The *price waterfall* was introduced by McKinsey and Company as a graphical way of illustrating the discounts that occur between the list price of a good and its pocket price. A consumer package goods (CPG) example is shown in Figure 2.1. In this case, there are 12 price reductions or discounts applied between the list price and the pocket price. These include an 8% competitive discount, 3% sales special, 1% exception deal, and so on,

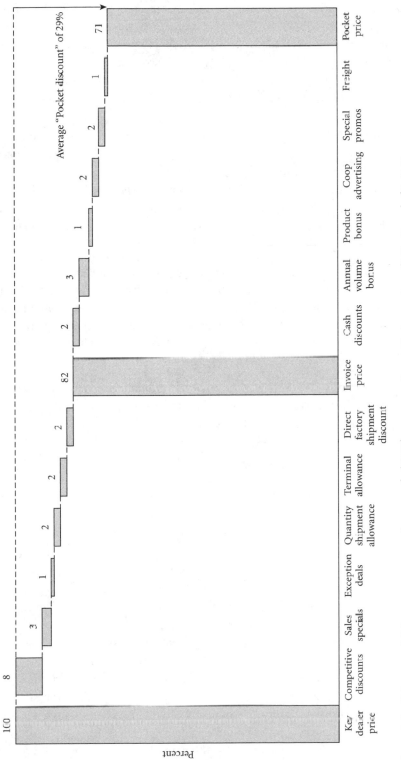

Figure 2.1 Price waterfall for a consumer package goods (CPG) company *Source:* Figure courtesy of Mike Keopel of A. T. Kearney.

down to a 1% freight allowance. The net result is that the pocket price for this customer is 29% less than the list price.

The price waterfall illustrates quite neatly that the pocket price paid by an individual customer is often not the result of a single decision, but the cumulative result of a series of decisions. In fact, for the majority of companies, many discounts are the results of independent decisions made by different parts of the organization, without consistent measurement or tracking. The competitive discount might have been authorized by the regional sales manager, while the product bonus was determined as part of a general marketing program and the freight allowance was given by the local salesperson in response to a last-minute call by the purchaser. As a result, no one is in charge. No one in the organization is responsible for the fact that the discount offered to this customer was 29% while that offered to another was 18%. In fact, not only is no one in charge, it is often remarkably difficult to determine what the pocket price paid by a particular customer even *is*. As Michael Marn and Robert Rosiello put it:

> The complexity and volume of transactions tend to create a smoke screen that makes it nearly impossible for even the rare senior managers who show an interest to understand what is actually happening at the transaction level. Management information systems most often do not report on transaction price performance, or report only average prices and thus shed no real light on pricing opportunities lost transaction by transaction. (Marn and Rosiello 1992, p. 86)

Without a consistent process of analysis and evaluation, the probability that a particular pocket price maximizes customer profitability is like the probability that a blindfolded dart player will hit a bulls-eye—not zero, but not very high. In fact, the situation can be even worse. Sophisticated buyers often understand a seller's pricing process better than the seller does himself. A sophisticated buying department, faced with a price waterfall such as that shown in Figure 2.1, would quickly learn how to "divide and conquer" in order to obtain the lowest pocket price. The buyer's procurement agent will call the local salesperson to get additional concessions, the senior salesperson to get relief from strict interpretation of volume purchase agreements, and even invoicing to get payment term changes. Smart buyers will detect a disorganized or dispersed pricing organization and play it to their advantage.

Management attention is often heavily concentrated on invoice prices or list prices. However, the price waterfall illustrates that the majority of important pricing adjustments often take place *after* the invoice price and certainly after the list price. A typical trucking company will sell less than 5% of its business at list price—all the rest involves discounting. Yet, in many cases, management will spend long hours preparing and analyzing list prices, despite the fact that list prices ultimately have little or no relationship to what most of their customers will be quoted, since all the important action occurs in the discounting. As Figure 2.1 shows, even companies that focus on the invoice price are still missing much of the important action. In this example, 11 points of discount occurred *after* the invoice price.

The distribution of pocket-price discounts given by a CPG company to its various customers over a year is shown in Figure 2.2. In this case, 9% of the customers were receiving a discount of greater than 40%, while 16% were receiving discounts between 35% and 40%,

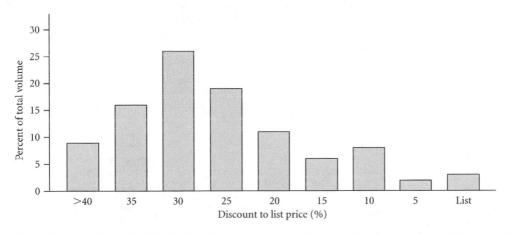

Figure 2.2 Pocket-price distribution for a consumer package goods company. *Source*: Figure courtesy of Mike Reopel of A. T. Kearney.

and only 3% were paying list price. This distribution represents a fairly typical spread of discounts for the CPG industry. This distribution in itself does not tell us anything about the quality of the pricing decisions being made by the company. However, it immediately demonstrates two facts.

1. *The item being sold is not a commodity.* The distribution of pocket prices means that customers are willing to pay a wide range of prices for the item.

2. *Only 3% of customers bought at list price.* For this item, setting list price is not the critical PRO decision. Rather, list price is being set high and discounts are being used to target prices to individual customers. The key decisions are what discounts to offer each customer.

It should be stressed that the existence of a pocket-price distribution such as the one shown in Figure 2.2 does not by itself say anything about the quality of the pricing decisions. A company practicing sophisticated PRO may also show a wide distribution of prices. After all, PRO is based on offering different prices to different customer segments. The question is: *Is the pocket-price distribution the result of a conscious corporate process based on sound analysis, or is it the result of an arbitrary process?*

A key measure of the quality of PRO decision making is the extent to which the pocket-price correlates with customer characteristics that are indicators of price sensitivity. For example, many companies believe they need to offer higher discounts to their larger customers. To the extent that larger customers have higher sensitivity to price, this is a sensible policy. In this case, a seller might expect discount levels as a function of customer size to fall within a band something like that shown in Figure 2.3A. However, the actual mapping of discount level against customer size for the CPG company is shown in Figure 2.3B. The correlation of discount to customer size was only about 0.09 for this company—statistically, indistinguishable from random.

Tools such as the price waterfall in Figure 2.1 and the pocket-price distribution histogram in Figure 2.2 are useful to help companies assess the current state of their pricing. The

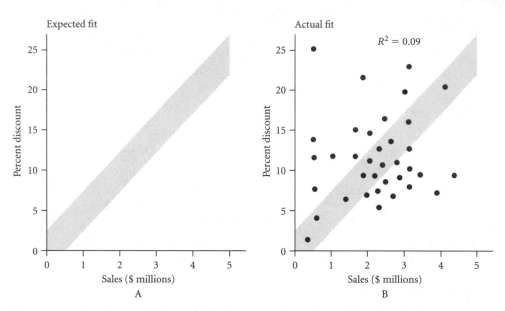

Figure 2.3 Correlation of discount with customer size—consumer package goods example. Part A shows management expectations; part B shows the actual distribution. *Source*: Figure courtesy of Mike Reopel of A. T. Kearney.

price waterfall can identify how pricing responsibilities are dispersed across the organization and where sophisticated buyers may be utilizing "divide and conquer" techniques to drive higher discounts. The pocket-price histogram can give an idea of the breadth of discounts being given to customers. An analysis such as that given in Figure 2.3 can show the extent to which discounts correlate to customer characteristics such as size of customer, size of account, and mix of customer business. This type of presentation often forms part of a preliminary diagnostic analysis and can be used to illustrate the need for better pricing decisions.

2.2 TRADITIONAL APPROACHES TO PRICING

Pricing and revenue optimization incorporates costs, customer demand (or willingness to pay), and the competitive environment to determine the prices that maximize expected net contribution. Other approaches to pricing tend to weigh one of these three aspects more than the others, as shown in Table 2.1. *Cost-plus pricing* calculates prices based on cost plus a standard margin. *Market-based pricing* bases prices on what competitors are doing. *Value-based pricing* sets prices based on an estimate of how customers "value" the good or service

TABLE 2.1
Alternative approaches to pricing

Approach	Based on	Ignores	Liked by
Cost-plus	Costs	Competition, customers	Finance
Market based	Competition	Cost, customers	Sales
Value based	Customers	Cost, competition	Marketing

being sold. The Finance Department tends to like cost-based pricing because it guarantees that each sale produces an adequate margin, which seems fiscally prudent. The Sales Department tends to like market-based pricing because it helps them sell against competition. The Marketing Department is often the natural supporter of pricing according to how customers value a product.

2.2.1 Cost-Plus Pricing

Cost-plus pricing is perhaps the oldest approach to setting prices and still one of the most popular. It has a compelling simplicity—determine the cost of each product and add a percentage surcharge to determine price. The surcharge is often calculated to reflect an allocation of fixed costs plus a required return on capital. It may also simply be based on tradition or a rule of thumb. For example, a common rule of thumb in the restaurant industry is "Food is marked up three times direct costs, beer four times, and liquor six times."[1]

The cost-plus pricing approach appears to be objective and defensible. If all competitors in a market have similar cost structures, it would appear to be a reasonable way to ensure consistency with the competition. Finally, it gives the appearance of financial prudence. After all, if all of our products are priced with the right surcharge, the company is guaranteed to make back the cost of production plus fixed costs plus the required return on capital. Everybody, including the shareholders, should be happy. It is not surprising that cost-based pricing, with its dual appeals to objectivity and financial prudence, often appeals to the Finance Department.

The major drawback of cost-plus pricing is widely recognized: It is an entirely inward-focused exercise that has nothing to do with the market. Calculating prices without any reference to what customers might (or might not) being willing to pay for your product is an obvious folly. Furthermore, it does not support price differentiation—the ability to charge different prices to different customer segments—which is at the heart of pricing and revenue optimization.

Another problem with cost-plus pricing is that the costs used as its basis are often nowhere near as "objective" as they seem (and as the Finance Department may believe them to be). The calculation of the variable and fixed costs involved in the production of a complex slate of products involves innumerable subjective judgments. Furthermore, all of the "hard" cost numbers available to the organization are based on historical performance—production costs in the future may be widely different as the mix of business changes and as production efficiency changes. Basing pricing decisions strictly on "costs" plus a surcharge can lead to highly distorted prices driving lower-than-expected results. This can yield results that often seem very puzzling, since the prices were based on seemingly objective costs. Cooper and Kaplan (1987) discuss several real-world examples of this effect.

Given these drawbacks, it should not be surprising that experts are uniformly harsh on cost-plus pricing.

- Nagle and Holden (1994, p. 3) decry the "cost-plus delusion" and state that the "problem with cost-driven pricing is fundamental."
- Dolan and Simon (1996, p. 38): "Cost-plus pricing is not an acceptable method."

- Lilien, Kotlar, and Murthy (1992, p. 207): "Does the use of a rigid, customary markup over cost make logical sense in the pricing of products? Generally, the answer is no."

Despite near uniform condemnation, cost-based pricing is surprisingly resilient. A 1984 survey of German industry found that about 70% of the companies used cost-based pricing in some form.[2] Other surveys have routinely found that up to 50% of businesses use cost-based pricing in the United States. Even in the age of e-commerce, cost-based pricing is alive and well: A 2002 survey of members of the Professional Pricing Society showed that 22% used cost-based pricing to price on the Internet.[3] Given that this was a survey of a sophisticated group of pricers, it is likely that the actual percentage is even higher.

2.2.2 Market-Based Pricing

Market-based pricing means different things in different contexts. We use it to refer to the practice of pricing based solely on the prices being offered by the competition. It is commonly applied by smaller players in situations in which there is a clear market leader—for example, a small cola brand might set its price based on the price of Coca-Cola. It is, of course, also the practice in pure commodity markets, such as bulk chemicals, or stocks, in which offerings are completely identical and there is rapid, perfect communications of transaction prices. In this case, there is no "pricing decision" per se—all companies take the price as given and adjust their production accordingly. For a commodity, there is no alternative to "market-based pricing."

Market-based pricing can also be an effective strategy for a low-cost supplier seeking to enter a new market. For example, Alamo Car Rental started as a low-cost rental car company targeting the price-sensitive leisure market. Alamo's initial strategy was to ensure they were always priced at least $1.00 lower than both Hertz and Avis on the reservation system displays used by travel agents. This strategy was effective at meeting the strategic goal of rapid growth and penetration of the leisure market.

While market-based pricing is appropriate in a commodity market, for small players in a market dominated by a large competitor, and as a way to drive market share, it is often used in cases where it is less appropriate. At its most extreme, it means letting the competition set our prices. Slavishly following competitive prices does not allow us to capitalize on the changing value perceptions of customers in the marketplace. Furthermore it does not allow us to capitalize on the differential perception that customers hold of us versus the competition. We should charge a higher price to customers who value our product or brand more highly. Monitoring competitive prices and making sure we maintain a realistic pricing relationship with key competitors is always important—but we also need to adjust our position relative to our competitors to reflect current market conditions if we want to maximize profitability.

2.2.3 Value-Based Pricing

Like market-based pricing, *value-based pricing* (or *value pricing*) means different things in different contexts. In its broadest sense it refers to the unexceptional proposition that price should relate to customer value. In its narrowest sense, it is sometimes used as a synonym for *personalized* or *one-on-one* pricing, in which each customer is quoted a different price based on her value for the product being sold. We use it to refer to the belief that customer value should be the key driver of price.[4] Historically, value-based pricing usually referred to the use of methodologies such as customer surveys, focus groups, and conjoint analysis to estimate how customers value a product relative to the alternatives, which is then used to determine price. This type of value-based pricing is employed most frequently for consumer goods—especially when a new product is being introduced.

There is absolutely nothing wrong with the basic idea behind value pricing. If we are a monopoly *and* we can determine the value each customer places on our product *and* charge them that value (assuming it is higher than our incremental cost) *and* not worry about arbitrage or cannibalization (or about being regulated), then that is what we should do in order to maximize profit.[5] This approach to pricing has a serious drawback: It is impossible. There is no way to discern individual customer value for a product at the point of sales. The possibility of arbitrage and cannibalization almost always limits the ability to charge different prices for different products. Finally, competitive pressure means that companies almost always have to price lower than they would like to any group of customers.

The competitive restriction on value-based pricing is worth emphasizing. There is a great difference between the "value" that a potential buyer might place on our product in isolation and what we can actually get that customer to pay in the market. A customer may value our product or services highly, but he also has alternatives. For example, management consulting firms routinely discuss changing from cost-based pricing (hours worked times rate per hour) to value-based pricing, under the belief that "a good consultant could boost earnings using a value-based model."[6] Yet, less than 5% of consultants use value-based pricing. Why should this be? Consider a brilliant management consulting organization that can provide services to a client that will lead to improved profitability of $2 million yet only cost $500,000 to provide. If the consulting company has a true monopoly, it should be able to close the deal at $1.95 million, leaving the client $50,000 ahead. But what if there is another, slightly less brilliant consulting company with the same cost structure that can provide similar services that would lead to improved profitability of only $1.5 million? That company could counterpropose a project at $1.4 million, which would be a better deal for the client, since it would leave them $100,000 ahead. The upshot is that competition can severely restrict the ability of a company to "value price" even when the competition is offering an inferior product. Even the existence of an inferior substitute will mean that a company cannot charge full value.

2.2.4 Summary

Cost-based pricing, market-based pricing, and value-based pricing are "purist" pricing approaches. In reality, most companies are not purists. While they may have a dominant philosophy, they do not use any one approach 100% of the time and will modify their approach to achieve different goals. According to Eric Mitchell of the Professional Pricing Society, when Xerox wanted to increase market share, they would put the pricing function under Sales. When they wanted to increase profits, they would move it into the Finance Department.[7] Other companies are less disciplined—their approach to pricing may change with the "flavor of the month": market-based when the emphasis is on market share, value-based when "focusing on the customer" comes into vogue.

Vacillating among pricing approaches is actually better than strict devotion to one approach. Any company that sticks tenaciously to any one of the three pure approaches would likely find itself in deep trouble very quickly. What is often seen in reality is a hybrid—companies espouse a particular philosophy but use pieces of all three, supplemented by a considerable amount of improvisation. The upshot is pricing confusion—there is rarely a consistent justification or approach applied across all pricing decisions.

2.3 THE SCOPE OF PRICING AND REVENUE OPTIMIZATION

Pricing and revenue optimization provides a consistent approach to pricing decisions across the organization. This means that a company needs to have a clear view of all the prices it is setting in the marketplace and the ways in which those prices are set. This defines the scope of pricing and revenue optimization.

2.3.1 The PRO Cube

The goal of pricing and revenue optimization is to provide the right price,

- for every product
- to every customer segment
- through every channel

and to update those prices over time in response to changing market conditions. The three dimensions of pricing and revenue optimization can be illustrated in a cube, as shown in Figure 2.4. Each element within the cube represents a combination of product, channel, and customer segment. Each element (or *cell*) has an associated price. For example, one element might be:

> *medium-size turbines sold to large customers in the northeast via the direct sales channel*

Another element might be:

> *Replacement gears sold to small companies via online sales*

In theory, each cell within the PRO cube could correspond to a different price. In practice, some cells may not be meaningful. Some products may not be offered through some channels, for example. It is also the case, of course, that the prices within the PRO cube will not always be independent of each other. Our ability (or desire) to charge different prices through different channels may be constrained either by practical considerations or by strategic goals. If we want to encourage small customers to purchase online rather than through our direct sales channel, we might institute a constraint that says that the online price for small customers for all products must be less than or equal to the direct sales chan-

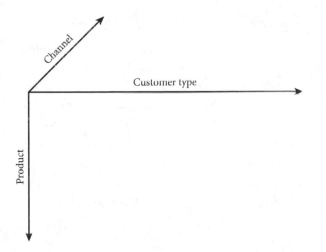

Figure 2.4 Dimensions of the pricing and revenue optimization cube.

nel price. These considerations are among the business rules that must be considered in the pricing and revenue optimization process described in Section 2.4.

Companies may offer even more prices than the PRO cube would imply. Certain products might be subject to tiered pricing or volume discounts. Or a company might offer bundles of products at different promotional rates or discounts that are not available for individual products. Each of these bundles or quantity combinations can be treated as an additional "virtual product" in the PRO cube.

The PRO cube is a useful starting point for a company seeking to understand the magnitude of the pricing challenge that it faces. Enumerating the combinations of products, market segments, and channels gives a rough estimate of the total number of prices a company needs to manage. Many companies are astonished at the sheer volume of prices they already offer. This astonishment is often the first step in realizing the need to establish a consistent pricing and revenue optimization process.

2.3.2 Customer Commitments

A core concept in pricing and revenue optimization is the idea of a *customer commitment*. Specifically, *a customer commitment occurs whenever a seller agrees to provide a customer with products or services, now or in the future, at a price*. The elements of a customer commitment include:

- The products and services being offered
- The price
- The time period over which the commitment will be delivered
- The time for which the offered commitment is valid i.e., how long the customer has to make up his mind
- Other elements of the contract or transaction (e.g., payment terms, return policy)
- Firmness of the commitment and risk sharing

Some examples of customer commitments include the following:

- A list price is possibly the most familiar form of customer commitment. A list price is a commitment that a buyer can obtain the item simply by paying the posted price. List price is often (but not always) a "take it or leave it" or "nonnegotiable" price. Common examples are the shelf prices at the grocery store and drugstore, price per gallon displayed on the gasoline pump, and many online retail prices.

- Coupons and other types of promotion are also forms of customer commitment. They allow certain customers to obtain a good at a price lower than list for some period.

- In a business-to-business setting, prices for large purchases are often individually negotiated. The seller may have published list prices, but, in many industries, items are rarely, if ever, purchased at the list price. Rather, each buyer negotiates an individual discount. The discount that a particular buyer receives can depend on the buyer's purchasing history with the seller, the skills of the purchasing agent and the salesperson, and the desire of the seller to make the sale. We describe an approach to optimizing such customized prices in Chapter 11.

- In other business-to-business settings, the buyer and seller negotiate a contract that establishes prices that will be in place for six months, a year, or longer. For example, in less-than-truckload (LTL) freight, shippers agree on a schedule of tariffs that will govern all the shipments they will make over the next year. These schedules are usually expressed in terms of a discount from a standard list tariff. Contracts are individually negotiated between each shipper and each carrier. Contracts may be exclusive (as they often are in package express), or a shipper may establish contracts with two or more carriers, as is common practice in trucking and container shipping.

- Contracts between electronics distributors, such as Ingram Micro and TechData, and wholesalers, such as Hewlett-Packard and Sun Microsystems, are often on a "tiered pricing" basis, where each tier includes a volume target and an incremental discount for hitting that target. An example is shown in Table 2.2. In this case, the purchaser will receive at least a 5% discount on each unit purchased during the current quarter. If she purchases at least 50,001 units, the discount increases to 6%. And if she purchases 80,001 units, the discount increases to 7%. This type of tiered pricing provides an incentive for the distributor to "push" the seller's products rather than those of its competitors. Tiered discounts can be based on either units sold or revenue sold. The increased discounts themselves can apply either to incremental sales above the tier or to all sales during the quarter.

- Online auction houses such as eBay enable a seller to establish a reserve price for an item they wish to sell. On eBay, the highest bidder above the reserve price will be sold the item at the maximum of the second highest bidder's price and the reserve price. The commitment by the seller is to honor this policy. In addition, the seller may establish a "buy now" price that allows immediate purchase. Auctions, either online or offline, are also common for many types of industrial goods.

TABLE 2.2
Tiered pricing

Quarterly units sold	Total discount (%)
0–50,000	5
50,001–80,000	6
80,001–110,000	7
≥110,001	8

The forms and types of commitments that sellers make (and buyers expect) vary from industry to industry. As a simple example, airline tickets were historically refundable, meaning that the airline took all the risk of a customer "no-show"—a risk the airlines sought to mitigate via overbooking. On the other hand, tickets to Broadway shows have historically been nonrefundable, meaning the customer takes on the risk of no-show. As a result, Broadway theaters do not overbook. The details of the types of commitments made in different industries are often the result of complex and contingent historical factors and may change over time—just as airlines are increasingly beginning to adopt nonrefundable ticketing.

In fact, it is not uncommon for individual sellers to be utilizing different approaches for different products through different channels. For example, an automobile manufacturer is likely to sell the majority of vehicles through dealers, utilizing a combination of "shelf price" (in this case, the wholesale price) and promotions. However, Ford Motor Company receives about 9% of its revenue in North America from group sales of cars to corporate, government, and industrial fleets. These sales are generally priced through individual negotiations or bids. Finally, a manufacturer may also be selling some cars directly to the public through a deal with an online channel. In this case, the manufacturer needs to apply pricing and revenue optimization across the entire range of its channels and pricing mechanisms in order to maximize total profitability.

2.4 THE PRICING AND REVENUE OPTIMIZATION PROCESS

Successful pricing and revenue optimization involves two components:

1. A consistent business process focused on pricing as a critical set of decisions
2. The software and analytical capabilities required to support the process

Much of the interest in pricing and revenue optimization has focused on its use of mathematical analysis. Quantitative analysis is indeed critical in most pricing and revenue optimization settings, but it cannot provide sustainable improvement unless it is embedded in the right process. An overview of such a process is shown in Figure 2.5. In this picture, the overall pricing and revenue optimization process has been divided into eight activities. Four of these activities are part of "operational PRO"—that is, they are executed every time the company needs to change the prices it is offering in the marketplace. The remaining four "supporting PRO" activities occur at longer intervals. As the figure shows, pricing and revenue optimization is a closed-loop process; that is, feedback from the market must be

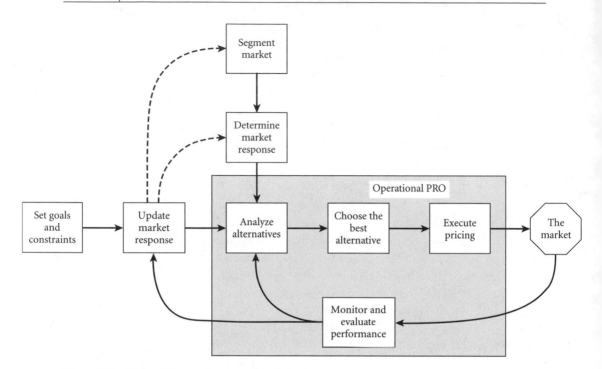

Figure 2.5 The pricing and revenue optimization process.

incorporated into both the operational activities and the more periodic activity of updating market response curves.

2.4.1 Operational PRO Activities

The operational PRO activities work continuously to set and update prices in the market-place. The timing of the decisions will depend on the application—airline revenue management systems can change fares from moment to moment. Revenue managers review the recommendations of the system on a daily basis. Other companies may update prices weekly or monthly. In any case, the core operational activities will be similar.

Analyze alternatives. This activity is the one most widely identified with pricing and revenue optimization or revenue management. Historically it has involved analysts' use of spreadsheets to compare pricing alternatives under different scenarios. More recently it has involved the use of software systems that solve the underlying optimization problem to recommend new prices for every element of the PRO cube.

Choose the best alternative. However prices are analyzed, a human being needs to be responsible for determining which prices should be set. For this reason, almost all pricing and revenue optimization software packages are equipped with a "what-if" capability that allows analysts to understand the reasons for their recommendations and the effect of different assumptions on the recommendations. In very rapidly changing environments such as the passenger airlines, the majority of prices will be updated automatically, with analysts only investigating the unusual or unexpected situations.

Execute pricing. Finally, the prices that have been calculated need to be communicated to the market. The mechanics of price transmission and distribution vary greatly from industry to industry, company to company, and even channel to channel within the same company. For an airline or hotel, prices are updated by opening or closing fare classes — a process discussed in more detail in Chapter 6. In other cases, a "pricing matrix" database specifies which prices are available to which customers through which channels. In other cases, new discount guidelines need to be communicated to the sales force. For a company with many products being sold through many channels, communicating the correct prices correctly can be a challenge in itself. A number of pricing execution or "pricing management" vendors, such as Vendavo and Metreo, sell software whose primary function is to ensure that complex pricing changes are correctly and efficiently transmitted through all channels.

Monitor and evaluate performance. As we receive the results from the marketplace, we need to compare the results with our expectations and evaluate overall performance against our goal. Are we achieving the lift we anticipated from a promotion? If not, why not? Was total market demand less than expected? Did the competition react more aggressively than we had anticipated? Were customers less responsive to price than we anticipated? Or was it a combination of all three?

Figure 2.5 shows that market feedback occurs at two levels. The most immediate feedback is to the analysis of alternatives. Here, the effects of the most recent actions should be monitored so that immediate action can be taken if necessary. The required actions may not always be directly related to pricing and revenue optimization. For example, the markdown management system utilized by a major retailer indicated that a particular style of pants was selling well below expectations. Investigation found that the pants had been hemmed improperly. Once the problem had been corrected, the pants began to sell at the rate initially expected.[8] In the more common case, a big difference between realized sales and expected sales is likely to be due to an unforseen change in the marketplace.

The second level of feedback updates the parameters of the market-response functions. If sales of some product are slower than expected, it may indicate that the market is more price responsive than expected and the future market-response curve for that product should be adjusted accordingly.

2.4.2 Supporting PRO activities

The primary role of the supporting activities is to provide key inputs to the operational PRO activities. The supporting activities occur on a much longer time frame. Typically goals and business rules will change quarterly at best. A new market segmentation may take place annually. Price-response curves will be updated much more frequently, typically weekly or monthly in the case of markdown management or customized pricing.

Set goals and business rules. A key initial step in pricing and revenue optimization is to specify the overall goal of the process. Without a clear goal it is impossible to make consistent decisions and it is impossible to evaluate decisions and improve the process over time. In general, the goal of pricing and revenue optimization is to maximize expected total contribution. However, at certain times, in certain markets, a company may wish to increase market share or attain a volume sales goal. Whatever the goal, it is most important that it be stated clearly and explicitly. As we discuss in Chapter 3, the corporate goal in a product/segment/channel combination determines the form of the objective function that will be used when optimizing that "cell" of the PRO cube.

Business rules apply whenever there is a restriction that may prevent us from pricing "optimally" in some market. Is there a minimum per-unit margin requirement we need to meet for all products within a category? Is there a minimum discount we need to offer to certain strategic customers? Do we want our retail list prices to be no lower than our Internet prices? Each of these types of business rule needs to be implemented as a constraint in the optimization problem at the heart of PRO.

Example 2.1

A heavy-equipment manufacturer wants to make sure that prices in the northeast are never more than 15% higher than the comparable model being offered by the leading competitor. This decision results in a constraint to be included in the PRO optimization problem:

Our price in the northeast ≤ 115% competitor A's price in the northeast.

We note that business rules are *inputs* into PRO — that is, they are decisions that are made not on the basis of short-term optimization but on the basis of other considerations a company wishes to include in its pricing.

Segment the market. An important theme within pricing and revenue optimization is segmenting the market in a way that maximizes the opportunity to extract profit. We discuss techniques for doing this in Chapter 4. The market segmentation needs to be updated periodically in order to reflect changes in the underlying market. However, this updating should be performed much less frequently than the operational PRO processes. For this reason, the "Segment Market" step in Figure 2.5 is shown with a dashed line outside the main process loop.

Determine price response. For each market segment identified we need to calculate the corresponding price-response functions. This step is performed in conjunction with segmenting the market.

Update price response. It is not sufficient merely to monitor the performance of PRO actions against expectations. A company needs to update its models to incorporate what they learn. As long as performance closely matches expectations, the parameters of the models need not be changed. However, if performance is significantly different from expectations, models need to be updated in order to reflect the new information.

The most critical message to take away from the pricing and revenue optimization process illustrated in Figure 2.5 is that PRO should be treated like any other business process. To make effective PRO decisions, we need to identify clearly what it is trying to achieve, the constraints we are facing, and the alternatives available. Based on our understanding of the market and the constraints, we choose the alternative most likely to achieve our goals. Once this alternative is implemented, we must monitor and measure the results against our expectations and update our understanding of the market so that we can make better decisions in the future. The PRO organization, responsibilities, systems, and data-capture methodologies all need to be able to support this process.

The PRO process presented in this section is highly general. We return to it in future chapters as we look at how pricing and revenue optimization is applied in specific pricing situations, such as revenue management, customized pricing, and markdown management.

2.4.3 The Time Dimension

Much of the growing interest in pricing and revenue optimization is being driven by the increasing velocity of pricing decisions. Where, in the past, prices changed once a quarter for many industries, now they change once a week, once a day, or even once an hour. Increased frequency and complexity of pricing within an industry creates its own momentum. A company that can change its prices more rapidly in response to changing market conditions will gain an advantage. This creates a strong incentive for other companies to match (or exceed) the frequency of change. E-commerce has been a proven driver of increased price velocity. As discussed in Chapter 1, the adoption of computerized distribution systems—an early form of e-commerce—by the passenger airlines was a direct contributor to the ability of the airlines to develop, manage, and update highly complex fare structures.[9]

Pricing has a different cadence in every industry. The rack (wholesale) price for gasoline fluctuates randomly, with little obvious trend. Fashion goods are priced high at the beginning of the season and are then subsequently marked down as the season progresses. Different pricing approaches need to be used in each of these markets. Gasoline rack prices are set using "dynamic pricing" approaches that primarily track changes in the underlying supply and demand imbalance. When supply is low (Iraqi oil production is interrupted) or demand is high (a cold winter in the northeast), the price tends to rise. Opposite conditions cause the price to fall. The price of a fashion item falls across the season, since such items become less valuable as the season progresses.[10] On the other hand, the passenger airlines have successfully segmented their customer base into early-booking leisure customers and later-booking business customers. To support this segmentation, ticket prices rise as departure approaches—a phenomenon we look at in much greater detail in Chapter 6. These different cadences lead to very different optimization approaches in different markets.

Frequent price changes creates a challenge for an organization. As price changes become more frequent and the pricing structure becomes more complex, it becomes less and less feasible for a company to apply in-depth analysis to each pricing decision. The "analyst with a spreadsheet" method of pricing decision making begins to break down. As the complexity and rapidity of pricing decisions continues to accelerate, many organizations find themselves overwhelmed. A common symptom is that despite expending more and more effort on pricing decisions, the company continually seems to be one step behind the market and the competition. At this point, most companies consider adopting some sort of computerized pricing support system.

2.4.4 The Role of Optimization

As the name implies, *optimization* clearly plays a central role in pricing and revenue optimization. As we see in Chapter 3, treating pricing decisions as constrained optimization problems is at the heart of pricing and revenue optimization. The formulation and solution of these constrained optimization problems draws on techniques from statistics, operations research, and management science.

While constrained optimization is at the heart of pricing and revenue optimization, it is also the case that no company in the world actually "optimizes" its prices. The reason is that determining the "optimal" price is, in general, impossible or at least well beyond our current ability to model and solve. All pricing and revenue optimization approaches (including those we will study) are based on solving stylized representations of the underlying problem. These representations include many of the important features of the real-world problem, but they will exclude others. For example, many hotel companies have become reasonably proficient at pricing and revenue optimization. Yet the following is a list of some of the factors often *not* incorporated in their pricing and revenue optimization decisions:[11]

- How the price we offer a potential customer now affects his propensity to consider this property (or this chain) in the future
- How group prices should be optimized to trade off the amount received from each group with the number of rooms they will take, considering that we may need to refuse bookings to future independent booking customers
- How the probability that this particular customer will cancel, understay (i.e., check out early), not show, or overstay (i.e., check out late) should influence the price we quote him
- How the price we quote to a customer should be influenced by the prices currently being offered by major competitors in this market
- How a group of properties serving a single location (e.g., all the Marriotts in Manhattan) should be priced to jointly optimize use of all the capacity
- How the expected booking order of future customers by length of stay affects the optimal price to offer this customer

The point is not that hotels are poor at pricing and revenue optimization. On the contrary, the industry has become increasingly sophisticated over the past two decades. The point is, rather, that hotels have been able to improve their pricing significantly without becoming "perfect."

As you go through the rest of the book, you will be introduced to pricing and revenue optimization models whose underlying assumptions are unrepresentative of the real world. As an example, the dynamic models used for capacity allocation in Chapter 7 and for markdown management in Chapter 10 assume that demand in different periods can be represented as *independent* random variables. This seems to be (and is) an unrealistic assumption. If we receive higher demand than anticipated in one period, we can generally expect higher demand in the next period. Yet the majority of pricing and revenue optimization models are based on this assumption.[12]

The justification for working with simplified representations of the underlying problem is that it works. Real-world applications have shown that this approach can lead to pricing decisions that generate additional profitability. By capturing 75% or so of the real-world complexity, mathematical analysis often does better than either human judgment or the other approaches to pricing described in Section 2.2. Of course, companies and vendors continue to invest to improve the sophistication of their pricing and revenue optimization systems. Over time, systems can capture more and more aspects of the real world, and pricing decisions continue to improve. However, it is unlikely that any system or approach will ever generate "perfect" recommendations. What pricing and revenue optimization really does is to use quantitative analysis to make better pricing decisions more quickly. Part of the philosophy of pricing and revenue optimization is that *good prices on time are far better than perfect prices late*. The improvement realized on any individual pricing decision may be small, but the aggregate effect over hundreds, thousands, or millions of pricing decisions can be very large indeed.

Finally, we should reemphasize the importance of the feedback loop in Figure 2.5. More than almost anything else, good pricing and revenue optimization is dependent on rapid and effective updating and monitoring. The faster and more effectively that prices can be adjusted to account for what is currently happening in a market, the higher the profit levels that will be generated.

2.5 SUMMARY

- For many companies, pricing involves a complex set of decisions that is poorly managed or unmanaged. In many cases, the "pocket prices" charged to customers are the result of a large number of uncoordinated and arbitrary decisions. The price waterfall and pocket-price histograms can be useful tools for understanding the current state of pricing management within a company.

- Traditional approaches to pricing include cost-plus, market based, and value based. Of these, cost-plus is the most common. Each approach ignores important aspects of the pricing problem. Most companies are not purists but rely on some combination of the approaches, with the emphasis changing over time.

- The scope of pricing and revenue optimization is to set and update the prices for each combination of product, customer segment, and channel—that is, each cell in the PRO cube.

- The approach used by pricing and revenue optimization must be tailored to the specifics of the underlying market structure. From the point of view of the seller, the key concept is what type of *customer commitment* is required in each market. Different types of customer commitments require different analytic approaches.

- Pricing and revenue optimization requires a consistent process for decision making, evaluation, and updating. A typical process is illustrated in Figure 2.5. This process includes both operational activities that involve setting and updating prices in response to market and cost changes and supporting activities that provide input to the operational activities.

2.6 EXERCISES

1. Brain and Company is a consulting group that offers a fool-proof pricing and revenue optimization service guaranteed to deliver $2 million in benefit to a customer. It costs Brain and Company $500,000 to provide this service. Unfortunately, they have a competitor, Dissenture, that provides a similar, but somewhat inferior, service that only delivers $1.5 million in guaranteed benefit. It also costs Dissenture $500,000 to provide this service.

   a. When competing with Dissenture, what price does Brain and Company need to charge in order to guarantee that they win the business? Assume that neither Dissenture nor Brain will price below cost and that both of them know each other's costs and the customer benefits in each case.

   b. How would Brain's price need to change if it only cost Dissenture $400,000 to provide their service?

1. Cited in Godin and Conley (1987, p. 58).
2. Cited in Dolan and Simon (1996, p. 38).
3. Reported in *The Pricing Advisor* of May 2002.
4. In the software industry, *value-based pricing* often refers to pricing policies that are based on usage or metrics other than the type of computer or the number of users. This practice was pioneered by the software vendor PeopleSoft, which priced its Human Resources module based on the number of employees in the licensed company and its Financial module based on the annual revenue of the licensee (Welch 2002). The goal of such approaches is to segment the market according to value in order to capture higher license fees from high-value customers. While PeopleSoft's experience was widely regarded as successful, other attempts to implement value-based pricing have been less successful, particularly when competition drives fees down.
5. This is called *perfect third-degree price discrimination by a monopolist.*
6. McLaughlin (2002).
7. Eric Mitchell, personal communication.
8. Rama Ramakrishnan, personal communication.
9. Boyd and Bilegan (2003) provide a good discussion of this history.
10. There are a number of other reasons why the prices of fashion goods tend to fall across a season; we discuss them in detail in Chapter 10.
11. Some hotels consider some of these elements, but no hotel considers all of them.
12. Some approaches use simple adjustments in the optimization to account for inter-temporal dependence.

BASIC PRICE OPTIMIZATION

In this section we introduce the basic elements of pricing and revenue optimization and show how the basic pricing revenue and optimization problem can be formulated as an optimization problem. The goal of the optimization problem—its objective function—is to maximize contribution: total revenue minus total incremental cost from sales. The key elements of this problem are the price-response function and the incremental cost of sales, both of which we introduce in this section. We then formulate and solve the pricing and revenue optimization function in the case of a single product in a single market without supply constraints and derive some important optimality conditions.

3.1 THE PRICE-RESPONSE FUNCTION

A fundamental input to any PRO analysis is the *price-response function*, or *price-response curve*, $d(p)$ which specifies how demand for a product varies as a function of its price, p. There is one price-response function associated with each element in the PRO cube—that is, there is a price-response function associated with each combination of product, market-segment, and channel. The price-response function is similar to the market demand function found in economic texts. However, there is a critical difference. The price-response function specifies *demand for the product of a single seller as a function of the price offered by that seller*. This contrasts with the concept of a *market demand curve*, which specifies how an entire market will respond to changing prices. The distinction is critical because different firms competing in the same market face different price-response functions. Referring to Table 1.2, the price-response function facing Amazon for *Bag of Bones* is likely to be quite different from the one facing ecampus.com. The differences in the price-response functions faced by different sellers are the result of many factors, such as the effectiveness of their marketing campaigns, perceived customer differences in quality, product differences, and location, among other factors.

In a perfectly competitive market, the price response faced by an individual seller is a vertical line at the market price, as shown in Figure 3.1. If the seller prices above the market

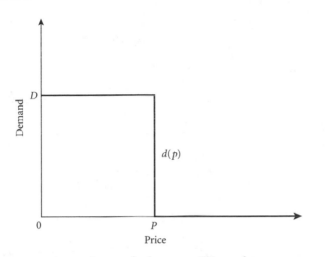

Figure 3.1   Price-response curve in a perfectly competitive market.

price, his demand drops to 0. If he prices below the market price, his demand is equal to the entire market. A standard example used in economics texts is wheat:

> The best example to keep in mind is that of a wheat farmer, who provides a minuscule percentage of the wheat grown in the world. Regardless of whether he produces 10 bushels or 1,000, he remains too small to have any impact on the going market price. . . . If he tries to charge even a fraction of a penny more, he will sell no wheat, because buyers can just as easily buy from someone else. If he charges even a fraction of a penny less, the public will demand more wheat from him than he can possibly produce—effectively an infinite quantity.[1]

In other words, wheat is a commodity—buyers are totally indifferent among the offerings of different sellers, they have perfect knowledge about all prices being offered, and they will buy the product only from the lowest-price seller. Furthermore, each seller is small relative to the total size of the market. In this situation, the seller has no pricing decision—his price is set by the operation of the larger market. To quote a popular text: "In a competitive market, each firm only has to worry about how much output it wants to produce. Whatever it produces can only be sold at one price: the going market price."[2] At any price below the market price, the demand seen by a seller would be equal to the entire demand in the market—the amount D in Figure 3.1. At any price above the market price he sells nothing. The seller of a true commodity in a perfectly competitive market has no need for pricing and revenue optimization—indeed, he has no need of any pricing capability whatsoever. However, true commodities are surprisingly rare. The vast majority of companies face finite customer responses to price changes and therefore have active PRO decisions.

The price-response functions that we consider—and those facing most companies most of the time—demonstrate some degree of smooth price response. An example is shown in Figure 3.2. Here, as price increases, demand declines until it reaches zero at some *satiating price P*. This type of smooth market-response function is usually termed a *monopolistic* or *monopoly* demand curve in the economics literature. The terminology is somewhat unfortunate, since the fact that a company faces some level of price response hardly means that

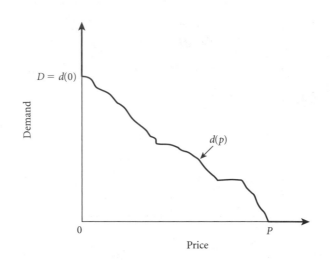

Figure 3.2 Typical price-response curve.

it is a "monopoly." Companies such as United Airlines, UPS, and Ford all face smooth price-response functions for their products, yet none of them would be considered a monopoly in the usual sense of the world.

3.1.1 Properties of the Price-Response Function

The price-response functions used in PRO analysis have a time dimension associated with them. This is in keeping with the dynamic nature of PRO decisions—we are not setting prices that will last "in perpetuity" but prices that will be in place for some finite period of time. The period might be minutes or hours (as in the case of a fast-moving e-commerce market), days or weeks (as in retail markets), or longer (as in long-term contract pricing). At the end of the period we have the opportunity to change prices. The demand we expect to see at a given price will depend on the length of time the price will be in place. Thus, we can speak of the price-response function for a model copier over a week or over a month, but without an associated time interval there is no single price-response function.

There are many different ways in which product demand might change in response to changing prices and, thus, many different possible price-response functions. However, all of the price-response functions we consider will be nonnegative, continuous, differentiable, and downward sloping.

Nonnegative. We assume that all prices are greater than or equal to zero; that is, $p \geq 0$.[3]

Continuous. We assume that the price-response function is *continuous*—there are no "gaps" or "jumps" in the market response to our prices. More formally, if $d(0) = D$ and P is the satiating price, that is, the lowest price for which $d(P) = 0$, then for every $0 < q \leq D$ there is a price $p \leq P$ such that $d(p) = q$. This implies that there is a price that will generate any level of demand between 0 and the maximum demand. This property, known as *invertability*, is often very useful.[4]

Differentiable. Differentiability means that the price-response function is smooth, with a well-defined slope at every point.[5] As with the assumption of continuity, this assumption involves taking a mathematical liberty, since prices are only defined for fixed increments.

However, differentiability allows us to use the tools of calculus to solve the constrained optimization problems that arise in PRO—a gain that outweighs the slight imprecision that results from using derivatives rather than difference equations.

Downward sloping. We assume that $d(p)$ is downward sloping whenever $d(p) > 0$—that is, that raising prices for a good during a period will decrease demand for that good during that period unless demand is already 0, in which case demand will remain at 0. Conversely, lowering prices can only increase demand.

The "downward sloping" assumption calls for a bit more discussion. First of all, it should be noted that downward-sloping demand curves do not mean that high prices will always be associated with low demand. A hotel revenue management will experience higher average rates when occupancy is high and lower average rates when occupancy is low. What the downward-sloping property does indicate is that, in any time period, demand would have been lower if prices had been higher, and vice versa. This corresponds both to economic theory (in which consumers maximize their utilities subject to a budget constraint) and to real-life experience.

Nonetheless, there are at least three cases in which the downward-sloping property may not hold.

1. *Giffen goods.* Economic theory allows for the possibility of so called *Giffen goods,* whose demand rises as their price rises because of substitution effects. An example might be a student on a strict budget of $8.00 per week for dinner. When hamburger costs $1.00 per serving and steak costs $2.00, he eats hamburger six times a week and steak once. If the price of hamburger rises to $1.10, to stay within his budget, he stops buying steak and buys hamburger seven times a week. In this case, a rise in the price of hamburger causes his consumption of hamburger to increase. While this behavior might conceivably occur at an individual level, a Giffen good requires that enough buyers act this way that they overwhelm other buyers who would buy less hamburger as the price rises. Giffen goods are almost never encountered in reality—in fact, many economists doubt whether they have ever existed.

2. *Price as an indicator of quality.* In some markets, price is used by some consumers as an indicator of quality: Higher prices signal higher quality. In this case, lowering the price for a product may lead consumers to believe that it is of lower quality, and demand could drop as a result. Typically, markets where this is an issue have a large number of alternatives and some "lazy" buyers who do not have the time or resources to research the relative quality of all the alternatives so that they use price as a proxy. Wine is a classic example: Faced with a daunting array of labels and varietals, many purchasers are likely to use a rule such as: a $10 bottle for dinner with the family, a $15 bottle if the couple next door is dropping by, and a $25 bottle if our wine-snob friends are joining us for dinner.[6] The "price-as-an-indicator-of-quality effect" can be particularly important when a new product enters the market. A medical-product company developed a way of producing a home testing device at a cost 75% below the cost of the prevailing technology. They introduced the new product at a list price 60% lower than the list price of the leading competitors, expecting to dominate the market. When sales were slow, they repackaged the product

and sold it at a price only 20% lower than the leading competitor. This time sales took off. Their belief is that the initial rock-bottom price induced customers to believe their product was inferior and unreliable. The higher price was high enough not to raise quality concerns but low enough to drive high sales.

3. *Conspicuous consumption.* Thorstein Veblen coined the term *conspicuous consumption* for the situation in which a consumer makes a purchase decision in order to advertise his ability to spend large amounts. It probably does not come as a shock that the reason some rock stars drink $300 bottles of Cristal champagne and drive Bentleys is not their finely honed appreciation of fine French champagne and British automotive engineering. Conspicuous consumption postulates a segment of customers who buy a product simply because it has a high price—and others know it. Dropping the price in this case may cause the product to lose its cachet and decrease demand.

While duly noting these three exceptions to downward-sloping demand curves, we will proceed to ignore them for the remainder of the book. In defense of this decision, we observe that for almost all items, almost all of the time, raising the price will lower demand and lowering the price will increase demand.

3.1.2 Measures of Price Sensitivity

It is often useful to have a simple characterization of the price sensitivity implied by a price-response function at a particular price. The two most common measures of price sensitivity are the *slope* and the *elasticity* of the price-response function.

Slope. The *slope* of the price-response function measures how demand changes in response to a price change. It is equal to the change in demand divided by the difference in prices, or

$$\delta(p_2, p_1) = [d(p_2) - d(p_1)]/(p_2 - p_1) \tag{3.1}$$

By the downward-sloping property, $p_1 > p_2$ implies that $d(p_1) \le d(p_2)$. This means that $\delta(p_1, p_2)$ will always be less than or equal to zero.

The definition in Equation 3.1 requires two prices to be specified, because the slope of a price-response function will be constant across all prices only if it is linear. However, it is common to specify the slope at a single price, say, p_1, in which case it can be computed as the limit of Equation 3.1 as p_2 approaches p_1. That is,

$$\delta(p_1) = \lim_{h \to 0} [d(p_1 + h) - d(p_1)]/h$$
$$= d'(p_1)$$

where $d'(p_1)$ denotes the derivative of the price-response function at p_1. By the differentiability property, we know that this derivative exists. The downward-sloping property means that the slope will be less than or equal to zero for all prices.

The slope can be used as a *local* estimator of the change in demand that would result from a small change in price. For small changes in price, we can write

$$d(p_2) - d(p_1) \approx \delta(p_1)(p_2 - p_1) \tag{3.2}$$

That is, a large (highly negative) slope means that demand is more responsive to price than a smaller (less negative) slope.

Example 3.1

The slope of the price-response function facing a semiconductor manufacturer at the current price of $0.13 per chip is $-1,000$ chips/week per cent. From Equation 3.2, he would estimate that a 2-cent increase in price would result in a reduction in demand of about 2,000 chips per week and a 3-cent decrease in price would result in approximately 3,000 chips/week in additional demand.

It is important to recognize that the quality of the approximation in Equation 3.2 declines for larger changes in prices and that the slope cannot be used as an accurate predictor of demand at prices far from the current price. It is also important to realize that the slope of the price-response function depends on the units of measurement being used for both price and demand.

Example 3.2

The price of a bulk chemical can be quoted in either cents per pound or dollars per ton. Assume that the demand for the chemical is 50,000 pounds at 10 cents per pound but drops to 40,000 pounds at 11 cents per pound. The slope of the price response function at these two points is

$$\delta(10, 11) = (50,000 - 40,000)/(10 - 11)$$

$$= -10,000 \text{ pounds/cent}$$

The same slope in tons per dollar would be $(25 - 20)/(0.1-0.11) = -500$ tons/dollar.

Price elasticity. Perhaps the most common measure of the sensitivity of demand to price is *price elasticity*, defined as the ratio of the percentage change in demand to the percentage change in price.[7] Formally, we can write

$$\epsilon(p_1, p_2) = -\frac{100\{[d(p_2) - d(p_1)]/d(p_1)\}}{100\{(p_2 - p_1)/p_1\}} \tag{3.3}$$

where $\epsilon(p_1, p_2)$ is the elasticity of a price change from p_1 to p_2. The numerator in Equation 3.3 is the percentage change in demand, and the denominator is the percentage change in price. Reducing terms gives

$$\epsilon(p_1, p_2) = -\frac{[d(p_2) - d(p_1)]p_1}{[p_2 - p_1]d(p_1)} \tag{3.4}$$

The downward-sloping property guarantees that demand always changes in the opposite direction from price. Thus, the minus sign on the right-hand side of Equation 3.4 guarantees that $\epsilon(p_1, p_2) \geq 0$. An elasticity of 1.2 means that a 10% *increase* in price would result in a 12% *decrease* in demand and an elasticity of 0.8 means that a 10% decrease in price would result in an 8% increase in demand.

$\epsilon(p_1, p_2)$ as defined in Equation 3.4 is sometimes called the *arc elasticity*. That it requires two prices to calculate reflects that the percentage change in demand resulting from changing prices will depend on both the old price and the new price. In fact, the percentage decrease in from a 1% *increase* in price will generally not even be the same as the percentage increase in demand that we would experience from a 1% *decrease in price*. For this reason, both prices need to be specified in order to fully characterize elasticity. However, as we did with slope, we can derive a *point elasticity* at p by taking the limit of Equation 3.4 as p_2 approaches p_1:

$$\epsilon(p_1) = -d'(p_1)p_1/d(p_1) \tag{3.5}$$

In words, the point elasticity is equal to -1 times the slope of the demand curve times the price, divided by demand. Since $d'(p) \leq 0$, the point elasticity $\epsilon(p)$ calculated by Equation 3.5 will be greater than or equal to zero. The point elasticity is useful as a local estimate of the change in demand resulting from a *small* change in price.

Example 3.3

A semiconductor manufacturer is selling 10,000 chips per month at $0.13 per chip. He believes that the price elasticity for his chips is 1.5. Thus, a 15% increase in price from $0.13 to $0.15 per chip would lead to a decrease in demand of about $1.5 \times 15\% = 22.5\%$, or from 10,000 to about 7,750 chips per month.

One of the appealing properties of elasticity is that, unlike slope, its value is independent of the units being used. Thus, the elasticity of electricity is the same whether the quantity electricity is measured in kilowatts or megawatts and whether the units are dollars or euros.

Example 3.4

Consider the bulk chemical whose price-response slope was estimated in Example 3.2. It showed a 20% decrease in demand (from 50,000 pounds to 40,000 pounds) from a 10% increase in price (from 10 cents to 11 cents). The corresponding elasticity is $0.2/0.1 = 2$—an elastic response. What if the units were euros and tons? It would still be a 20% decrease in demand (from 25 tons to 20 tons) from a 10% increase in price.

Like slope, point elasticity is a *local* property of the price-response function. That is, elasticity can be specified between two different prices by Equation 3.4 and a point elasticity can be defined by Equation 3.5. However, the term *price elasticity* is often used more broadly and somewhat loosely. Thus, statements such as "gasoline has a price elasticity of 1.22" are imprecise unless they specify both the time period of application and the reference price. In practice, the term *price elasticity* is often used simply as a synonym for *price sensitivity*. Items with "high price elasticity" have demand that is very sensitive to price while "low price elasticity" items have much lower sensitivity. Often, a good with a price elasticity greater than 1 is described as elastic, while one with an elasticity less than 1 is described as inelastic.

Elasticity depends on the time period under consideration, and, as with other aspects of price response, we must be clear to specify the time frame we are talking about. For most products, *short-run elasticity* is lower than *long run elasticity*. The reason is that buyers have more flexibility to adjust to higher prices in the long run. For example, the short-run elasticity for gasoline has been estimated to be 0.2, while the long-run elasticity has been estimated at 0.7. In the short run, the only options consumers have in response to high gas prices are to take fewer trips and to use public transportation. But if gasoline prices stay high, consumers will start buying higher mile-per-gallon cars, depressing overall demand for gasoline even further. A retailer raising the price of milk by 20 cents may not see much change in milk sales for the first week or so and conclude that the price elasticity of milk is low. But he will likely see a much greater deterioration in demand over time. The reason is that customers who come to shop for milk after the price rise will still buy milk, since it is too much trouble to go to another store. But some customers will note the higher price and switch stores the next time they shop.

On the other hand, the long-run price elasticity of many durable goods—such as automobiles and washing machines—is lower than the short-run elasticity. The reason is that customers initially respond to a price rise by postponing the purchase of a new item. However, they will still purchase at some time in the future, so the long-run effect of the price change is less than the short-run effect.

Finally, it is important to specify the level at which we are calculating elasticity. Market elasticity measures total market response if all suppliers of a product increase their prices—perhaps in response to a common cost change. Market elasticity is generally much lower than the price response elasticity faced by an individual supplier within the market. The reason is simple: If all suppliers raise their price, the only alternative faced by customers is to purchase a substitute product or to go without. On the other hand, if a single supplier raises its price, its customers have the option of defecting to the competition.

Table 3.1 shows some elasticities that have been estimated for various goods and services. Note that a staple such as salt is very inelastic—customers do not change the amount of salt they purchase very much in response to *market* price changes. On the other hand, we would expect that price elasticity of the market-response function faced by any individual seller of salt to be quite large—since salt is a fungible commodity in a highly competitive market.

TABLE 3.1
Estimated price elasticities for various goods and services

Good	Short-run elasticity	Long-run elasticity
Salt	0.1	—
Airline travel	0.1	2.4
Tires	0.9	1.2
Restaurant meals	2.3	—
Automobiles	1.2	0.2
Chevrolets	4.0	

This effect can be seen in Table 3.1 in the difference between the short-run elasticity for automobile purchases (1.2) and the much larger elasticity (4.0) faced by Chevrolet models. The table also illustrates the fact that long-run elasticity is greater than the short-run elasticity for airline travel (where customers respond to a price rise by changing travel plans in the future and traveling less by plane), but the reverse is true for automobiles (where consumers respond to price rises by postponing purchases).

3.1.3 Price Response and Willingness to Pay

So far, we have treated the price-response function as simply given. In reality, demand is the result of thousands, perhaps millions, of individual buying decisions on the part of potential customers. Each potential customer observes our price and decides whether or not to buy our product. Those who do not buy our product may purchase from the competition, or they may decide to do without. The price-response function specifies how many more of those potential customers would buy if we lowered our price and how many current buyers would not buy if we raised our price. Thus the price-response function is based on assumptions about customer behavior. We usually cannot directly track the thousands or even millions of individual decisions that ultimately manifest themselves in demand for our product.[8] However, it is worthwhile to understand the assumptions about customer behavior that underlie the price-response functions so that we can judge if the price-response function is based on assumptions appropriate for the application. The most important of such models of customer behavior is based on *willingness to pay*.

The willingness-to-pay approach assumes that each potential customer has a *maximum willingness to pay* (sometimes called a *reservation price*) for a product or service. A customer will purchase if and only if the price is less than her maximum willingness to pay. (We will use *willingness to pay*, sometimes abbreviated *w.t.p.*, to mean "maximum willingness to pay.") For example, a customer with a willingness to pay of $253 for an airline ticket from New York to Miami will purchase the ticket if the price is less than or equal to $253 but not if it is $253.01 or more. In this case, $d(253)$ equals the number of customers whose maximum willingness to pay is at least $253. A customer with a maximum willingness to pay of $0 (or less) will not buy at any price.

Define the function $w(x)$ as the w.t.p. distribution across the population. Then, for any values $0 \leq p_1 < p_2$:

$$\int_{p_1}^{p_2} w(x)\, dx = \text{fraction of the population that has w.t.p. between } p_1 \text{ and } p_2$$

We note that $0 \leq w(x) \leq 1$ for all nonnegative values of x. Let $D = d(0)$, the maximum demand achievable. Then we can derive $d(p)$ from the w.t.p. distribution from

$$d(p) = D \int_{p}^{\infty} w(x)\, dx \tag{3.6}$$

We can take the derivative of the corresponding price-response function to obtain

$$d'(p) = -Dw(p)$$

which is nonpositive, as required by the downward-sloping demand curve property. Conversely, we can derive the willingness-to-pay distribution from the price-response function [9] using

$$w(x) = -d'(x)/d(0)$$

Example 3.5

The total potential market for a spiral-bound notebook is $D = 20,000$, and willingness to pay is distributed uniformly between \$0 and \$10.00 as shown in Figure 3.3. This means that

$$w(x) = \begin{cases} 1/10 & \text{if } 0 \le x \le \$10 \\ 0 & \text{otherwise} \end{cases}$$

We can apply Equation 3.6 to derive the corresponding price-response curve:

$$\begin{aligned} d(p) &= 20,000 \int_{p}^{10} (1/10) \, dx \\ &= 20,000(1 - p/10) \\ &= 20,000 - 2,000p \end{aligned}$$

The price-response curve $d(p) = 20,000 - 2,000p$ is a straight line with $d(0) = 20,000$ and a satiating price of \$10.00.

Example 3.5 illustrates a general principle:

A uniform willingness-to-pay distribution corresponds to a linear price-response function, and vice versa.

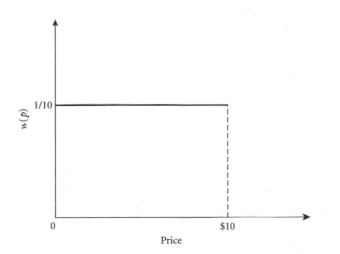

Figure 3.3 Uniform willingness to pay distribution.

One of the advantages of Equation 3.6 is that it partitions the price-response function into a total-demand component D and a willingness-to-pay component $w(x)$. This is often a convenient way to model a market. For example, we might anticipate that total demand varies seasonally for some product while the willingness-to-pay distribution remains constant over time. Then, given a forecast of total demand $D(t)$ for a future period t, our expected price-response function in each future period would be

$$d(p(t)) = D(t) \int_{\underline{p}}^{\overline{p}} w(x) \, dx \tag{3.7}$$

This approach allows us to decompose the problem of forecasting total demand from the problem of estimating price response. It also allows us to model influences on willingness to pay and total demand independently and then to combine them. For example, we might anticipate that a targeted advertising campaign will not increase the total population of potential customers, $D(t)$, but that it will shift the willingness-to-pay distribution. On the other hand, if we open a new retail outlet, we might anticipate that the total demand potential for the new outlet will be determined by the size of the population served, while the willingness to pay will have the same distribution as existing stores serving populations with similar demographics.

Of course, a customer's willingness to pay changes with changing circumstances and tastes. The maximum willingness to pay for a cold soft drink increases as the weather gets warmer—a fact that the Coca-Cola company considered exploiting with vending machines that changed prices with temperature (see Chapter 12 for a discussion of the "temperature-sensitive vending machine" idea). Willingness to pay to see a movie is higher for most people on Friday night than on Tuesday afternoon. A sudden windfall or a big raise may increase an individual's maximum willingness to pay for a new Mercedes Benz. To the extent that such changes are random and uncorrelated, they will not effect the overall w.t.p. distribution, since increasing willingness to pay on one person's part will tend to be balanced by another's decreasing willingness to pay. On the other hand, systematic changes across a population of customers will change the overall distribution and cause the price-response function to shift. Such systematic changes may be due to seasonal effects, changing fashion or fads, or an overall rise in purchasing power for a segment of the population. These systematic changes need to be understood and incorporated into estimating price response and future price response.

A disadvantage of the willingness-to-pay formulation is that it assumes that customers are considering only a single purchase. This is a reasonable assumption for relatively expensive and durable items. However, for many inexpensive or nondurable items, a reduction in price might cause some customers to buy multiple units. A significant price reduction on a washing machine will induce additional customers to buy a new washing machine, but it is unlikely to induce many customers to purchase two. However, a deep discount on socks may well induce customers to buy several pairs. This additional induced demand is not easily incorporated in a willingness-to-pay framework—willingness-to-pay models are most applicable to "big ticket" consumer items and industrial goods.

3.1.4 Common Price-Response Functions

Linear price-response function. We have seen that a uniform distribution of willingness to pay generates a linear price-response function. The general formula for the linear price-response function is

$$d(p) = D - mp \qquad (3.8)$$

where $D > 0$ and $m > 0$. $D = d(0)$ is the *demand at zero price*. The general linear price-response function is shown in Figure 3.4. The *satiating price*—that is, the price at which demand drops to zero—is given by $P - D/m$. The slope of the linear price-response function is $-m$ for $0 < p < P$ and 0 for $p \geq P$. The elasticity of the linear price-response function is $mp/(D - mp)$, which ranges from 0 at $p - 0$ and approaches infinity as p approaches P, dropping again to 0 for $p > P$.

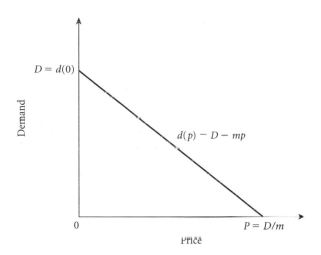

Figure 3.4 Linear price-response function.

We will use the linear price response function in many examples because it is a convenient and easily tractable model of market response. However, it is not a realistic *global* representation of price response. The linear price-response function assumes that the change in demand from a 10-cent increase in price will be the same, no matter what the base price might be. This is unrealistic, especially when a competitor may be offering a close substitute. In this case, we would usually expect the effect of a price change to be greatest when the base price is close to the competitor's price.

Constant-elasticity price-response function. As the name implies, the constant-elasticity price-response function has a point elasticity that is the same at all prices. That is,

$$d'(p)p/d(p) = -\epsilon \qquad \text{for all } p > 0 \qquad (3.9)$$

where $\epsilon > 0$ is the elasticity. The price-response function corresponding to Equation 3.9 is

$$d(p) = Cp^{-\epsilon} \qquad (3.10)$$

where $C > 0$ is a parameter chosen such that $d(1) = C$. For example, if we are measuring price in dollars and $d(\$1.00) = 10,000$, then $C = 10,000$. The slope of the constant-elasticity price-response function is

$$d'(p) = -C\epsilon p^{-(\epsilon+1)}$$

which is less than zero, confirming that constant-elasticity price-response functions are downward sloping. Some examples of constant-elasticity price-response functions are shown in Figure 3.5. Note that constant-elasticity price-response functions are neither finite nor satiating. Demand does not drop to zero at any price, no matter how high, and demand continues to approach infinity as price approaches zero. For these reasons, constant elasticity is usually not a good *global* assumption for price response.

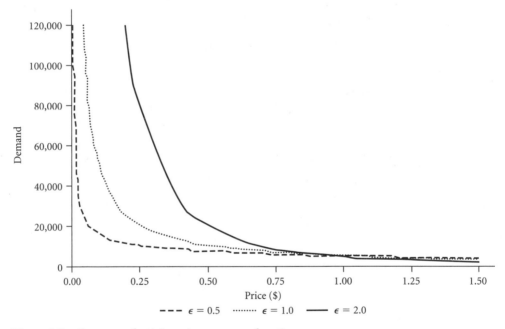

Figure 3.5 Constant-elasticity price-response functions.

It is interesting to analyze the impact of price on *revenue* for a seller facing constant-elasticity price response. Let $R(p)$ denote total revenue at price p. Then $R(p) = p\,d(p)$ and, for the constant-elasticity price-response function given by Equation 3.10,

$$R(p) = pCp^{-\epsilon}$$
$$= Cp^{(1-\epsilon)}$$

Taking the slope of this function gives

$$R'(p) = (1-\epsilon)Cp^{-\epsilon}$$
$$= (1-\epsilon)\,d(p)$$

Since $d(p) > 0$, the direction of the slope is determined by the $(1 - \epsilon)$ term. If $\epsilon < 1$ (that is, if demand is inelastic), then $R'(p) > 0$. This means that the seller facing constant *inelastic* price response can always increase his revenue by increasing price. In fact, he can also increase total operating margin by increasing price, so we would never expect to find a company maximizing operating margin setting its price such that the local elasticity is less than 1. If $\epsilon > 1$, a seller can increase revenue by decreasing price. In fact, the seller can maximize revenue by setting the price as close to zero—without actually becoming zero—as possible! If $\epsilon = 1$, then $R(p) = C$ for any value of p—revenue will not change at all as price changes. Revenue as a function of price for three different constant-elasticity price-response cases is illustrated in Figure 3.6.

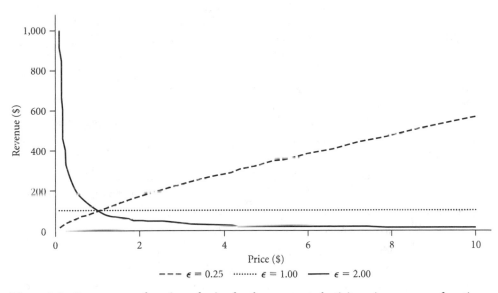

Figure 3.6 Revenue as a function of price for the constant-elasticity price-response function.

These properties make the constant-elasticity function problematic as a global price-response function. It is certainly the rare market in which a seller can maximize his revenue by either increasing his price toward infinity or dropping it as close to zero as possible. For these reasons, constant elasticity is a better representation of local price response than for use as a global price-response function. In real-world situations, we would expect price elasticity to change as price changes.

The constant-elasticity price-response function in Equation 3.10 corresponds to the willingness-to-pay distribution given by

$$w(x) = \epsilon x^{-(\epsilon+1)}$$

This distribution is given in Figure 3.7 for different values of ϵ. The figure shows that the constant-elasticity price-response function corresponds to a distribution of willingness to pay that is highly concentrated near zero.

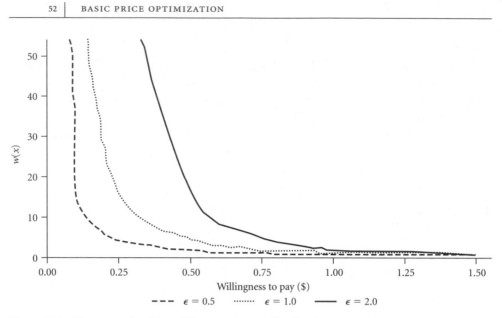

Figure 3.7 Constant-elasticity willingness-to-pay distributions.

The logit price-response functions. Both the linear and the constant-elasticity price-response functions are useful local models of price response. However, they have rather severe limitations as global models of customer behavior. This can be seen by considering their corresponding willingness-to-pay distributions. The linear price-response function assumes that w.t.p. is uniformly distributed between 0 and some maximum value. The constant-elasticity price-response function assumes that the distribution of willingness to pay drops steadily as price increases, approaching, but never reaching, zero. Neither of these functions would seem to represent customer behavior very realistically.

How would we expect customers to react to changes in price? Consider the case where we are selling a compact car. Assume that competing models are generally similar to ours and are selling at a market price of about $13,000. If we price well above the market price, say, at $20,000, we won't sell many cars. But the few customers who are buying from us at $20,000 must be very loyal (or very ignorant)—we would not expect to lose very many more of them if we increased our price from $20,000 to $21,000. In other words, the elasticity of the price-response function is low at this price. On the other hand, if we priced well below the market price—say, at $9,000 —we would expect to sell lots of cars. At this price, almost anyone who wants to buy a compact car and is not incredibly loyal to another brand (or incredibly averse to ours) would be buying from us. Lowering our price another $1,000 is unlikely to attract many new customers. Again, price elasticity is low.

What happens when we are close to the market price? In this case, we would expect small changes in our price to lead to substantial shifts in demand. There are a lot of customers who are more or less indifferent between our offering and that of the competition. Many of these customers can be persuaded to purchase our car if we ask only $250 less than the market price, and even more will shift if we ask $500 less than the market price. Similarly, if we charge $250 above the market price we are likely to lose a lot of demand to the competition. In other words, price elasticity is highest when we are at (or near) the market price.

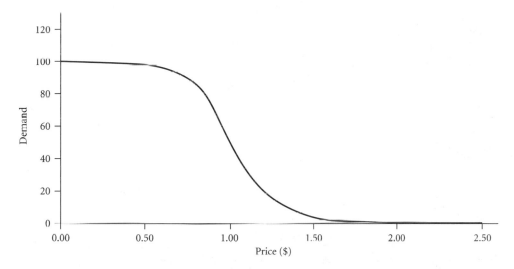

Figure 3.8   (Reverse) S-shaped, or sigmoid, price-response curve.

This kind of consumer behavior generates a response curve of the general form shown in Figure 3.8. When we price very low, we receive lots of demand, but demand changes slowly as we change price. In the area of the "market price," demand is very sensitive to our price—small changes in price can lead to substantial changes in demand. At high prices, demand is low and changes slowly as we raise prices further. The price-response curve has a sort of reverse S shape. Empirical research has shown that this general form of price-response curve fits observed price response in a wide range of markets.

The most popular price-response function of this form is the *logit* price-response function:

$$d(p) = \frac{Ce^{-(a+bp)}}{1 + e^{-(a+bp)}} \tag{3.11}$$

Here, a, b, and C are parameters with $C > 0$ and $b > 0$. a can be either greater than or less than 0, but in most applications we will have $a > 0$. Broadly speaking, C indicates the size of the overall market and b specifies price sensitivity. Larger values of b correspond to greater price sensitivity. The price-sensitivity curve is steepest at the point $\hat{p} = -(a/b)$, as indicated in Figure 3.8. This point can be considered to be approximately the "market price."

The logit price-response curve is shown for different values of b in Figure 3.9. Here we have fixed $\hat{p} = \$13,000$, so $a = -\$13,000 \times b$ for each curve. Demand is very sensitive to price when price is close to $\hat{p}$. Higher values of b represent more price-sensitive markets. As b grows larger, the market approaches perfect competition. In other words, the price-response curve increasingly approaches the perfectly competitive price-response function in Figure 3.1.

Some of the characteristics of the logit price-response function are shown in Table 3.2. Logit willingness to pay follows a bell-shaped curve known as the *logistic distribution*. The logistic distribution is similar to the normal distribution, except it has somewhat "fatter tails"—that is, it approaches zero more slowly at very high and very low values. An example of the logistic w.t.p. distribution is shown in Figure 3.10. The highest point (mode) of the logistic willingness-to-pay distribution occurs at $\hat{p} = -(a/b)$, which is also the point at which

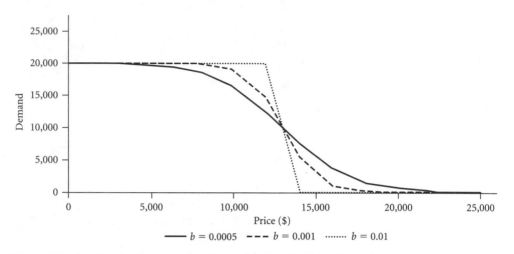

Figure 3.9 Logit price-response functions with $C = 20,000$ and $p = \$13,000$.

TABLE 3.2
Properties of the logit price-response function

Demand at 0	$d(0) = \dfrac{Ce^{-a}}{1 + e^{-a}}$
Slope	$d'(p) = \dfrac{-Cbe^{-(a+bp)}}{(1 + e^{-(a+bp)})^2}$
Elasticity	$\epsilon(p) = \dfrac{bp}{1 + e^{-(a+bp)}}$
Willingness-to-pay distribution	$w(x) = \dfrac{Ke^{-(a+bx)}}{(1 + e^{-(a+bx)})^2}$

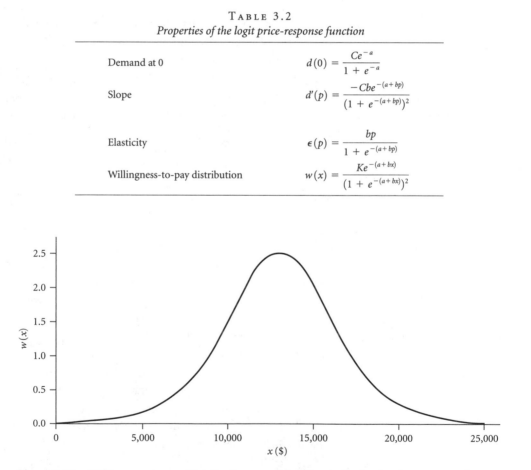

Figure 3.10 Willingness-to-pay distribution corresponding to the logit price-response function in Figure 3.9 with $b = 0.0005$. The y-axis has been scaled by a factor of 20,000.

the slope of the price response is steepest. This is a far more realistic w.t.p. distribution than those associated with either the constant-elasticity or linear price-response functions. For that reason, the logit is usually preferred to linear or constant-elasticity price-response functions when the effects of large price changes are being considered.[10]

3.2 PRICE RESPONSE WITH COMPETITION

So far we have not given much attention to the issue of competition. We have mentioned a "market price" as the steepest point in the logit price-response function, but we have not made an explicit link with competition. Yet competition is an important—some may say the most important—fact of life in any market of interest. Most managers identify competition as the number-one factor influencing their pricing. Many complain about being at the mercy of their competitors who have "stupid" or "irrational" pricing. How should we factor competition into our calculation of price response?

There are three different levels at which competition might be included in PRO. In increasing levels of sophistication and difficulty they are: incorporating competition in the price-response function, explicitly modeling consumer choice, and trying to anticipate competitive reaction.

3.2.1 Incorporating Competition in the Price-Response Function

In many cases, competitive prices may not be available at the time prices need to be optimized. This is especially true in business-to-business markets, when the pocket price of the customer may include discounts that are never made visible to the competition. But it is also true in many consumer markets. Retailers generally have a good idea of what their major competitors are charging at any particular time, but they usually don't have the time or resources to do exhaustive research on a daily or weekly basis.

Is there any hope of optimizing prices if we don't know what the competition is doing? The answer is yes. First of all, the price-response function we will be using in a market will be based on history. To this extent, *it already includes "typical" competitive pricing.* (Indeed, it would be difficult, if not impossible, to estimate a price-response function that did not include competition.) To the extent that our competitors will behave in a similar fashion in the future as they have in the past, the price-response function will be a fair representation of market response—including competitive response.

What if the market has changed? Then, in part, we must rely on the "fast-feedback loop" in the PRO process, as illustrated in Figure 2.5. If we have a competitor who responds more aggressively to a price action than in the past, this will be manifested in the demand we see in the next period. We have the opportunity to adjust our price-response function and re-optimize accordingly.

3.2.2 Consumer-Choice Modeling

Of course, if we have access to current competitive prices, we should be able to use that information to help us better predict customer response to our own price. This information is increasingly available, particularly for online markets. For example, the Online Petroleum

Information System (OPIS) posts a daily list of prices for different grades of petroleum products offered by different sellers in all major markets in the United States and Canada. How can this type of information be used by sellers in setting their prices?

Consumer-choice modeling is based on the situation in which a number of competitors are providing similar products or services to some population of customers. Each of the competitors sets a price for the product. Each customer has a vector of willingnesses to pay (or reservation prices), one for each product. These different w.t.p.'s represent the different values that she places on the features and "brand value" associated with each product—a more desirable product will have a higher associated w.t.p. The *surplus* for each customer and each product is defined as the difference between the customer's willingness to pay and the price of each product. Each customer purchases the product with the highest positive surplus. If none of the products has a positive surplus for a customer, she will not purchase at all.

Example 3.6

A customer is shopping for stereo amplifiers at the local Stereo Hut store. Stereo Hut sells five amplifiers at the following prices:

Model	Price	Willingness to pay	Surplus
Audio Two	$400	$250	−$150
Koshiba	$650	$950	$300
Takata and Fuji	$500	$550	$50
Soundmaster	$750	$950	$200
Cacophonia	$1,200	$1,300	$100

This customer would purchase the Koshiba amplifier since it provides her with the highest surplus.

Note that, in the example, the customer does not buy either the cheapest alternative (Audio Two) or his favorite alternative (Cacophonia). Rather, she purchases the alternative that yields the highest surplus. We would expect that each customer would have a different set of reservation prices based on the value she places on the various features of each alternative or her preference for a particular brand. As before, we can imagine that the reservation prices would be distributed across the population in an n-dimensional bell-shaped curve. Assume now we have a fixed population of potential buyers and that each of these buyers has positive surplus for at least one of the alternatives. Then, the market share that will be obtained by a particular alternative is

$$\text{Market share of alternative } i = \text{Fraction of buyers for whom}$$
$$w_i - p_i > w_j - p_j \text{ for all } j$$

The idea behind consumer-choice modeling is to predict the share of each alternative given all of the prices. Let $p = (p_1, p_2, \ldots, p_n)$ be the vector of prices for the alternatives and let μ_i be the market share of alternative i. Then, a market-share function determines $\mu_i = f_i(p)$ for all i. A market-share function will have the following characteristics:

- $0 \leq f_i(p) \leq 1$. The market share of each alternative is between 0 and 1.
- $\sum_{i=1}^{n} f_i(p) = 1$. Every buyer chooses some alternative.
- $\partial f_i(p)/\partial p_i < 0$. Increasing the price of a product decreases its market share.
- $\partial f_i(p)/\partial p_j > 0$ for $i \neq j$. Increasing the price of a product increases the market share of other products. (The products are substitutes.)

Given a market-share function and a total demand D, the demand for product i is given by

$$d_i(p) = D\mu_i = Df_i(p) \tag{3.12}$$

The multinomial logit. The most widely used consumer choice model is the *multinomial logit* (MNL), defined by

$$\mu_i(p) = \frac{e^{-b_i p_i}}{\sum_{j=1}^{n} e^{-b_j p_j}} \tag{3.13}$$

where $b_j > 0$ is a parameter that varies by alternative. It is easy to see that $\mu_i(p)$ in Equation 3.13 satisfies all the conditions for a valid market-share function. The b_j are a measure of price responsiveness for each alternative — a high value of b_j means that alternative j is highly price sensitive, while a lower value of b_j indicates a lower value of price sensitivity.

Example 3.7

Statistical analysis of historical purchases has determined that the MNL provides a good fit to customer choices at Stereo Hut. The values of b_j for each amplifier are shown here along with the predicted market share at the current prices.

Model	Price	b_j	Market share
Audio Two	$400	2.5	0.31
Koshiba	$650	3.077	0.11
Takata and Fuji	$500	2.4	0.25
Soundmaster	$750	2.4	0.14
Cacophonia	$1,200	1.25	0.19

Note that the Koshiba amplifier has a high level of price sensitivity and achieves a market share considerably lower than the Cacophonia, even though its price is almost 50% lower.

Relation of the multinomial logit to the logit price-response function. You may have guessed that there must be some relationship between the MNL and the logit price-response function. And indeed there is: *In the case where competitive prices are constant, the MNL reduces to the logit price-response function.* To see this, assume that prices $p_2, p_3, \ldots, p_n$ are held constant. Then we can replace the competitive-price term in Equation 3.13 with a constant. That is, we can set

$$K = \sum_{i=2}^{n} e^{-b_i p_i}$$

giving us

$$d_1(p_1) = \frac{De^{-b_1 p_1}}{e^{-b_1 p_1} + K} = \frac{De^{-b_1 p_1}/K}{e^{-b_1 p_1}/K + 1} = \frac{De^{-b_1 p_1} e^{-(\ln K)}}{e^{-b_1 p_1} e^{-(\ln K)} + 1} = \frac{De^{-(a + b_1 p_1)}}{e^{-(a + b_1 p_1)} + 1} \tag{3.14}$$

where we have set $a = \ln(K)$ and we use the fact that $\ln(1/K) = -\ln(K)$. This is the same as the logit price-response function specified in Equation 3.11. If we anticipate that competitive prices will be largely stable, the MNL provides little or no additional predictive value over a logit price-response function.

Strengths and weaknesses of consumer-choice modeling. There is a vast literature on consumer-choice modeling, and the issues involved with estimating the parameters of consumer-choice models have been much studied. Statistical software packages such as SAS include procedures for estimating the parameters of the logit or probit market-share functions. This is a great strength of the consumer-choice approach to price-response estimation.

There are a number of weaknesses to consumer-choice modeling as well. One is that, at least as we have posed it, the models assume that all customers purchase some alternative. However, it may be that some customers choose not to purchase at all, since their willingness to pay for every alternative may be below the price of that alternative. Thus, the estimation of the total market D is not really independent of the prices being offered. Indeed, it seems intuitive that an aggressive discount by one supplier would not only siphon customers away from competitors but actually induce customers into the market who might not have purchased from any alternative.

Another drawback of the consumer-choice modeling approach is that, in theory, it requires information on all competitive prices. However, in most markets, companies typically identify two to five companies they consider important competitors. For example, Table 11.2 lists the annual percentage rates (APRs) for unsecured consumer lenders for 16 different banks in the United Kingdom. While all of these 16 banks (and even more) compete in some sense for the loan business, in reality any lender would only consider four or five of them to be important competition. Other surveys have shown that in many consumer markets three or four major brands dominate a category, although there may be scores of smaller competitors. In these cases, one commonly used approach is to derive a *competitive index price* by weighting the prices offered by the major competitors and using this index as a single competitive price in a multinomial logit.

3.2.3 Anticipating Competitive Response

Even extensive consumer-choice modeling would seem to take us only partway to Nirvana. After all, if we are taking competitive prices into account in setting our prices, we should anticipate that our competitors will take our price into account when they set their prices. If we drop a price, we should anticipate the possibility that competitors will match, possibly erasing much of the additional demand we might otherwise predict. The results of raising a price would certainly be different depending upon whether or not our competitors decided to match.

Attempts to predict competitive response and incorporate it into current pricing decisions falls within the realm of decision analysis, or game theory. While these approaches have their applications to strategic pricing, they are far less relevant to the tactical decisions of pricing and revenue optimization. For example, there is a vast literature on the use of game theory in pricing. This literature has little application to the day-to-day tactical pricing issues that fall within the scope of pricing and revenue optimization. There does not appear to be a single pricing and revenue optimization system that explicitly attempts to forecast competitive response using game theory as part of its ongoing operation. There are many reasons for this, but I believe there is one that is particularly important. Pricing and revenue optimization is based on playing the "best response" (i.e., finding the expected contribution-maximizing price) to whatever the competitors are currently doing. Theoretical examinations of markets find that this is almost always a good thing to do and often the best possible that can be done. For example, if customers in a market choose a supplier based on the multinomial logit price-response model described in Section 3.2.2, then the best each supplier can do is to set the price that maximizes expected contribution given the prices set by the competition. More sophisticated strategies cannot yield more.[11]

The philosophy of pricing and revenue optimization is to make money by many small adjustments, searching for and vacuuming up small and transient puddles of profit as they appear in the marketplace. It is about making a little more money from each transaction. It is not about finding the great pricing move that will stagger the competition with one blow. Many of the price adjustments called for by pricing and revenue optimization are likely to fall below the radar screen of the competition and may not trigger any explicit response whatsoever.

This does not mean that competitive response need never be considered in pricing. The potential competitive responses to major "bet-the-company" bids or substantial changes in pricing strategy need to be carefully considered. For example, in the early 1990s, Hertz Rent-a-Car initiated the use of a sophisticated pricing optimization system. Previously, Hertz, like other national rent-a-car companies, had changed prices only rarely. Whenever one of the rental car companies dropped a price, the others were likely to follow immediately—often with even larger drops—precipitating an industrywide fare war. Hertz took great pains to communicate to the industry that its new system would be changing prices much more commonly than before—some prices would go up, some would go down, but all would change much more frequently. The communication was successful: Hertz was able to initiate its revenue management program without inciting retaliatory price wars. Once Hertz initiated revenue management, it was able to generate additional revenue through thousands of small adjustments to prices that its competitors were unable to match.

3.3 INCREMENTAL COSTS

Costing seems like it should be the easy part of pricing and revenue optimization. After all, a company may not know the price-response function it faces, but surely it should know its own costs. Unfortunately, things are not quite so simple. With any exposure to the field of accounting one will quickly realize that the simple question "How much did this product cost?" usually does not have a simple answer. Rather, the "cost" of producing even a simple product depends on who wants to know and what they are going to use the answer for. Accountants have derived a host of product-costing methodologies, including fully allocated costs, partially allocated costs, marginal costs, avoided costs, and financial costs, to name just a few.

While each costing methodology has its place, pricing and revenue optimization decisions are based on the *incremental cost* of a customer commitment, where incremental cost is defined as follows.

> *The incremental cost of a customer commitment is the difference between the total costs a company would experience if it makes the commitment and the total cost it would experience if it doesn't.*

Calculating incremental cost for a customer commitment depends critically on the context and nature of the commitment. Here are some examples.

- An airline is considering whether or not to sell a single seat to a passenger on a future flight. The incremental cost is the additional meal and fuel cost that would be incurred from flying an additional passenger plus any commissions or fees the airline would pay for the booking.

- A retailer buys a stock of fashion goods at the beginning of the season. Once he has bought the goods, he cannot return them and cannot reorder. During the season he wants to set and update the prices that will maximize the total revenue he will receive from the fashion goods. Since the cost of the goods is sunk and selling a unit will not drive any additional future sales, his incremental cost per sale is zero.[12]

- A drugstore sells bottles of shampoo and replenishes its stock weekly. Because selling a unit will result in an additional unit order, the incremental cost for selling a bottle of shampoo is the wholesale unit cost.

- A distributor is bidding for a year-long contract with a hospital to be the preferred provider for disposable medical supplies. From previous experience, the distributor knows that this hospital is an expensive customer requiring high levels of customer support, wide variances in orders, and high rates of product returns. The expected incremental cost of the contract includes not only the expected cost of the items the hospital will purchase, but also the expected cost of customer service, operating costs and holding costs driven by the wide variance in orders, and the expected costs of returns.

These examples illustrate some of the key characteristics of incremental cost. These characteristics can be summarized as follows.

- *Incremental cost is forward looking*. It is based on the effect a customer commitment will have on future costs. Costs that have already been taken or that are driven by decisions already made prior to the customer commitment are sunk and do not enter into the calculation of incremental cost.

- *Incremental cost is marginal.* It is the expected cost of making *this* customer commitment. The incremental cost of making this commitment may not be the same as the average cost of similar commitments made in the past.

- *Incremental cost is not fully allocated cost.* Only costs that change as the result of a customer commitment are part of the incremental cost. Overhead, or fixed costs of staying in business, may not be allocated to any specific commitment. As a result, the incremental cost of a customer commitment is usually less than the fully allocated cost. Further, the sum of the incremental costs of all commitments will be less than the total operating cost of the company, since there will remain an unallocated residual fixed cost after all the incremental costs have been totaled.

- *The elements of incremental cost can depend on the type, size, and duration of the commitment.* Specifically, if the customer commitment is a multiunit order, then order-based or setup costs need to be allocated across all the units in the order.

- *The incremental cost of a commitment can be uncertain.* Trucking companies such as Roadway Express and Yellow Freight sell contracts to shippers. Each contract covers the next year and commits the trucking company to carry all the freight tendered by the customer at an agreed-on tariff. The incremental cost associated with one of these contracts is likely to be highly uncertain at the time the commitment is made. First of all, the amount, timing, and origin and destination of the freight the customer will tender over the next year is uncertain. In addition, the cost of moving the customer's freight will depend on the freight the company will move for other customers, which is also uncertain. This cost will depend in part on what portion of the customer's freight is *backhaul* business, which can utilize excess capacity on existing trucks, and what portion will be *headhaul* freight, which will require running new trucks.

In each case, the calculation of incremental cost requires understanding the nature of the customer commitment and then estimating the additional costs that would be generated by making the commitment—or, equivalently, the costs that would be avoided by not making the commitment. The methodology behind calculating incremental costs is closely related to activity-based costing (ABC). Activity-based costing is a management accounting approach to allocating costs to their underlying causes in order to give a clearer view of the real sources of cost within an organization. A good introduction to activity-based costing is *Cost & Effect* by Kaplan and Cooper (1997).

3.4 THE BASIC PRICE OPTIMIZATION PROBLEM

The difference between the price at which a product is sold and its incremental cost is called its *unit margin* or just *margin*. The sum of the margins of all products sold during a time period is called the *total contribution*. In most cases, the seller's goal is to maximize total contribution. When the supplier is selling a single product at a single price, her total contribution will be

$$m(p) = (p - c)\, d(p) \tag{3.15}$$

where $m(p)$ is total contribution and c is incremental cost. The basic price optimization problem is

$$\max_p (p - c)\, d(p) \tag{3.16}$$

The total contribution function $m(p)$ is hill shaped, with a single peak, as shown in Figure 3.11. The top of this peak is the maximum total contribution the supplier can realize in the current time period, and p^* is the price that will maximize the total contribution. Note that there is a fundamental lack of symmetry in the total-contribution curve: The supplier can lose money by pricing too low (below incremental cost), but she cannot lose money by pricing too high—the worst that can happen is that she drives demand to zero.

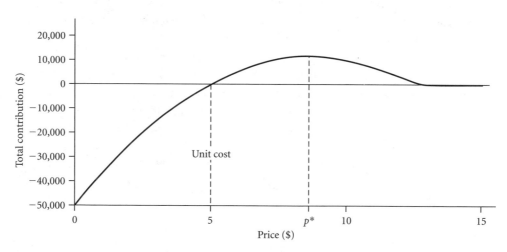

Figure 3.11   Total contribution as a function of price.

3.4.1 Optimality Conditions

The problem in Equation 3.16 is an unconstrained optimization problem, and standard optimization theory tells us that it can be solved by taking the derivative of $m(p)$ and setting it equal to zero.[13] The derivative of $m(p)$ with respect to price is given by

$$m'(p) = d'(p)(p - c) + d(p) \tag{3.17}$$

To find the price that maximizes total contribution, we set $m'(p) = 0$, or

$$d'(p)(p - c) + d(p) = 0$$

Thus, a p^* satisfying

$$d(p^*) = -d'(p^*)(p^* - c) \tag{3.18}$$

will maximize total contribution.[14]

Condition 3.18 is not particularly insightful in itself, but it can be used to derive two standard conditions for optimal prices.

Marginal price equals marginal cost. We can rewrite Equation 3.18 as

$$p^* \, d'(p^*) + d(p^*) = c \, d'(p^*) \tag{3.19}$$

The term on the left-hand side of Equation 3.19 is *marginal revenue*—the derivative of total revenue with respect to price. This is the amount of additional revenue the seller could achieve from a small increase in price. Typically, marginal revenue is greater than zero at low prices but less than zero at higher prices. When price is low, increasing price leads to increased total revenue because the reduced demand is outweighed by increased margin. But at some price, the effect of raising price further is to decrease total revenue as demand begins to drop more quickly than margin increases.

The term on the right-hand side of Equation 3.19 is *marginal cost*: the amount of additional cost the seller would incur from a small increase in price. Note that marginal cost is always less than or equal to zero—an increase in price results in lower demand (by the downward-sloping property), which in turn leads to lower total costs. Equation 3.19 states that contribution is maximized when marginal revenue equals marginal cost.

Example 3.8

The marginal-revenue and marginal-cost curves are shown in Figure 3.12 for a seller with a price-response function given by $d(p) = 10,000 - 800p$ and incremental cost of $5.00. The marginal-revenue curve corresponding to this price-response function is $R'(p) = 10,000 - 1,600p$, and the marginal cost curve is a horizontal line at $-$4,000$. The contribution maximizing price occurs where the marginal-revenue curve intersects the marginal-cost curve in Figure 3.12, in this case at $p^* = 8.75.

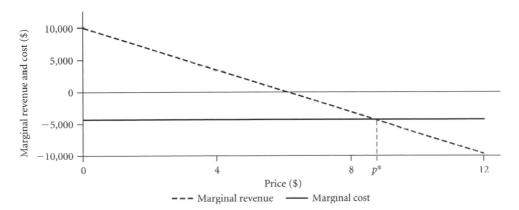

Figure 3.12 Marginal revenue and marginal cost.

We can state this important condition as follows.

Total contribution is maximized in the basic price optimization problem at the price at which marginal revenue equals marginal cost.

Equation 3.19 provides further useful guidance on price changes that could improve total contribution. If marginal revenue is greater than marginal cost, then the supplier can increase his contribution by increasing price. If, on the other hand, marginal revenue is lower than marginal cost, he should decrease his price to increase contribution.

Optimal contribution margin and elasticity. We can also relate the optimal price to point elasticity. Rewrite Equation 3.17 as

$$m'(p) = d(p)\left[\frac{d'(p)p}{d(p)} + 1\right] - d'(p)c$$

$$= d(p)[1 - \epsilon(p)] - d'(p)c \qquad (3.20)$$

where $\epsilon(p)$ is point elasticity as defined in Equation 3.5. In Equation 3.20, the second term, $-d'(p)c$, will always be greater than or equal to zero since $d'(p) \le 0$. If $d(p) > 0$, then $m'(p)$ will always be greater than zero if $\epsilon(p) < 1$. In other words,

If the point elasticity at our current price is less than 1, we can increase total contribution by increasing price.

Of course, since point elasticity changes as we change price, we cannot expect total contribution to continue increasing forever as we increase price. Typically, as price increases, elasticity will increase as well, until we reach a point where lost sales outweigh increased unit margins. We can express the corresponding condition in terms of point elasticity by combining Equation 3.20 with the condition that $m'(p^*) = 0$ for p^* to maximize total contribution. Then

$$d(p^*) = -d'(p^*)(p^* - c)$$
$$-d'(p^*)/d(p^*) = 1/(p^* - c)$$
$$-d'(p^*)p^*/d(p^*) = p^*/(p^* - c)$$
$$\epsilon(p^*) = p^*/(p^* - c) \qquad (3.21)$$

The quantity $(p - c)/p$ is the margin per unit expressed as a fraction of price. It is known as the *contribution margin ratio* or sometimes as the *gross margin ratio*. For a retailer purchasing an item at \$150 and selling it at \$200, the contribution margin ratio is (\$200 − \$150)/\$150 = 0.33. In words, Equation 3.21 says

At the optimal price, the price elasticity is equal to the reciprocal of the contribution margin ratio.

Of course this is equivalent to

At the optimal price, the contribution margin ratio is equal to the reciprocal of elasticity.

A convenient formula relating the optimal price to elasticity and cost is

$$p^* = \frac{\epsilon(p^*)}{\epsilon(p^*) - 1} \times c$$

This relationship provides a particularly convenient way to calculate the optimal price in the face of a constant elasticity price-response function.

Example 3.9

An electronics goods retailer faces a constant-elasticity price-response function with an elasticity of 2.5 for a popular model of television. It costs him $180 apiece to purchase the televisions wholesale. At the optimum price, he should achieve a contribution margin ratio of $1/2.5 = 40\%$ per unit. This means he should price the televisions at $(2.5/1.5) \times \$180 = \$300$ in order to maximize total contribution.

Imputed price elasticity. Equation 3.21 implies that we can derive local price elasticity in a market from the contribution margin at the optimal price.

Example 3.10

A seller believes he is pricing optimally, and his contribution margin ratio is 20%. This can only be true if the price elasticity is 5.

Imputed price elasticity is a good "reality check" on the credibility of a company's current pricing.

3.4.2 Applying Basic Price Optimization

We can illustrate basic price optimization with a simple example.

Example 3.11

A widget maker is looking to set the price of widgets for the current month. Assume that the widget maker's unit production cost c is a constant $5.00 per widget and that his demand for the current month is governed by the linear price-response function

$$d(p) = (10{,}000 - 800p)^+$$

This means that the demand for widgets will be $10{,}000 - 800p$ for prices between zero and $12.50 and that the demand will be 0 for prices over $12.50. (We use the notation $(x)^+$ to denote the maximum of x and 0, where x may be either a single variable or a mathematical expression.) This linear price-response function is shown in Figure 3.13.

In this simple example, $d'(p) = 800$. Substituting into Equation 3.18, we can see that the optimal price p^* must solve

$$\$10{,}000 - 800p^* = 800(p^* - \$5.00)$$

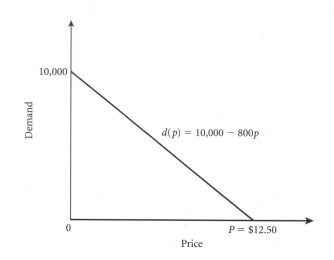

Figure 3.13   Price-response curve for widgets.

or, after a little algebra,

$$1{,}600p^* = 14{,}000 \quad \text{or} \quad p^* = \$8.75$$

At the optimal price of $8.75, total widget sales will be $10{,}000 - 800(\$8.75) = 3{,}000$ units, total revenue will be $3{,}000 \times \$8.75 = \$26{,}250$, and total contribution will be $3{,}000(\$8.75 - \$5.00)$, or $11,250. Figure 3.11 shows how total contribution varies as a function of price. Note that total contribution is zero at $p = c = \$5.00$, rises to a maximum at $p^* = \$8.75$, and drops to zero again at $p = \$12.50$.

3.4.3 Marginality Test

One way to check the optimality of p^* is to use the *marginality test*, which states that a particular price can only be optimal if raising the price by a penny or lowering the price by a penny results in reduced margin contribution. The principle of marginality should be pretty obvious—if we could increase contribution by changing the price, then the current price would not be optimal—but it is a useful check nonetheless. Table 3.3 shows the results of varying the price in Example 3.11 from $8.74 to $8.76. As expected, the price of $8.75 results in the highest margin of the three alternatives. However, the pattern of change among the prices is instructive: At $8.74 we are selling eight more units per month, but this is not enough to make up for the lost margin per unit. At $8.76 we are making a penny more per unit sold, but this is offset by the loss of sales of eight units. The optimal price, $8.75,

TABLE 3.3
Impact of price on margin contribution near the optimal price

Price	Demand	Unit margin	Margin contribution
$8.74	3008	$3.74	$11,249.92
$8.75	3000	$3.75	$11,250.00
$8.76	2992	$3.76	$11,249.92

exactly balances the gain in units sold from the potential loss of margin from raising prices further.

3.4.4 Maximizing Revenue

In some cases, a company might wish to maximize total revenue (rather than total contribution). In this case, the objective function will be

$$\max_{p} R(p) = d(p)p \tag{3.22}$$

It is easy to see that this is equivalent to Equation 3.16 when $c = 0$. A company with incremental cost of zero can maximize net contribution by maximizing revenue. There are some service industries, such as movie theaters, video rentals, and sporting events, in which the incremental costs are close to zero. Some of these are discussed in Section 6.7.1. Also, incremental costs are zero (or very small) in many cases in which a company has already purchased a fixed amount of perishable, nonreplenishable inventory. This is the situation faced by many fashion-goods retailers, who purchase inventory for an entire season ahead of time. Once the inventory has been purchased, the incremental cost of a sale is zero—and the seller should set prices accordingly. Many of these situations count as *markdown opportunities* and are discussed in Chapter 10.

The revenue-maximizing price, p', can be found by differentiating $R(p)$ and setting the derivative equal to 0. Specifically,

$$R'(p') = d'(p')p' + d(p') = 0 \tag{3.23}$$

implying that p' solves

$$-\frac{d'(p')p'}{d(p')} = \epsilon(p') = 1 \tag{3.24}$$

In other words, the revenue-maximizing price occurs where the elasticity of the price-response function is equal to 1.[15] This implies that there is no unconstrained revenue-maximizing price associated with a constant-elasticity price-response function unless the price elasticity happens to be exactly 1—in which case, revenue is constant at all prices.

Equation 3.19 says that contribution is maximized when marginal revenue is equal to marginal cost (which is less than zero). Equation 3.23 says that contribution is maximized when marginal revenue is equal to zero. Typically, marginal revenue is a decreasing function of price (at least in the region of the optimal price). In this case, we can show how marginal revenue and marginal cost can be used to compute the revenue-maximizing and contribution-maximizing prices in Figure 3.14. Specifically, we can see that, as long as the marginal revenue curve is decreasing, *the revenue-maximizing price is lower than the contribution-maximizing price.*

Example 3.12

The CEO of the widget-making company decides that the firm's goal for the next month will be to maximize revenue from widget sales as part of the

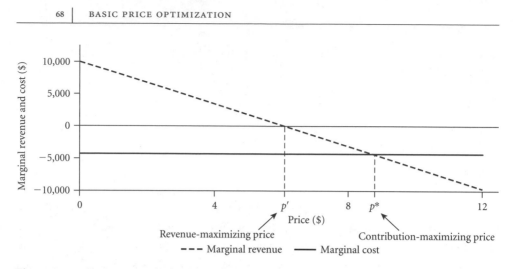

Figure 3.14 Revenue maximization and contribution maximization.

long-term strategy to increase market share. The revenue-maximizing price can be found by solving Equation 3.23. The resulting revenue-maximizing price is equal to $6.25, with corresponding sales of 5,000 units. The corresponding per-unit margin is $1.25, and the total contribution margin is $5,000 \times \$1.25 = \$6,250$. We can compare this to the maximum margin contribution of $11,250 and conclude that to maximize total revenue, the company needs to give up $11,250 - \$6,250 = \$5,000$ of contribution margin.

The decision that management needs to make in Example 3.12 is whether or not it is worth giving up a total contribution of $5,000 per month to "buy" an additional 2,000 units of demand. Since the revenue-maximizing price is lower than the contribution-maximizing price, there is no guarantee that the revenue-maximizing price will provide a reasonable margin—or even a positive margin—if incremental cost is greater than zero. For this reason, it is dangerous to maximize total revenue without including a constraint that ensures that the resulting price is greater than incremental cost.

3.4.5 Weighted Combinations of Revenue and Contribution

In some cases, a company might wish to maximize a weighted combination of total contribution and revenue. Some pricing and revenue optimization systems use "slider bars" to determine how much to weight revenue relative to contribution. The most common approach to combining revenue contribution is to use a weighting parameter α, with $0 \leq \alpha \leq 1$, resulting in a weighted objective function $Z(p)$ given by

$$Z(p) = \alpha(p - c)\, d(p) + (1 - \alpha)p\, d(p) \tag{3.25}$$

For $\alpha = 1$, $Z(p)$ equals total contribution; for $\alpha = 0$, $Z(p)$ equals revenue. Values of α between 0 and 1 will maximize a weighted combination of the two, with higher values of α resulting in a higher weighting for contribution relative to total revenue.

Applying some algebra to Equation 3.25 gives

$$Z(p) = (p - \alpha c)\, d(p) \tag{3.26}$$

which shows that maximizing a weighted combination of the revenue and total contribution is the same as maximizing contribution with a discounted cost. For example, a value of $\alpha = 0.5$ implies equal weights for total revenue and total contribution. Equation 3.26 shows that the price that maximizes this weighted objective function can be found by maximizing total contribution with cost reduced by 50%. Equation 3.25 allows us to state a general principle.

> *The price that maximizes a weighted combination of revenue and contribution is greater than or equal to the revenue-maximizing price and less than or equal to the contribution-maximizing price.*

In the absence of other constraints, we would only be interested in prices greater than the revenue-maximizing price and less than the contribution-maximizing price. In other words, there is no reason for an unconstrained seller to consider pricing outside of this range.

3.5 SUMMARY AND EXTENSIONS

1. The core problem in PRO can be formulated as a constrained optimization problem where the objective function is to maximize total contribution. The constraints are the result of either business rules (e.g., the desire to maintain a minimum market share in a certain market) or constraints on capacity or inventory.

2. A key input into any PRO problem is the price-response function that relates price to demand. The price-sensitivity function is typically nonnegative, continuous, and downward sloping.

3. Two common key measures of price sensitivity are the slope and elasticity of the price-response function, where the slope is defined as the derivative of the price-response function and elasticity is the (approximate) percentage change in demand that would result from a 1% change in price. Both slope and elasticity are *local* properties of the price-response function, in that they can be used to estimate the effects of small changes in price but not large changes.

4. In many cases, price-response functions can be considered as the measure of the number of people whose maximum willingness to pay (or reservation price) is greater than a certain price. In this case, a price-response function corresponds to a particular distribution of willingness to pay across a population. For example, a linear price-response function corresponds to a uniform distribution on willingness to pay.

5. Linear and constant-elasticity price-response functions are both commonly used in analysis. However, both tend to be unrealistic when applied to large changes in price. In such cases, a reverse S-shaped model, such as the logit, may be more appropriate.

6. There are three broad approaches to incorporating competitive pricing into price optimization. The first is to assume that competitive pricing is already incorporated into the estimation of the price-response function. This approach is quite common when the competitive environment is quite stable and/or competitive prices are

not available at the time when prices need to be set. The second approach is to explicitly include competitive prices into a broader price-response model. The final approach is to attempt to try to anticipate competitive response to one's pricing actions. This is typically only done when a major pricing change is contemplated.

7. The cost used in pricing and revenue optimization is the *incremental cost* of a customer commitment. It is the difference between the total costs a company would incur from satisfying the commitment. The incremental cost will vary with the duration and size of the commitment and is not a fully allocated cost.

8. The following are equivalent optimality conditions for the unconstrained price optimization problem:

Marginal revenue equals marginal cost.

The derivative of total contribution with respect to price is zero.

The contribution margin ratio is equal to 1 over the price elasticity.

Any of these three conditions can be used to compute the optimal price. However, these conditions may not hold if the price optimization problem is constrained. Constraints may be due to limits on supply or capacity or may be due to business rules limiting the prices that can be charged.

9. The price that maximizes revenue can be found by setting marginal revenue to zero. It is always lower than the price that maximizes total contribution (unless incremental costs are zero, in which case they are the same).

3.6 EXERCISES

1. Consider a seller seeking to maximize contribution. Under what relative values of his current price p, his cost c, and his point elasticity $\epsilon(p)$ should the seller raise his price to increase contribution? Under what conditions should he lower his price? Keep his price the same?

2. A retailer is currently charging a price of $147.52 for a Hewlett-Packard OfficeJet printer that costs him $112.00 per unit. He determines that the point price elasticity of this model of printer is 5.1 at its current price.

   a. If he wants to maximize net contribution, is he better off raising his price, lowering his price, or keeping it the same?

   b. If the elasticity of 5.1 is valid over at least a range of $20.00 on either side of his current price, what is his optimal (contribution-maximizing) price?

3. An auto manufacturer can manufacture compact cars for an incremental cost of $5,000 apiece. She faces a logit price-response function for sales in the next month, with parameters $C = 40,000$, $b = 0.0005$, and $\hat{p} = \$12,000$. What price will maximize the total contribution? How many cars will she sell during the month?

4. (*Giffen Good*) A penurious graduate student has a food budget of $100.00/week. To survive with sufficient energy to attend classes, he knows that he needs to consume

50 protein units per week. The only two foods he can stand to eat on a regular basis are beans and hamburger. He derives twice as much pleasure per protein unit from eating hamburger as he does from beans.

a. Assume that hamburger costs $3.00 per protein unit and beans cost $1.00 per protein unit. Formulate the student's diet problem as a linear program. (You can assume he wants to maximize his "total utility" from his diet and that he gets 1 utile from each protein unit of beans he consumes and 2 utiles from each protein unit of hamburger.) What is the optimal consumption of beans and hamburger in this case?

b. Plot the student's price-response curve for beans as the price of beans goes from $0.01 to $2.00, assuming that everything else (including the price of hamburger) stays constant. Note that his individual price-response function is indeed upward sloping. Why? What happens when the price of beans exceeds $2.00 per unit?

c. The student receives a scholarship that enables him to spend $300 a week on food. What is his price-response function for beans now?

5. The average ticket prices for concerts held by six different artists in 2000–2001 are as follows:[16]

Artist	Ticket price
Barbra Streisand	$483.61
Luciano Pavarotti	$105.70
The Eagles	$89.22
Bruce Springsteen	$65.20
George Strait	$48.60
Phish	$30.50

Given that the incremental costs of mounting a show are roughly the same for all performers, what do you think accounts for the wide variation in the average ticket price commanded by the artists? Do you believe that all of these artists are seeking to maximize expected revenue from their concerts? If not why not, and what might they be trying to do?

1. Landsburg (1989).

2. Varian (1987, p. 132).

3. In economic terms, it means that what we are selling is a *good*—something people are willing to buy—rather than an *illth*—something people are willing to pay to get rid of. This is not a restrictive assumption—we can convert an illth with negative price to a good with positive price by exchanging the buyer and the seller. Thus, instead of assuming that people "sell" trash (an illth) at a negative price, it is more natural to assume that people buy "trash removal" (a good) at a positive price.

4. In reality, strict continuity of price-response functions often does not hold. In particular, prices for most items sold in the United States do not vary by less than 1 cent and most items are sold in discrete units. We could easily have the situation where $d(\$5.11) = 5,000$ and $d(\$5.10) = 5,010$. In this case, price response is not technically continuous or invertible—there is no price such that $d(p) = 5,005$. However, as long as these jumps are small relative to overall demand, we can act as if the price-response function is continuous between consecutive prices and round to the nearest penny once we have solved for the right price, knowing that our final price will be off by at most 1 cent.

5. We will sometimes use piecewise linear price-response functions. Technically, piecewise linear functions are differentiable "almost everywhere"—specifically, they are differentiable everywhere except where the linear segments join together.

6. Several restaurants have noted that a disproportionate number of customers tend to order the second-cheapest chardonnay on the menu—and they tailor their pricing accordingly.

7. Here, we will be considering *own-price elasticity*—the response of the demand for a product to its *own* price.

8. An important exception is e-commerce, in which programs can actively track the number of visitors to the Web site or the number of people who clicked to get a price quote on an online loan.

9. This assumes that the price-response function is finite.

10. You might wonder why we haven't considered a price-response function based on a normal distribution of willingness to pay. There is such a price-response function; it is called the *probit*. However, it is difficult to work with since there is no closed-form version. Also, the two distributions (and their corresponding price-response functions) behave in a very similar fashion in the region around the market price. In fact, "by judicious adjustment of the coefficients logit and probit models can be made to virtually coincide over a fairly wide range . . . and it is practically impossible to choose between them on empirical grounds" (Cramer 2003, p. 26). Because the logit is easier to work with and is much more commonly used in practice, we will couch the majority of our analysis here and in Chapter 11 in terms of the logit. Train (2003) and Aldrich and Nelson (1984) also provide good comparisons of logit and probit models.

11. For a fairly technical proof of this, see Vives (2001).

12. See Chapter 10 for more details on pricing in this situation.

13. Appendix A reviews some basic optimization theory.

14. We also need the second derivative of contribution, $m''(p)$, to be less than zero for a $p*$ satisfying Equation 3.18 to maximize (rather than minimize) total contribution. This condition will be satisfied if $m''(p*) = d''(p*)(p* - c) + 2\,d'(p*) < 0$.

15. We have assumed that the second-order condition $R''(p') = d''(p')p* + 2\,d'(p') \leq 0$ holds.

16. Figures from Wild (2002).

4 | PRICE DIFFERENTIATION

In this chapter we treat one of the most fundamental concepts in PRO—*price differentiation*. Price differentiation refers to the practice of a seller charging different prices to different customers, either for exactly the same good or for slightly different versions of the same good. Price differentiation is a powerful way for sellers to improve profitability. It also adds a new level of complexity to pricing, often creating a need to use analytical techniques to improve the calculation and updating of prices over time.

We use the term *price differentiation* to refer to the ways that additional profit can be extracted from a marketplace by charging different prices. Tactics for price differentiation include charging different prices to different customers (or groups of customers) for *exactly* the same product, charging different prices for different versions of the same product, and combinations of the two. The term *price discrimination* is used in the economics literature to refer to much the same thing. We use the term *price differentiation*, rather than the more common *price discrimination*, in part to avoid the negative connotations associated with the word *discrimination*. However, we also want to stress that price differentiation includes not only charging different prices to different customers for the same product (group pricing) but also the less controversial strategies of product versioning, regional pricing, and channel pricing.

There is both art and science to price differentiation. The art lies in finding a way to divide the market into different segments such that higher prices can be charged to the high-willingness-to-pay segments and lower prices to the low-willingness-to-pay segments. There is no one way to segment customers that applies to all possible markets. Instead, there is a variety of techniques that can be applied in different ways, depending on the characteristics of a market, the competitive environment, and the character of the goods or services being sold. The science lies in setting and updating the prices in order to maximize overall return from all segments.

We start by using a simple example (based on the widget maker from Chapter 3) to illustrate the economic principles behind price differentiation.

4.1 THE ECONOMICS OF PRICE DIFFERENTIATION

Let us return to the case of the widget maker in Section 3.4.2. The widget maker, looking for a way to increase his profitability, might start by taking a close look at his price-response function, as illustrated in Figure 3.13. He would see that 10,000 customers are willing to pay some amount greater than zero for his widget, 5,000 are willing to pay $6.25 or more, 3,000 are willing to pay $8.75 or more (the contribution-maximizing price), and 1,200 are even willing to pay $11.00 or more. The marketing department might see an opportunity to improve profitability. After all, there are 2,000 customers willing to pay $10.00 or more who are purchasing at $8.75. This is a good deal for these customers, but it is also at least $1.25 in additional revenue "left on the table" from each sale. Furthermore, 3,000 customers are willing to pay more than the production cost ($5.00) but less than $8.75—the sales price. Each of these is a potentially profitable sale lost because the price is too high. What if the seller could determine the maximum amount that each customer would be willing to pay and could charge that amount to everyone willing to pay more than the per unit cost of $5.00? This would be pricing nirvana—the ultimate in "one-to-one" pricing.

The total potential opportunity for profit improvement from price differentiation is shown in Figure 4.1. With a single price, the widget maker will charge $8.75 per unit and realize a total profit of ($8.75 − $5.00) × 3,000 = $11,250. This is the area of region A in Figure 4.1. "Perfect" price differentiation would enable the seller to charge each customer willing to pay more than $8.75 per unit her exact willingness to pay. This would provide the additional revenue in region B in the figure. There is an additional opportunity to sell widgets to customers who are willing to pay more than $5.00, the unit production cost, but less than $8.75. This potential profit is shown as region C in the figure. The sum of the three regions is the total contribution that the widget maker would realize *if* he were able to charge every potential customer exactly at her willingness to pay. This is an upper bound on what

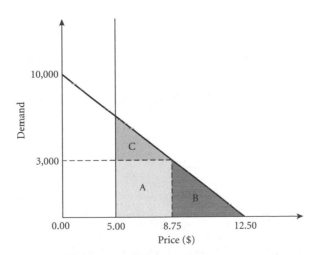

Figure 4.1 Contribution opportunity from price differentiation.

could possibly be realized under any price differentiation program. Charging every customer exactly her willingness to pay is known as *third-degree price discrimination* in the economics literature.

While it is unrealistic to assume that this total potential could ever be captured, the sheer magnitude of the potential gain means there is a powerful motivation for sellers to tailor different prices to different buyers according to their willingness to pay. Assume that the widget maker finds he can divide his market into two segments. One segment consists of all customers willing to pay more than $7.00 for widgets. The other segment consists of all the customers willing to pay $7.00 or less. The corresponding price-response curves are:

$$d_1(p_1) = \min[4{,}400, (10{,}000 - 800p_1)^+]$$
$$d_2(p_2) = (5{,}600 - 800p_2)^+$$

where $d_1(p_1)$ is the price-response curve for customers with a high willingness to pay and $d_2(p_2)$ is the price-response curve for customers with the lower willingness to pay. These two price-response curves are shown in Figure 4.2. The sum of these two curves is the original price-response curve in Figure 3.13. These two segments taken together make up the same total market that the widget maker faced before. The difference is that now he can offer a different price to each of the two segments. We assume for this example that the widget maker can perfectly identify customers as belonging to one group or the other and can then offer each customer the appropriate price, without any opportunity for resale or arbitrage between the two groups.

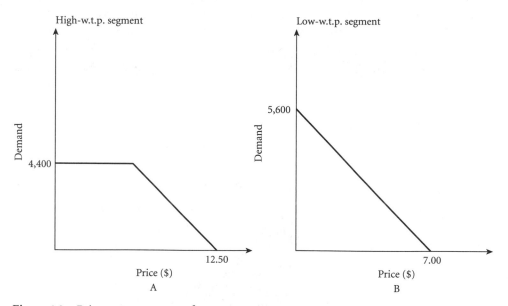

Figure 4.2   Price-response curves for two segments.

The widget maker can determine the optimal prices for each segment by solving Equation 3.18 twice—once for each segment. The results (along with a comparison to the unsegmented case) are shown in Table 4.1. Dividing his customers between those with w.t.p.

TABLE 4.1
Impact of market segmentation

	Unsegmented	Segment 1	Segment 2	Total	Change (%)
Average price	$8.75	$8.75	$6.00	$8.17	−6.6
Demand	3,000	3,000	800	3,800	26.7
Revenue	$26,250	$26,250	$4,800	$31,050	18.3
Gross contribution	$11,250	$11,250	$800	$12,050	7.0
Net contribution	$1,250	—	—	$2,050	85

greater than $7.00 and those with w.t.p. less than $7.00 and charging the optimal prices to the different segments enables the widget maker to increase his revenues by 18% and his total contribution by 7%. It is interesting to note that customers benefit as well. The same 3,000 customers who would buy under a single price at $8.75 still get to buy at $8.75. In addition, 800 additional customers get to purchase at the new low price of $6.00. These 800 customers are priced out of the market if the seller can only charge a single price. In this case, price differentiation is a win-win situation since the seller is certainly better off and all of the buyers are at least as well off as before. However, price differentiation is not always such a boon for consumers, as we discuss in Section 4.6.

4.2 LIMITS TO PRICE DIFFERENTIATION

If price differentiation is such a powerful way for sellers to increase contribution, why don't all of them do it? The reason is that there are powerful real-world limits to price differentiation.

1. *Imperfect segmentation.* The brain-scan technology required to determine the precise willingness to pay of each customer has not yet been developed. The best that can be done is to create market segments such that the *average* willingness to pay is different for each segment.

2. *Cannibalization.* Under differential pricing, there is a powerful motivation for customers in high-price segments to find a way to pay the lower price. In the widget example, there is a strong motivation for high-willingness-to-pay customers who are being charged $8.75 per widget to "masquerade" as low-willingness-to-pay customers and pay only $6.00 per widget.

3. *Arbitrage.* Price differentials create a strong incentive for third-party *arbitrageurs* to find a way to buy the product at the low price and resell to high-w.t.p. customers below the market price, keeping the difference for themselves.

The presence of any one of these factors can eliminate the benefits of price differentiation.

Example 4.1

Assume that the widget seller has segmented his market and is charging the two prices shown in Table 4.1. If 300 — that is 10%— of the high-willingness-to-pay customers are able to find a way to purchase widgets at the lower cost of $6.00, it would totally eliminate the benefits of price differentiation.

The deterioration of benefits in Example 4.1 could arise from imperfect segmentation, cannibalization, arbitrage, or a combination of any of them.

4.3 TACTICS FOR PRICE DIFFERENTIATION

The previous section established two properties of price differentiation.

1. Price differentiation allows sellers to increase profitability by charging different prices to customers with different willingness to pay.

2. Cannibalization, imperfect segmentation, or arbitrage can destroy—or even reverse—the benefits of price differentiation.

The first property means that sellers have a tremendous incentive to find creative ways to position and price their products differently to different market segments. The second means that price differentiation needs to be carefully planned and managed in order to be successful. In this section we describe some of the most common and effective approaches to price differentiation used in different markets.

4.3.1 Group Pricing

Group pricing is the tactic of offering different prices to different groups of customers for exactly the same product.[1] The idea is to offer a lower price to customers with a low willingness to pay and a higher price to those with a high willingness to pay. In practice, "pure" group pricing requires determining whether or not a prospective buyer belongs to a particular group and using that information to determine which price to charge. Examples of pure group pricing include:

- Student discounts
- Senior citizen discounts
- "Ladies' Night" specials
- Family specials
- Discounts for favored customers
- Favorable terms offered by manufacturers or wholesalers to large retailers such as Wal-Mart
- Lower prices offered to government, educational, and nonprofit organizations by suppliers

Four criteria must hold for group pricing to be successful.

- *There must be an unambiguous indicator of group membership*. Examples of such indicators include a student ID card or a driver's license that lists age. Furthermore, it must be difficult or impossible for members of one group to masquerade as members of another. Otherwise, cannibalization could easily reduce or destroy the benefits of price differentiation.

- *Group membership must strongly correlate with price sensitivity.* Senior citizen discounts are predicated on the belief that senior citizens, *as a whole*, are more price sensitive than the public in general.

- *The product or service should not be easily traded or exchanged among purchasers.* This is necessary to avoid *arbitrage*—in which customers with access to low prices resell to customers who are quoted higher prices.

- *The segmentation must be both culturally and legally accepted.* While group pricing on the basis of age is broadly accepted, differentiating prices on the basis of other characteristics, such as race and gender, are controversial or illegal. The Robinson-Patman Act prohibits many forms of group pricing that wholesalers might want to use to charge differential prices to retailers.

Taken together, these criteria are so stringent that pure group pricing is relatively rare in direct consumer sales. It is most common in services. Services are often sold directly by the supplier so that Disneyworld, for example, can check a customer's age before selling a child's ticket. Furthermore, many services, such as health care and haircuts, are intrinsically non-transferable, so arbitrage is not an issue. Airlines originally began checking passenger identification not for security reasons but to prevent arbitrage.

Pure group pricing is also common in business-to-business sales. In Chapter 11 we discuss how businesses can estimate price responsiveness and develop customized prices for different business segments. Customized pricing in business-to-business sales is often combined with some form of product versioning, particularly in industries where individual orders are very complex and/or configurable.

4.3.2 Channel Pricing

Channel pricing is the practice of selling the same product for different prices through different distribution channels. Here are some examples.

- Barnes and Noble sells books for different prices online than through its outlets.

- Special "Web-only" fares for airline tickets are available through the Internet but not through travel agencies.

- Many fashion and home furnishing merchants offer lower prices for merchandise through mail-order catalogs than for the same merchandise sold through retail outlets.

As with other price differentiation schemes, there can be more than one reason why a seller might charge different prices through different channels. One is cost—for many companies, selling through the Internet is cheaper than selling through traditional channels. Continental Airlines calculated that distribution costs for a $325 ticket are about $43 when the ticket is sold through a travel agent versus only $18 when the same ticket is sold through Continental's Web site. This difference in itself would be sufficient reason for Continental to charge lower prices on its Web site.

However, it is also the case that customers arriving via different channels have different price sensitivities. For personal loans, it has been shown that customers inquiring through the Internet are more price sensitive than those contacting a call center, who are in turn more price sensitive than those who apply for a loan at a retail branch. Furthermore, Internet customers who access a consolidator Web site or use a shopping 'bot tend to be more price sensitive than those who go directly to a bank's Web site. This is not surprising given the characteristics of the channels—it is generally easier and more convenient to shop and compare prices during a single Internet session than by making many phone calls. Thus differential willingness to pay is also a motivation for channel pricing.

4.3.3 Regional Pricing

Regional pricing is an extremely common price differentiation technique. Here are some examples.

- In Latin America, McDonalds sells hamburgers for higher prices in wealthy neighborhoods than in poorer ones.[2]

- A roundtrip New York–Tokyo ticket purchased in Japan will usually cost more for many airlines than the same ticket purchased in the United States.

- A glass of beer costs more at an airport bar than at the corner bar.

In each case, the price difference is based on the supplier's desire to exploit differences in price sensitivity between locations. After all, travelers at an airport are essentially a captive market and have few alternatives.

4.3.4 Couponing and Self-Selection

We have seen that group pricing is often both difficult and unpopular—difficult because it requires the seller to categorize customers on the basis of price sensitivity before quoting them a price, and unpopular because it often seems "unfair" to consumers. It is often much more convenient to differentiate prices in ways that allow customers to self-select. In a self-selection approach, both the list price and a discounted price are available to all customers, but it takes additional time, effort, or flexibility to obtain the discounted price. The idea is that those willing to make the additional effort to get the discount are generally more price sensitive than those who are not. Here are some examples.

- Retailers commonly offer discount coupons through newspapers, direct mail, and magazines.

- Retailers often offer mail-in rebates for purchasers of a good.

- Movie theaters charge lower prices for a weekday matinee than for a Saturday night show.

- Brand-name retailers such as Ralph Lauren, the Gap, and Liz Claiborne operate outlet stores in somewhat out-of-the-way locations in which merchandise is available for a substantial discount.

The common thread among these examples is that the seller has chosen a mechanism that allows customers to self-select, depending on the value they place on time or flexibility. Any customer can obtain an item at a discount if she is willing to take some additional effort. Research has shown that users of coupons are more price sensitive than nonusers of coupons.[3] Locating outlet stalls away from large cities segments the market between those who are willing to spend additional time shopping and those who aren't. Peak-load, day-of-week, and time-of-day pricing segments the market between those who have the flexibility to change their plans in order to save some money and those who are not willing to do so. Since these mechanisms are based on self-selection, they are far more acceptable to most consumers than mechanisms in which the seller unilaterally selects customers to receive discounts.

4.3.5 Product Versioning

When pure group pricing is not feasible, companies use other strategies to differentiate prices. The most notable of these is designing or developing products (either virtual or real) that may have only minor differences but enable the seller to exploit differences in price sensitivity among customer segments. This can involve developing an "inferior" variant and/or a "superior" variant of an existing product. We will discuss examples of both strategies as well as their logical extension into the creation of a product line.

Inferior goods. Consider the following cases.

- Well-known international brand names such as Mobil/Exxon and Shell sell excess gasoline in bulk at low prices to so-called "off-brand" independent dealers who resell it under their own brands.

- A well-known premium wine producer sells some of its production under a different label at about half the price.

- Brand-name vegetable canners sell their products under their own brand but also sell to retailers who sell the product to consumers as a "house brand" or a generic brand.

While the specifics of each of these cases differ, the motivation on the part of the seller is the same—a desire to sell a product cheaply to customers with lower willingnesses to pay without cannibalizing sales of the full-price product. This is achieved in each case by creating an inferior version of the "standard product."

A particularly extreme example of inferior goods is the category of so-called *damaged goods*. This is a term coined to refer to the situation in which a manufacturer or supplier creates an inferior good by damaging, degrading, or disabling a standard good (Deneckere and McAfee 1996). Since this process starts with the standard good, the supplier is actually paying more to create the inferior good it will sell at a lower price. One example is the 486SX processor developed and sold by Intel Corporation.

The 486SX processor of Intel Corporation was initially produced in a curious way. Intel began with a fully functioning 486DX processor, then *disabled the math coprocessor,* to produce a chip that is strictly inferior to the 486DX but more expensive to produce. Nevertheless, in 1991, the 486DX sold for $588, and the 486SX for $333, a little over half the price of the chip that is less expensive to produce.[4]

Complex application software packages such as supply-chain software or enterprise resource planning (ERP) software are often sold at different prices, depending on the number of features purchased by a customer—the more features purchased, the more expensive the license. In many cases, the software is configured for a particular customer by starting with the complete package and then disabling the features that the customer did not purchase.

The concept of "damaging" a good in order to create an inferior good to be sold at a lower price may initially seem somewhat bizarre. However, it is really only a special case of the more general category of "inferior" goods. There can be a tremendous gain from offering an inferior good at a lower price, even if the supposedly inferior product is more expensive to produce. Starting from a standard product and then paying to have it "damaged" is only a special case of this more general principle.

Superior goods. Spendrups is the largest brewery in Sweden. Traditionally Spendrups brewed medium- or low-priced lagers aimed at the mass market. In the 1980s, they created Spendrups Old Gold, which they advertised as a premium beer and sold in a special, highly distinctive bottle. Although Old Gold did not generally fare better than Spendrups' other brands in comparative taste tests, Spendrups was able to establish Old Gold as a premium brand and maintain a price 25% to 50% higher than that of its other brands. This is the obvious complement to the inferior-good strategy: creating a superior good in order to extract a higher price from less price-sensitive customers.

Another example of the superior-good strategy was employed by Proctor-Silex. In 1985, Proctor-Silex priced a top-of-the-line iron at $54.95, while their next best model was priced at $49.95. The only difference between the two was that the top model had a small light indicating when the iron is ready to use. The difference in manufacturing cost between the two models was only $1.00, yet Proctor-Silex was able to maintain a $5.00 price difference because, as a Proctor-Silex marketing manager put it, "There is a segment of the market that wants to buy the best, despite the cost."[5] By creating a "superior" product, Proctor-Silex enabled the less price-sensitive segment of the market to self-select and extracted an additional $4.00 in contribution margin from each high-end buyer. In some ways, a superior-good strategy is safer than an inferior-good strategy because it does not threaten cannibalization of existing sales. Of course, it presumes an ability to create and establish a product that the market perceives as truly superior to the existing product and that there is a customer segment willing to pay a premium for the superior product.

Product lines. Establishing a product line is the natural extension of creating inferior or superior products. A product line is a series of similar products serving the same general market but sold at different prices. For our purposes, we will consider *vertical* product lines, where almost all customers would agree that a higher-priced product is superior to a lower-priced one. This applies, for example, to a hotel that charges more for an ocean-view room than a parking-lot-view room—almost all customers would prefer the ocean view to the parking lot view. It also applies to personal computers offered by Dell, where each product in the line has higher performance (faster CPU, more memory, etc.) than the product just below it in the line. This can be contrasted to *horizontal* product lines, where different customers would prefer different products within the line, even at the same price. Coca-Cola offers a horizontal profit line with "Classic" Coke, Diet Coke, Cherry Coke, Diet Cherry Coke, etc. This is a horizontal product line because no one of the products is unambiguously higher quality or more desirable than another.

An example of a vertical product line is shown in Table 4.2, which gives prices for four versions of the QuickBooks financial software offered by Intuit. The software comes in four "editions," ranging from the Basic Edition, which costs $199.95, to the Enterprise Solutions, which costs $3,500. In between are the Pro Edition, which is described as including "all the features of Basic plus advanced tools and customization options to boost efficiency and accuracy" and the Premier Edition, which includes "all the features of Pro and comprehensive tools for greater insight into your business." The top-of-the-line Enterprise Solutions package is described as "Our most comprehensive business management tool for growing businesses, with all the features of Pro and Premier."[6]

TABLE 4.2
Online prices offered by Intuit for the QuickBooks product family (August 2004)

Product	Price
Basic Edition	$199.95
Pro Edition	$299.95
Premier Edition	$499.95
Enterprise Solutions	$3,500.00

In all likelihood, there is only a tiny difference (if any) in the marginal cost of producing and delivering the four different versions of QuickBooks software. Yet the Enterprise Solutions package is priced more than 15 times higher than the Basic Edition. The rationale for the product line and the broad difference is market segmentation—very small businesses that need less functionality and have fewer users are presumably more price sensitive than larger businesses with more users. The establishment of a series of products allows Intuit to segment its market via self-selection on the part of its customers.

Another example of product-line pricing is illustrated in Table 4.3, which shows the one-day rates on display through Expedia for a Hertz one-day rental from the Seattle airport on a midweek day in May. Hertz lists six different products, with prices ranging from $53.99 per day for an economy rental to almost $100 for a luxury car. By providing a menu of alternatives at different prices Hertz allows customers to self-select: There are those who are entirely budget-focused and will choose the Economy or Compact cars and those who prefer (and are willing to pay for) greater levels of driving comfort. It is important to stress that the range of rates offered by Hertz for these different products is not driven by cost differences. Life-cycle costs do not vary much among models. More important, there is little or no difference in the daily incremental cost to Hertz from renting out an economy car or a

TABLE 4.3

Rates offered by Hertz through Expedia for one-day rentals of different car types at the Seattle airport on a midweek day in May 2004

Car type	Representative model	Rate
Economy	Hyundai Accent	$53.99
Compact	Ford Focus	55.99
Mid-size	Mazda 626	60.99
Standard	Mustang V6	63.99
Full-size	Ford Taurus	69.99
Premium	Mercury Grand Marquis	89.99
Luxury	Lincoln Town Car	99.99

luxury car. The spread in daily rates is driven almost entirely by Hertz's desire to segment its market and charge different prices to different segments.

For service companies like Hertz, creation of a product line has an important side benefit—it creates opportunities for *upgrading*. A rental car company or a cruise line has the ability to oversell lower-quality car types and upgrade customers into higher-quality types. Not only does this provide the company with greater flexibility to manage its inventory, but being upgraded is usually viewed favorably by customers. An important advantage of pricing differentiation by establishing a product line is that consumers perceive it as *fair*. The pricing menus offered by Hertz and Intuit are openly communicated and available to all comers.[7] Consumers get to choose among the alternatives, and the concept of "paying more to get more" is widely accepted. This makes product-line pricing more acceptable than group pricing in most customers' minds.

4.3.6 Time-Based Differentiation

Time-based differentiation is a very common form of product versioning. Here are some examples.

- Amazon offers 5- to 9-day "Super-saver" shipping free while charging $3.97 for "standard shipping."

- Passenger airlines offer discount rates to customers who book a week or more prior to departure.

- Software- and hardware-support contracts charge more for "two-hour response" than for "two-day response."

- Fashion goods cost more during the beginning of the season and are marked down toward the end of the season.

In each of these cases, companies have created differentiated products that allow customers to self-select. In the case of Amazon, customers who are willing to wait for delivery can pay less. For passenger airlines, customers who have the flexibility to book earlier can pay less. Of course, it may be that the higher price charged by Amazon for early delivery exactly matches the incremental cost. But it is highly likely that Amazon is also using time of delivery as a segmentation variable, relying on the fact that some of their customers will willingly pay a premium in order to have the product in their hands sooner.

Time-based differentiation plays a very important role at passenger airlines, hotels, and rental car companies, in which time of booking and other factors, such as willingness to accept a Saturday night stayover, are used as indicators of whether or not a potential customer is traveling for leisure purposes or business purposes. Those traveling for leisure purposes are presumed to be more price sensitive than those traveling for business. This segmentation is the foundation of revenue management in those industries, and we discuss it in detail in Chapter 6. The willingness of some customers to wait in order to purchase fashion goods at a discount is the basis of markdown management, which we treat in detail in Chapter 10.

4.3.7 Product Versioning or Group Pricing?

We have treated product versioning and group pricing as separate strategies for price differentiation. In reality, there is no clear line separating the two approaches and many price differentiation strategies contain elements of both. For example, consider the classic airline example (which we explore in more detail in Chapter 6) of a roundtrip ticket from San Francisco to Chicago costing $250 if purchased a week in advance and including a Saturday stayover versus $750 if purchased at the last minute without restrictions. Is this group pricing or product versioning? Disgruntled customers might argue that it is simply group pricing, since different customers are paying different amounts for exactly the same service, namely, a roundtrip coach seat San Francisco–New York. This is the "Why am I paying $500 more than the person sitting beside me for exactly the same flight?" objection. The airline would reply that the two types of tickets are distinct products and that the added cost of the full-fare ticket is fully justified by the flexibility of being able to purchase late and return without staying over a Saturday night.

The reality is, of course, that airline pricing—like many successful examples of price differentiation—includes elements of both group pricing and product versioning. The airlines consciously created restricted discount fares as an inferior product. They did so, however, as a way to enable them to offer different fares to different customer groups: lower fares to leisure travelers, who are more price sensitive but more flexible; and higher fares to business travelers, who are less price sensitive but less flexible. Viewed one way, we could say that the airlines created an inferior product as the most efficient and least controversial way to institute group pricing.

The airline example illustrates a very important point. Pure group pricing is very difficult to pull off in consumer markets. There are few cases in which consumers can unambiguously be identified as belonging to a particular group. Airlines have no reliable objective marker to tell them whether a particular customer is flying for business or for pleasure. In the absence of such a marker, they rely on the very imperfect criterion of whether or not a customer can book early. This works well enough, but it is imperfect. For example, there are plenty of highly price-sensitive leisure customers who would love to book late. Furthermore, the airlines have lots of empty seats they would like to fill with these customers even at a very low price. But, at least until recently, there has been no systematic way to sell to these customers without cannibalizing the full-fare business customers.

4.4 VOLUME DISCOUNTS

Volume discounting is a time-honored and very popular tactic. "Buy more to save more" is a common motto. Some examples follow.

- A six-pack of beer purchased from the supermarket costs less than six times the cost of a single bottle, and a case (12 bottles) usually costs less than two six-packs.

- Larger boxes of laundry detergent cost less per ounce than smaller boxes.

- Verizon offers residential long-distance plans in which the cost per minute declines with the number of minutes. A plan allowing 30 minutes per month charges 10 cents per minute, one allowing 300 minutes per month charges 7 cents per minute, and one allowing 1,000 minutes per month charges 4 cents per minute.

Volume discounting is as prevalent, if not more prevalent, in wholesale and business-to-business selling. Table 4.4 shows three typical price schedules.[8] In each case, the sellers offer significantly lower unit prices to customers who are buying more units. And the price decreases as the number of units in the order increases.

TABLE 4.4
Price schedules for Opera software, St. Louis Commerce Magazine,
and Horton Brass Products in August 2004

OPERA SOFTWARE		ST. LOUIS COMMERCE MAGAZINE		HORTON BRASS PRODUCTS	
Order size	Price per copy	Order size	Unit price	Order size	Discount
1–9	$39.00	5–50	$2.75	1–11	0 (list price)
10–19	$37.00	51–100	$2.50	12–47	Approx. 8% off[†]
20–29	$35.00	101–250	$2.25	48–199	Approx. 15% off[†]
30–50	$33.00	251–500	$1.75	200–999	20% off
51 or more	*	501 or more	$1.50	1,000–2,499	25% off
				2,500 or more	30% off

* "Volume contracts negotiated directly with Opera software."
[†] Actual discount is calculated using a pricing table.
SOURCES: http//www.opera.com, http//www.stlcommercemagazine.com, http//www.horton-brasses.com.

There are at least three reasons why companies offer volume discounts:

1. *Transaction or order costs.* If there are substantial costs associated with fulfilling an order independent of size, the order cost per unit will decrease as the size of the order increases. Therefore, it may make sense for the seller to charge a lower price per unit for large orders.

Example 4.2

A software seller has a fixed cost of $1,000 per installation and a variable cost of $40 per user. His total cost for an installation with 10 users is $1,400, or $140/user, compared with a total cost of $5,000, or only $50/user, for an installation with 100 users. Even if large users and small users have the same price sensitivity, it will make sense to charge less per user to large users.

2. *Decreasing marginal utility.* In many cases, the marginal utility to a buyer decreases as the number of units purchased increases. A hot and thirsty customer walking into a convenience store places more value on the first can of cold soft drink than she does on the second. Decreasing marginal utility is also often seen in business-to-business sales.

Example 4.3

A company wants to purchase copies of a financial analysis software package for its employees to use. There is wide variation in the value the company will gain from having different employees have access to the software. The company is able to determine that there are 500 employees who would use the package and that the value to the company from their access is uniformly distributed between 0 and $250 per year. This means that the software vendor is essentially facing a "demand curve" of $d(p) = 500 - 2p$ for the number of copies it can sell at a single annual license fee to this company. The vendor can set a single annual license fee of $125 and sell 250 copies for total revenue of $31,250 — the maximum revenue from a single price. However, if it adopted a two-tier pricing scheme and licensed the first 250 copies for $125 each but dropped the price to $75 for each additional sale, it will sell an additional 100 copies at $75 for additional revenue of $7,500.

3. *Increasing price sensitivity.* Customers purchasing larger amounts are often more price sensitive than customers purchasing smaller amounts. Corporate purchasers who buy large volumes are likely to be following a formal procurement process in which they carefully compare alternatives. A contractor who spends millions of dollars on galvanized pipe annually is much more likely to spend time and effort finding a good deal than a homeowner who is buying a length of pipe at the hardware store. Volume discounting is one way that a seller can differentiate among large-volume, highly price-sensitive buyers and smaller-volume, less price-sensitive buyers.

There are numerous schemes for volume discounting, many of which are often grouped under the general category of *nonlinear pricing*. The *nonlinear* refers to the fact that the total price paid is not a linear function of the number of units ordered as it would be with a single price. Figure 4.3 shows how the total order price for *St. Louis Commerce Magazine* varies with the number of copies ordered. The sharp downward jumps are at the price-points when deeper and deeper discount levels kick in. Without the volume discounts, the total cost would be a linear function of the number ordered. This type of discounting has the well-known drawback that the price-jumps can create a situation in which a buyer can actually pay less money by purchasing more units. Thus, an order of 250 copies would cost $562.50 while an order of 260 copies would only cost $455.00. In essence, the magazine is paying the buyer almost $9.00 apiece to take an additional 10 copies. Despite this seemingly irrational aspect, this type of volume discount is extremely common in practice.

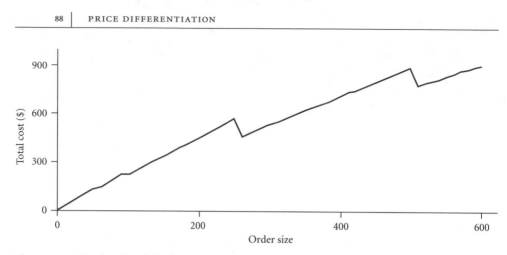

Figure 4.3 Total order price for *St. Louis Commerce Magazine* as a function of the number of copies ordered based on the schedule in Table 4.4. *Source*: Data from http://www.stlcommercemagazine.com, August 2004.

Volume discounts can either be applied to an entire order, as in the three price schedules shown in Table 4.4, or incrementally. In incremental discounting, additional discounts are only applied to additional units—not to the entire order. A common example of incremental pricing in consumer markets is "Buy one, get the second at half price." In this case, the discount is applied only to the second unit purchased, not to the first. Incremental discounts avoid the downward price jumps seen in Figure 4.3. However, they can also be harder to communicate to buyers.

Volume discounts are often applied based on total volume of business over some period, rather than on size of a single order. This is often accomplished in consumer markets by "frequent buyer" schemes such as the airlines' frequent-flyer programs. My local coffee shop keeps track of my purchases and gives me every 10th cup free. The stated purpose of such programs is to reward loyal customers, but they also serve the purpose of lowering the real price seen by frequent purchasers, who are likely to be more price sensitive. This practice is extremely common in business-to-business sales, in which discounts are often applied based on sales volume in a quarter or other period. For example, electronics distributors resell electronics goods to retailers, government, and educational institutions. A manufacturer (such as Hewlett-Packard) selling through the distributor will offer a progressive end-of-quarter rebate based on how much of their product the distributor has sold during the quarter. For example, Acme Electronics might offer a 0.5% rebate if the distributor sells between $1 million and $1.499 million worth of Acme products during the quarter, a 0.75% rebate if the distributor sells between $1.5 million and $1.999 million, and a 1% rebate if the distributor sells over $2 million. In freight transportation, a carrier will often offer a higher discount if a shipper commits to a higher volume of business over some future period.

Combining different terms and discount structures can lead to an extremely wide variety of volume discount schemes. Some of these are discussed in Nagle and Holden (1994) and in Wilson (1993). All of these schemes are designed to exploit the decreasing marginal value of purchasers and/or the higher price sensitivity of large purchasers. In the case of decreasing marginal values, a seller could, in theory, capture the maximum contribution by pricing each additional unit at the willingness to pay of the customer for that unit. Of course, this is impossible because the seller is actually selling to a mixture of customers with different w.t.p.'s and the exact w.t.p. of each customer is unknown. However, given overall demand curves for purchases of different sizes, a seller can derive a volume discounting scheme that will increase contribution over a single price.

Like any market segmentation scheme, volume discounts provide opportunities for arbitrage. Referring to the price schedule in Table 4.4, an enterprising arbitrageur could purchase 50 copies of Opera software at $33.00 and then resell them at $38.00, undercutting the single-copy list price of $39.00. Software companies often require users to register to receive future support and maintenance, in part to avoid the possibility of such arbitrage (not to mention out-and-out piracy). In other cases, bulk and volume purchasers are required to sign a contract that prohibits them from reselling for profit. On the other hand, wholesalers such as the *St. Louis Commerce Magazine* should presumably be largely indifferent to arbitrage since they are using volume discounts to encourage the largest number of sales possible.

Volume discounting should be distinguished from *oligopsony* or *monopsony*—the exercise of market power by purchasers so large that they represent a significant fraction of the entire market. Historically, the "big three" U.S. automakers could often virtually dictate prices to some of their suppliers, since they were the only game in town. Similarly, very large freight consolidators can use their size to negotiate favorable tariffs from freight carriers, and Wal-Mart uses its status as the largest retailer in the world to extract very low prices from its suppliers. Branches of the U.S. government often require as terms of their procurement contracts that suppliers provide them "most favored buyer" status—that is, they must sell to the government at a price at least as low as the lowest price given to any other customer. Pressure exerted by a monopsonist to extract price concessions is not the same as a seller using differentiated prices to maximize profit.

4.5 CALCULATING DIFFERENTIATED PRICES

If market segments are completely independent (i.e., no cannibalization) and the seller faces no capacity constraints, then calculating differentiated prices is quite simple—the seller simply finds the contribution-optimizing price for each segment. This is the right approach whether the underlying differentiation is based on channel, geography, or pure group pricing.

Example 4.4

An electronics distributor sells portable MP3 players through its exclusive retail outlets and on its Web site. The unit cost for each MP3 player is $200. The additional cost per sale through the Internet is $35.00, including shipping, but $70 through the retail stores. Through price testing, the distributor has discovered that price elasticity is 2.5 for Internet customers versus 2.2 for retail customers. Using Equation 3.21, the distributor calculates the contribution-maximizing price as $(2.5/1.5) \times (\$200 + \$35) = \$392$ for Internet sales and $(2.2/1.2) \times (\$200 + \$70) = \$495$ for retail sales.

4.5.1 Optimal Pricing with Arbitrage

Unfortunately for sellers, perfect price differentiation is usually impossible. Cannibalization is likely whenever customers cannot be perfectly segmented according to willingness to pay. Arbitrage is likely whenever a third party can purchase the product at a low price and resell it at a high price. Regional pricing is subject to arbitrage whenever a product can be purchased in a low-price region and transported cheaply to be resold at a higher price elsewhere. For this reason, global companies often set price bands for various markets to avoid resales from low-price countries that would cannibalize sales in higher-price countries.

Example 4.5

A computer chip manufacturer finds that the contribution-maximizing prices for his chips are \$2.54 in the United States and \$2.43 in Brazil. However, if it costs \$0.08 per unit to ship chips from Brazil to the United States, he will not be able to charge those prices due to the potential for arbitrage between the two countries. He needs to set prices for both countries that do not vary by more than \$0.08.

The regional pricing problem with arbitrage can be formulated as a constrained optimization problem. Assume that a manufacturer is selling a common product to n different locations. These could be cities or regions, but for purposes of discussion we will consider them to be countries. The delivered cost (including transportation) in country i is c_i. The cost of an arbitrageur to transport the product from country i to country j is a_{ij}.[9] To avoid arbitrage, the supplier needs to set prices such that $p_j \leq p_i + a_{ij}$ for each i and j. Otherwise, the supplier faces the possibility that an arbitrageur will purchase product in country i, transport the product to country j, and sell it for a price $\hat{p}_j$. If $\hat{p}_j < p_j$ and $\hat{p}_j > p_i + a_{ij}$, then the arbitrageur can undercut the supplier in country j while still turning a profit. It is clear that a contribution-maximizing supplier would usually like to avoid this situation.[10]

Let p_i be the price in country i and $d_i(p_i)$ be the price-response curve faced by the supplier in country i. Then the problem of optimizing international prices under the possibility of arbitrage can be formulated as

$$\max_p \sum_{i=1}^{n} (p_i - c_i)\, d_i(p_i)$$

subject to

$$p_j \leq p_i + a_{ij} \qquad \text{for } i = 1, 2, \ldots, n; j = 1, 2, \ldots, n; i \neq j$$

$$p_i \geq 0 \qquad \text{for } i = 1, 2, \ldots, n$$

This problem will not, in general, be a linear program. However, if the price-response curve for each country is continuous and downward sloping, it will have a single optimum and will be easy to solve using standard optimization approaches. In many cases, global companies do not always solve the full optimization problem, but rather determine prices for major markets (e.g., North America, Western Europe, Japan) and then use price bands to determine prices for smaller markets that are close enough to major market prices to eliminate the potential for trans-shipment.

4.5.2 Optimal Pricing with Cannibalization

Cannibalization presents a somewhat different problem than arbitrage. To analyze differentiated pricing with cannibalization, let's return to the case in which we divided widget customers into those with w.t.p. $\geq$ \$7.00 and those with w.t.p. $<$ \$7.00. The corresponding price-response curves, shown in Figure 4.2, assume perfect differentiation—the company can perfectly distinguish between those customers willing to pay more than \$7.00 and those willing to pay less than \$7.00 and can charge the optimal price to each group. What if some of the higher-willingness-to-pay customers find a way to buy at the lower price? Let α be the *cannibalization fraction*—the fraction of higher-willingness-to-pay customers who find a way to buy at the lower price. $\alpha = 0$ corresponds to the case of perfect differentiation—none of the high-w.t.p. customers buy at the lower price—while $\alpha = 1$ corresponds to no differentiation—*all* of the customers buy at the lower price. Values of α between 0 and 1 represent different segmentation efficiencies. Given a value of α, the price-response curves for each of the two segments are given by.[11]

$$d_1(p_1) = (1 - \alpha) \min(4{,}400, (10{,}000 - 800p_1)^+)$$

$$d_2(p_2) = (5{,}600 - 800p_2)^+ + 4{,}400\alpha$$

The second term in the equation for $d_2(p_2)$ reflects the fact that there are 4,400 total customers with a w.t.p. greater than \$7.00 and that a fraction α of them will find a way to buy at the lower price, p_2.

To find the values of p_1 and p_2 that maximize total contribution, we need to solve the optimization problem

$$\max_{p_1, p_2}(p_1 - c)(1 - \alpha) \min(4{,}400, (10{,}000 - 800p_1)^+)$$

$$+ (p_2 - c)[(5{,}600 - 800p_2)^+ + 4{,}400\alpha]$$

subject to

$$p_2 \leq \$7.00$$

The prices that maximize total contribution in this case are:

$$p_1^* = \$8.75$$

$$p_2^* = \min(\$6.00 + \$2.75\alpha, \$7.00)$$

When $\alpha = 0$ (no cannibalization), $p_2^* = \$6.00$. As α increases, cannibalization increases and p_2^* increases as well. This corresponds to intuition—the more our low-price product is cannibalizing our high-price product, the higher we need to price the low-price product to maximize total contribution. When $\alpha = 0.36$ (i.e., 36% of the high-w.t.p. customers find a

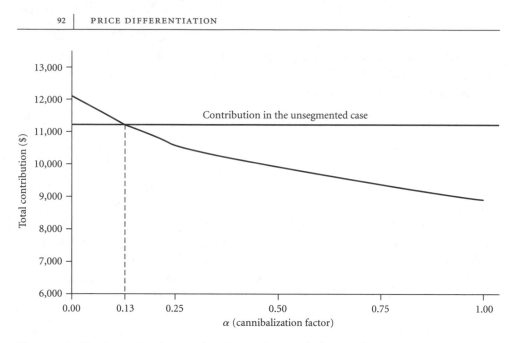

Figure 4.4   Total contribution as a function of the cannibalization fraction α.

way to pay the lower price), the optimal low price has risen to $7.00. At this point, none of the low-w.t.p. customers are buying any more (since their w.t.p. is less than $7.00) and the only low-price customers are cannibalized high-w.t.p. customers.

Figure 4.4 shows optimal total contribution as a function of α. As α increases, total contribution decreases as more and more high-w.t.p. customers are cannibalized by the lower price. At a value of α of about 13%, total contribution is $11,250, the same total contribution that could be achieved with no segmentation. In this simple example, if more than 13% of our high-willingness-to-pay customers will be cannibalized, we are better off offering only a single price than trying to differentiate and offer different prices to the different segments.

While the figure of 13% is specific to this example, the lesson is general: Even fairly low rates of cannibalization can outweigh the benefits of price differentiation. This means that when establishing customer segments and determining the optimal prices, it is critical that we understand the potential for cannibalization and price accordingly within each segment. Otherwise, we can end up in a situation where we are worse off than if we had simply established a single price to the entire market.

4.5.3 *Finding the Best Segmentation

The ability of a seller to segment his market depends upon two things:

1. Ability to identify groups of customers that have different willingnesses to pay
2. Ability to price independently to those two groups

Simply identifying customers with different w.t.p.'s for a product is not useful (at least from a PRO point of view) if we cannot find a way to charge different prices to those groups. This usually requires some ingenuity as well as a deep understanding of the overall market. However, since we are currently considering an imaginary "widget world" we can ask the question: If the widget maker could choose the ideal way to divide the market into two seg-ments, how should he do so in order to maximize contribution? Specifically, if he could choose a particular willingness to pay, v, such that he can offer one price, p_1, to everyone with w.t.p. greater than v and a different price, p_2, to everyone with w.t.p. less than or equal to v, what value of v would he choose? For any v, we write $d_1(p_1; v)$ as the price-response curve for the segment with w.t.p. greater than v and $d_2(p_2; v)$ as the price-response curve for the seg-ment with w.t.p. less than or equal to v. The problem that the seller wants to solve is to find the value of v that maximizes

$$m^*(v) = \max_{p_1, p_2}[(p_1 - c)\, d_1(p_1; v) + (p_2 - c)\, d_2(p_2; v)]$$

subject to

$$p_1 \geq v \qquad v \geq p_2 \geq 0$$

We know that the optimal value of v will be greater than $5.00 (the unit cost) and less than $12.50 (the maximum price). We have already seen that for $v = 7.00$, $p_1^*(v) = 8.75$, $p_2^*(v) = 6.00$, and $m^*(v) = 12,050$. Further results for values of v ranging from $5.00 to $12.50 are shown in Table 4.5. Among the options in the table, the ideal segmentation would be to differentiate between those customers with w.t.p. greater than $10.00 and those with w.t.p. less than $10.00. The widget maker would charge the first (higher-w.t.p.) group $10.00 and the second (lower-w.t.p.) group $7.50, with a corresponding total contribution of $15,000—33% higher than without any segmentation but still substantially below the "one-to-one" pricing total contribution of $22,500.[12]

TABLE 4.5
Impact of market segmentation

v	$p_1^*(v)$	$d_1(p_1^*; v)$	m_1^*	$p_2^*(v)$	$d_2(p_2^*; v)$	m_2^*	$m^*(v)$
$5.00	$8.75	3,000	$11,250	$5.00	0	0	$11,250
$6.00	$8.75	3,000	$11,250	$5.50	400	$200	$11,450
$7.00	$8.75	3,000	$11,250	$6.00	800	$800	$12,050
$8.00	$8.75	3,000	$11,250	$6.50	1,200	$1,800	$13,050
$9.00	$9.00	2,800	$11,200	$7.00	1,600	$3,200	$14,400
$10.00	$10.00	2,000	$10,000	$7.50	2,000	$5,000	$15,000
$11.00	$11.00	1,200	$7,200	$8.00	2,400	$7,200	$14,400
$12.00	$12.00	400	$2,800	$8.50	2,800	$9,800	$12,600
$12.50	$12.50	0	$0	$8.75	3,000	$11,250	$11,250

4.6 PRICE DIFFERENTIATION AND CONSUMER WELFARE

We have seen that price differentiation can be good for sellers. But is it good for buyers? This is not merely an academic exercise. Price differentiation can be very unpopular among cus-tomers. As we shall see in Chapter 12, a differential pricing scheme can be viewed as unfair. This is true even if it makes customers, as a whole, better off. Any differential pricing scheme based strictly on making customers pay more is not only likely to be unpopular. It may also invite regulatory action. A differential pricing scheme that improves (or does not decrease) total consumer welfare is more defensible both to the public and to potential regulators.

The key concept in measuring the effect of pricing policy on consumer welfare is *consumer surplus*. The surplus of an individual consumer is the difference between his willingness to pay and the price at which he purchases, if he purchases, and is zero if he does not purchase.[13] The surplus associated with a customer who does not purchase is zero. The total consumer surplus in the market is the sum of the individual surpluses. Since a customer will only purchase if his willingness to pay is greater than the price, total consumer surplus in a market will always be greater than or equal to 0. Consumer surplus is important because, at least according to most theories of social welfare, one pricing scheme is better than another for consumers as a whole if it results in a greater total consumer surplus.[14] When there is a single price, consumer surplus is equal to the area of the section under the price-response curve above the sales price. For the widget seller in Section 4.1, total consumer surplus is equal to the area of the triangle labeled B in Figure 4.1.

At first thought, it might seem that price differentiation can only make customers worse off. After all, if a seller could perfectly differentiate, he would charge a price to each customer exactly equal to her willingness to pay (or just a penny below). If this were possible, it would result in total consumer surplus of 0—the seller would grab all of the consumer surplus in the market for himself. In terms of Figure 4.1, the seller would have taken all of areas A, B, and C as profit, leaving no consumer surplus.

However, it turns out that price differentiation *can* make consumers better off. Consider the case where the widget maker is able to divide his market into two segments, with the two price-response curves shown in Figure 4.2. As shown in Table 4.1, the seller's optimal policy in this case is to charge \$8.75 to the high-willingness-to-pay segment and \$7.00 to the low-willingness-to-pay segment, with a concurrent increase in contribution of \$800 relative to the best he can do charging a single price. The total consumer surplus under this new policy is the old surplus, denoted by region C_1 in Figure 4.5, plus the new surplus, C_2, enjoyed by the customers paying \$7.00. The seller's profit is the sum of regions A_1 and A_2. Comparison with Figure 4.1 shows that this two-price policy has resulted in both more

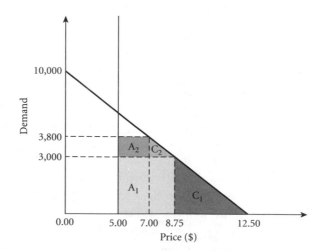

Figure 4.5 Profit and consumer surplus from the two-price case.

profit for the seller *and* higher total consumer surplus for the buyers than the single-price policy. In other words, in this case price differentiation is a win-win for buyers and sellers.

The case in Figure 4.5 is notable because some customers are better off and no customer is worse off than with a single price. The customers who paid $8.75 with the single price still pay $8.75, so they are unaffected. Customers who pay $7.00 under the two price policy are better off since they would not have purchased with a single price. And the seller is better off since he makes more money. A more common situation is illustrated by the case in which the seller charges two prices: $8.00 and $10.00. With perfect segmentation, the seller sells 2,000 units at $10.00, for a gross contribution of $10,000, and 1,600 units at $8.00, for an additional gross contribution of $4,800. His gross contribution is $14,800—much higher than the $12,050 he achieved by pricing at $7.00 and $8.75. However, not all buyers are better off relative to the single-price policy. Those who purchase at $8.00 are definitely happier because either they would have purchased at $8.75 and are saving $0.75 or they wouldn't have purchased at all. But the buyers now purchasing at $10.00 are worse off—they are each paying $1.25 more than they would have paid under a single-price policy.

It is easy to see that total consumer surplus is less under this two-price policy than under the single-price policy. The surplus gained by the 1,600 purchasers at $8.00 is less than or equal to $0.75 each (why?). Those purchasing at $10.00 are each paying $1.25 more, so they lose $1.25 each in consumer surplus. The difference in consumer surplus between the two-price policy and the single-price policy is

$$\Delta CS \leq \$0.75 \times 1,600 - \$1.25 \times 2,000$$

$$\leq -\$1,300$$

Since this is less than zero, the net effect of price differentiation in this case is to reduce total consumer surplus.

This example is typical, in the sense that most price differentiation schemes result in both winners and losers among customers. However, it is not the case that price differentiation always either increases or decreases total consumer surplus. The total effect on consumer surplus of a price differentiation scheme depends on the situation.

There is one general rule: *If a price differentiation scheme increases profits for a seller but does not result in additional production, it must reduce total consumer surplus.* This rule is most relevant when capacity is constrained—if a theater is already selling out at a single price and it goes to a two-price system that increases revenue, then it has done so by making customers, *on the average*, worse off. Again, this does not mean that there are not customers who are better off under the new scheme—it simply means that the total consumer surplus is less under the new scheme than under the old. If, on the other hand, a theater that is not full finds that it can increase total revenue by a price differentiation tactic, then the effect of the differentiation on total consumer surplus will depend on the situation. A study of the effects of pricing and consumer behavior for an actual Broadway show concluded that price differentiation increased both attendance and profit by about 5% while having a "negligible" effect on consumer surplus (Leslie 2004).

4.7 SUMMARY

- Price differentiation is the tactic of charging different customer segments different prices for the same (or nearly the same) product or service. It can be a powerful way for a seller to increase contribution.

- The effectiveness of price differentiation can be limited by imperfect segmentation, cannibalization, or arbitrage. A poorly conceived or executed price differentiation scheme may not only fail, it can result in lower contribution than a single-price scheme.

- There is a wide variety of price discrimination schemes, ranging from group pricing through channel and regional pricing to volume discounting and product versioning. The best approach or combination of approaches depends on the market.

- Product-versioning tactics are better accepted by customers and less susceptible to cannibalization and arbitrage than group pricing. Developing a "virtual product" is a common tactic, particularly in service industries.

- The methods for calculating differentiated prices when the supplier does not face capacity or supply restrictions are extensions of the methods introduced in Chapter 3 for a supplier pricing a single product. The possibilities of cannibalization and arbitrage need to be specifically incorporated in order for the prices to be correct.

- The effects of price differentiation on consumer welfare (as measured by consumer surplus) can be either positive or negative, depending on the market and on the differentiation scheme. If a price differentiation scheme does not increase supply, it cannot increase total consumer surplus.

We will return to theme of price differentiation again and again. In particular, price differentiation is the basis of revenue management (Chapter 6), markdown management (Chapter 10), and customized pricing (Chapter 11).

4.8 EXERCISES

1. (*Arbitrage*) A supplier is selling hammers in two cities, Pleasantville and Happy Valley. It costs him $5.00 per hammer delivered in each city. Let p_1 be the price of hammers in Pleasantville and p_2 be the price of hammers in Happy Valley. The price-response curves in each city are:

    Pleasantville: $d_1(p_1) = 10{,}000 - 800p_1$

    Happy Valley: $d_2(p_2) = 8{,}000 - 500p_2$

    a. Assuming the supplier can charge any prices he likes, what prices should he charge for hammers in Pleasantville and Happy Valley to maximize total contribution? What are the corresponding demands and total contributions?

    b. An enterprising arbitrageur discovers a way to transport hammers from Pleasantville to Happy Valley for $0.50 each. He begins buying hammers in

Pleasantville and shipping them to Happy Valley to sell. Assuming the supplier does not change his prices from those given in part a, what will be the optimal price for the arbitrageur to sell hammers in Happy Valley? How many will he sell? What will his total contribution be? (Assume that Happy Valley customers will buy hammers from the cheapest vendor.) What will happen to the total sales and contribution for the supplier? (Remember that he is now selling to the arbitrageur too.)

c. The supplier decides to eliminate the arbitrage opportunity by ensuring that his selling price in Happy Valley is no more than $0.50 more than the selling price in Pleasantville (and vice versa). What is his new selling price in each city? What are his corresponding sales and total contribution?

d. From among the Pleasantville buyers, the Happy Valley buyers, and the seller, who wins and who loses from the threat of arbitrage?

2. Assume that it costs Hertz $20 per day for every car it rents out, regardless of model. What is the implied price elasticity of customers for each of the seven car types listed in Table 4.3?

1. We use the term *group pricing* in the sense of Shapiro and Varian (1992). This should be distinguished from use of the term to offer lower rates to groups of customers in industries such as the passenger airlines, hotels, and cruise lines. This is actually a form of volume discounting, which is treated in Section 4.4.

2. "Big Mac's Makeover," *The Economist*, Oct. 16, 2004, pp. 63–65.

3. Narasimhan (1984).

4. From Deneckere and McAfee (1996). Italics in the original.

5. Quoted in Birnbaum (1986).

6. All descriptions from http://quickbooks.intuit.com.

7. This does not, of course, mean that Hertz and Intuit are not also offering even deeper discounts to favored customers.

8. Opera software sells fast Web-browsing software to businesses. Horton Brass Company sells metal fittings to retailers, contractors, and furniture manufacturers.

9. In many cases, this cost will be symmetrical—that is, $a_{ij} = a_{ji}$. However, this is not always the case. For example, one country may charge a higher import duty on the product.

10. There is an important exception—when the arbitrageur has access to lower-cost transportation than the supplier. In this case, it may be optimal for the supplier to allow the arbitrage or, possibly, to reach an agreement by which the arbitrageur serves as a transporter or distributor for the supplier.

11. We are assuming that $p_2 \leq \$7.00$.

12. The results from the widget maker example can be generalized to any seller facing a *linear* price-response function. For such a seller, the optimal total contribution he can derive without market segmentation is $(m - bc)^2/4$. The total contribution he could realize from the market if he could do perfect "one-to-one" pricing and charge each customer exactly their willingness to pay is $(m - bc)^2/2$—exactly twice what he can realize without segmentation. If he is able to divide the market optimally into two segments based on willingness to pay and charge each segment the optimal price, he can realize total contribution of $(m - bc)^2/3$—a 33.3% increase over no segmentation. If price response is not linear, segmentation will still result in increased total contribution; however, the magnitude of the increase will be different.

13. We assume for simplicity that no customer purchases more than a single unit.

14. This section provides only a high-level treatment of consumer surplus. Fuller treatment can be found in most microeconomics texts, such as Varian (1992) and Nicholson (2002).

5 | PRICING WITH CONSTRAINED SUPPLY

In Chapter 3 we saw how a seller can calculate the optimal single-period price when he has the freedom to produce (or order) as much of a good as he wants and he knows with certainty the price-response curve he faces. In this case the seller can maximize expected profit by charging the price at which his marginal cost equals his marginal revenue or, equivalently, the price at which his contribution margin ratio equals 1 over the elasticity. Unfortunately, things are a bit more complicated in the real world: Sellers have the freedom to adjust prices over many periods, they are unsure how customers will respond to different prices, and they face constraints on their ability to satisfy demand. Sellers need to be able to set prices in a dynamic, uncertain, and constrained world. In this chapter we focus on the influence of constrained supply on optimal prices.

When the supply of a good is constrained for any reason, the approaches presented in Chapter 3 do not necessarily give the price that maximizes net contribution. Return for a moment to the example of the widget maker. With only a single period to consider and with perfect knowledge of his market, the optimal actions for him were to set his price at $8.75 and produce 3,000 units. In this case, he sells all 3,000 units and makes a total contribution of $11,250. This solution assumes that supply is totally flexible *and* demands are deterministic *and* he is only going to operate during a single period. What should he do if he can only manufacture 2,800 widgets? What price should he set? That is the sort of question we address in this chapter.

We start by discussing the nature of supply constraints and the situations in which they occur. We then discuss how a seller can determine the optimal price to charge when faced by a supply constraint, and we introduce the important concept of *opportunity cost*. We extend the calculation of optimal prices to the case when a supplier has a segmented market and faces supply constraints. This leads to the tactic of variable pricing, which is used when a supplier has multiple units of constrained capacity and can change prices in order to balance supply and demand.

5.1 THE NATURE OF SUPPLY CONSTRAINTS

Most sellers face supply constraints at least some of the time. For example, most retailers replenish their stock of inventory at fixed intervals—often weekly. In between replenishment times, they are limited to selling their current inventory—in other words, they have a fixed supply. However, in most cases, retailers stock enough inventory that a stock-out is unlikely. A drugstore will typically have enough toothpaste, shaving cream, and aspirin in stock that it will not sell out except in cases of an extraordinary run on a particular item—bottled water prior to a hurricane, for example. In this case, the seller may technically have a limited amount of inventory on hand, but he does not need to consider a supply constraint when setting price. There are, however, many cases in which a seller needs to consider the constrained nature of supply in order to calculate the optimal price.

1. *Service providers* almost always face capacity constraints. A hotel is constrained by the number of rooms, a gas pipeline by the capacity of its pipes, and a barbershop by the number of seats (and barbers) it has available.

2. *Manufacturers* face physical constraints on the amount they can produce during a particular period. For example, Ford Motor Company in North America can produce about 475,000 vehicles per month.[1] In any particular month, Ford can only sell 475,000 vehicles plus whatever inventory it had on hand at the beginning of the month.

3. *Retailers and wholesalers* often sell goods that are not replenishable. These include fashion goods that are typically ordered once or electronic goods that are near the end of their life cycle.

4. *Intrinsically scarce or unique items*, such as beachfront property, flawless blue diamonds, van Gogh paintings, and Stradivarius violins, command premium prices because of their scarcity. In these cases, marginal cost is not an important determinant of price either because it is meaningless (as in the case of van Gogh paintings) or extremely low relative to the scarcity rent that sellers can command (as in the case of diamonds).

The treatment of a supply constraint depends on its nature. A *hard* constraint is one that cannot be violated at any price. Typically hotels and gas pipelines face hard constraints. On the other hand, air freight carriers often have the option to lease space on other carriers to carry cargo in excess of their capacity. The freight carrier's physical capacity is thus a *soft* constraint. Whether a supply constraint is hard or soft will, in part, depend on timing. An airline that learns two months in advance that it will be facing very high demand for a particular flight may be able to assign a larger aircraft. However, it may not have any option to increase capacity if it only learns about the high demand a week before departure.

5.2 OPTIMAL PRICING WITH A SUPPLY CONSTRAINT

In Section 3.4.2, the optimal unconstrained price of widgets was $8.75, with corresponding demand of 3,000 units and a total contribution of $11,250. This is optimal only if the seller is able to manufacture all 3,000 units—or order them from a third party. But what if he cannot satisfy all the demand at the optimal unconstrained price? Perhaps he has a supply chain bottleneck that limits his production. Perhaps he is a reseller with a fixed monthly quota he cannot exceed. In any case, the widget maker faces a rationing problem—he needs to determine which customers will be served and which will not. He has three basic options:

1. Do nothing—Keep the price at $8.75 and let customers buy on a first-come/first-served basis until supply is exhausted.

2. Allocate the limited supply to favored customers.

3. Raise the price until demand falls to meet supply.

Alternatives two and three are not mutually exclusive—the seller could use a combination of allocations and price rises to manage the shortage. And, if he has segmented his market effectively, he could raise his average selling price by allocating most or all of the limited supply to higher-paying customers—this is the basic idea behind revenue management, which we discuss in Chapter 6.

If the widget maker cannot segment his market (allocating favored customers is a form of segmentation), his only options are to sell on a first-come/first-served basis or to raise the price. Let's assume he decides to raise the price in order to maximize his short-run contribution margin. Then he needs to solve the constrained optimization problem:

$$\max d(p)(p - c)$$

subject to

$$d(p) \leq b$$

where b is the maximum supply available. Let p^* be the optimal unconstrained price. If $d(p^*) \leq b$, the supplier doesn't need to do any further calculations: p^* is also the optimal constrained price. If, on the other hand, he finds that $d(p^*) > b$, then he needs to charge a *higher* price in order to maximize contribution. This situation is illustrated in Figure 5.1. Here, the capacity constraint is a horizontal line—the supplier can only produce quantities below that line. At the optimal unconstrained price, p^*, demand $d(p^*)$ exceeds capacity.

When the optimal unconstrained price generates demand that exceeds capacity, the supplier needs to calculate the *runout price*, that is, the price at which demand would exactly equal the supply constraint. In Figure 5.1, the runout price is the price $\hat{p}$ at which the price-response curve intersects the capacity constraint. In other words, it is the price at which $d(\hat{p}) = b$.

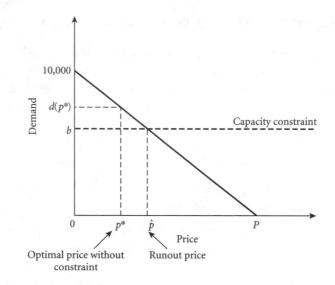

Figure 5.1 Pricing with a capacity constraint.

Example 5.1

Assume the widget seller faces the price-response curve $d(p) = 10,000 - 800p$ but can only supply a maximum 2,000 widgets during the upcoming week. Demand at the optimal unconstrained price of $8.75 is 3,000 widgets. Therefore, the supply constraint is binding and he needs to price at the runout price. The runout price of $\hat{p} = \$10.00$ can be found by solving $d(\hat{p}) = 10,000 - 800\hat{p} = 2,000$.

The general principle behind calculating the optimal price with a supply constraint is the following.

> *The profit-maximizing price under a supply constraint is equal to the maximum of the runout price and the unconstrained profit-maximizing price. As a consequence, the profit-maximizing price under a supply constraint is always greater than or equal to the unconstrained profit-maximizing price.*

The effects of different levels of capacity constraint on price and total revenue are shown in Table 5.1. For a binding capacity constraint, $b < 3,000$, the runout price can be found by inverting the price-response function:

$$\hat{p} = d^{-1}(b) = (10,000 - b)/800 \qquad \text{for } b < 3,000$$

Table 5.1 shows the results of reducing capacity at increments from 3,000 units per month to 1,000 units per month. The optimal price increases steadily as the capacity decreases. The benefits of reoptimizing price in response to constrained capacity also increases steadily. As capacity becomes increasingly constrained, there is more and more pressure on the seller to increase the price.

5.3 OPPORTUNITY COST

Everything else being equal, imposing a supply constraint can only reduce contribution. An auto manufacturer that experiences a strike that takes 25% of capacity out of production for a month will likely see lower profits for that month. A 200-room hotel that takes 50 rooms out of service for two months to be refurbished is likely to give up some potential revenue. Furthermore, the deeper or more binding a supply constraint cuts, the greater the hit the seller is likely to take on his contribution. Taking 75 rooms out of service for two months will lead to less overall contribution than taking 50 rooms out of service for the same period of time.

The reduction in contribution resulting from a supply constraint is called the *opportunity cost* associated with that constraint. It is the difference between the maximum contribution the supplier could realize without the constraint and the maximum contribution with the constraint. Since the constrained contribution can never be greater than the unconstrained contribution, total opportunity cost will always be greater than or equal to zero.

Example 5.2

In Example 5.1 the optimal price for widgets with a supply constraint of 2,000 widgets per week was $10.00 per widget, with a total contribution of ($10.00 − $5.00) × 2,000 = $10,000. The optimal unconstrained price of widgets is $8.75, with demand of 3,000 and corresponding total contribution of ($8.75 − $5.00) × 3,000 = $11,250. The total opportunity cost of the supply constraint is $11,250 − $10,000 = $1,250.

Total opportunity cost is the amount the seller would be willing to pay to eliminate his supply constraint entirely. In many cases, the more interesting question is how much the supplier would be willing to pay for one additional unit of supply or capacity. This is the *marginal opportunity cost*.

Example 5.3

The marginal opportunity cost for the widget seller facing a constraint of 2,000 widgets per week can be found by solving the constrained optimization problem with a supply constraint of 2,001 and subtracting the optimal contribution with a supply constraint of 2,000. When the supply constraint is 2,001, the optimal contribution is $10,002.50. Thus, the marginal opportunity cost of the supply constraint is equal to $10,002.50 − $10,000.00 = $2.50.

Optimal contributions, prices, and marginal opportunity costs for the widget example are shown in Table 5.1. Note that as the amount of available capacity decreases (i.e., the supply constraint becomes more binding), the optimal price and the marginal opportunity cost both increase. The marginal opportunity cost is zero when the capacity constraint is not binding—which is the case for any constraint above 3,000 units. This is an illustration of the following general principle.

TABLE 5.1

Impact of constrained capacity on optimal price, contribution, and opportunity cost

Available capacity	Contribution at $8.75	Optimal price	Optimal contribution	% Change	Marginal opportunity cost
≥3,000	$11,250	$8.75	$11,250	0	$0.00
2,500	$9,375	$9.38	$10,950	16.8	$1.25
2,000	$7,500	$10.00	$10,000	33.3	$2.50
1,000	$3,750	$11.25	$6,250	66.7	$5.00

> *Total and marginal opportunity costs are only nonzero when there is a supply or capacity constraint that is binding at the optimal unconstrained price. Otherwise they are zero.*

The opportunity cost is an important input to other corporate decisions. From Table 5.1 we can see that the marginal opportunity cost faced by the supplier is $2.50 per widget when supply is limited to 2,000 units. This means that the widget maker would be willing to pay up to $2.50 in rent for an additional unit of capacity that allowed him to make one more widget at a cost of $5.00. Alternatively he would be willing to pay up to $2.50 + $5.00 to buy another widget from a wholesaler. Fundamentally, the opportunity cost associated with constrained capacity is an economic measure of how much the company would be willing to pay for additional capacity. By calculating and utilizing this information in its supply decisions, companies can drive higher returns than they could from optimizing their pricing and their supply decisions in isolation.

5.4 MARKET SEGMENTATION AND SUPPLY CONSTRAINTS

Market segmentation can be a powerful tool for increasing profitability when supply is constrained. To see how, let's use an example.[2]

Example 5.4

The football game between Stanford and the University of California at Berkeley (a.k.a. "the Big Game") is going to be held at Stanford Stadium, which has 60,000 seats. Customers can be segmented into students (those carrying a student ID card) and the general public. We assume that the price-response curves for each of these segments is:

General public: $\quad d_g(p_g) = (120{,}000 - 3{,}000p_g)^+$ $\qquad$ (5.1)

Students: $\qquad d_s(p_s) = (20{,}000 - 1{,}250p_s)^+$ $\qquad$ (5.2)

where p_g is the price charged to the general public and p_s is the student price. What if Stanford can only charge a single price to all? In this case, the aggregate demand curve is $d(p) = (120{,}000 - 3{,}000p)^+ + (20{,}000 - 1{,}250p)^+$ and the optimal price will be $20.00. At this price, Stanford would sell exactly 60,000 tickets, grossing $1,200,000. Note that all ticket sales would be to the general public. The students are priced out of the market, since the highest willingness to pay of any student is 20,000/1,250 = $16.00.

Now, what if Stanford could charge different ticket prices to students versus the general public? Then finding the optimal price requires solving the constrained optimization problem

$$\text{maximize } p_g(120,000 - 3,000p_g)^+ + p_s(20,000 - 1,250p_s)^+ \qquad (5.3)$$

subject to

$$(120,000 - 3,000p_g)^+ + (20,000 - 1,250p_s)^+ \leq 60,000$$

We could, of course, solve this problem directly. However, we gain more insight by using the principle established in Chapter 3: Prices should be set for the two different segments so that the marginal revenues from both segments are equal. When supply is unconstrained, marginal revenues should all be set to the marginal cost. When supply is constrained, marginal revenues should still be equated, but they need to be set so the supply constraint is satisfied.

Example 5.5

We want to find the revenue-maximizing prices for students and the general public. The marginal opportunity cost is $2p_g - 40$ for the general public and $2p_s - 16$ for students. Equating the two marginal revenues and simplifying gives $p_g = p_s + 12$. In other words, the ticket price for the general public will be $12.00 higher than the ticket price for students. The other condition that must be satisfied is that the total demand from both students and the general public be equal to the capacity of the stadium; that is $(120,000 - 3,000p_g)^+ + (20,000 - 1,250p_s)^+ = 60,000$, which, when simplified, gives $3p_g + 1.25p_s = 80$. Solving both conditions simultaneously gives $p_s = \$10.35$ and $p_g = \$22.35$. At these prices, Stanford will sell 52,941 tickets to the general public and 7,059 seats to students, generating revenue of $1,256,471, a 4.7% increase over the best that could be achieved with a single ticket price.

Note that the profit-maximizing price for the general public is more than double the student price. The stadium is sold out and there are thousands of people who would be willing to pay much more than the student price. Yet the profit-maximizing decision for Stanford is to sell more seats to students at a deep discount. Note also that the effect of market segmentation is that students win while the general public loses. That is, market segmentation reduces the price of tickets for the more price-sensitive students while increasing the price for the less price-sensitive general public.

The optimal prices assumed that the marginal costs—and ancillary revenues—of serving both students and general public were the same. Differences in either marginal costs or ancillary revenues between the two market segments would lead to different optimal prices (see Exercise 3). The results also relied on the fact that the "fence" between students and the general public was perfect. The optimal prices and revenues would also change if student sales cannibalized sales to the general public (see Exercise 1).

5.5 VARIABLE PRICING

Consider the following pricing tactics.

- Most local telephone companies charge different rates for calls by time of day. For example, one plan might charge 3 cents per minute from 6:00 AM to 6:00 PM, 2 cents per minute from 6:00 PM to 11:00 PM, and 1 cent per minute from 11:00 PM to 6:00 AM.

- The San Francisco Opera charges a lower price for weeknight performances than for weekend performances. The most expensive box seats cost $175 for a Wednesday performance and $195 for a Saturday performance, while the least expensive balcony side tickets cost $25 for a Wednesday performance and $28 for a Saturday performance.

- The Colorado Rockies baseball team uses the four-tier pricing system for their home games shown in Table 5.2. Lower prices for games in April, May, and September are justified by the fact that the weather is more likely to be bad during these months, resulting in lower demand.[3]

TABLE 5.2

2002 Home ticket prices for the Colorado Rockies baseball team

Tier	Description	Average price
Value	Weekday games against low-drawing opponents during April, May, and September	$16.97
Standard	Weekday games against division rivals during April, May, and September	$18.00
Premium	Weekend games in May, June, July, and August	$20.07
Classic	Opening day, games against the N.Y. Yankees, fireworks games	$21.58

- The Gulf Power Company is an electric utility serving more than 370,000 retail customers in northwestern Florida. The majority of these retail customers pay a flat rate of $0.057 per kilowatt hour for electricity. However, Gulf Power offers residential customers the alternative of purchasing their electricity under their Residential Select Variable Pricing (RSVP) program. Under the RSVP program, each weekday is divided into an off-peak, a shoulder, and an on-peak period. Electricity costs $0.035 per kilowatt hour (kWh) during the off-peak period, $0.046 during the shoulder period, and $0.093 during the on-peak period. In the summer the on-peak period is from 11:30 AM to 8:30 PM, while in the winter the on-peak period is from 6:00 AM to noon. The summer off-peak period is from 10:30 PM to 6:00 AM and the winter off-peak period is from 10:00 PM to 5:30 AM. All other hours are shoulder period. In addition to these three periods, with a half hour's notice Gulf Power can declare a "critical period" during which electricity costs $0.290 per kWh. Under the RSVP program, Gulf Power can declare up to 88 hours of critical period per year.[4]

What do these four pricing tactics have in common? They are all cases in which a seller with constrained capacity adjusts prices in response to anticipated changes in demand in order to maximize return from fixed capacity. We call this tactic *variable pricing*. Industries where variable pricing is employed share four characteristics:

- Demand is variable but follows a predictable pattern.

- The capacity of a seller is fixed in the short run (or is expensive to change).

- Inventory is perishable or expensive to store—otherwise buyers would learn to predict the variation in prices and stockpile when the price is low.

- The seller has the ability to adjust prices in response to supply/demand imbalances.

Under these conditions, sellers can use variable prices to shape demand to meet fixed capacity (or supply) by exploiting differences in customer preference. Weekday opera performances are less popular than weekend performances. The Rockies know that a game against the Yankees will generate more demand than a game against the Cincinnati Reds. The highest electricity and telephone prices correspond to the periods of highest use and the lowest prices to the periods of lowest use.

Note that variable pricing is not pure group pricing, since it allows customers to self-select based on a menu of alternatives.

5.5.1 The Basics of Variable Pricing

Consider a hypothetical theme park that can serve up to 1,000 customers per day. The theme park charges a single admission price, and all rides are free after admission. During the summer, demand follows a stable and predictable pattern, with higher demand on weekends than during weekdays. We assume that demands for different days of the week are independent; that demand curves are linear, with intercepts, slopes, and satiating prices as shown in Table 5.3; and that the theme park has a marginal cost of zero per customer.

TABLE 5.3
*Intercepts and slopes for the price-response curves
in the theme park example*

Day of week	Intercept (D_i)	Slope (m_i)
Sunday	3,100	−62
Monday	1,500	−50
Tuesday	1,400	−40
Wednesday	1,510	−42
Thursday	2,000	−52.6
Friday	2,500	−55.6
Saturday	3,300	−60

What price should the theme park charge without variable pricing? Since its marginal cost is zero, it maximizes contribution by maximizing revenue. The revenue-maximizing single price can be found by solving the non-linear optimization problem

$$\max_{p, x} p \sum_{i=1}^{7} x_i$$

subject to

$$x_i \leq D_i + m_i p \qquad \text{for } i = 1, 2, \ldots, 7$$

$$x_i \leq C \qquad \qquad \text{for } i = 1, 2, \ldots, 7$$

$$p \geq 0$$

where p is the optimal single price, x_i is attendance on each day, D_i and m_i are, respectively, the intercept and slope of the price-response function for day i, and C is total daily capacity (in this case 1,000). The optimal single price is $25.00 per ticket. The corresponding attendance and revenue for each day are shown in the columns labeled "Single Price" in Table 5.4. With a single price, the theme park serves a total of 4,796 customers during the week, with total revenue of $119,890. What is striking in Table 5.4 is the wide variation in attendance across the week. The park is full on Friday, Saturday, and Sunday, but it operates at only 25% of capacity on Monday and 40% of capacity on Tuesday. Furthermore, potential customers are being turned away on Friday, Saturday, and Sunday—500 on Saturday alone.

TABLE 5.4
Theme park daily prices, attendances, and revenues under constant pricing and under variable pricing

Day of week	SINGLE PRICE			VARIABLE PRICING		
	Price	Attendance	Revenue	Price	Attendance	Revenue
Sunday	$25.00	1,000	$25,000	$33.87	1,000	$33,870
Monday	$25.00	250	$6,250	$15.00	750	$11,250
Tuesday	$25.00	400	$10,000	$17.50	700	$12,250
Wednesday	$25.00	461	$11,535	$18.01	755	$13,590
Thursday	$25.00	684	$17,105	$19.00	1,000	$19,000
Friday	$25.00	1,000	$25,000	$27.00	1,000	$27,000
Saturday	$25.00	1,000	$25,000	$38.33	1,000	$38,333
TOTAL		4,796	$119,890		6,205	$155,294

These two conditions—wide variation in utilization and a large number of turndowns—are indications that contribution could be improved through variable pricing. In the case of the theme park, this means charging a different price for each day. When demands are independent—as we have assumed—the optimal daily prices can be calculated by solving independent optimization problems for each day. The resulting daily prices, attendances, and revenues are shown in the columns labeled "Variable Pricing" in Table 5.4. With variable pricing, daily prices range from a low of $15.00 on Monday to a high of $38.33 on Saturday. The total number of customers served during the week rises 29% from 4,796 to 6,205 and total revenue rises 30% to $155,294. Note that variable pricing levels utilization across days of the week and increases overall utilization. Attendance on the low days of Monday and Tuesday increases from 250 and 400 to 750 and 700, respectively. The weekly utilization of the park (its *load factor*) increases from 4,796/7,000 = 68.5% to 6,205/7,000 = 89%.

The *average* price paid by all customers increases only slightly under variable pricing—from $25.00 to $25.03. This is typical—variable pricing can often lead to a major increase in total revenue with only a small increase in the average price paid by customers.

5.5.2 Variable Pricing with Diversion

We have seen that variable pricing can increase operating contribution when demands are independent among periods. However, variable pricing can also shift demand from peak periods to off-peak periods—a phenomenon called *diversion* or *demand shifting*. Diversion occurs when at least some customers are flexible and will shift their consumption among periods if they can save money by doing so. Diversion can be illustrated by an example due to Robert Cross (1997). His local barbershop was overcrowded and turning customers away on Saturdays, while Tuesdays were very slow. Some of the Saturday customers were working people who could only come on Saturday; others were retirees and schoolchildren, who could get their hair cut any day of the week. By raising prices 20% on Saturday and reducing them by 20% on Tuesday, the shop induced some of the Saturday customers to shift to Tuesday. As a result of this simple peak-pricing action, turnaways decreased, Saturday service improved, and total revenue increased by almost 20%.

Variable pricing segments the market for a generic product (a haircut) between those with strong preferences for a particular date and those who are relatively indifferent. Since customer preferences are not evenly distributed—more people want to see an opera, attend a theme park, or get their hair cut on a weekend—while capacity is fixed, using price to shift indifferent customers to less popular dates can increase both revenue and utilization and reduce turnaways. In the case of the Colorado Rockies, the four-tiered pricing system segments the market between customers who badly want to see a specific popular game (such as one against the Yankees) from those who just want a night out at the ball park. Furthermore, variable pricing is generally well accepted, since it segments via self-selection: Customers choose the product and price combination they prefer.

While diversion is an important element of variable pricing, it can be a two-edged sword. Raising the price for peak capacity and lowering it for off-peak capacity will shift customers from the peak to the off-peak period. This is good (at least in moderation) because the overall gain from extracting higher prices from the remaining peak customers outweighs the lower price received for off-peak customers. However, if the price differential becomes too great, we would expect more and more peak customers to defect to the off-peak period. If the barbershop drops Tuesday prices too low and raises Saturday prices too high it might end up with a Tuesday peak and very slow Saturdays. Ultimately the loss from peak customers who shift to the cheaper off-peak period (cannibalization) can outweigh the benefits of off-peak demand induction and higher peak rates.

While diversion is easy to describe, it is difficult to model. One approach is to presume that every customer has a separate willingness to pay for each alternative. Each customer would compare his w.t.p.'s for each alternative with the price and purchase the alternative that provided the highest positive surplus—assuming that such an alternative exists.

Example 5.6

Under the separate-willingness-to-pay model, each customer would have a separate w.t.p. for attendance on each day at the theme park. The willingness to pay of each customer can be represented as a vector, so a customer with w.t.p.

vector of ($30, $18, $22, $19, $14, $18, $32) would have a $30 w.t.p. for Sunday attendance, an $18 w.t.p. for Monday attendance, and so on. We can represent the vector of prices in the same fashion: ($33.87, $15.00, $17.50, $18.01, $19.00, $27.00, $38.33). The consumer surplus vector for this customer is the difference between his w.t.p. and the price for each day, here ($-$3.87, $3.00, $4.50, $.99, $-$5.00, $-$9.00, $-$6.33). In this case, the customer would attend on Tuesday because that provides him with the highest surplus ($4.50). For comparison, the consumer surplus for this customer under a constant price of $25.00 would be ($5.00, $-$7.00, $-$3.00, $-$6.00, $-$11.00, $-$7.00, $7.00), which means he would attend on Saturday. The effect of variable pricing on this customer is to shift his attendance from Saturday to Tuesday.

While the willingness-to-pay point of view helps us understand how an individual consumer might act, it is difficult to extend to a useful model of total market price responsiveness. If we knew the distribution of customer w.t.p.'s across the population, we could, in theory, use that information to derive a multidimensional demand function. One problem is that this model would require seven own-price elasticities (one for each day of the week) and 42 cross-price elasticities (one for each combination of days of the week). It is unlikely that the theme park (or most other companies) would have the data available to estimate a credible model with this many parameters.

We can use a much simpler approach to incorporating diversion in the theme park example—we will assume that eight customers will shift from one day to another for every $1 difference in price. Thus, if the base prices for Monday and Tuesday were $20 and $22, respectively, we would first calculate a base demand for each day using their individual linear price-response curves and then shift 16 people from Tuesday to Monday. When applied across the whole week, this means that demand will shift from days with higher-than-average prices to those with lower-than-average prices. Under this model, the unconstrained demand the theme park will see on day i is given by

$$d_i = D_i + m_i p_i + \sum_{j=1}^{7} 8(p_j - p_i)$$

where d_i is the unconstrained demand, p_i is the price, D_i is the demand at zero price, and m_i is the slope of the linear demand curve for day i. Demand for each day now depends not only on the price for that day but on the price for all the other days of the week. We can now formulate the optimal pricing problem as a non-linear optimization problem:

$$\max_{p,x} \sum_{i=1}^{7} p_i x_i$$

subject to

$$x_i \leq D_i + m_i p_i + \sum_{j=1}^{7} 8(p_j - p_i)$$

$$x_i \leq C$$

$$p_i \geq 0 \qquad \text{for } i = 1, 2, \ldots, 7$$

The optimal prices, attendance, and revenue under this model are shown in Table 5.5. Base demand is the number of customers calculated using the demand curves for each day, and net diversion is the net number of customers induced to shift to or from each day by differential pricing. A positive net diversion means that more customers shifted to that day than shifted away; a negative net diversion means the opposite. Variable pricing shifted a total of 838 customers from the peak days of Friday, Saturday, and Sunday to the off-peak days of Monday through Thursday. Furthermore, the theme park served 6,600 total customers during the week, resulting in a 94% utilization and total revenue of $156,536—a dramatic improvement over the single-price case.

TABLE 5.5
Theme park daily prices, attendances, and revenues using variable pricing and assuming demand switching

Day of week	Price	Base demand	Net diversion	Attendance	Revenue
Sunday	$28.92	1,307	−307	1,000	$28,920
Monday	$18.12	594	298	892	$16,163
Tuesday	$19.58	617	216	833	$16,310
Wednesday	$19.80	680	204	884	$17,503
Thursday	$21.29	880	120	1,000	$21,290
Friday	$25.21	1,099	−99	1,000	$25,210
Saturday	$31.14	1,432	−432	1,000	$31,140
TOTAL		6,609	0	6,609	$156,536

Of course, the theme park operator might not want to set prices exactly as shown in Table 5.5. For simplicity, he may want to reduce the total number of prices and only offer prices in increments of $5. In this case, it is easy to see that he would still gain significant revenue from a three-tier pricing policy of $30 on weekends, $25 on Friday, and $20 on Monday through Thursday, as opposed to setting a constant price of $25.

5.6 VARIABLE PRICING IN ACTION

Variable pricing does not need to be implemented within list prices. The theme park could implement two-tier pricing by establishing a $30 list price but distributing $10-off coupons redeemable only on weekdays. Even more effectively, the theme park might establish a $35 price for weekends and Friday, a $20 price for Monday through Thursday, and distribute $5-off coupons redeemable only for Monday admissions. In this case, variable pricing has been implemented through a combination of variable list pricing and couponing. With this in mind, we can see how variable pricing is used in three different industries—airlines, electric power, and broadcast advertising.

5.6.1 Sporting Events

Variable pricing is increasingly being adopted by sports team owners eager to find ways to increase revenue. Variable pricing is particularly attractive to baseball owners, since each team has 81 home games that vary widely in fan appeal. The Colorado Rockies are widely credited with pioneering variable pricing in baseball. In addition to the Rockies, variable pricing at some level of sophistication is used by the New York Mets, Anaheim Angels, New York Yankees, Atlanta Braves, Cleveland Indians, and San Francisco Giants in baseball and the Ottawa Senators and Pittsburgh Penguins of the National Hockey League. Popular variable-pricing techniques include higher prices for weekend games and for games against rivals and popular visiting teams.

Sporting teams like variable pricing because it can increase total revenue without increasing ticket prices. This is attractive in an environment where ticket price increases are likely to be condemned by fans and sportswriters as evidence of "greedy owners and players gouging loyal fans." In 2003 the New York Mets adopted a variable-pricing plan under which the price was increased $10 for the 17 most popular games while lowering or holding prices unchanged for 43 games. "That allowed the Mets, who finished last in their division in 2002, to trumpet the plan as holding ticket price increases to only 4% on average"(Fatsis 2002).

While more and more teams are adopting some form of variable pricing, there are risks. Complex pricing schemes often draw criticism from fans. Furthermore, determining high-valued opponents before the season opens can be difficult. Some baseball teams have increased prices for games against the San Francisco Giants because there are a large number of fans willing to pay extra to see Barry Bonds play. However, an early season injury to Bonds would mean that these games would be suddenly overpriced and unlikely to sell out.

However, the potential gains are large enough that more and more clubs in more and more sports are adopting some form of variable pricing. The San Francisco Giants claim that their variable-pricing schemed netted them additional ticket revenue of $1 million in 2002, a year in which their total profit was only $100,000.

5.6.2 Passenger Airlines

Passenger airlines certainly meet the criteria for variable pricing—constrained capacity with demand that fluctuates over time. Southwest Airlines implements variable pricing directly by changing fares for their departures in order to match demand with the restricted capacity. However, the major "nondiscount" airlines also practice variable pricing. They do so by opening and closing the availability of various fare classes on different flights. Figure 5.2 shows average fares and load factors on a flight of a major airline from the Midwest to Florida during the winter. For operational reasons, the airline has scheduled the same aircraft on the flight each day. The airline is charging a higher average price on high-demand days (Saturday and Sunday) and lower prices on low-demand days (Tuesday, Wednesday, and Thursday). In this case, the airline is adjusting the average fare not by changing the list price but by opening and closing fare classes. When total demand is anticipated to be high, the airline will restrict availability of discount fares, causing the average fare to increase. When total demand is anticipated to be low, the airline will open availability of deep discounts, causing the average fare to drop. It is continually monitoring demand using its revenue management system to determine which classes to open and close on each flight. We describe how this is done in some detail in Chapters 6 and 7.

Discount airlines use variable pricing even more directly. If demand at Southwest Airlines begins to rise more quickly or more slowly than anticipated, Southwest may change

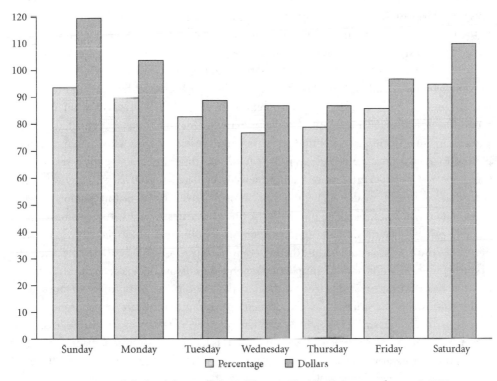

Figure 5.2 Average daily load factors for a Midwest–Florida flight on a domestic U.S. discount carrier. *Source*: Figure courtesy of Garrett J. van Ryzin, Professor, Columbia University.

the price. Southwest does not attempt to use prices to segment customers between "high-elasticity" and "low-elasticity" segments—rather, it is using variable pricing without segmentation to maximize the return from each flight and, to some extent, to smooth demand through demand diversion from high-fare/high-utilization flights to low-fare/low-utilization flights.

5.6.3 Electric Power

Electric power would seem to be an obvious candidate for variable pricing. Suppliers have constrained capacity, and electricity is difficult and expensive to store. Demand follows predictable patterns, and many customers have the flexibility and willingness to adjust their usage in response to prices. In fact, electric utilities have a further motivation to vary prices: There are tremendous cost differences between generation during peak and off-peak periods. For many utilities, it can be 10 times more expensive to generate power during a peak period than during an off-peak period. During a peak period, even a slight reduction in demand can lead to a substantial reduction in marginal production cost. In some cases, a 5% reduction in demand would reduce the marginal cost of production by 55%. This reduction would benefit all customers, not just those who responded to the variable price.[5]

Despite the obvious benefits that electric suppliers (and, potentially, consumers) could realize from time-of-day pricing, utilities in the United States have been slow to adopt programs that would adjust the price of electricity in response to changes in demand. Some of the reasons are technical, relating to the unique characteristics of electric power transmission and distribution. However, the most powerful reasons are political and historical. Historically, electric utilities were granted service monopolies over a certain territory and guaranteed a reasonable return on their investments in generation capacity and transmission. In return, they submitted to government regulation of their prices to avoid abuses of monopoly power in pricing. While some jurisdictions are moving to less regulated regimes and seeking to encourage competition, the transition from fully regulated to a more competitive market for electric power has proven to be very difficult, and in some cases, a political disaster. The failed attempt by California to deregulate its electricity market was a debacle that was one of the drivers behind the California governor recall and election of 2003.

Despite the political barriers, many electric power utilities have instituted some form of variable-pricing program. Most of these programs are aimed at industrial customers, who often have the flexibility to schedule their operations to take advantage of variable prices. In a typical program, the electricity supplier will charge the customer for electricity on an hour-by-hour basis, with expected prices for the next day announced 24 hours in advance. This enables industrial customers to reschedule their operations to minimize consumption costs. Programs to charge variable prices to residential customers are much rarer—the Gulf Power RSVP program described earlier is typical. It is likely that, despite setbacks, the trend toward more competitive power markets in the United States will continue and that the need for variable-pricing methods will only increase.

5.6.4 Television Advertising

Television advertising spots vary widely in terms of desirability and demand. A half-minute spot during a hit prime-time show is far more valuable than a half-minute spot during a 2:00 AM screening of *The Horror of Party Beach*. Consequently, a network charges more for the prime-time slot than for the "insomnia" slot. Pricing advertising inventory is a classic variable-pricing problem—broadcasters have a fixed and perishable inventory of slots, with wide variations in demand for specific slots. The industry is highly competitive. The major networks (ABC, NBC, CBS, Fox) compete not only with each other but with a growing number of cable networks (Showtime, HBO, ESPN, CNN, etc.) as well. But in a larger sense, broadcasters compete for advertising dollars with other media, such as newspapers, magazines, and the Internet. In this environment, it is critical that broadcasters price intelligently to maximize return on their fixed inventory.

The problem is made more complex by the fact that the inventory the networks have to sell does not correspond precisely with what advertisers want to buy. The broadcaster's inventory consists of advertising slots—generally three *pods*, consisting of 2.5 minutes of consecutive commercials per 30-minute program. But most buyers are more interested in purchasing *impressions*: the number of viewers ("eyeballs") watching their advertisement. Furthermore, they want those "eyeballs" to fall within certain demographics.[6]

The broadcast and cable networks sell advertising during two periods: the *upfront* market and the *scatter* market. The upfront market occurs in conjunction with the announcement of the fall schedule in May or June and lasts for one to three weeks.[7] Broadcasters sell the majority of their inventory—typically between 60% and 80%—in the upfront market. About $17.1 billion of advertising space was sold by network, cable, and syndicated television stations in the 2003 upfront market.[8] The remaining inventory is sold in the scatter market, much closer to the actual time the advertising is to appear—for example, advertisers may purchase time in October for commercials to run in November and December.

Broadcasters face many constraints and complexities in selling in the upfront market.

- Most of the inventory sold during the upfront market comes with a "guaranteed audience," meaning the broadcaster guarantees a minimum number of impressions. If this number is not met by the base schedule, the broadcaster will provide additional spots (called *makeups*). Scatter market sales are usually at a lower price than upfront sales, but they do not include any guarantees.[9] If a network delivers more impressions than agreed on, it is simply a bonus to the advertiser—there is no additional payment to the network.

- A particular buyer may request a mix of specific slots, program quality, and demographics. The seller needs to be able to understand the best way to supply this request. He also needs to know how to compare requests from different advertisers on an "apples vs. apples" basis.

- While a broadcaster knows his inventory of slots, he does not know with certainty the impressions that will be generated by any show. If he "oversells" impressions on the upfront market, he will be forced to provide makeups. On the other hand, if he "undersells" impressions, he ends up giving away some capacity for free that could have generated revenue.

- Placement of advertisements into slots is subject to a number of complex constraints. For example, competing advertisements for automobiles, beverages, or fast food usually cannot run in the same pod. An advertiser purchasing 10 slots per week may want no more than three of them to run on any particular night. These constraints on ad placement make the overall problem more difficult.

The goal of the broadcaster is to maximize total revenue from its inventory of slots. In this sense, broadcasters face a classic variable-pricing problem—they can maximize total revenue only if they price each unit of inventory (slot) in order to maximize its return. However, the variable-pricing problem is complicated by the fact that purchasers are buying not individual units of inventory, but bundles that can include hundreds of different units of inventory. Furthermore, the needs of a specific buyer can often be served using different combinations of slots. Uncertainty about the number of impressions a particular slot will receive adds to the complexity. Nonetheless, the basic principles of variable pricing hold: The prices of the highest-demand slots are set at the point where demand equals capacity, while the prices of the low-demand slots should be set to maximize revenue from those slots.

These pricing decisions need to be made during an extremely hectic period in which a broadcaster may need to evaluate and price thousands of proposals during a one- or two-week period. While each broadcaster establishes a "rate sheet" for her product, the vast majority of slots are sold at significant discounts from the rate sheet. An increasing number of broadcasters are using automated pricing or "revenue management" systems to support upfront sales. These systems serve two functions. First, as "bookkeeping" systems, they enable the broadcaster to keep track of the status of their inventory of slots and impressions as proposals are sold in a way similar to airline reservation systems. Second, they provide recommendations on how individual proposals should be priced given anticipated supply/demand balances for each slot. Broadcasters who have adopted such systems include the American Broadcasting Company (ABC), TV New Zealand, the Canadian Broadcasting Company (CBC), and the Seven Network (Australia). A description of how the revenue management system works at the National Broadcasting Company (NBC) can be found in Bollapragada et al. (2002).

5.7 SUMMARY

- Supply constraints are commonplace in many industries. They can arise due to limited inventory or because capacity itself is physically constrained. Whenever there is a significant chance that demand might exceed available supply, then the supply constraint needs to be explicitly incorporated in determining the optimal price.

- With a single market segment, the optimal constrained price is the maximum of the runout price and the optimal unconstrained price. The optimal price with a supply constraint is always at least as high as the optimal unconstrained price.

- With multiple market segments, the optimal price can be found by solving a constrained-optimization problem. At the optimal price, the marginal revenue will be the same for all segments, but it will not be equal to marginal cost if the constraint is binding.

- A supply constraint has an associated *total opportunity cost*, defined as the additional operating profit the business could achieve if the supply constraint were eliminated. *Marginal opportunity cost* is defined as the additional operating profit the seller would realize if one additional unit of supply were available. Both the total and the marginal opportunity costs associated with a supply constraint are zero if the constraint is not binding.

- Variable prices can be used when capacity is constrained and demand changes over time in a predictable fashion. Variable pricing can increase profitability when demands are independent by adjusting demand to meet supply. It is even more effective when some customers are flexible, because it can shift demand from peak to off-peak periods.

- Optimal variable prices can be found by solving a constrained-optimization problem. The marginal values associated with the supply constraints are the opportunity costs of additional capacity.

- Some industries in which variable pricing is used are sporting events, concerts, passenger airlines, electric power, and television and online advertising.

The pricing and revenue optimization problems we address in later chapters build on the basic techniques of pricing with constrained supply. Capacity allocation (Chapter 7) is based on opening and closing availabilities to different market segments in order to maximize return from fixed and perishable capacity when willingness to pay increases over time. Network management (Chapter 8) extends this concept to the case when customers are buying multiple resources. Overbooking (Chapter 9) deals with the question of how many total units to offer for sale when capacity is fixed. And markdown management (Chapter 10) addresses the case of setting and updating prices for a fixed stock of perishable goods over time. In each of these problems, much of the complexity of the pricing problem comes from the fact that supply is constrained.

5.8 EXERCISES

1. We return to the Stanford Stadium pricing problem in Section 5.4, assuming a capacity of 60,000 seats and the demand curves for students and for the general public as given in Equations 5.1 and 5.2. Assume that 5% of the general public will masquerade as students (perhaps using borrowed ID cards) in order to save money. Assuming that Stanford knows that, what are the optimal prices for student tickets and general public tickets it should set in this case? What is the total revenue, and how does it compare to the case without cannibalization? What does this say about the amount that Stanford would be willing to pay for such devices as photo ID cards in order to eliminate cannibalization?

2. An earthquake damages Stanford Stadium so that only 53,000 seats are available for the Big Game. What is the optimal single price and the total revenue? What are the optimal separate prices to charge for students and the general public and the corresponding total revenue? What is the "opportunity cost" per seat for the 7,000 unavailable seats in both cases?

3. (*Ancillary Revenue*) Stanford Stadium has been repaired so that it again seats 60,000 people. Now assume that, on average, each member of the general public will consume $20 worth of concessions, resulting in a $10 contribution margin, while each student only consumes $10, resulting in a $5 contribution margin. Assuming no cannibalization, what are the prices for students and the general public that maximize total contribution margin (including, of course, ticket revenue)?

4. A barber charges $12 per haircut and works Saturday through Thursday. He can perform up to 20 haircuts a day. He currently performs an average of 12 haircuts per day during the weekdays (Monday through Thursday). On Saturdays and Sundays, he does 20 haircuts per day and turns 10 potential customers away each day. These customers all go to the competition. The barber is considering raising his prices on weekends. He estimates that for every $1 he raises his price, he will lose an additional 10% of his customer base (including his turnaways). He estimates that 20% of his remaining weekend customers would move to a weekday in order to save $1, 40% would move to a weekday in order to save $2, and 60% would move to a

weekday in order to save $3. Assuming he needs to price in increments of $1, should he charge a differential weekend price? If so, what should the weekend price be? (Assume he continues to charge $12 on weekdays.) How much revenue (if any) would he gain from his policy?

5. The optimal prices for theme park admission in Table 5.4 are based on the assumption that admission fees are the only source of revenue for the park. However, the owner determines that visitors to the theme park spend an average of $12 per person on concessions, generating an average concession margin of $5 per person. Under the same assumptions about capacity and demand, what is the single-admission price the theme park should charge to maximize total weekly margin (admission price plus concession margin)? What are the individual daily prices he should charge under a variable-pricing policy, assuming independent daily demands? What is the impact on total weekly admissions? What is the impact on total weekly margin from explicitly including concessions in the optimization relative to optimizing prices on the basis of admission revenue alone?

6. Assume that the theme park owner invested in expanding his park so that he could accommodate up to 1,500 customers each day.

   a. What single price would maximize his total revenue, assuming he faces independent demands for each day and that the price-response curves per day are as specified in Table 5.3? What is his corresponding attendance and revenue per day?

   b. Under the same assumptions, what would be the variable prices he should charge for each day to maximize expected revenue, and what are the corresponding attendance and revenue per day?

7. The theme park owner performs some market research and determines that his customers can best be represented by the following model.

   i. Base customer demand for each day of the week is linear and is specified by the parameters in Table 5.3.

   ii. Weekend (Saturday and Sunday) customers will switch to the other weekend day at the rate of 10 customers for every $1 difference in price. They will not switch to weekdays at any price.

   iii. Weekday customers will switch to any other day (including a weekend day) at the rate of 8 customers for every $1 difference in price.

   What are the optimal daily prices the theme park should charge?

1. Total North American annual production capacity for Ford in 2003 was 5.7 million vehicles annually (Hakim and Berryman 2003).

2. This example is modified from one originally developed by Jeremy Bulow of the Stanford Business School.

3. Grovel (2003).

4. Electric Power Research Institute (2002).

5. Hirst and Kirby (2001).

6. While the most desirable demographics for an advertiser depend on the product or service being sold, the two most desirable demographics overall are women ages 18 to 49 and adults age 25 to 54.

7. Television has a fall schedule because the auto manufacturers deliver new models in the fall. The networks originally started offering new shows in the fall as a way to entice viewers as they competed for automobile advertising dollars supporting the new model year.

8. Downey (2003).

9. Spots for special events such as the Olympics and the Superbowl are often exceptions. They are sold in the scatter market but in some cases can command much higher rates than the upfront market.

6 | REVENUE MANAGEMENT

Revenue management (RM) refers to the strategy and tactics used by a number of industries—notably the passenger airlines—to manage the allocation of their capacity to different fare classes over time in order to maximize revenue. Revenue management is applicable under the following conditions.

1. The seller is selling a fixed stock of perishable capacity.
2. Customers book capacity prior to departure.
3. The seller manages a set of fare classes, each of which has a fixed price (at least in the short run).
4. The seller can change the availability of fare classes over time.

Revenue management can be considered a special case of pricing with constrained supply. However, the final two conditions give revenue management its special flavor. Revenue management is not based on setting and updating prices but on setting and updating the availability of fare classes, where each fare class has an associated fare (price) that remains constant through the booking period. This distinctive feature is a legacy from revenue management's origin. The passenger airlines that pioneered revenue management in the 1980s needed to utilize the capabilities they had at hand. This meant using the booking controls embedded in their reservation systems as the primary mechanism for controlling the fares displayed to customers at any time. Following the success at the airlines, revenue management has been adopted by a number of other industries, including hotels, rental cars, freight transportation, and cruise lines—many of whom use the same (or similar) reservation systems as the passenger airlines.

We use *revenue management industries* as a generic term for industries meeting the conditions listed earlier and *revenue management companies* to refer to companies that make use of booking controls and fare classes. While these companies use revenue management in its purest fashion, the techniques can be applied to any situation in which a seller needs to determine how to allocate a fixed supply among different channels or customer segments paying different prices.

This chapter serves as an introduction to revenue management. It is a prelude to the next three chapters, which address specific aspects of revenue management in more detail. We start by relating some of the history of revenue management and then outline revenue management strategy as an application of some of the price differentiation techniques introduced in Chapter 4. We then introduce revenue management tactics—the ways in which companies can manage their capacity to maximize return once they have chosen a strategy. Computerized reservation systems and global distribution systems play major roles in the way that revenue management is actually implemented. We describe their interaction and operation in Section 6.4. We describe the functions and operations of revenue management systems and how they operate in Section 6.6.2. Finally we discuss how the effectiveness of a revenue management program can be measured and cover the current status and future prospects of revenue management.

Since this chapter is introductory, it may feel a bit lacking in algorithms and computations. This will be made up in the following chapters, each of which addresses a specific aspect of tactical revenue management in detail: capacity allocation in Chapter 7, network management in Chapter 8, and overbooking in Chapter 9.

6.1 HISTORY

Prior to 1978, the airline industry in the United States was heavily regulated. Both schedules and fares were tightly controlled by the Civil Aeronautics Board (CAB). Fares were held sufficiently high to guarantee airlines a reasonable return on their investments. In 1978, Congress passed the Airline Deregulation Act. The act specified that the industry would be deregulated over four years, with complete elimination of restrictions on domestic routes and new service by December 31, 1981, and the removal of all fare regulation by January 1, 1983. The result was a shock from which the industry has not yet fully recovered.

One of the reasons Congress passed the Airline Deregulation Act was to inspire and encourage creative new entrants into the passenger airline business. One of the first new airlines to arise after deregulation was PeopleExpress. PeopleExpress was not unionized, and it offered a bare-bones service, with passengers paying extra for baggage handling and onboard meals. As a result, its cost structure was significantly lower than those of American and the other major airlines, such as United and Delta. By offering fares up to 70% below the majors, PeopleExpress filled its planes with passengers from a previously untapped market segment: price-sensitive students and middle-class leisure travelers who were induced to travel by the existence of fares far lower than anything the industry had seen before. PeopleExpress built its business initially by entering underserved markets, where its competition was primarily bus or car travel. PeopleExpress experienced four years of phenomenal growth and, in 1984, began service on Newark–Chicago and New Orleans–Los Angeles routes—key markets for American Airlines.

The choice American Airlines faced was stark. If it matched People's low fares, it could retain its customer base but would not be able to cover its costs. If it did not match People's fares, most of its customer base would be siphoned off by the low-price competitors. And, of course, in the deregulated environment, nothing could keep a successful PeopleExpress from moving in on all of American's core markets. American Airlines seemed doomed—its only choice appeared to be between a slow death and a rapid one. However, Robert Crandall, CEO of American Airlines, formulated a counterattack: American would compete with PeopleExpress on low fares and simultaneously sell some of its seats at a higher fare as well.

In January 1985, American Airlines announced its "Ultimate Super Saver Fares" program. Ultimate Super Saver Fares matched PeopleExpress prices, with two key differences:

- For a passenger to qualify for an "Ultimate Super Saver" discount fare on American, he would need to book at least two weeks before departure and stay at his destination over a Saturday night. Passengers not meeting this restriction would be charged a higher fare. In contrast, PeopleExpress put no restrictions on their discount fares—every passenger paid a low fare.

- American restricted the number of discount seats sold on each flight in order to save seats for full-fare passengers who would be booking within the last two weeks prior to departure. PeopleExpress allowed every seat to be sold at a low fare.

American's two-pronged approach was carefully thought out and turned out to be the perfect counter to People's challenge. The booking restrictions ensured that the vast majority of the discount passengers buying American were leisure passengers who were able to book early and who were more price sensitive. The later-booking passengers who paid full fare were primarily business travelers who were less price sensitive but needed seat availability at the last minute. Both groups of passengers preferred American's superior service to People's bare-bones approach. In effect, American Airlines had segmented the market between leisure and business travelers and used differentiated pricing to attack a competitor.

The impact of American's actions was dramatic. American announced the new fares and new structure in January 1985. By March of that year, PeopleExpress was struggling and by August it was on the verge of bankruptcy. In September, Texas Air bought PeopleExpress for less than 10% of the market value it had enjoyed a year before. PeopleExpress' flamboyant CEO, Donald Burr, put the blame for his airline's demise squarely on American's superior yield management capability: "We had great people, tremendous value, terrific growth. We did a lot of things right. But we didn't get our hands around the yield management and automation issues." [1]

This was the origin of revenue management (or *yield management* as it was called at the time). American's success prodded other major airlines in the United States to develop revenue management capabilities of their own. Throughout the remainder of the 1980s and well into the 1990s, carriers such as United, Delta, and Continental invested millions of dollars in implementing computerized revenue management systems and establishing revenue management organizations. As world aviation markets were increasingly deregulated, carriers in Europe and Asia began to adopt revenue management as well. Hotels and rental car companies followed the airlines in adopting revenue management. Marriott was a pioneer in hotel revenue management, and Hertz and National were pioneers in rental car revenue management. Vendors such as PROS and Talus Solutions developed and sold commercial revenue management software packages. The next wave of adopters included cruise lines, passenger trains, and various modes of freight transportation. Development and investment in revenue management continues in many of these industries today.

6.2 LEVELS OF REVENUE MANAGEMENT

Successful revenue management requires consistent execution at three levels, as shown in Table 6.1. *Revenue management strategy* is the identification of customer segments and the establishment of products and prices targeted at those segments. Once products and prices have been established, *revenue management tactics* require setting and updating limits on how much of a particular product can be sold at a particular fare to each segment for some period of time—say, a day or a week. *Booking control* is the moment-to-moment determination of which booking requests should be accepted and which should be rejected.

TABLE 6.1
The three levels of revenue management decisions

Level	Description	Frequency
Strategic	Segment market and differentiate prices	Quarterly or annually
Tactical	Calculate and update booking limits	Daily or weekly
Booking control	Determine which bookings to accept and which to reject	Real time

In most cases, booking control is a simple, mechanical process of checking whether a booking can be accepted given the booking limits currently in place. For airlines, hotels, rental car companies, and cruise lines, booking control is a function of the reservation system. Tactical revenue management is the "brains" of the process. It is where future demand is forecast, optimization algorithms run, and booking limits set and updated.

We first discuss the strategy of revenue management and how it applies in different industries. We then turn to a somewhat detailed discussion of booking control—the "real-time" face of revenue management. With this background in place, the next three chapters deal with elements of tactical revenue management—capacity control, network management, and overbooking.

6.3 REVENUE MANAGEMENT STRATEGY

Revenue management strategy consists of the identification of customer segments and the establishment of products targeted at those segments. A fundamental element of revenue management strategy at many hotels, rental car companies, and airlines is the distinction between leisure customers and business customers first recognized by American Airlines. The different characteristics of leisure and business customers are shown in Table 6.2. The airlines used these characteristics to segment their market and create virtual products oriented toward the different segments. A typical approach is shown in Table 6.3. Here, an airline has identified five customer segments, two business and three leisure, with at least one product targeted toward each segment. The leisure products have various restrictions (early purchase, Saturday night stay) that make them unattractive or unavailable to many business

TABLE 6.2

Characteristics of business vs. leisure customers at the passenger airlines

Leisure	Business
Highly price sensitive	Less price sensitive
Book earlier	Book later
More flexible to departure and arrival times	Less flexible
More accepting of restrictions such as Saturday night stayovers	Less accepting of restrictions

TABLE 6.3

Typical airline market segmentation

	SEGMENT				
	BUSINESS ORIENTED			LEISURE ORIENTED	
Price sensitivity	Low	Moderate	Sensitive	Moderate	Very high
Schedule flexibility	Need	Important	Somewhat	Prefers	Very flexible
Inventory	Last seat	Somewhat restricted	Restricted	Restricted	Very limited
Product	Unrestricted Business	Corporate Discount	Discount Business	Regular Leisure	Sale fares Web only Priceline.com

travelers. In the terminology of Section 4.3, the airlines used artificial restrictions to create an inferior product that they could sell at a lower price to a more price-sensitive segment of the market.

Product versioning is not the only price differentiation tactic used by the airlines. They also use most of the other tactics described in Section 4.3 in some form or other. Airlines sell products targeted to many segments such as government, senior citizens, groups, tour operators, and cruise lines. International airlines are great believers in regional pricing. They will sell the same tickets for different prices in different countries (even after adjusting for exchange rates) in order to exploit differences in price sensitivity. Airlines are also enthusiastic channel pricers; ticket prices on the Internet are often cheaper than through travel agents.

Other revenue management companies followed the airlines in segmenting their market, creating virtual products and establishing a wide range of prices. Hotels and rental car companies establish and manage products and different prices oriented toward various groups: corporate, leisure, and business segments. As a simple example, many hotels in Hawaii maintain so-called *kamaaina* rates for local residents.[2] These rates are often far lower than the standard rates, and hotel revenue managers make them available during slack periods in order to fill their properties. Only customers who can prove Hawaiian residency qualify for a kamaaina rate. This is a classic example of group pricing. By confining availability to locals, hotels ensure that the low kamaaina rates do not cannibalize their high-paying business from the mainland United States and Asia.

Cruise lines do not have late-booking business customers, but they do sell to the *incentive segment*—bulk purchases of cruise capacity by companies to be used as incentives for their employees. For example, a medical supply company might purchase 20 berths on a particular sailing to reward the 20 top North American sales managers. This incentive business is booked earlier and is sold at lower fares than individual cruises. Cruise lines also charge different rates for customers from different cities. Managing availability by city is one way they can maximize contribution from each sailing.[3]

6.4 THE SYSTEM CONTEXT

American Airlines was able to outmaneuver PeopleExpress in part because it had a developed a *computerized reservation system* called SABRE that allowed it to save seats for later-booking business passengers—a capability PeopleExpress lacked. When it was turned on in 1964, SABRE was a technological marvel. Not only did it replace the colored index cards in revolving trays that American and other airlines had used since the 1930s to manage their reservations, it gave American Airlines the ability to distribute its products and fares globally and to receive bookings from anywhere in the world.

SABRE combines the functions of a *computerized reservation system* (CRS) and a *global distribution system* (GDS). The key function of a reservation system is to serve as the repository of all the bookings that have been accepted for future flights. The reservation system also contains the controls that specify how many bookings from different fare classes the airline will accept on future flight departures. A reservation system is a critical capability for any revenue management company. Many large airlines, hotels, and rental car companies have developed their own systems, while many smaller companies are "hosted" by commercial providers of reservation services.

Figure 6.1 illustrates some of the distribution channels for a typical airline. At one time, more than 80% of the bookings for a major airline would be communicated through a global distribution system. Several airlines owned their own systems: American Airlines

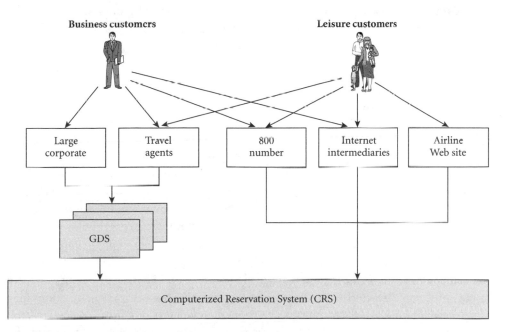

Figure 6.1 Distribution channels for a typical airline.

owned SABRE, United Airlines owned Galileo (then called Apollo), and Northwest Airlines owned Worldspan. Other global distribution systems, such as ABACUS, were owned by consortia of airlines. However, following a series of Justice Department rulings that eliminated the ability of an airline to give preferential treatment to its own flights on its GDS, airlines largely divested themselves of their global distribution systems.

Global distribution systems provide a conduit connecting the reservation system and a number of important sales outlets—particularly travel agents. There are currently over 180,000 GDS terminals worldwide. Most of these terminals are placed with travel agents, but some are in the travel offices of large companies (Marvel 2004). The four most important global distribution systems are AMADEUS, Galileo, SABRE, and Worldspan.[4] Each GDS distributes schedule, fare, and booking availabilities to the agencies and transmits bookings and cancellations from the agencies to the airlines. Most airlines, major hotel chains, major rental car companies, and cruise lines have contracts with most or all of the global distribution systems allowing them to distribute and sell their products. There are exceptions: Both Southwest Airlines and JetBlue Airways subscribe only to SABRE and do not accept bookings through any other GDS (Kontzer 2004).

This system background is important because airlines did not choose to pursue a revenue management strategy and then design reservation systems to support that strategy. Rather, reservation systems were developed first and revenue management capabilities were added later. SABRE went operational in 1964—14 years before the airlines were deregulated and 21 years before American first did battle with PeopleExpress. The computerized reservation systems were among the most sophisticated and complex transaction-processing systems of their day. But they were not very flexible. Since they were built on large mainframes using 1960s-vintage software, major modifications were (and are) expensive and time consuming. As a result, the way airlines and other travel companies manage their inventory is still dictated by the capabilities of these systems. And at the heart of these systems are the booking control mechanisms that determine moment by moment which fare classes are available for sale and which are not.

6.5 BOOKING CONTROL

Booking control is the real-time face of revenue management. The function of booking control is to determine whether or not each booking request received should be accepted or rejected.[5] As shown in Figure 6.1, booking requests stream into the reservation system from many different channels. Within a very short time (typically less than 200 milliseconds), the reservation system needs to send a message whether or not that request can be accepted. Given the short time available, reservation systems typically rely on very simple, mechanical procedures for determining whether or not to accept a request.

When a booking request is received—say, for a seat for a future flight or a hotel room for some future dates—the request is assigned to a fare class. This assignment may be based on the time and characteristics of the request (e.g., whether it meets the qualifications for a deep discount), the channel through which the request was received, the market segment of the customer (e.g., group versus individual), or combinations of all of these. The fare classes are typically assigned letters, so we can speak of a B-Class or M-Class booking request.[6]

The reservation system includes a *booking limit* for each fare class on each product. When a booking request is received, the reservation system checks the booking limit for the associated fare class. If there is sufficient availability, the request will be accepted; if not, the request will be rejected.

Example 6.1

An airline receives a B-Class request for 3 seats on Flight 137 from Houston to Miami, departing in two weeks. The current B-Class booking limit for this flight is 2. Because there is insufficient availability, the request is rejected.

At each time, the booking limits currently in place will determine which booking requests will be accepted and which rejected. When a new booking is accepted or a previously accepted booking cancels, the reservation system automatically updates the booking limits for that product. This is all done very rapidly, consistent with the need of the reservation systems to work in a real-time environment.

6.5.1 Allotments

An obvious way to manage bookings would be to divide the available capacity into discrete chunks and to allocate each chunk to a fare class. This is known as the *allotments* approach, and the size of the chunk allocated to each fare class is called its allotment. Under this approach, bookings are accepted in a class until the allotment for that class is exhausted.

Example 6.2

A 100-seat aircraft is being managed using allotments. Thirty seats have been allotted to deep-discount bookings (B-Class) with a $125 fare, 45 seats to full-fare coach (M-Class) with a $200 fare, and 25 seats to business class (Y-Class) with a $560 fare. Two weeks before departure, 25 B-Class bookings, 45 M-Class bookings, and 10 Y-Class bookings have been accepted. The remaining allotments are 5 seats for B-Class, no seats for M-Class, and 15 seats for Y-Class.

While the allotments approach is easy to understand, it has a major drawback: It doesn't work very well. In particular, it can result in high-fare customers being rejected while lower fare customers are still being accepted. In Example 6.2, once the M-Class allotment closed, the airline would be accepting customers paying $125 while rejecting $200 bookings. This is a prime revenue management sin—we cannot maximize revenue by rejecting high-fare customers in order to save seats for low-fare customers. For this reason, most revenue management companies "nest" their inventory so that high-fare customers have access to all of the inventory available to lower-fare customers.

6.5.2 Nesting

Nesting was developed to avoid the situation in which high-fare bookings were rejected in favor of low fare bookings. To describe nesting, we number fare classes so that 1 is the highest fare class and n is the lowest. We define b_i as the booking limit for class i. With nested booking controls, booking limits are always nondecreasing; that is,

$$b_1 \geq b_2 \geq b_3 \geq \cdots b_n \tag{6.1}$$

Furthermore, at each time, every fare class has access to all of the inventory available to lower fare classes. This avoids the possibility of accepting low-fare bookings while rejecting high-fare bookings.[7] The booking limit for the highest class, b_1, is an upper bound on the total number of bookings that will be accepted. If the airline is not expecting any no-shows or cancellations, then b_1 would equal the capacity of the flight. When there is a possibility that bookings will cancel or not show, then it may be optimal to *overbook*, that is, to accept more bookings than available capacity.[8]

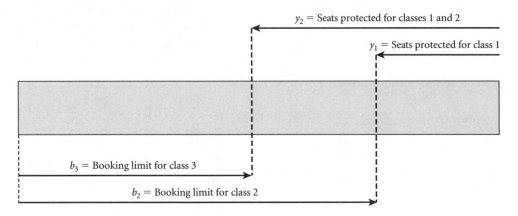

Figure 6.2 Nested booking limits and protection levels.

We can also describe nesting in terms of *protection levels*. The protection level for class i is the total number of seats available to class i and all higher classes. Let y_j be the protection level for class $j = 1, 2, 3, \ldots, n - 1$. The relationship among booking limits and protection levels with nested booking controls is illustrated in Figure 6.2. From this figure it should be evident that

$$y_j = b_1 - b_{j+1} \qquad \text{for } j = 1, 2, \ldots, n - 1 \tag{6.2}$$

and $y_n = b_1$; that is, the protection level for the lowest fare class is equal to the total booking limit for the flight. Combining Equation 6.2 with Condition 6.1, we can see that protection levels decrease for higher fare classes; that is,

$$0 \leq y_1 \leq y_2 \leq \cdots \leq y_{n-1}$$

as can be seen in Figure 6.2.

6.5.3 Dynamic Nested Booking Control

What happens when we accept a booking when limits are nested? One approach is to decrement all nonzero booking limits by 1 every time we book a seat. Once a booking limit for a class reaches zero it remains there, at least until the next reoptimization.

Example 6.3

A flight has a total booking limit of 100 and five fare classes with booking limits of $(b_1, b_2, b_3, b_4, b_5) = (100, 73, 12, 4, 0)$. Note that this flight is currently not accepting any bookings from class 5. Any booking class with a limit of 0 is said to be *closed*. We can derive the corresponding protection levels using Equation 6.2: $(y_1, y_2, y_3, y_4, y_5) = (27, 88, 96, 100, 100)$.

Table 6.4 shows a series of booking requests, whether or not each request would be accepted, and the updated booking limits and protection levels, starting from the booking limits specified in Example 6.3. Each line of the table lists the booking limits and protection levels just prior to receiving the request. The last column shows the corresponding action for each request.[9]

TABLE 6.4
Dynamics of booking limits and protection levels

	BOOKING LIMITS					PROTECTION LEVELS					Request	Action
	1	2	3	4	5	1	2	3	4	5		
1	100	73	12	4	0	27	88	96	100	100	2 seats in Class 5	Reject
2	100	73	12	4	0	27	88	96	100	100	5 seats in Class 2	Accept
3	95	68	7	0	0	27	88	95	95	95	1 seat in Class 2	Accept
4	94	67	6	0	0	27	88	94	94	94	1 seat in Class 4	Reject
5	94	67	6	0	0	27	88	94	94	94	3 seats in Class 3	Accept
6	91	64	3	0	0	27	88	91	91	91	4 seats in Class 3	Reject
7	91	64	3	0	0	27	88	91	91	91	2 seats in Class 3	Accept
8	89	62	1	0	0	27	88	89	89	89	4 seats in Class 3	Reject
9	89	62	1	0	0	27	88	89	89	89	1 seat in Class 3	Accept
10	88	61	0	0	0	27	88	88	88	88	2 seats in Class 2	Accept
11	86	59	0	0	0	27	86	86	86	86	2 seats in Class 3	Reject

Note that the protection levels for the higher classes are preserved while bookings are being accepted for the lower classes. Even after 14 total bookings have been accepted, 27 seats are still protected for Class 1 demand. Nesting implies that a class can be closed as a result of accepting bookings for a higher class. In Table 6.4, this happens with the second booking request received—accepting five Class 2 bookings led to the closure of Class 4. Finally, nesting guarantees that fare classes close in order, from lowest to highest.[10]

6.5.4 *Managing Cancellations

Since almost 30% of airline bookings are cancelled before departure, the bookings management process at a passenger airline needs to be able update booking limits for cancellations. The obvious way to do this would be to treat a cancellation as the opposite of a booking; that is, when a single-seat booking cancels, increase all the positive booking limits by 1, just as we decreased all the positive booking limits by 1 when we accepted the booking. This is, in fact, the way that many reservation systems treat cancellations.

There is a problem with this approach, however. Let's say we have a booking limit of three seats in the lowest booking class and we accept a booking for four seats in some higher class. Then, the lowest class would close. Now, assume that 10 seconds later the booking for four seats is cancelled (perhaps the original request was an error). Under the approach described earlier, the four seats would be added back to the open booking classes and the lowest booking class would remain closed. This seems wrong. After all, we have the same available capacity and the same forecasts for future demand that we had 10 seconds before—why should our booking limits change?

Another way of viewing the issue is that, under the process we have so far described, the closure of a booking class is irreversible, at least until reoptimization occurs.[11] For this reason, we call the procedure illustrated in Table 6.4 an *irreversible* process. Recognizing the shortcomings of an irreversible process, some reservation systems enable a *reversible* bookings management process. The trick in creating a reversible process is to allow the booking limits to go below zero. In a reversible process, new bookings are subtracted from all booking limits and cancellations are added back to all booking limits. As before, a booking request is accepted only if the corresponding booking limit is greater than the number of seats requested. This means that a class with a negative booking limit is closed. With a reversible process, a cancellation can then result in availability going from zero (or less than zero) to positive, opening a previously closed class.

These two approaches to treating cancellations are illustrated in Table 6.5, which shows a sequence of booking requests and cancellations and the corresponding evolution of the booking limits for four booking classes under both approaches. The initial set of booking limits is (73, 12, 4, 0). The second entry in each row of Table 6.5 is either a booking request or a cancellation. The other entries in each row are the booking limits just prior to the event under both approaches and the action (if any) that the airline would take. Since an airline cannot "reject" a cancellation, there are no actions associated with cancellations.

From Table 6.5 we can see that the reversible approach sometimes opens previously closed booking classes. This means that it accepts more low-fare bookings than the irreversible approach. While this may seem appealing, the other side of the coin is that the irreversible approach saves more seats for later high-fare bookings. Generally, it is felt that the reversible approach provides higher revenue, since a booking request that immediately cancels will not

TABLE 6.5
Dynamics of booking limits and protection levels

	Event	BOOKING LIMITS				Action	BOOKING LIMITS				Action
		1	2	3	4		1	2	3	4	
1	Request 2 seats in Class 3	73	12	4	0	Accept	73	12	4	0	Accept
2	Request 2 seats in Class 3	71	10	2	0	Accept	71	10	2	−2	Accept
3	2 bookings cancel	69	8	0	0		69	8	0	−4	
4	Request 5 seats in Class 3	71	10	0	0	Reject	71	10	2	−2	Reject
5	Request 3 seats in Class 2	71	10	0	0	Accept	71	10	2	−2	Accept
6	Request 2 seats in Class 3	68	7	0	0	Reject	68	7	−1	−5	Reject
7	3 bookings cancel	68	7	0	0		68	7	−1	−5	
8	Request 2 seats in Class 3	71	10	0	0	Reject	71	10	2	−2	Accept
9	Request 2 seats in Class 3	71	10	0	0	Reject	69	8	0	−4	Reject
10	2 bookings cancel	71	10	0	0		69	8	0	−4	
11	Request 1 seat in Class 2	73	12	0	0	Accept	71	10	2	−2	Accept
12	Request 1 seat in Class 3	72	11	0	0	Reject	70	9	1	−3	Accept
	Final state	72	11	0	0		69	8	0	−4	

change the booking limits. (For an example of this, see event numbers 2 and 3 in Table 6.5 and the resulting changes in booking limits under the two approaches.) However, which approach is used is often determined by the capabilities of its reservation system rather than by considerations of relative benefit.[12]

6.6 TACTICAL REVENUE MANAGEMENT

The job of tactical revenue management is to calculate and periodically update booking limits. These booking limits are transmitted to the reservation system, which then uses them to determine which booking requests to accept and which to reject based on the logic described in Section 6.5.

To introduce the tactical revenue management problem in its most general form, it is useful to define *resources, products, and fare classes*.

- *Resources* are units of capacity managed by a supplier. Examples of resources are a flight departure, a hotel room night, and a rental car day. Each resource is constrained—the flight departure has a limited number of seats, the hotel only has a limited number of rooms it can sell, and a rental car company has only so many cars it can rent out on a particular day.

- *Products* are what customers seek to purchase. A product may require use of one or more resources. A seat on Flight 130 from St. Louis to Cleveland on Monday, June 30, is a product that uses only a single resource. A two-night stay at the Sheraton Cleveland for a customer arriving on March 19 and departing on March 21 is a product that uses two resources: a room night on March 19 and a room night on March 20.

- There are one or more *fare classes* associated with each product. Each fare class is a combination of a price and a set of restrictions on who can purchase the product and when. As discussed in Section 6.3, different fare classes can be used to establish different virtual products, for group pricing, for regional pricing, or for combinations of all of these.

Table 6.6 shows how the resource/product approach applies in four different revenue management industries. A *resource unit* is the smallest unit of capacity that can be sold: a single seat for an airline, a room night for a hotel. A company may sell several different *types of resource*: airlines sell coach, business, and first-class seats; rental car companies offer subcompact, compact, mid-size, and luxury cars; and a hotel may sell five or six different room types. While resources are the assets a company needs to manage, products are what customers actually want to *buy*. An airline's products are direct and connecting flight combinations. A hotel's products are combinations of arrival date and length of stay. A customer reserving a two-night stay starting next Wednesday is buying a different product than one reserving a two-night stay starting next Thursday.

The resource/product/fare class terminology enables us to formulate the tactical revenue management problem in a very general manner.

TABLE 6.6
Revenue management in four different industries

	Passenger airlines	Hotels	Rental car companies	Cruise lines
Resource	Flight leg	Property	Location	Sailing
Resource unit	Seat	Room night	Rental day	Berth
Resource types	Service classes	Room types	Car types	Berth classes
Number of types	1–3	1–many	3–10	5–10
Products	Itineraries	Arrival date/ length of stay	Arrival date/ length of rental	Cruise
Products per resource	Many for hub-and-spoke airline	Many	Many	Few

A supplier controls (1) a set of resources with fixed and perishable capacity, (2) a portfolio of products consisting of combinations of one or more of the resources, and (3) a set of fare classes associated with each of the products. The tactical revenue management problem is to choose which fare classes should be open and which closed for sale at each moment in order to maximize expected total net contribution.

The fact that revenue management is based on opening and closing fare classes does not make a big difference from the customer's point of view—customers just see the lowest available fare changing over time. The focus on opening and closing fare classes is partly due to the design of the reservation systems. It is also based on the competitive dynamics of the airline market. Specifically, most airlines believe they need to match the advertised, or "headline," fares offered by their competition in key markets in order to drive demand for bookings. However, as bookings arrive, revenue management enables them to "shape" demand to the limited capacity of each flight. Revenue management supplements rather than replaces pricing.

6.6.1 Components of Tactical Revenue Management

As we have seen, the point of tactical revenue management is to determine which fare classes should be open and which closed for all products in order to maximize return from a fixed set of resources. This general problem can be decomposed into three constituent problems.

1. *Capacity allocation.* How many customers from different fare classes should be allowed to book?

2. *Network management.* How should bookings be managed across a network of resources, such as an airline hub-and-spoke system or multiple-night hotel stays?

3. *Overbooking.* How many *total* bookings should be accepted for a product in the face of uncertain future no-shows and cancellations?

Table 6.7 gives a general view of the relative importance of each of these problems in different industries.

Capacity allocation is important whenever a company sells the same unit of constrained

TABLE 6.7
Relative importance of revenue management problems among industries

Industry	Capacity allocation	Network management	Overbooking
Passenger airlines			
Hub-and-spoke	****	***	****
Point-to-point	**	N/A	****
Hotels			
Business	***	****	***
Resort	**	**	*
Rental cars	***	****	***
Cruise lines	****	*	*
Passenger rail	**	****	*
Air freight	***	**	***
Event ticketing	****	N/A	N/A

* = little importance, ** = can be important in some cases, *** = usually important,
**** = of great importance, N/A = not applicable.

capacity or inventory at two or more different prices. In this case, the company needs to determine how many units to sell at the lower price(s) and how many to reserve for sale at a higher price. The major passenger airlines need to determine how many seats to sell to early-booking groups and discount customers and how many to reserve for later-booking business customers. Rental cars and hotels face similar challenges. Sporting teams need to determine how many tickets to sell on discounts or promotions versus holding to sell at full price. Air freight carriers have agreements with different customers that specify different rates—the carriers want to make sure that high-paying customers do not find themselves shut out because all capacity was reserved by lower-paying customers. On the other hand, resort hotels, discount carriers such as Southwest, and passenger trains may only maintain a small number of prices for the same inventory. For these companies, capacity allocation tends to be less important than other aspects of revenue management.

Network management is important for companies that sell products consisting of combinations of resources. It is the single most important component of revenue management for passenger railways and for rental cars and business hotels, where managing length of stay has more impact on total revenue than managing rate classes. It is important for airlines that operate hub-and-spoke systems but not as important as capacity allocation or overbooking. It is of little or no importance in industries in which each product sold uses only a single resource, such as cruise lines, point-to-point airlines, sporting events, and theater.

Overbooking is important whenever bookings are allowed to cancel or not show with little or no penalty. Since airline tickets are typically sold in this way, overbooking has been a major component of airline systems. It has become somewhat less important as the fraction of nonrefundable tickets has increased, but it is still a very important component of revenue management at most airlines, as it is at business hotels and rental car companies. On the other hand, most resort hotels and cruise lines do not overbook because of the high perceived cost of denying service to a customer who may have planned his entire vacation (or even honeymoon) around staying at a particular resort or departing on a particular cruise. It is generally not used for sporting events and theater, where tickets are nonrefundable and seats are individually assigned.

6.6.2 Revenue Management Systems

The primary job of a revenue management system is to calculate and update the booking limits within the reservation system. Typically a revenue management system is separate from the reservation system but linked to it, as shown in Figure 6.3. The revenue management system receives a feed of bookings and cancellations from the reservation system and, in turn, calculates booking limits that are transmitted periodically to the reservation system. The revenue management system will then send messages to update the booking limits in the global distribution systems.

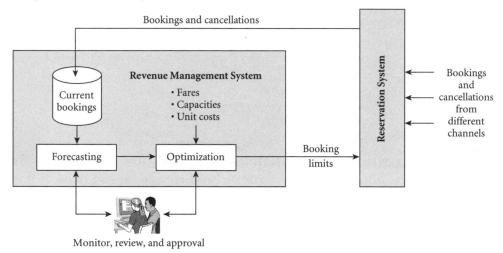

Figure 6.3 Schematic overview of a typical revenue management system.

The revenue management system includes a database with information on current bookings on all flights. It also includes a database incorporating fares for all product/fare class combinations, capacities on all flight legs, and passenger variable costs by product. This information is typically extracted from other computer systems, specifically the pricing system, the scheduling system, and various accounting systems.

The *forecasting* module generates and updates forecasts for all product/fare class combinations for all future dates. Generally, an initial forecast will be generated about one year prior to departure—the time when most airlines first allow bookings for a future flight. This forecast will be updated periodically as bookings and cancellations are received over time. Typically, a forecast will be updated monthly when a flight is six months or more from departure and more frequently as departure approaches. Forecasts are typically updated daily for flights that are within two weeks of departure.

The forecasts generated by the revenue management system are *probabilistic*; that is, they predict both a mean and a standard deviation for future demand. Uncertainty plays a major role in the calculation of optimal booking limits.

Example 6.4

A typical forecast generated by a revenue management system would be that expected future B-Class bookings on Fight 47 from Chicago to Grand Rapids,

Michigan, departing at 9:30 two weeks from today is 13 passengers with a standard deviation of 9, while expected M-Class bookings will be 22 passengers with a standard deviation of 10.

These forecasts are based on current and recent bookings for this flight, historic booking performance for this flight, and general demand trends for all flights. Most systems also forecast cancellations and no-shows in order to support overbooking calculations.[13] Standard forecasting techniques are used to generate the initial forecast and to update the forecasts as bookings and cancellations are received over time. Chapter 9 of Talluri and van Ryzin (2004) describes some of the leading forecasting techniques used to support revenue management. Makridakis, Wheelwright, and Hyndman (1997) is a good general introduction to forecasting.

The probabilistic forecasts are the primary input used by the optimization module to generate the booking limits. As described in Chapters 7 and 8, booking limits are calculated by estimating the economic tradeoff between accepting more discount bookings now versus having more capacity available to serve future bookings. Typically, booking limits are automatically recalculated whenever the demand forecasts are updated.

Revenue management systems recommend booking limits for each product/fare class combination. Effective revenue management requires that these recommendations be continually monitored and reviewed. For example, Delta Airlines employs a group of more than 30 "revenue management analysts" who continually monitor the forecasts and booking limits generated by Delta's revenue management system. Monitoring and adjusting forecasts is a particularly important part of the process. For example, the revenue management system will not know that the Super Bowl will be held in New Orleans this year. It is the job of the revenue management analyst to adjust the forecasts for January flights in the New Orleans market to reflect the additional demand generated by the Super Bowl.

6.6.3 Updating Booking Limits

Most RM companies set initial booking limits based on resource capacities, the demand forecasts for each booking class, and the economic tradeoffs among the classes. Most reservation systems begin to accept bookings about a year prior to a flight departure or room rental date. At this time an airline sets initial booking limits for fare classes on those departures. The initial booking limits are loaded into the reservation system and decremented as bookings are accepted. Periodically, demand is reforecast and new booking limits are calculated based on the new forecast of demand and remaining unbooked capacity. This is known as a *reoptimization* or an *update*. Updates can be triggered in three different ways.

1. *Periodic updates* occur at scheduled intervals. These intervals are typically long (say, monthly) when the flight is far from departure and booking requests are rare. As the flight approaches departure and the bookings pace increases, periodic updates are scheduled more frequently—daily or even more often during the last two weeks prior to departure.

2. *Event-driven updates* are triggered by events such as a booking class closing, a change in aircraft, and an unanticipated spike in demand.

3. *Requested updates* may be launched at any time by a flight controller or revenue manager based on competitive actions, changes in fares, anticipated changes in future demand, or any other reason.

Each time booking limits are updated for a flight, the new booking limits are loaded into the reservation system and the booking management process resumes immediately starting from the new limits.

6.7 NET CONTRIBUTION IN REVENUE MANAGEMENT

Revenue management decisions—like other pricing and revenue optimization decisions—are usually based on maximizing *expected net contribution*. The expected net contribution of a customer commitment is the price (fare) minus the incremental cost of the commitment. When passenger airlines in the United States first began to adopt revenue management, they were in the happy situation that their fares were well above their incremental costs (or *passenger variable costs*, as they are called in the airline industry). The earliest generation of airline revenue management systems ignored incremental costs (or assumed they were zero) and focused on maximizing expected revenue (hence the name *revenue management*). As a result, much of the revenue management literature is couched in terms of maximizing revenue instead of maximizing contribution.

As long as revenue management was confined to the passenger airlines *and* fares remained high relative to incremental cost, this didn't make much difference; maximizing expected revenue led to virtually the same decisions as maximizing expected net contribution. However, in the 1990s, two things began to happen. First, discount fares began a steady decline, to the point where by 2001, the difference between the deepest discount fares and incremental cost was small. Second, revenue management began to be adopted by new industries. In some industries, such as freight transportation and cruise lines, the incremental cost associated with a customer commitment could be significant. Contribution in these industries could be maximized only if incremental costs were incorporated explicitly into revenue management decisions.

6.7.1 Computing Incremental Costs

Table 6.8 shows some of the elements of incremental cost and a subjective estimate of the importance of incremental cost in several revenue management industries. As noted, incremental costs are relatively high (and thus important) in cruise lines and container shipping. Food is a major expense for cruise lines, and the amount of food they purchase and load for a sailing depends on the number of passengers booked. At the other end of the spectrum, incremental costs are relatively low (and therefore generally unimportant) in theater and sporting events. It generally costs little more to stage a play in front of a full theater versus an empty one—not counting, of course, the psychic cost to the actors of playing before an empty house. In between these two extremes fall hotels, rental car companies, and

TABLE 6.8
Incremental cost elements in some revenue management industries

Industry	Incremental cost elements	Relative importance
Passenger airlines	Commissions, incremental fuel, meal costs, passenger fees	Moderate
Hotels	Commissions, room cleaning, wear and tear	Low
Rental cars	Commissions, check-in/check-out, wear and tear	Moderate
Cruise lines	Commissions, food, cleaning costs	High
Container shipping	Repositioning, handling, incremental fuel	High
Sporting events and theater	Commissions	Very low

passenger airlines. In all cases it becomes more important to estimate incremental costs accurately and to incorporate them into revenue management decisions when prices are low.

Incremental costs may vary by channel and market segment. In particular, commissions and distribution fees are important components of incremental cost in many revenue management industries. SABRE charges $3 to $4 per flight segment for an airline booking and about $4 per room for a typical hotel booking. In addition, travel agents receive a commission of about 10% for every booking they make. On the other hand, the variable cost of a direct reservation on a hotel's own Web site is about $1.50 (Marvel 2004). Figure 6.4 shows distribution costs for a $325 ticket sold through different channels for a major U.S. airline in 2002. The cost per booking varies from less than $10 for an opaque ticket to almost $45 for a booking sold through a travel agency.[14]

The range of costs shown in Figure 6.4 represents a channel-pricing opportunity. It also provides an expanded opportunity for revenue management—airlines and hotels can establish fare classes based on the channel of a booking request and determine whether or not

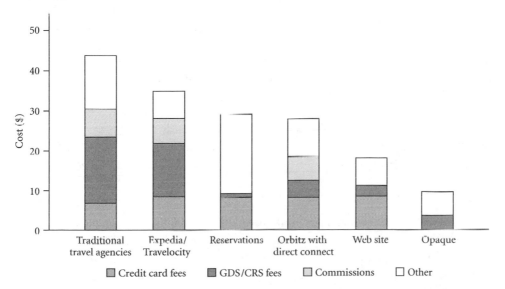

Figure 6.4 Per-ticket distribution costs by channel for a $325 ticket for a major U.S. airline (2002). *Source:* Figure courtesy of Continental Airlines.

to provide availability through that channel. Furthermore, it provides a tremendous economic incentive for revenue management companies to steer demand as much as possible through lower-cost channels. While online travel has been booming, the global distribution systems still account for about 60% of bookings for a typical airline and about 68% for a typical hotel, leaving plenty of scope for future savings (Grossman 2004).

Calculation of incremental costs for a particular booking request requires an activity-based incremental costing model. A typical activity-based costing model for a fictional rental car company (Rent-a-Lemon) is shown in Table 6.9. Three types of cost element are represented: a transaction cost that is generated by every booking, a daily cost that depends on the number of days in the rental, and a commission. The commission is 15% for bookings through travel agents and 0 for bookings through Rent-a-Lemon's 800 number or at one of its airport counters.

TABLE 6.9
Incremental cost elements for Rent-a-Lemon

Cost element	Units	Value	Description
Commissions	$/$	15%	Commission paid for bookings through travel agents
		0%	Commission paid for bookings through other channels
Transaction cost	$/Rental	$8.25	Paperwork, cleaning costs, check-in and check-out costs for each rental
Daily cost	$/Day	$4.32	Wear and tear per day of rental

Example 6.5

Both Mr. Smith and Mrs. Jones want to rent a car for two days from the Rent-a-Lemon location at the Topeka airport. The rate available to both Smith and Jones is $28.00/day. Mr. Smith is making his request at the Rent-a-Lemon counter at the Topeka airport, while Mrs. Jones is requesting the rental through a travel agency. The expected unit cost for Mr. Smith's two-day rental is $8.25 + ($4.32 × 2) = $16.89, while the expected unit cost for the same rental to Mrs. Jones is $16.89 + 0.15 × (2 × $28.00) = $25.29. The difference is due to the commission that Rent-a-Lemon will pay to the travel agent if it rents to Mrs. Jones.

The type of activity-based cost model in Table 6.9 is fairly typical for both hotels and rental car companies. The passenger airlines usually estimate a separate incremental cost for each flight leg in their system.

6.7.2 Ancillary Products and Services

It is common in revenue management industries that the fare received from a customer is not the only source of revenue. An airline passenger may also purchase a beer or duty-free goods aboard his flight. Hotels charge for a wide range of goods and services, such as outgoing calls, minibar, and room service. Insurance is a highly profitable sideline for rental car companies. These additional sources of contribution from a customer above and beyond the prices he pays are called *ancillary products* or *services*.[15] Examples of ancillary products

TABLE 6.10
Ancillary products and services in some revenue management industries

Industry	Ancillary products and services	Importance
Passenger airlines	Duty-free sales, beverage sales	Low
Hotels	Food and beverage, minibar, telephone fees	Medium
Rental cars	Insurance, gasoline	Medium
Cruise lines	Gambling, onboard sales	Medium to high
Freight transportation	Sorting, call before delivery, special handling	Medium
Sporting events, theater	Food and beverage, merchandise sales	High
Hotel/casinos	Gambling	Very high

in various revenue management industries along with their relative importance are shown in Table 6.10. While ancillary products are not particularly important for the passenger airlines, they play an important role in many hotels and rental car companies as well as for sporting events and theater—not to mention hotel/casinos, where gambling is the dominant source of revenue and profitability.

Ancillary contribution is the net contribution from sales of ancillary products or services. To maximize expected contribution, a revenue management company needs to include the estimated ancillary contribution for each booking request. This can be challenging because the amount of ancillary contribution that will be received from a prospective booking is typically unknown at the time a pricing or availability decision needs to be made. Expected ancillary contribution must be estimated based on the customer, product, and channel.

Example 6.6

Harrah's Entertainment uses its CRM system to track the gaming patterns of 28 million customers who belong to its Total Rewards loyalty program. These customers are classified into 64 segments based on gaming habits, and Harrah's forecasts daily hotel room demand for each of its properties for each of these segments. The ancillary contribution for each segment is the anticipated gaming profit that Harrah's will realize. Incorporating this contribution into its revenue management system enables Harrah's to ensure that rooms are available for late-booking high-value customers.[16]

6.7.3 Calculating Expected Net Contribution

The expected net contribution associated with a passenger commitment includes the price (or fare) plus the ancillary contribution minus the incremental cost, as shown in Equation 6.3:

$$\text{Net contribution} = \text{Price} + \text{Ancillary contribution} - \text{Incremental cost} \quad (6.3)$$

Example 6.7

Both Mr. Smith and Mrs. Jones want to rent a car from Rent-a-Lemon for two days for the advertised rate of $28 per day. The incremental costs for Mr. Smith and Ms. Jones are $16.89 and $25.29, respectively. Rent-a-Lemon's CRM system shows that Mr. Smith always takes out insurance when he rents a car while Ms. Jones never takes out insurance. The net profit from insurance for a two-day rental is $7.20. Therefore, the net contribution of renting to Mr. Smith would be $2 \times \$28 + \$7.20 - \$16.89 = \$53.51$ and the net contribution of renting to Ms. Jones would be $\$2 \times \$28 - \$25.29 = \$30.71$.

Note in Example 6.7 that the expected net contribution from renting to Mr. Smith is almost 80% higher than that for Ms. Jones, even though they are paying the same price. If Rent-a-Lemon had only one car available in Topeka, they would be better off renting to Smith than to Jones.

6.8 MEASURING REVENUE MANAGEMENT EFFECTIVENESS

Before deregulation in 1983, airlines could only change their fares after a lengthy regulatory review process. Without direct control over fare, the point of most airline marketing was to fill the planes. The Civil Aeronautics Board always set fares sufficiently high that more passengers meant more money and therfore more profit. Furthermore, there was little or no price differentiation allowed, so there was no scope to perform revenue management. In this environment, the airlines used *load factor* as their primary performance measure. Load factor is defined as the number of seats sold on a flight divided by the number of available seats. A 150-seat flight that departs with 105 passengers on board has experienced a $105/150 = 70\%$ load factor. Load factor was a sensible performance measure in the regulated world. Prices were regulated at a level such that if an airline filled about 75% of its seats on each flight—the so-called *break-even load factor*—they would meet their total costs. Each passenger above the break-even load factor represented additional profit. A marketing program was successful if it increased load factors.

Following deregulation, the issue of performance metrics became more complex. In a multifare world, load factor could no longer pass muster as a leading performance metric. The reason is easy to see—in response to the rise of discount carriers, the major airlines had introduced deep discounts that induced vast amounts of leisure demand on many flights. It would be easy to maximize load factor for these flights—simply allow deep-discount customers to book all the seats. But this would be counter to the entire purpose of tactical revenue management—which is to maximize revenue by reserving seats for late-booking business passengers. Since load factor ignores revenue, it is the wrong metric for a revenue management world. In fact, it is worse than that: Policies designed to maximize load factor would lead to planes filled with deep-discount passengers and massive denial of availability to business passengers—the airlines' highest-paying customers.

To get a better view of the revenue picture, airlines began to look at *yield* in addition to load factor. Yield is simply revenue per passenger mile. Like load factor, it can be measured at any level from flight to market to entire airline. It was sometimes stated that the goal of managing bookings should be to increase yield—hence the term *yield management*, which was the original name for what is now more commonly called *revenue management*. Unfortunately, yield alone is a very imperfect metric since it ignores flight capacity. The strategy for increasing the yield from a flight is the exact opposite from that for increasing load factor—reject all early-booking demand and accept only late-booking high-yield passengers. This policy would maximize yield but would be disastrous for the airline, since it would result in flights that were empty except for a few high-paying business passengers.

What the airlines really needed was a metric that combined the capacity focus of load factor with the revenue focus of yield and recognized that the goal of revenue management is to maximize the return from resources. For an airline, these resources are seats, and the airline needs to maximize *revenue from available seats*. Since prices for products are at least somewhat proportional to distance, it helps to normalize by distance and to measure *revenue per available seat mile*, or RASM. An airline that flies a 100-seat aircraft on an 1,800-mile flight (about the distance from Chicago to San Francisco) with a total revenue of $50,000 has just achieved an RASM of $50,000/(100 × 1,800) = $0.28 for that flight. Note that RASM is indifferent to how the revenue was distributed among passengers on the flight. Fifty passengers paying $1,000 each (a 50% load factor) would result in the same RASM as 100 passengers paying $500 each (a 100% load factor). This is the right focus from the revenue management point of view—a policy that has resulted in $51,000 from the flight is more successful than one that resulted in $50,000, even if the first policy resulted in a lower load factor.[17]

Revenue per available seat mile can also be expressed in terms of net yield and load factor:

$$RASM = Net\ yield \times Load\ factor$$

Revenue per available seat mile is the leading metric currently used by airlines to measure effectiveness of pricing and revenue management. Similar approaches are also employed at other RM companies: *revenue per available room night* (often abbreviated *REVPAR*) at hotels, *revenue per available rental day* at rental car companies, and *revenue per berth* for cruise lines. The RASM metric enables comparison of revenue performance across markets and within a single market over time. Speaking broadly, flights that are achieving high RASM are generating a higher return to the company's assets than those with low RASM. And RASM also provides a useful performance benchmark among different airlines. Those airlines achieving high RASMs are generating more revenue from their assets in general than those with lower RASMs. However, high RASM does not guarantee high profitability (or any profitability at all), since it is strictly a revenue-based metric and ignores costs entirely.

6.9 REVENUE MANAGEMENT IN ACTION

By most measures, revenue management has been a success. Every major airline, hotel, rental car company, or cruise line has a revenue management department or a revenue management function. These departments rely on computerized systems to recommend actions based on sophisticated mathematical algorithms. The benefits of revenue management at the airlines have been widely acknowledged—so much so that at most major airlines, revenue management is considered a key management function. The practice of revenue management has spread to many other industries, including hotels, rental car companies, cruise lines, railroads, tour operators, broadcasting, and freight transportation. There is active research in many areas. An important area of current research is on how to better incorporate customer behavior, lifetime customer value, and competitive response into revenue management decisions. This research continues within RM companies, at universities, and at consulting companies and system vendors. In addition, there are numerous efforts to adapt revenue approaches to the needs of new industries, ranging from oil and gas pipelines to health care to made-to-order manufacturing. In each of these industries, constrained perishable capacity plays a major role, and revenue management has the potential to supplement existing pricing approaches, often leading to substantial improvements in profitability.

It would be nice to end the story on this note. On the other hand, as we enter the new century, it seems that the airlines, which are the most sophisticated in revenue management, are among those suffering the most. In early 2003, United Airlines declared bankruptcy, while American Airlines lost more than $3 billion in 2002 and was asking for federal funding to survive. Meanwhile, the only U.S. airlines making money are the low-cost, low-fare carriers, such as JetBlue and Southwest. It seems to be a complete reversal of the American Airlines/PeopleExpress story—this time it is the carriers with expensive and sophisticated revenue management systems that are going bankrupt while their low-cost, low-fare rivals thrive. What does this say about the future of revenue management?

TABLE 6.11
Comparison of the Big 6 versus low-cost carriers (2002 annual results)

	Average Big 6	Southwest	JetBlue	AirTran	Low-cost average
RASM	10.5	8.4	7.7	9.1	8.4
CASM	11.1	7.5	6.3	8.5	7.4
Net contribution per seat mile	(0.6)	0.9	1.4	0.6	1.0

Some insight into this question is provided by Table 6.11, which shows the average performance of the "Big 6" airlines in the United States (American, Continental, Delta, Northwest, United Airlines, and US Airways) versus three low-cost airlines (Southwest, JetBlue, and AirTran) during 2002.[18] In Table 6.11, CASM stands for *cost per available seat mile*— the *total* operating cost (including fixed operating costs such as crew salaries) divided by the total available seat margin. *Net contribution per seat mile* is simply RASM minus CASM. As can been seen from the table, the Big 6 airlines managed to maintain an average RASM 25% higher than their low-cost competitors. This is an impressive achievement in an environment in which airline seats are rapidly becoming a commodity and the Internet is enabling unprecedented fare visibility. Unquestionably, superior revenue management is a major element enabling the Big 6 to maintain this revenue gap. But while the Big 6 may be winning the revenue game, they are getting clobbered in the cost game. Their average cost per available seat mile is 50% higher than that of the low-cost carriers, overwhelming their revenue advantage. The result is that, in 2002, the low-cost carriers made a penny on average for every seat mile they flew, while the Big 6 lost six-tenths of a cent.

The revenue advantage the Big 6 have been able to maintain is a strong indication of the continuing importance of revenue management. However, it is also unquestionably true that the game is changing rapidly—not only for airlines but for other RM companies—and revenue management practices are going to need to change as well. Much of this change is being driven by the rise of the Internet as a distribution channel. Retail travel is unquestionably an e-commerce success story: Travel accounted for 36% of retail purchase on the Internet, well ahead of any other category.[19] It is a measure of the success of travel sales on the Internet that some of the leading on-line travel retailers are actually profitable.

From the airlines' point of view, the success of the Internet as a distribution channel has been a mixed blessing. On the one hand, it has enabled the airlines to slash their distribution costs by cutting out the middleman—especially the travel agencies, who used to be the dominant distribution channel for travel products. On the other hand, the Internet has posed a set of new challenges that the major airlines have been struggling to meet.

- The Internet has provided unprecedented fare visibility to consumers. Instead of relying on travel agents or 800 numbers, price-conscious shoppers can surf the net for bargains on their own time, 24 hours a day, seven days a week. This increases the pressure for airlines and others to continually manage their prices and availabilities. It is also eroding some of the traditional "product fences" that have allowed airlines to maintain separate products for leisure and business travelers.

- While the Internet has been a disaster for the traditional travel agency distribution channels, it has led to the rise of new online intermediaries, such as Expedia, Travelocity, and Priceline. These intermediaries and their various competitors are all striving to be the dominant retailer of travel products on the Internet. Naturally, the airlines are leery of the prospect of any intermediary gaining a dominant position, so a consortium of U.S. airlines created Orbitz to be their own online retailer. For the foreseeable future, airlines will need to manage pricing and availability through a variety of online retailers as well as through their own Web sites and the traditional channels.

- The Internet has also created new opportunities for the airlines to create and sell more "inferior" products. For example, Priceline allows customers to bid for travel without knowing the exact departure time or airline they are purchasing. Priceline has explicitly marketed this as an "inferior" product that the airlines can safely sell at a high discount without cannibalizing their mainstream products. Other airlines and hotels are experimenting with selling "distressed inventory" (i.e., empty capacity close to departure) at deep discounts. The need to manage these additional discount products adds further complexity to revenue management.

- As we have seen, revenue management was shaped by the design of the global distribution systems the airlines developed in the 1960s. These systems maintain a relatively small number of fare classes for each product, and the focus of revenue management has been on which of these classes to open and close at different times. Travel agents were trained in the parlance of booking classes and product restrictions that the airlines had established. But the Internet is much more suited to real-time pricing than to availability management. Online shoppers do not care about fare class availabilities; they simply want to find the lowest price for their desired travel. This means that the entire machinery of protection levels and booking limits behind classical revenue management is becoming less relevant.

While everyone agrees that revenue management needs to change in response to these trends, there is little agreement on what kind of change is needed and how it will occur. But under any scenario, revenue management companies will need to manage a large portfolio of products and market segments through many different channels for some time to come. Until the flexible airplane and hotel is invented, airlines and hotels will need to maximize net contribution from fixed and perishable capacity. The capability to determine who gets to purchase at what fares will be an important driver of market success for some time to come.

It is also clear that the traditional airlines will need to continue to adjust their pricing tactics in response to the challenge of the discount airlines. Already, many of the major airlines have needed to simplify and reduce their fares on routes where they face discount competition. Making a virtue of a necessity, in 2004 Alaska Airlines advertised in their onboard magazine that: "We're proud to announce the retirement of our random & lame-brained fare generator . . ." by "closing the gap between the highest fares and lowest fares in all our markets." Other major airlines were making similar moves, albeit with less fanfare.

Revenue management is in the process of a major paradigm shift. The airlines (and other RM companies) have become experts in managing availabilities. In the new world, they will need to become equally expert in understanding customer price response. Meanwhile, industries outside the travel industry are adopting revenue management approaches to managing availability. The ultimate result may be a convergence of approaches combining revenue management's treatment of availability management with sophisticated customer price-response models.

6.10 SUMMARY

- *Revenue management* is the name given to the ways by which a number of industries maximize expected contribution from their constrained resources. It is applicable to any situation in which:

    The seller is selling a fixed stock of perishable capacity.

    The seller offers a set of fare classes, each of which has a fixed price (at least in the short run).

    The seller can change the availability of fare classes over time.

    Customers book capacity prior to usage.

    High-fare customers book later than low-fare customers.

    Revenue management is used in its purest form by passenger airlines, hotels, rental car companies, cruise lines, passenger trains, apartment rental managers, and various forms of freight transportation. Many of the core concepts are also applicable in other industries.

- Revenue management needs to be implemented at three levels. At the strategic level it requires identifying customer segments and creating "virtual products" and other differentiated prices. At the booking-control level it requires determining in real time whether or not booking requests should be accepted or rejected. At an intermediate level, tactical revenue management periodically recalculates and updates the booking limits used for booking controls.

- The primary revenue management segmentation at the passenger airlines is between early-booking price-sensitive leisure travelers and later-booking, less price-sensitive business customers. The airlines, hotels, and rental car companies use time-based product differentiation to create products oriented toward each of these segments. In addition, revenue management companies typically have products tailored to other segments, such as groups and large corporations. Finally, they may also use channel pricing and regional pricing to further segment the market. This can lead to pricing structures of great complexity.

- In general, a revenue management company controls a set of constrained resources that can be combined to create products. Each product has a range of discrete fare classes with different associated fares. These fare classes reflect the price differentiation tactics being used by the seller and the set of products and fares the seller has established. Tactical revenue management requires updating booking limits on these fare classes over time.

- Tactical revenue management consists of three interrelated problems:

    Capacity allocation—How should fare class booking limits be set for a single-resource product?

    Network management—How should bookings for multiresource products be controlled?

    Overbooking—How many total bookings should be allowed for a resource?

    These three problems are not independent. However, they have different levels of importance within different revenue management industries.

- The main job of a revenue management system is to set initial booking limits and to perform the periodic reoptimization of the booking limits. A revenue management system includes a forecasting module that derives probabilistic forecasts of future demand and an optimization module that uses those forecasts along with other information to determine the optimal booking limits.

- Early revenue management programs aimed to maximize expected revenue. In an environment where incremental costs are low relative to prices, this is a reasonable assumption. However, as prices have fallen and revenue management has been adopted by new industries, it has become increasingly important to estimate incremental costs and include them in the objective function. Further, ancillary products play an important role in many revenue management industries, and their expected contribution needs to be incorporated into revenue management decisions.

- The best measure of overall revenue management performance is contribution per available unit of resource. The metric most typically used at the airlines is

RASM—revenue per available seat mile. Equivalent metrics exist in other revenue management industries. For example, REVPAR—revenue per available room—is the preferred metric for revenue management performance in the hotel industry.

- Revenue management has been a highly effective tactic at the major airlines since the mid-1980s. However, the major airlines are increasingly finding themselves challenged by low-cost carriers. While the major airlines have been able to maintain higher revenues per available seat mile than the low-cost carriers, this revenue advantage has not been able to overcome the cost advantage of the low-cost carriers. It is likely that, at least in the airlines, revenue management will increasingly evolve toward dynamic pricing, with less emphasis on capacity allocation.

The next three chapters address each of the three tactical revenue management problems in more detail. Chapter 7 deals with capacity allocation, Chapter 8 with network management, and Chapter 9 with overbooking.

6.11 EXERCISE

1. A restaurant has 25 tables, each of which can seat up to four people. Typically, it can do three seatings per table during the dinner period from 6:00 to 10:00 PM. The restaurant has a fairly predictable demand pattern, with Fridays and Saturdays the busiest nights and Sundays and Mondays the least busy. The restaurant is always booked to capacity on Fridays and Saturdays and sometimes on Wednesdays and Thursdays but virtually never on Sunday or Monday. It has implemented a revenue management program under which it will sometimes turn down booking requests for one or two people on Fridays and Saturdays if it believes it can fill the restaurant with bookings for larger parties of three and four people. What performance measure should it use to evaluate the effectiveness of its revenue management program?

1. The quote from Donald Burr and the story of American versus PeopleExpress is told in Chapter 4 of Robert Cross' book *Revenue Management: Hard-Core Tactics for Market Domination* (1997).

2. *Kamaaina* is the Hawaiian word for "native."

3. Lieberman and Dieck (2002) describe the approach used by one cruise line to managing availability by city of origin.

4. Most global distribution systems also provide reservation system functionality, as SABRE does for a number of airlines, including American.

5. This is something of a simplification. An airline needs to deal with both booking requests and availability requests. The *booking request* is a request for an actual booking. An *availability request* is a check on what fares are available for a particular product. Many availability requests are from travel agents or from customers who are "just shopping." For simplicity, we will continue to speak of booking requests.

6. As a consequence, some reservation systems limit the number of booking classes per product to a maximum of 26.

7. This is true at least when fare classes have independent demand. We will show later that when demands are dependent there are cases in which it can be optimal to reject high-class bookings while accepting bookings from lower fare classes.

8. Approaches to overbooking are described in Chapter 9.

9. Some airline reservation systems use different variations of this booking management process. For example, some systems would decrement the protection level for Class 2 when a Class 2 booking is accepted. There is no consensus on which variation provides the best overall performance.

10. Note that two or more of the lowest open classes can close simultaneously *if* they all have the same booking limit.

11. There is one exception: Most reservation systems will reopen the highest class when cancellations occur on a totally booked flight.

12. Once again, different reservation systems use slightly different approaches to update booking limits and protection levels in the face of cancellations and there is no consensus on the "best" approach.

13. Chapter 9 describes how these forecasts are used to set overbooking levels.

14. *Opaque tickets* are a form of inferior product under which the customer purchases a ticket for a specified origin and destination on a particular departure date from a company such as Hotwire or Priceline. When purchasing the ticket, he does not know the identity of the airline, the exact time of departure, or the number of stops. Opaque tickets enable the airlines to sell a very inferior product to leisure travelers while minimizing cannibalization of the full-fare business product.

15. Sometimes ancillary revenue is called *incidental revenue*.

16. Information about Harrah's from Phillips and Krakauer (2002), Kuyumcu (1999), and Binkley (2004).

17. From an overall PRO point of view, *net contribution per available seat mile* (NCASM) would be an even better metric. For the example flight, assume there is a per-passenger operating cost of $50. Then, 100 passengers paying $500 each would result in an operating margin of $50,000 − 100 × $50 = $45,000, for an NCASM of $0.25, while 50 passengers paying $1,000 apiece would result in an operating margin of $50,000 − 50 × $50, for an operating margin of $47,500 and an NCASM of $0.26. The higher operating margin per available seat mile (OMASM) accurately reflects the superior operating margin of the second case, which is not reflected in RASM. However, for RM companies where the fares are much higher than the operating costs, RASM is close enough to NCASM to provide an effective metric.

18. Donofrio (2002).

19. Consumer electronics was in second place, with 15% of sales.

7 CAPACITY ALLOCATION

7.1 INTRODUCTION

Capacity allocation is the problem of determining how many seats (or hotel rooms or rental cars) to allow low-fare customers to book when there is the possibility of future high-fare demand. Capacity allocation is particularly important among passenger airlines because many airlines have based their revenue management strategy on segmenting the market between early-booking, low-fare leisure customers and later-booking, higher-fare business customers, as discussed in Chapter 6. Capacity allocation is also an issue for any revenue management company that has the opportunity to restrict early low-price bookings in order to reserve capacity for later higher-price bookings. The techniques described in this chapter are used *mutatis mutandi* in many industries, including rental car companies, hotels, cruise lines, freight transportation, and made-to-order manufacturing, among others.

We introduce the capacity allocation problem by analyzing the two-class model in some detail. We then move on to the multiclass problem, with an emphasis on the widely used expected marginal seat revenue (EMSR) heuristics. We then discuss the dynamic multiclass problem when fare classes are nested. We then relax the independence assumption and discuss how booking limits could be set when demand in different fare classes can depend on which classes are currently open. Finally we discuss how the performance of a capacity allocation program can be measured and evaluated.

7.2 THE TWO-CLASS PROBLEM

In the two-class capacity allocation problem, a flight (or other product) with fixed capacity serves two classes of customers: discount customers who book early and full-fare customers who book later. Discount customers each pay a fare $p_d > 0$, and full-fare customers each pay a higher fare $p_f > p_d$. In the basic two-class model we assume that all discount booking requests occur before any full-fare passengers seek to book. We have a limited number of seats. The static two-class capacity allocation problem is: How many discount customers (if any) should we allow to book? Or, equivalently: How many seats (if any) should we protect for full-fare customers?

The standard approaches to the capacity allocation problem we describe in this section are formulated as if the goal were to maximize expected revenue—that is, incremental costs and ancillary contribution are zero. This streamlines the discussion and is consistent with the revenue management literature. But, in reality, companies will be (or should be) maximizing expected total contribution, including incremental cost or ancillary contribution. The approaches in this section can be made consistent with maximizing total contribution by substituting *net contribution*, as defined by Equation 6.3, wherever *price* or *fare* appears in an algorithm or equation.

The goal of two-class capacity allocation is to determine a *discount booking limit*—the maximum number of discount bookings that will be allowed. When there are only two classes, the protection level for full-fare bookings is equal to the capacity minus the booking limit: $y = C - b$, where C is capacity. Obviously it is straightforward to calculate the booking limit given the protection level and capacity, and vice versa.

7.2.1 The Decision Tree Approach

At the heart of the capacity allocation problem is the tradeoff between setting the booking limit too high and setting it too low. If we set the discount booking limit too low, we will turn away discount customers but not see enough full-fare demand to fill the plane. The plane will depart with empty seats even though we turned away bookings. This is called *spoilage*, since the empty seats become spoiled inventory at the moment the flight departs. On the other hand, if we allow too many discount customers to book, we run the risk of turning away more profitable full-fare customers. This is called *dilution*, since we diluted the revenue we could have received from saving an additional seat for a high-fare booking. The challenge of capacity allocation is to balance the risks of spoilage and dilution to maximize expected revenue.

The tradeoffs in the two-class problem are shown as a decision tree in Figure 7.1 for a flight with total capacity C. $F_f(x)$ is the probability that full-fare demand is less than or equal to x and $F_d(x)$ is the probability that discount demand is less than or equal to x. Assume we

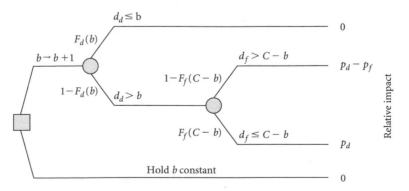

Figure 7.1 Two-class capacity allocation decision tree.

have currently set a booking limit of b. The decision we face is whether or not to increase the booking limit by one seat (or, equivalently, to reduce the protection level by one seat). What would be the change in expected revenue if we increase the booking limit from b to $b + 1$? If discount demand d_d is less than or equal to b, there will be no effect on expected revenue. (Recall that booking classes are nested, so all of the seats that are not sold to discount customers are available to full-fare customers.) In this case, the net change in expected revenue of increasing the booking limit by one seat is 0, as shown on the top branch of the tree.

Only when discount demand is greater than b do things get interesting. In that case [which occurs with probability $1 - F_d(b)$], increasing the booking limit from b to $b + 1$ results in an additional discount passenger. The net effect on revenue depends on full-fare demand. If full-fare demand is greater than $C - b$ (which happens with probability $1 - F_f(C - b)$), the additional discount booking will displace a full-fare passenger. This is *dilution*, and the resulting change in total revenue is $p_d - p_f < 0$. The other possibility is that discount demand is greater than b and full-fare demand is less than the protection level, $C - b$. In this case, we accept an additional discount passenger but do not displace a full-fare passenger. The gain is p_d: Increasing the discount booking limit has reduced spoilage.

The expected change in revenue from changing the booking limit from b to $b + 1$ is the probability-weighted sum of the possible outcomes, or

$$E[h(b)] = F_d(b)0 + [1 - F_d(b)]\{[1 - F_f(C - b)](p_d - p_f) + F_f(C - b)p_d\}$$
$$= [1 - F_d(b)]\{p_d - [1 - F_f(C - b)]p_f\} \tag{7.1}$$

If the term on the right-hand side of Equation 7.1 is greater than zero, then we can increase expected profitability by increasing the discount booking limit from b to $b + 1$. On the other hand, if the term is less than zero, expected revenue will decrease if we increase the discount booking limit.[1]

The key term in Equation 7.1 is $p_d - [1 - F_f(C - b)]p_f$. As long as this term is greater than zero, we should increase the discount booking allocation. With a booking limit of b, there will always be *at least* $C - b$ seats available for full-fare passengers. If discount demand is less than b, there will be even more seats available for full-fare passengers. $1 - F_f(C - b)$ is the probability that full-fare demand will exceed the protection level. It is shown as a function of b in Figure 7.2. The term $1 - F_f(C - b)$ is small when the protection level is large (that is, the discount booking limit is small) and gets larger as we decrease the protection level (that is, increase the discount booking limit). If $p_d < [1 - F_f(C - b)]p_f$, then we should not allocate *any* seats for discount passengers—we are better off saving all seats for full-fare passengers. If $p_d > [1 - F_f(C - b)]p_f$, then we are better off allocating at least one seat for discount passengers.

Example 7.1

An airline has set a discount booking limit of 80 seats on a 150-seat aircraft for a certain flight departure. The corresponding protection level is 70 seats. If the airline substituted a 100-seat aircraft for that flight and neither the fares nor the

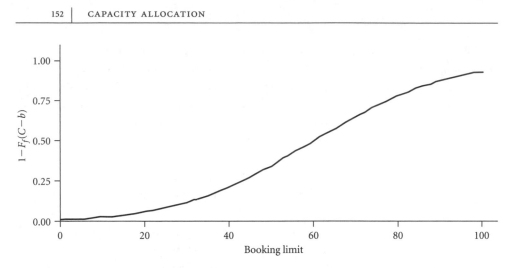

Figure 7.2 Probability that full-fare demand will exceed the protection level as a function of booking limit for a 100-seat aircraft.

full-fare demand forecast changed, then the optimal protection level would still be 70 seats. The optimal discount booking limit with the smaller aircraft would be $100 - 70 = 30$ seats.

This marginal analysis suggests the following simple "hill-climbing" algorithm for calculating the optimal booking limit b^*.

Algorithm for Computing Optimal Discount Booking Limit

1. Set $b = 0$.
2. If $b = C$, set $b^* = C$ and stop. Otherwise, go to step 3.
3. Calculate $E[h(b)] = p_d - [1 - F_f(C - b)]p_f$.
4. If $E[h(b)] \leq 0$ or $F_d(b + 1) = 1$, set $b^* = b$ and stop.
5. If $E[h(b)] > 0$ and $F_d(b + 1) < 1$, set $b \leftarrow b + 1$ and go to step 2.

This algorithm involves adding one seat at a time to the discount booking limit (or, equivalently, removing one seat at a time from the full-fare protection level) and continuing as long as adding one more seat increases expected revenue. However, there is a simpler way to get to the same point.

7.2.2 Littlewood's Rule

The sequential algorithm finds the value of b^* such that

$$1 - F_f(C - b^*) = p_d/p_f \tag{7.2}$$

or, equivalently,

$$1 - F_f(y^*) = p_d/p_f \tag{7.3}$$

where y^* is the optimal protection level for full-fare demand.[2]

Condition (7.2) for the optimal two-class discount booking limit was first described in 1972 by Kenneth Littlewood, an analyst at British Overseas Airways Company (BOAC) (a predecessor to British Airways), and is known as *Littlewood's rule*. The quantity on the left-hand side of Equation 7.2, $1 - F_f(C - b^*)$, is the probability that full-fare demand will exceed the protection level. Littlewood's rule states that, to maximize expected revenue, the probability that full-fare demand will exceed the protection level should equal the fare ratio p_d/p_f. If the discount fare is 0, Littlewood's rule states that we should set the protection so high that there is no chance that full-fare demand would exceed it. In other words, the optimal discount booking limit would be 0. This is intuitive—if discount passengers are not paying us, there is no reason we should give them any seats! As p_d increases, the optimal number of seats to protect decreases until, when $p_d = p_f$, it is optimal to set the discount booking limit to C. This is also intuitive—if discount passengers are paying as much as full-fare passengers, there is nothing to be gained by turning away a discount booking as long as there are still empty seats.

Almost always, the function $F_f(y)$ will be a strictly increasing function of the protection level y. In this case, F_f will be invertible and we can write Littlewood's rule as

$$y^* = \min[F_f^{-1}(1 - p_d/p_f), C] \qquad (7.4)$$

where F_f^{-1} refers to the inverse cumulative distribution function of full-fare demand. At the point where $y^* = F_f^{-1}(1 - p_d/p_f)$, the risks of protecting too much capacity for full-fare demand and protecting too little are exactly balanced.

One fact you may find surprising about Littlewood's rule is that the optimal protection level—and, hence, the optimal discount booking limit—does not depend in any way on the forecast of discount demand. The distribution of discount demand $F_d(D_d)$ does not appear in Equation 7.4. Doubling (or halving) the discount demand forecast will not change the optimal booking limit. In addition, Equation 7.4 shows that the optimal protection level does not depend on the capacity, except to the extent that it never makes sense to "protect" more seats than the capacity of the plane. The economic tradeoffs embodied in Littlewood's rule only depend on the two fares and the distribution of expected full-fare demand.

Example 7.2

The mean full-fare demand for a flight with a 100-seat aircraft is 50 with a standard deviation of 100. For any fare ratio, f_d/f_f, the corresponding optimal booking limit is the smallest value of b for which $1 - F_f(C - b) \geq f_d/f_f$. Table 7.1 illustrates the key calculation in the optimal two-class discount booking limit algorithm for a 100-seat flight. For a fare ratio of 0.4, the optimal booking limit is 25, for a ratio of 0.5, it is 50, and for a ratio of 0.6, it is 76. Since discount demand does not enter into Littlewood's rule, these limits are independent of the discount demand forecast.

In Example 7.2 the booking limit increases with the fare ratio, as expected. Notice that if the fare ratio is less than 0.309, we would not allow any discount passengers to book—we would be better off protecting the entire plane for full-fare passengers. On the other hand,

TABLE 7.1
The value of $1 - F_f(C - b)$ *as a function of b when total capacity is 100 seats
and the mean full fare demand is 50 with a standard deviation of 100*

b	$1 - F_f(C - b)$	b	$1 - F_f(C - b)$	b	$1 - F_f(C - b)$	b	$1 - F_f(C - b)$
0	0.309	24	0.397	49	0.496	75	0.599
1	0.312	25	0.401	50	0.500	76	0.603
5	0.326	26	0.405	51	0.504	80	0.618
10	0.345	30	0.421	55	0.520	85	0.637
15	0.363	35	0.440	60	0.540	90	0.655
20	0.382	40	0.460	65	0.560	95	0.674
23	0.394	45	0.480	70	0.579	100	0.691

if the fare ratio is greater than 0.691, we would open the entire flight to discount passenger bookings. In either case, the airline might want to consider revisiting its fare structure—in the first case the discount fare is probably too low, and in the second case it is probably too high relative to the full fare.

The tradeoffs involved in setting the discount booking limit are shown in Figure 7.3 for a 100-seat flight with mean full-fare demand of 50 and standard deviation of 25—the same values as in Table 7.1. The discount fare is $100, and the full fare is $200, so the fare ratio is 0.5. The top curve is total expected revenue—the sum of the expected revenue from full-fare passengers and discount passengers. The dotted curve is expected discount revenue, and the difference between expected total revenue and expected discount revenue is expected full-fare revenue. As we increase the discount booking limit from zero, the expected revenue from discount passengers increases, with very little decrease in expected full-fare passenger revenue. As we continue to increase the discount booking limit, we begin to displace more and more full-fare passengers. The point at which the decrease in expected full-

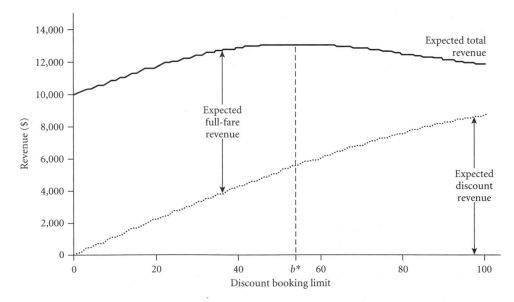

Figure 7.3 Expected discount, full-fare, and total revenues as a function of booking limit.

fare passengers exactly balances the gain from expected additional discount passengers is the optimal booking limit calculated by Littlewood's rule.

To summarize, Littlewood's rule determines the optimal discount booking limit in the case when discount demand books before full-fare demand. The optimal booking limit depends only on the forecast of full-fare demand, the aircraft capacity, and the fare ratio. It is not affected by the forecast of discount demand. However, the forecast of discount demand has a big impact on the sensitivity of expected revenue to the booking limit. When the forecast of discount demand is low, expected revenue is usually not very sensitive to the booking limit, within reasonable ranges. But when the forecast of discount demand is high, expected revenue becomes very sensitive to the booking limit. The lesson is that it is most critical to calculate precise booking limits when we forecast high levels of discount demand.

7.2.3 Littlewood's Rule with Independent Normal Demands

The two-class discount booking limit algorithm will find the optimal booking limit given any distribution of full-fare demand. But there is a particularly simple way to calculate the optimal discount booking limit when full-fare demand is normally distributed.[3] In this case,

$$F_f(x) = \Phi\left(\frac{x - \mu_f}{\delta_f}\right)$$

where $\Phi(x)$ is the standard cumulative normal distribution and μ_f and δ_f are the mean and standard deviation of full-fare demand, respectively. Littlewood's rule then implies that we want to find the value of b such that

$$\Phi\left(\frac{C - b - \mu_f}{\delta_f}\right) = 1 - \frac{p_d}{p_f}$$

We can see that the optimal discount booking limit and protection level satisfy

$$b^* = [C - \delta_f \Phi^{-1}(1 - p_d/p_f) - \mu_f]^+ \tag{7.5}$$

$$y^* = \min[\mu_f + \delta_f \Phi^{-1}(1 - p_d/p_f), C] \tag{7.6}$$

where $\Phi^{-1}(x)$ is the *inverse cumulative normal distribution*.[4]

Figure 7.4 shows $\Phi^{-1}(1 - p_d/p_f)$ as a function of the fare ratio p_d/p_f. From this figure and Equation 7.6 we can derive a number of important characteristics of the optimal discount booking limit. First of all, $\Phi^{-1}(1 - p_d/p_f)$ is a decreasing function of the fare ratio. This means that b^* is an *increasing* function of the fare ratio. Note that $\Phi^{-1}(1/2) = 0$, which means that $p_d = p_f/2$ implies that $b^* = C - \mu_f$; that is, it is optimal to set a protection level exactly equal to expected full-fare demand when the fare ratio is 1/2. For $p_d/p_f < 1/2$ it is optimal to protect *more* seats for full-fare demand than we expect to receive, and for $p_d/p_f > 1/2$ it is optimal to protect *fewer* seats than expected full-fare demand. In other words, the fare ratio determines whether we should save more or fewer seats than expected demand for full-fare passengers.

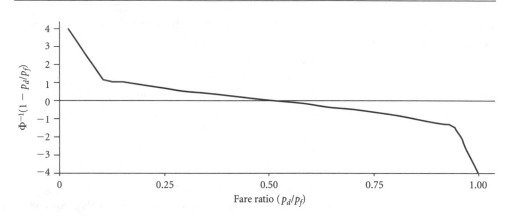

Figure 7.4   Inverse cumulative normal function of $1 - p_d/p_f$.

Example 7.3

A flight has a capacity of 100 seats and two fare classes. The full fare is $300, and full-fare demand is normally distributed with a mean of 70. If the discount fare is $150, the airline should protect exactly 70 seats for full-fare customers and set a booking limit of 30 for discount-fare demand. If the discount fare is $180, the airline should protect fewer than 70 seats for full-fare demand; if the discount fare is $120, the airline should protect more than 70 seats for full-fare demand. The optimal protection levels for each case can be determined from Equation 7.6.

Equation 7.6 shows that the optimal protection level is equal to the expected full-fare demand μ_f plus the standard deviation of full-fare demand δ_f times a term. Recall that $\delta_f > 0$ is a measure of the uncertainty in our forecast of full-fare demand. A higher value of δ_f means a flatter distribution and more uncertainty. What impact does it have on the optimal booking limit? First of all, notice that $\delta_f = 0$ implies that $b^* = [C - \mu_f]^+$. If we knew full-fare demand with certainty, we would protect exactly μ_f seats for full-fare demand.[5] Because we know that $d_f = \mu_f$ when $\delta = 0$, this is clearly the policy that will maximize expected revenue.

Of course, things would be too easy (and there would be no need for sophisticated revenue management) if companies knew future full-fare demand with certainty, so we need to consider the case when the standard deviation is greater than zero.[6] From Equation 7.6, we can see that y^* is a linear function of the standard deviation when full-fare demand is normally distributed. The effect of the standard deviation on the optimal protection level when mean full-fare demand is 50 is shown in Figure 7.5 for different values of the fare ratio, p_d/p_f.

The dependence of the protection level on full-fare standard deviation and the fare ratio is summarized in Table 7.2. When the fare ratio is exactly 1/2 or the standard deviation of full-fare demand is zero, then the optimal protection level for full-fare demand is equal to mean full-fare demand. If the fare ratio is less than 1/2, the optimal protection level will be greater than μ_f, and increasing the standard deviation will increase the protection level. If the fare ratio is greater than 1/2, the optimal protection level will be less than μ_f and will fall as the standard deviation increases.

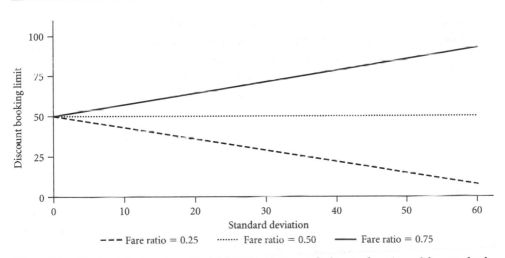

Figure 7.5 Optimal discount booking limit for a 100-seat flight as a function of the standard deviation of full-fare demand.

TABLE 7.2
Dependence of protection level y^* on the standard deviation of full-fare demand when full-fare demand is normally distributed

Fare ratio	Dependence of protection level
$p_d/p_f > 0.5$	y^* is less than mean full-fare demand and decreases with δ_f
$p_d/p_f = 0.5$	$y^* =$ mean full-fare demand
$p_d/p_f < 0.5$	y^* is greater than mean full-fare demand and increases with δ_f

7.2.4 Relation to Newsvendor Problem

Littlewood's rule has a close relationship to the so-called *critical fractile* (or *critical ratio*) solution to the optimal replenishment problem for perishable goods that is studied as part of operations management. Both capacity allocation and replenishment of perishable goods are themselves special cases of a classic problem known as the *newsvendor problem*. The newsvendor problem well predates revenue management; it was first identified and studied as early as 1888.

The newsvendor problem considers the situation in which a purchaser needs to order a quantity of some good in the face of uncertain demand. The problem got its name from the example of a newspaper salesperson who needs to determine how many newspapers to purchase at the beginning of the day to satisfy the day's uncertain demand. The key to this decision is that the newsvendor faces different "costs" if he purchases too much or too little. If he buys too many newspapers, then at the end of the day he will have unsold, worthless copies that he discards. If he buys too few, he will sell out of papers and turn away potentially profitable customers. The purchaser might be a retailer deciding how many units of a fashion good to order, or it might be a manufacturer ordering raw materials.

The solution to the newsvendor problem can be expressed in terms of the *overage cost* and the *underage cost* of the decision. The overage cost is the cost per unit of purchasing too many items; the underage cost is the unit cost of purchasing too few. Assume that the newsvendor buys newspapers for 20 cents apiece and sells them at 25 cents. His overage cost is 20 cents per unsold paper; his underage cost is the 5 cent profit that he forgoes for each missed sale. (Note that the overage cost is an actual monetary cost, while the underage cost is an opportunity cost.) If U is the underage cost and O is the overage cost, the optimal order quantity for the newsvendor is the value of Y such that

$$F(Y) = \frac{U}{U + O} \tag{7.7}$$

where $F(y)$ is the cumulative distribution on demand.

Example 7.4

When newspapers cost 20 cents and are sold for 25 cents, Equation 7.7 implies that the number of newspapers the vendor should purchase would be the smallest value of Y such that $F(Y) \geq 5/(20 + 5) = 0.2$.

Finding the optimal discount booking limit in the two-class case is analogous to the newsvendor problem. The airline needs to determine how many seats to protect (i.e., "order") to satisfy unknown full-fare demand. The airline's unit overage cost from protecting too many seats is a displaced discount fare: $O = p_d$. The underage cost is the revenue from a lost full-fare booking minus the discount fare: $U = p_f - p_d$. Substituting into Equation 7.7 means that the airline should set the protection level such that

$$F(y) = \frac{U}{U + O}$$

$$= \frac{p_f - p_d}{p_f}$$

$$= 1 - \frac{p_d}{p_f}$$

This is Littlewood's rule.

7.3 CAPACITY ALLOCATION WITH MULTIPLE FARE CLASSES

Littlewood's rule finds the optimal discount allocation in the case of two classes when the lower fare class books first. However, as discussed in Section 6.3, airlines are prolific price differentiators, often offering tens if not hundreds of different fares on a flight, such as special discount fares, corporate fares, and group fares in addition to the standard discount fares and full fare. An airline needs to manage the availability of all of these fares to maximize total contribution. The same holds true for any revenue management company selling multiple fare classes. More specifically, they need to set the nested booking limits within a booking control structure, as described in Section 6.5.2. This is the *multiclass capacity allocation* problem, and, predictably, it is more difficult to solve than the two-class model.

To analyze the multiclass model we make the following assumptions.

- A product has n fare classes, each with an associated fare. Fare classes are numbered in descending fare order, that is, $p_1 > p_2 > \cdots > p_n$. A fare class is called higher than another if it has a higher fare—thus, class 1 is the highest class and class n is the lowest class.

- Demand in each class is an independent random variable. We denote the demand in fare class i by d_i. Demand in class i follows a probability distribution $f_i(x)$ defined on integer $x \geq 0$, where $f_i(x)$ is the probability that demand for fare class i will be x. $F_i(x)$ denotes the probability that $d_i \leq x$.

- Demand books in increasing fare order. That is, the lowest-fare passengers (those paying p_n) book first, followed by the second-lowest-fare passengers and so on, so that the highest-fare passengers (those paying p_1) book last.

- There are no no-shows or cancellations.

- The objective function is to maximize expected revenue.[7]

The time convention for the multiclass model is shown in Figure 7.6. During the first period the airline sees only booking requests from the lowest-fare passengers, those paying p_n. At the end of this first booking period, the airline has accepted some number of bookings from these passengers, say, $x_n \geq 0$. During the second period, passengers paying the next-highest fare, p_{n-1}, start to book, and so on, until the last period, in which the highest-fare passengers—those paying p_1—seek to book. Note that the indices of the fare classes decrease as the time of departure approaches. (It may help to think of a countdown to departure as a way to remember this convention.)

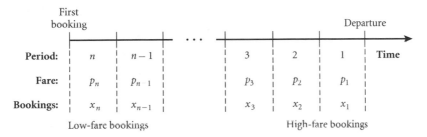

Figure 7.6 Booking process assumed in simple multiclass model.

The airline's decision at the start of each booking period j is how many bookings of type j it should accept. It knows how many bookings it has already accepted, namely, $\sum_{i=j+1}^{n} x_i$. Since there are no no-shows or cancellations, $C_j = [C - \sum_{i=j+1}^{n} x_i]$ is the unbooked capacity remaining at the beginning of period j. The airline also knows the demand distributions for future booking periods. Given this information, the airline needs to find the maximum number of bookings from class j to accept in order to maximize expected revenue. We call this quantity the *class j booking limit* and denote it by b_j. In this model, the airline only needs to calculate one booking limit at the start of each period, since it will receive bookings from only one fare class during the coming period. The airline can wait until it sees how many bookings it accepts in this period before setting the booking limits for the next higher class.

7.3.1 The Decision Tree Approach

To solve the multiclass booking limit problem, we work backwards. At the beginning of the final period the airline has C_1 seats remaining. Since there are no no-shows or cancellations, it is clearly optimal for the airline to allow all remaining seats to be booked. So $b_1 = C_1$. Next we consider period 2—the penultimate period before departure. At the beginning of period 2 the airline has C_2 seats remaining. It should be clear that the problem the airline faces at the beginning of the second period is exactly the two-fare-class problem we solved in Section 7.2. Therefore, the airline can maximize revenue by applying Littlewood's rule (Equation 7.2): The optimal booking limit is the smallest value of $0 \leq b_2 \leq C_2$ such that $F_1(C_2 - b_2) < 1 - p_2/p_1$.

Things get more complicated when we move backwards one period to calculate b_3. Conceptually, the tradeoff is similar to the two-class case: If we increase the booking limit in period 3, one of two things can happen. Either we receive an additional "type 3" passenger booking or we don't. If we don't, the net impact on total revenue of increasing the booking limit will be zero. If we do book an additional customer in period 3, we will receive a fare of p_3, but we run the risk of displacing a later-booking customer who would pay a higher fare—either p_1 or p_2. There is no easy way to calculate either the probability that we will displace a booking or the conditional probability of which type of booking will be displaced. However, the fundamental tradeoff remains the same as in the two-class case—we want to set the booking limit that balances the risks of spoilage and dilution.

The period 3 problem is illustrated in Figure 7.7, where q_2 is the probability that increasing the class 3 booking limit will displace a class 2 passenger and q_1 is the probability that it will displace a class 1 passenger. From this tree we can see that the optimal class 3 booking limit depends on the probability that an additional class 3 booking would displace a higher fare booking and the fare of the booking that would be displaced. If we knew the displacement probabilities q_1 and q_2, it would be straightforward to roll back the decision

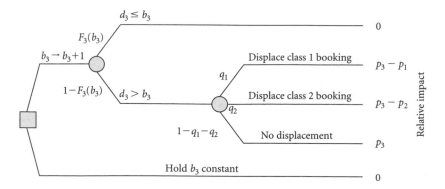

Figure 7.7 Capacity allocation decision tree for period 3 prior to departure.

tree to solve for the optimal b_3 (Exercise 1). Unfortunately, there is no easy way to calculate the displacement probabilities for three or more fare classes. As a result, the solution techniques for finding the optimal booking limits for three or more fare classes require the use of dynamic programming.[8]

While the techniques for finding the optimal booking limits and protection levels in the multiclass problem are not mathematically difficult, they can be computationally intensive, particularly when they need to be applied to thousands of flights in a limited period of time. For this reason, airlines, hotels, rental car companies, and their revenue management brethren typically do not calculate the *optimal* multiclass booking limits. Rather, they utilize a heuristic to determine good but not necessarily optimal booking limits. The most popular of these heuristics are the expected marginal seat revenue (EMSR) approaches, especially EMSR-a and EMSR-b. These are very fast and almost always find booking limits that generate expected revenue very close to the theoretical optimum.

7.3.2 Expected Marginal Seat Revenue (EMSR) Heuristics

Expected marginal seat revenue (EMSR) comes in (at least) two flavors: EMSR-a and EMSR-b. Both EMSR-a and EMSR-b were introduced by Peter Belobaba in his PhD dissertation and a series of subsequent papers (Belobaba 1987, 1989). Both are based on approximating the multiclass problem by a series of two-class problems and applying Littlewood's rule to obtain a solution.

EMSR-a. Expected marginal seat revenue—version a is the most well-known heuristic for the capacity allocation problem. It is based on the idea of calculating protection levels for the current class relative to each of the higher classes using Littlewood's rule. These protection levels are then summed to create the protection level for the current class. For example, if we are in class 3, EMSR-a would calculate a protection level for class 3 against class 1 (which we denote by y_{31}) using the form of Littlewood's rule in Equation 7.3:

$$y_{31} = F_1^{-1}\left(\frac{p_1 - p_3}{p_1}\right)$$

and a protection level for class 3 against class 2, which we denote by y_{31} according to

$$y_{32} = F_2^{-1}\left(\frac{p_2 - p_3}{p_2}\right)$$

(Recall that C_3 is the unbooked capacity we have at the beginning of booking period 3.) The EMSR-a protection level for class 3, y_3, is calculated as the sum of these two protection levels; that is,

$$y_3 = y_{31} + y_{32}$$
$$= F_1^{-1}\left(\frac{p_1 - p_3}{p_1}\right) + F_2^{-1}\left(\frac{p_2 - p_3}{p_2}\right)$$

or

$$b_3 = \left[C_3 - F_1^{-1}\left(\frac{p_1 - p_3}{p_1} \right) - F_2^{-1}\left(\frac{p_2 - p_3}{p_2} \right) \right]^+$$

EMSR-a can be generalized to any number of fare classes. For $j \geq 2$, the EMSR-a protection level y_j is

$$y_j = \sum_{i=1}^{j-1} F_i^{-1}\left(\frac{p_i - p_j}{p_i} \right) \tag{7.8}$$

If demands are normally distributed for each fare class, the EMSR-a protection level for class j is

$$y_j = \sum_{i=1}^{j-1} \mu_i + \delta_i \Phi^{-1}\left(\frac{p_i - p_j}{p_i} \right)$$

which is quite easily computed using standard cumulative normal distribution tables. It is easy to confirm that EMSR-a reduces to Littlewood's rule in the case of two fare classes.

EMSR-b. Expected marginal seat revenue—version b assumes that a passenger displaced by an additional booking would be paying a fare equal to a weighted average of future fares. EMSR-b creates an "artificial class" with demand equal to the sum of the demands for all the future periods and a fare equal to the average expected fare from future bookings. It then uses Littlewood's rule to calculate the booking limit of the current class j with respect to the artificial class. EMSR-b assumes that the "expected fare" of the displaced booking is equal to the expected fare of future demand. This is an approximation because limits will also be set on higher-fare booking, so the demand accepted won't generally be equal to the mean.

To formalize EMSR-b, assume that demand in all classes follows a normal distribution, with the demand in class i having a mean of μ_i and a standard deviation of δ_i. Assume we are at the beginning of period $j \geq 2$ and want to calculate the booking limit b_j. EMSR-b then proceeds as if we were solving a two-class problem. EMSR-b assumes that demand for the artificial class is normally distributed with mean demand μ, average fare p, and standard deviation δ given by

$$\mu = \sum_{i=1}^{j-1} \mu_i, \qquad p = \sum_{i=1}^{j-1} p_i \mu_i / \mu, \qquad \delta = \sqrt{\sum_{i=1}^{j-1} \delta_i^2}. \tag{7.9}$$

(The formulas for the mean and the standard deviation are standard for the sum of any independent random variables. See Appendix B for more details.) We can use the version of Littlewood's rule for normal distributions in Equation 7.6 to write

$$y_j = \min\left[\mu + \delta \Phi^{-1}\left(\frac{p - p_j}{p} \right), C \right] \tag{7.10}$$

as the formula for EMSR-b when demands are normally distributed. Again, it is easy to confirm that EMSR-b reduces to Littlewood's rule in the case of two fare classes.

Comparison of EMSR heuristics. It is difficult to make definitive statements about the relative merits of the two EMSR heuristics. There are cases when EMSR-a gives higher booking limits than EMSR-b and cases when the opposite is true. More pertinently, there are cases when EMSR-a results in higher revenue than EMSR-b, and vice versa. Both appear to give solutions close to the optimal booking limits in most realistic cases, and both generally capture a high percentage of the optimal revenue. One set of studies has showed that EMSR-b was consistently within 0.5% of the optimal revenue, while EMSR-a led to revenues that were more than 1.5% lower than optimal in some cases (Belobaba 1992). Other studies (and much practical experience) has shown that both EMSR heuristics tend to perform well in almost all realistic cases and that neither strictly dominates the other.

Example 7.5

Talluri and van Ryzin (2004) ran a series of simulations comparing the performance of the two EMSR heuristics with the optimal policy for a single flight with four fare classes and independent normal demands. The fares, mean demand, and standard deviation of demand for each class are shown in Table 7.3 along with the protection levels calculated by each policy. The results of the simulations are shown in Table 7.4 for different levels of total seating capacity. In this case, EMSR-b performed slightly better than EMSR-a; however, both policies performed within 1% of the optimal revenue for all values of seating capacity. This high level of performance is a good indication of why the EMSR heuristics are so popular in practice.

It is widely felt that the additional revenues from solving the optimal booking control problem do not generally justify the extensive additional computations that would be required relative to using an EMSR heuristic. As a result, EMSR-b has become the standard for calculating booking limits for a single resource.[9]

TABLE 7.3
Fares, demand data, and protection levels for Example 7.5.

| Class (j) | Fare (p_j) | DEMAND STATISTICS | | PROTECTION LEVELS | | |
		Mean (μ_j)	Std. Dev. (δ_j)	Optimal	EMSR-a	EMSR-b
1	$1,050	17.3	5.8	9.7	9.8	9.8
2	$950	45.1	15.0	54.0	50.4	53.2
3	$699	39.6	13.2	98.2	91.6	96.8
4	$520	34.0	11.3			

SOURCE: From Talluri and van Ryzin (2004).

TABLE 7.4
*Revenue from the optimal policy and the two EMSR heuristics
as a function of total capacity for Example 7.5*

| Capacity | Optimal Revenue | EMSR-A | | EMSR-B | |
		Revenue	% Optimal	Revenue	% Optimal
90	$74,003	$73,950	99.3	$74,000	100
100	$79,429	$79,164	99.67	$79,426	100
110	$84,884	$84,554	99.61	$84,862	99.7
120	$89,879	$89,668	99.77	$89,875	100
130	$95,054	$94,899	99.84	$95,054	100

SOURCE: From Talluri and van Ryzin (2004).

7.3.3 Bid Pricing

We have seen that optimal nested booking limits have the property that if one fare class is open, then all higher fare classes will be open. This means that one of three conditions must hold when the allocations for a resource are optimized; either

1. All fare classes are open, or

2. All fare classes are closed, or

3. There is an open fare class such that all higher classes are open and all lower classes are closed.

This suggests the following rule:

> *Accept a single-seat booking request if its associated fare is greater than or equal to the fare in the lowest open class. Otherwise reject it.*

Example 7.6

A flight departure has six fare classes. Two weeks before departure, fare classes 1, 2, and 3 are open while classes 4, 5, and 6 are closed. The class 3 fare is $250 and the class 4 fare is $210. If the next booking request has a fare greater than or equal to $250, it will be accepted; otherwise it will be rejected.

This simple rule to control bookings is called *bid pricing*, and the minimum acceptable fare is called the *bid price*. In bid pricing, the fare of a booking request is compared to a *hurdle rate* (the bid price) for a product and accepted if and only if the fare exceeds the bid price. When the bid price is zero, any booking request with positive net contribution will be accepted—this is equivalent to having all fare classes open. When the bid price is set to any number higher than the highest fare, no booking requests will be accepted—this is equivalent to having all fare classes closed. The seller can use the bid price as an intensity control, raising the bid price when he wishes to reduce sales and increase average price and lowering the bid price when he wishes to increase sales and accept a lower average price.

Bid pricing has an appealing simplicity to it. It requires only calculating and updating a single number—the bid price. It avoids the complexity involved in recalculating multiple booking limits. *If* bid prices are continually updated *and* each request is for a single unit of resource (i.e., a single airline seat or a single hotel room night) *and* demand for different fare classes were independent, a system under which booking requests are evaluated only against a bid price could capture at least as much revenue as the standard booking limit approaches.

The bid price criteria should remind you of the rule we established in Section 5.3 that a request for a constrained resource should be accepted only if the associated price exceeds the opportunity cost of the resource. There is a reason for this—the bid price for a resource is the opportunity cost for that resource. The decision tree approach described in Section 7.2.1 makes this explicit—we should accept a booking only if its fare exceeds the expected revenue we could realize from that unit of capacity in the future, i.e., its opportunity cost. Bid pricing exploits the following equivalence.

$$\text{Bid price for a resource} = \text{Fare in the lowest open fare class}$$

$$= \text{Opportunity cost for the resource}$$

Bid pricing is simply an actualization of the rule that a unit of a constrained perishable resource should be sold only if the price received is greater than the opportunity cost.

Despite the appealing simplicity of bid pricing, most revenue management companies do not use "pure" bid pricing systems. Rather, they rely upon booking limits, as described in Section 6.5.2. If bid pricing is so good, why is it not used by more revenue management companies? There are three main reasons.

1. Bid prices give only *marginal* guidance — that is, a bid price can only tell us whether or not we should accept a booking request for a single seat. The bid price does not give a definitive answer to the question of whether or not we should accept a booking request for more than one seat.[10]

2. The bid price for a resource jumps upward any time a booking is accepted and decreases any time an existing booking is cancelled. For bid prices to provide optimal control, they would need to be calculated at least every time a booking or cancellation takes place. This would be computationally infeasible given the volume of bookings and cancellations that an airline, rental car company, or large hotel chain needs to process.

3. As described in Chapter 6, booking limits were built into the airline reservation systems from their inception. The nested booking controls described in section 6.5 were the only way available to airlines and other revenue management companies to implement capacity allocation.

Despite these practical concerns, bid pricing is an important concept. Since the bid price on a leg approximates the opportunity cost for a resource, it is a good estimate of the additional revenue that could be achieved by acquiring an additional unit of resource. Second, bid prices play an extremely important part in network revenue management, as we see in Chapter 8.

7.4 CAPACITY ALLOCATION WITH DEPENDENT DEMANDS

The models we have considered so far assume that demand in each fare class is independent of demand in the other fare classes. Perhaps even more surprising, they assume that demand in each fare class is independent of whether other classes are opened or closed. This is the assumption of perfect market segmentation (see Chapter 4). Standard capacity allocation models, such as Littlewood's rule and the EMSR heuristics, assume no cannibalization — opening a discount class has no effect on full-fare demand. Full-fare passengers are either unwilling or unable to purchase at the discount fare, and none of the discount passengers would purchase the product at the full fare.

The assumption of fare class independence does not reflect the real world. In reality, there are no such things as "full-fare customers" and "discount customers"; there are only potential buyers searching for the alternative that best meets their needs. In fact, the assumption of independence fails even at the most basic level of airline segmentation. There are business travelers who book early in order to take advantage of discount fares, just as there are leisure travelers who would be willing to pay full fare for travel but are more than happy to purchase at the discount fare. This means that some fraction of the customers who are refused when we close the discount fare will go on to purchase at the full fare and that we cannot really treat the two demands as independent. Rather, the full-fare demand will depend on whether or not the discount fare class is opened or closed. When we close discount fares, we would expect more full-fare demand because some of the discount-fare customers will go ahead to purchase at full fare when the discount fare is not available.

As revenue management systems became more widely used, flight controllers noticed that closing a discount fare class would often lead to increased demand in higher classes. This phenomenon was termed *buy-up* or *sell-up*. By the same token, opening a discount fare class would often lead to decreased demand in higher classes—cannibalization. Revenue controllers would close discount classes earlier than recommended by the revenue management system because they knew that they would gain benefits from buy-up.

Buy-up and cannibalization are not separate phenomena. As Bill Brunger, vice president of revenue management for Continental Airlines, put it, "Passengers do not come with Y-Class or M-Class stamped on their foreheads." Rather, customers search for the best combination of fare and travel option that meets their needs. The Internet increased visibility of all airline fares and their accessibility to all customers. As a result, the difference between full-fare and discount fares has grown tremendously—by one estimate the average full fare paid in 2002 was *seven times* the average discount fare for the same trip (Donofrio 2002). This provides a tremendous incentive for all customers to shop for lower fares.

The assumption of fare class independence was built into revenue management from the beginning. The reasons for this were twofold. First of all, the most pressing need facing the airlines was to develop systems quickly that enabled them to respond to the challenge of low-cost competitors and to manage the exploding number of fares in the marketplace. Rapidly implementing relatively simple approaches was more important than waiting to solve every aspect of the problem. The second reason was that, in many cases, the assumption of perfect segmentation was not too bad. The booking fences between discount and full-fare segments were felt to be fairly effective. Furthermore, for international airlines, regional pricing was a major part of revenue management strategy. In the 1980s, the fare paid in Japan for a ticket would often be 50% more than the same ticket purchased in Europe or the United States. In the 1990s, one European airline estimated that 100% of its profit was due to its ability to sell tickets in certain overseas markets at fares higher than its own market. Prior to the rise of the Internet, this geographical discrimination was quite powerful and not subject to high levels of cannibalization.

7.4.1 Demand Dependence with Two Fare Classes

We can modify the marginal analysis approach of Figure 7.1 to find the optimal booking limit under imperfect segmentation with two fare classes. We assume as before that the discount fare is p_d and the full fare is p_f, with $p_f > p_d$. For this analysis, use new definitions of demand:

$$d_d = \text{Total discount demand}$$

$$d_f = \text{Total full-fare demand } \textit{assuming all discount bookings are accepted}$$

In addition, we will define α as the fraction of rejected discount demand that will seek to book a full fare, with $0 \leq \alpha \leq 1$, if discount seats are not available. The actual full-fare demand the airline sees will be a function of the discount booking limit and can be written as

$$\hat{d}_f = d_f + \alpha[d_d - b]^+$$

This means that increasing the booking limit b will decrease expected full-fare demand by α if discount demand exceeds the booking limit and will have no effect on full-fare demand otherwise.

We can relate this model to the willingness-to-pay approach discussed in Chapter 3. Specifically, this model is equivalent to assuming that there are d_d customers with a w.t.p. for the discount product that is greater than p_d. Of these, αd_d also have a w.t.p. for the full-fare product than is greater than p_f: If the discount product is not available, they will buy the full-fare product. $\alpha - 0$ corresponds to the case of perfect segmentation. Finally, there are d_f customers who have a w.t.p. for the full-fare product that is greater than p_f and whose willingness-to-pay for the discount product is lower than p_d. Of course, we would expect d_d, d_f, and α to change if we changed the fares p_d and p_f.

The decision tree for the two-class model with demand dependence is shown in Figure 7.8. The only difference from the basic two-class allocation model in Figure 7.1 occurs when discount demand is greater than the booking limit *and* full-fare demand is less than the protection level, $C - b$. In this case, increasing the booking limit by 1 leads to an additional discount booking, but there is a probability of α that this increased discount booking cannibalizes a future full-fare booking. The net impact on expected profitability is $p_d - \alpha p_f$.

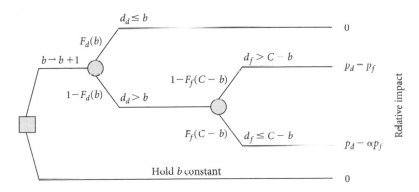

Figure 7.8 Two-class capacity allocation with demand dependence.

It is apparent that the expected marginal impact of increasing the booking limit by 1 in this case is given by

$$E[h(b)] = F_d(b)0 + [1 - F_d(b)]\{[1 - F_f(C - b)](p_d - p_f) + F_f(C - b)(p_d - \alpha p_f)\}$$
$$= [1 - F_d(b)][p_d - \alpha p_f - (1 - F_f(C - b))(1 - \alpha)p_f] \qquad (7.11)$$

As usual, the direction of the change in expected profit will be determined by the sign of the term $p_d - \alpha p_f - F_f(C - b)(1 - \alpha)p_f$. If this term is greater than zero, increasing the booking limit by 1 will lead to increased expected revenue. If it is less than zero, increasing the booking limit will lead to decreased expected revenue. Note that if $\alpha \geq p_d/p_f$, the term on the right will be less than or equal to zero for all values of b. This corresponds to the case where cannibalization overwhelms demand induction. In this case, we know immediately that the optimal booking limit is $b^* = 0$.

Assume now that $p_d > \alpha p_f$. From Equation 7.11 we can see that we are looking for the protection level y^* that solves

$$1 - F_f(y^*) = \frac{p_d - \alpha p_f}{(1 - \alpha)p_f} \qquad (7.12)$$

Note that Equation 7.12 reduces to Littlewood's rule when $\alpha = 0$.

We can also write Equation 7.12 as

$$1 - F_f(y^*) = \frac{1}{1 - \alpha}\left(\frac{p_d}{p_f} - \alpha\right) \qquad (7.13)$$

We call $\left[\frac{1}{1 - \alpha}\left(\frac{p_d}{p_f} - \alpha\right)\right]^+$ the *modified fare ratio*. Note that Equation 7.13 is the same as Littlewood's rule using $\frac{1}{1 - \alpha}\left(\frac{p_d}{p_f} - \alpha\right)$ instead of the fare ratio p_d/p_f. Since the modified fare ratio is less than the actual fare ratio, the impact of demand dependence is to reduce the discount booking limit (equivalently, increase the full-fare protection level) from the case with no demand dependency.

Note that when full-fare demand is normally distributed, the optimal protection level is

$$y^* = \mu + \delta\Phi^{-1}\left[\frac{1}{1 - \alpha}\left(1 - \frac{p_d}{p_f}\right)\right]$$

7.4.2 Modified EMSR Heuristics

Both EMSR-a and EMSR-b can be modified to incorporate imperfect segmentations. The modifications are based on the assumption that when a class closes, rejected demand for that class may buy up to the next highest class—but not to any higher classes. For example, if we close class 3, some class 3 demand may seek to buy in class 2 but not in class 1. We can easily derive modified versions of the EMSR heuristics under this simple assumption.

Define α_j for $j = 2, 3, \ldots, n$ as the fraction of class j customers who would purchase in the next-higher class $j - 1$ if class j is closed. Thus, α_3 is the fraction of class 3 customers who would "buy up" to class 2 if they find class 3 closed when they request a booking. α_j is referred to as the *buy-up factor* for class j. Note that there is no buy-up factor for the highest fare class. Then, for the case of normal demand distributions, EMSR-a and EMSR-b can be extended to incorporate buy-up factors as follows:

EMSR-a with buy-up:
$$y_j = \mu_{j-1} + \delta_{j-1}\Phi^{-1}\left[\frac{1}{1-\alpha}\left(1 - \frac{p_j}{p_{j-1}}\right)\right]$$
$$- \sum_{i=1}^{j-2}\left[\delta_i\Phi^{-1}\left(1 - \frac{p_j}{p_i}\right) - \mu_i\right]$$

EMSR-b with buy-up:
$$y_j = \mu + \delta\Phi^{-1}\left[\frac{1}{1-\alpha}\left(1 - \frac{p_j}{f}\right)\right]$$

where μ, p, and δ for the modified EMSR-b algorithm are as defined in Equation 7.9.

Modified EMSR-a calculates the protection levels for class j against every higher class under the assumption that buy-up will only occur to the next-highest class, $j-1$, if we close j. It then subtracts the sum of all these protection levels from the remaining capacity to determine the booking limit for class j. EMSR-b assumes that buy-up will occur to the "aggregate class" consisting of all the higher classes and calculates the booking limit using the version of Littlewood's rule in Equation 7.16.

These two modifications to the EMSR heuristics have been studied by Belobaba and Weatherford (1996) who showed that the modified EMSR heuristics provide additional revenue when buy-up is present. The modified EMSR heuristics are easy to implement, and versions of them have been used by many revenue management companies. However, they have some disadvantages. They require a set of $n-1$ buy-up factors to be estimated and stored for each flight. They also require redefining the demand for each fare class as the demand that would be received if the next-higher class is open. They do not incorporate the possibility of buy-up from class j to classes higher than $j-1$.

Perhaps more fundamentally, the modified EMSR approaches are a "heuristic grafted on to another heuristic." They are not derived from a fundamental model of consumer choice. Rather, they assume that passengers have M-Class and Y-Class stamped on their heads and that only some of the M-Class passengers will buy up to Y-Class if M-Class is closed. Development of more fundamental models including consumer choice is an active research area.

7.5 CAPACITY ALLOCATION IN ACTION

We have described several techniques for calculating booking limits. These techniques need to be used within the context of a booking control structure, as described in Section 6.5. In practice, booking limits are periodically calculated offline for a flight and transmitted to the reservation system where they are used to control bookings. The combination of periodic recalculation of booking limits and the nested booking limits within the reservation system defines a *dynamic booking control process*.

Dynamic Booking Control Process

1. Calculate the initial booking limits for a flight.

2. When a booking request for class j is received, compare the number of seats requested with the current booking limit for the class.

3. If the number of seats requested exceeds the booking limit for class j, reject the request and go to step 6.

4. If the number of seats requested is within the booking limit for class j, accept the request. Depending on the capabilities of the reservation system, either (a) decrement the booking limits for classes with positive availability by the number of seats accepted or (b) decrement the booking limits for *all* classes by the number of seats accepted.

5. When a booking cancels, either (a) increment the booking limits for classes with positive availability by the number of seats cancelled (irreversible) or (b) increment to booking limits for *all* classes by the number of seats cancelled (reversible).

6. Periodically recalculate all booking limits based on total bookings and demand expected in each class until departure. (This recalculation is often called a *reoptimization*.)

This dynamic booking control process makes no assumption about the nature of the reoptimization approach being used or the frequency with which reoptimizations occur. And, in fact, there is considerable variation among companies in the optimization approaches used and the frequency and situations under which they are applied. There is a general belief that frequent reoptimization is important—particularly when demand is changing rapidly or departure is approaching and bookings and cancellations are being received at a high rate. Often, the tradeoff is between using a more complex algorithm and reoptimizing less often and using a simpler algorithm and reoptimizing more often. These issues are the topics of ongoing research and are by no means settled.

7.6 MEASURING CAPACITY ALLOCATION EFFECTIVENESS

We saw in Chapter 6 that revenue per available seat mile (RASM) is the metric most widely used to measure the overall effectiveness of revenue management at an airline. RASM is a good high-level measure, but it does not tell the entire story. It is often not immediately clear why RASM is high or low in a particular market. Are we achieving a high RASM in a particular market relative to the competition because we have superior service? superior marketing? better revenue management? all of these? RASM by itself does not address the important need to isolate and measure the effects of revenue management separately from all other influences in a market. The need to understand the effects of revenue management is important because revenue management software systems are expensive, usually requiring millions of dollars of investment in software and hardware. Revenue management programs are also expensive to operate—a major airline may have a department of 50 or more people dedicated to running the revenue management system and reviewing and updating its forecasts and recommendations. How can management be convinced that this expensive and somewhat esoteric department is yielding results that justify this investment? A metric specifically targeted at measuring revenue management effectiveness is required.

The most popular approach to measuring revenue management effectiveness is the *rev-*

enue opportunity model originally developed by American Airlines.[11] The revenue opportunity model assumes we have a record of all the booking requests we received for a flight—those we accepted and those we rejected. We then measure the revenue that could be achieved from a specific flight under two extreme cases. In the base case, bookings are accepted in the order in which they are received until the capacity constraint is reached or demand is exhausted, whichever comes first. The revenue achieved in the base case is the flight's performance without any revenue management. In the "perfect revenue management" case, bookings are accepted in decreasing order of revenue until demand is exhausted or the capacity constraint is reached. This represents a case in which we achieved as much revenue as possible given the demands for different fare classes. Of course, this level of performance is not achievable because it would require perfect foresight on future demand.

It should be clear that the revenue achieved under "perfect revenue management" will always be greater than or equal to the revenue achieved under "no revenue management." If the flight is full, the revenue achieved under any actual revenue management program will generally lie between these extremes—better than no revenue management but never better than perfect revenue management.[12] The *total revenue opportunity* on a flight is the difference between the revenue achieved from perfect revenue management and the revenue achieved from no revenue management. Then the *revenue opportunity metric* is the revenue actually achieved from that flight minus the revenue that would have been achieved under no revenue management expressed as a percentage of the total revenue opportunity.

Example 7.7

If the maximum possible revenue for a flight is $50,000, revenue from "no revenue management" is $35,000, and an airline actually realized $45,000 from the flight, then the revenue opportunity metric (ROM) for that departure would be

$$\text{ROM} = (\$45,000 - \$35,000)/(\$50,000 - \$35,000) = \$10,000/\$15,000 = 67\%$$

ROM has been used by airlines, hotels, and other RM companies to measure the effectiveness of their revenue management programs. American Airlines claimed that their systemwide ROM increased from 30% in 1988 to 49% in 1990 as the result of better revenue management systems and processes (Smith et al. 1992). ROM has also proven useful in evaluating the performance of different forecasting and optimization algorithms as well as in measuring the performance of revenue managers. However, it can be sensitive to changes in market conditions. For example, the ROM for a flight with very low demand will always be close to 100%, since every booking will be accepted. On the other hand, a flight with high uncertainty in high-fare demand (a high standard deviation) will tend to have a lower ROM than one with the same expected high-fare demand but less uncertainty (a lower standard deviation). This means that changes in ROM for a flight or group of flights may be due to changes in the underlying structure of demand rather than to changes in revenue management effectiveness.

7.7 SUMMARY

- The capacity allocation problem is how to regulate booking requests for a product consisting of a single resource over time in order to maximize revenue. For most revenue management companies, this is the problem of periodically setting and updating booking limits for a nested booking control structure, as described in Section 6.5.2. The problem is typically posed assuming that bookings occur in order of increasing fare.

- At the heart of the two-class problem is the tradeoff between accepting too many discount bookings and cannibalizing future full-fare demand and accepting too few discount bookings and leaving with empty seats. Littlewood's rule finds the booking limit that balances these two risks in order to maximize total expected contribution.

- The underlying tradeoff when there are multiple fare classes is the same as in the two-class problem: Accepting too many early discount bookings may cannibalize future full-fare bookings, whereas accepting too few may lead to empty seats. However, when there are more than two fare classes, there is no easy closed-form solution for finding the optimal booking limits. Rather, airlines and other revenue management companies typically rely on various heuristic approaches, of which EMSR-a and EMSR-b are the best known.

- The basic EMSR approaches to multiple-fare class booking control do not incorporate the fact that opening or closing a fare class will change the anticipated demand in other fare classes for the same product. Typically, the EMSR heuristics are modified to incorporate the phenomenon of dependent demand, also known as *buy-up* and *sell-down*.

- Typically, the decision whether or not a particular booking request is accepted is based on whether or not there is sufficient availability for that class in the booking system. The function of the revenue management system is to periodically update the booking limits in the system based on current bookings and changes in the market.

- A common way for airlines and other revenue management companies to measure the effectiveness of their capacity allocation is by using the revenue optimization metric, or ROM. ROM measures the revenue actually achieved as a percentage of the maximum revenue that could have been achieved if the supplier had "perfect" forecasts of future demand. ROM is not so much an absolute measure, because underlying uncertainty in demand ensures that 100% ROM can never be achieved. But it is a good relative measure of how well different flights are being managed.

Capacity allocation is the first of the constituents of revenue management we will study. Network management, which is treated in the next chapter, extends the ideas from this chapter to the case in which a company is selling products that consist of more than one resource. Overbooking, treated in Chapter 9, extends the idea of capacity allocation still further, to the situation in which bookings can cancel or not show.

7.8 EXERCISES

1. Roll back the decision tree in Figure 7.7 to determine a formula for the period 3 booking limit that would maximize expected net revenue given the displacement probabilities q_1 and q_2.

2. Granite State Airlines serves the route between New York and Portsmouth, NH, with a single-flight-daily 100-seat aircraft. The one-way fare for discount tickets is $100, and the one-way fare for full-fare tickets is $150. Discount tickets can be booked up until one week in advance, and all discount passengers book before all full-fare passengers. Over a long history of observation, the airline estimates that full-fare demand is normally distributed, with a mean of 56 passengers and a standard deviation of 23, while discount-fare demand is normally distributed, with a mean of 88 passengers and a standard deviation of 44.

   a. A consultant tells the airline they can maximize expected revenue by optimizing the booking limit. What is the optimal booking limit?

   b. The airline has been setting a booking limit of 44 on discount demand, to preserve 56 seats for full-fare demand. What is their expected revenue per flight under this policy? (Hint: Use a spreadsheet.)

   c. What is the expected gain from the optimal booking limit over the original booking limit?

   d. A low-fare competitor enters the market and Granite State Airlines sees its discount demand drop to 44 passengers per flight, with a standard-deviation of 30. Full-fare demand is unchanged. What is the new optimal booking limit?

3. Granite State Airlines also serves the route between Washington, DC (National), and Portsmouth, NH, with a single flight daily. The airline sells both discount-fare and full-fare tickets. The airline has assigned a 100-seat aircraft to the flight. Using Littlewood's rule, the airline has determined that the optimal discount-fare booking limit for a flight departing in two weeks is 40.

   a. What is the protection level for the flight?

   b. The flight controller has learned that the annual Yorkshire Terrier Fancier's Convention will be held in Portsmouth in two weeks. As a result, he increased the forecast of mean discount-fare demand by 50% over its previous value. The full-fare forecast remained the same. What are the new booking limits and protection levels for this flight?

   c. Right after learning about the Yorkshire Terrier Fancier's Convention, the flight controller learned that, due to maintenance problems, there will also be a switch of aircraft on the flight. Instead of a 100-seat aircraft, the flight will be served by a 120-seat aircraft. What are the new booking limits and protection levels for this flight?

d. The full fare for this flight is $200 and the discount fare is $100. What is the expected full-fare demand for this flight, assuming that both discount-fare and full-fare demand follow normal distributions?

NOTES

1. We assume $F_d(b) < 1$; that is, there is some probability that discount demand will exceed the current booking limit. Otherwise, changing the booking limit has no effect on expected revenue.

2. Technically, the sequential algorithm finds the smallest *integer* value of b such that $F_f(C - b^*) < 1 - p_d/p_f$. However, it is much more convenient to work with the equality version in Equation 7.2, with the understanding that the solution will need to be rounded to an integer before it can be implemented.

3. We will be using the *discrete* version of the normal distribution here, so some of the expressions that follow need to be treated with care. See Appendix B for details.

4. That is, if $\Phi(y) = x$, then $\Phi^{-1}(x) = y$. Some properties of the normal distribution are discussed in Appendix B.

5. This assumes that $\mu_f \leq C$: If $\mu_f > C$, we would set the discount booking limit to zero and protect the entire plane for full-fare bookings.

6. Airlines typically find that the standard deviation of future demand ranges from 25% to 75% or more of the expected demand. This is equivalent to saying that the *coefficient of variation*, defined as δ_f/μ_f, ranges from 0.25 to 0.75.

7. As before, we can extend this to maximizing expected contribution by using net contribution instead of fare.

8. See Curry (1990), Wollmer (1992), and Brumelle and McGill (1993) for three different solution approaches. A comparison among these three approaches is given by Li and Oum (2002).

9. See Boyd and Bilegan (2003) and Talluri and van Ryzin (2004) for useful surveys on industry practice.

10. To be clear, if the average fare associated with a multiple-seat booking is less than the bid price, it is optimal to reject the request. But if the fare is greater than the bid price, it is not necessarily optimal to accept the request.

11. The revenue opportunity model was first described by Smith, Leimkuhler, and Darrow (1992).

12. It is possible for achieved revenue to be lower than the "no revenue management" case if too many early-booking requests were rejected in anticipation of future bookings that did not materialize.

8 | NETWORK MANAGEMENT

8.1 BACKGROUND AND INTRODUCTION

When every product offered by a supplier uses only a single resource, the supplier can maximize total profitability by maximizing the profitability of each resource independently. For example, a Broadway show can maximize total revenue over a season by setting prices and availabilities that maximize revenue independently for each performance.[1] Once a seller with constrained capacity begins selling products that use multiple resources—such as an airline selling tickets on connecting flights or a hotel selling multiple-night stays—the revenue management problem becomes much more complex. The seller can no longer maximize total contribution by maximizing contribution from each resource independently. Rather, he needs to consider the interactions among the various products he sells and their effect on his ability to sell other products. This is the challenge of *network management*—the topic of this chapter.

Chapter 7 describes the techniques used to maximize expected profitability for a single resource. This is all that is needed by airlines such as Southwest, JetBlue, and Ryan Air that only allow single-leg bookings. These airlines—like the Broadway show—can maximize total profitability by maximizing the profitability of each resource independently. However, this approach will not maximize system profitability for airlines that offer passengers the opportunity to buy tickets for two or more connecting flight legs. Hotels and rental car companies also sell multiple-resource products, since hotel guests can stay for more than one night and rental car customers can rent for more than a day. *Network management* is applicable to any company controlling a set of constrained and perishable resources and selling products that consist of combinations of those resources.

In Section 8.2 we introduce the network management problem and the types of industries in which it applies. We give some idea of the complexity of the problem and show why a simple and intuitive "greedy heuristic" does not work. We then present various solution approaches to the network management problem. One approach is linear programming. However, it is a computationally intensive procedure that can only be run on a periodic basis. In the interim, most airlines use some version of *virtual nesting* to manage booking requests. We will discuss virtual nesting and the important concept of *net local fare*, which is a consistent way to rank (and hence nest) network booking requests. We will then present *bid pricing*, an important alternative to linear programming for network management. Section 8.7 discusses the issues involved in implementing network management.

8.2 WHEN IS NETWORK MANAGEMENT APPLICABLE?

Network management is important in any revenue management industry that sells products consisting of more than one resource. As shown in Table 6.7, there are some revenue management industries, such as cruise lines and sporting events, in which multiresource products do not play a major role.[2] In the industries shown in Table 8.1, network management can lead to substantial increases in profitability over managing revenue by fare class alone.

TABLE 8.1
Examples of multiresource products from various revenue management industries

Industry	Resource unit	Multiresource product
Passenger Airline	Seat on a flight leg	Multi-leg itinerary
Hotel	Room Night	Multi-night stay
Rental Car	Rental Day	Multi-day rental
Passenger Train	Leg	Multi-leg trip
Container Shipping	Leg	Multi-leg routing

As shown in Table 6.7, network management is very important to business hotels and rental car companies (and indeed to any company that rents out capacity for periods of varying duration). Network management is also important to airlines that offer connecting service. This can be seen from Figure 8.1, which shows the distribution of passengers by fare

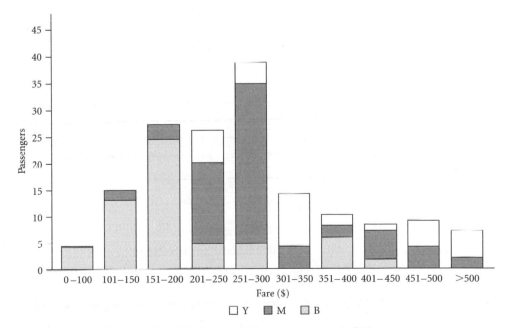

Figure 8.1 Distribution of total fares by fare class on an example flight.

class and total fare paid on a flight departure from San Francisco to Chicago. There are three fare classes on this flight: full fare (Y), discount (M), and deep discount (B). In general, Y-Class passengers tend to pay more than M-Class passengers, who tend to pay more than B-Class passengers. However, fare class is not a perfect proxy for fare. There are some B-Class passengers paying more than $400 and some Y-Class passengers paying less than $250. Managing this flight based strictly on fare class does not maximize revenue. First of all, if this airline closes B-Class, it will still be accepting Y-Class (and M-Class) passengers who are paying less that $250 while rejecting B-Class passengers willing to pay more than $400 for a seat. Furthermore, managing by fare class does not allow the airline to take advantage of the spread of fares within each class. If capacity on this flight were constrained, the airline might want to accept only passengers paying more than, say, $200.

San Francisco and Chicago are hubs for this airline. This means that the San Francisco-to-Chicago flight carries passengers traveling from many origins to many destinations. Only a small fraction of the passengers are actually flying from San Francisco to Chicago; the majority are connecting in either San Francisco or Chicago (or both). For example, the highest fares on the flight (those with total fare over $3,000) might be flying from Tokyo to Chicago via San Francisco or from San Francisco to Paris via Chicago. Other passengers might be flying from San Francisco to Chicago to Grand Rapids or from Fresno to San Francisco to Chicago, and so on. Each origin-destination combination can be purchased in different fare classes, adding even more complexity. The fare for an M-Class Tokyo-to-Chicago passenger is likely to be higher than a Y-Class San Francisco–to-Chicago passenger. Yet, leg-based capacity allocation would not allow the airline to accept the M-Class Tokyo-to-Chicago passenger while rejecting the Y-Class San Francisco-to-Chicago passenger. The goal of network management is to improve revenue by managing the mix of products as well as the mix of fare classes being sold for each product.

Airlines have estimated that network management adds 0.5% to 1% of additional revenue on top of the revenue gains from optimal capacity allocation and overbooking. This may not sound like much, but for a $5 billion airline such as the Scandinavian Airline System, it is $25 million to $50 million per year in additional profit. Network management is even more critical for hotels and rental car companies. In these industries, managing the mix of bookings by length of stay (or length of rental) provides more leverage than managing by fare class alone. For a hotel, it is usually more important not to accept short-stay bookings that will force it to reject future longer-stay booking requests than it is to worry about the rate mix of any individual booking length. For this reason, unlike the airlines, the first successful hotel (and rental car) revenue management systems included network management capabilities.

8.2.1 Types of Network

In the 1960s, major airlines in the United States began to establish *hub-and-spoke* networks as a way to better leverage their operations. Figure 8.2 shows a hub-and-spoke network with two *hubs* and 13 *spoke cities*. Each spoke city is connected to one or more of the hubs. Arrivals and departures at the hubs are timed so that passengers arriving from cities to the west of the hub can connect to cities to the east, and vice versa. The hub-and-spoke network allows an

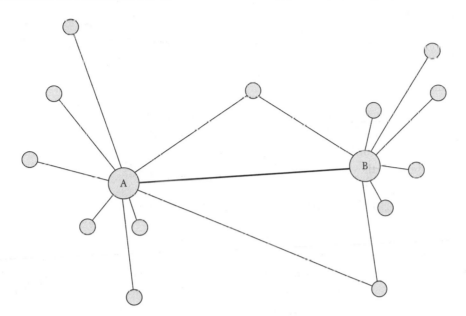

Figure 8.2 Example of a hub-and-spoke network. Nodes A and B are hubs; the remaining nodes are spoke cities.

airline to offer a large number of products with a relatively small number of flights. With 20 eastbound flights into a hub connecting with 20 westbound flights, an airline can offer 440 products (all possible connections plus the direct flights in and out of the hub) with only 40 total flights. While hub-and-spoke airlines offer some direct flights between spoke cities, the vast majority of their traffic touches at least one hub—either as an origin or destination or as a connecting point. Airlines operating hub-and-spoke networks include American, Continental, Delta, United, Air France, British Airways, and Singapore Airlines, among many others. During the 1980s, most large airlines organized their operations around the hub-and-spoke model and saw their connecting traffic soar. For example, American Airlines reported that its fraction of connecting passengers grew from about 10% of total traffic in 1980 to more than 60% by 1986.[3]

The resources for a hotel are room nights, and its products are all possible combinations of arrival date and length of stay. In a *linear network*, such as the one shown in Figure 8.3, each room night connects to the preceding night and to the following night. A passenger railway network is also linear; for example, Amtrak's *California Zephyr*, which starts at Emeryville, CA, and terminates in Chicago, makes 33 intermediate stops along the way. A passenger boarding the *Zephyr* at Emeryville can get off at any one of 34 stops (the 33 intermediate stops plus Chicago); a passenger boarding at the second stop (Martinez, CA) can get off at any one of 33 stops; and so on. Each of the 34 legs is a resource, and each combination of origin and destination is a product. The capacity and passenger load by leg for the *Zephyr* are shown in Figure 8.4. The typical passenger railroad has a linear network similar to the hotels and rental car companies, but with the length of the network equal to the number of legs being offered.

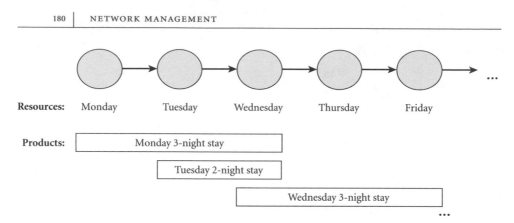

Figure 8.3 A linear network, typical of hotels and rental car companies.

Each product in a network has one or more associated fare classes. The network management problem is to determine which booking requests to accept for every possible combination of product and fare class at every time. We use the term *origin-destination fare class* (or ODF) for a product/fare class combination.[4] While ODF is an airline term, we will use it to refer to a combination of product and fare class in any industry. Thus, for a hotel, a four-night *rack-rate*[5] booking arriving June 13 is a different ODF than a three-night discount booking arriving June 14. The goal of network management is to manage and update the availability of all ODFs over time in order to maximize expected contribution.

The number of products being offered by a hotel or rental car company at one time can be very large—much larger, in fact, than the number of rooms in the hotel. A hotel accepting reservations for customers arriving for the next 365 days with stays from 1 up to 15 days in length is offering $15 \times 365 = 5{,}475$ different products. In fact, the number of products can

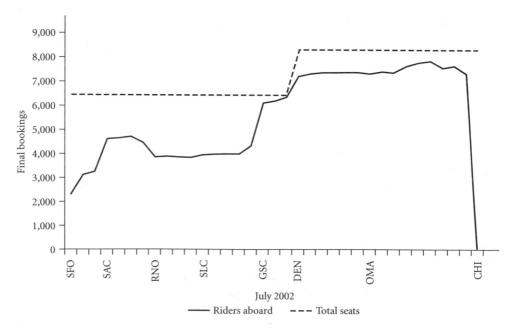

Figure 8.4 Capacity and passengers by leg for the *California Zephyr* train (July 2002).
Source: Amtrak.

be even larger, since each room type creates an entirely new product dimension. A particular hotel might have four different types of room (for example, standard, deluxe, deluxe view, and suite), for which it can charge different rates. Since a customer can book any one of these room types for any arrival date and length of stay, the number of products being offered by the hotel is actually $4 \times 15 \times 365 = 21,900$. In other words, a hotel may well be offering 100 times more products than it has rooms! On the other hand, cruise lines typically offer only one or two options for embarkation and disembarkation per sailing. The different products on a particular sailing are determined by the different cabin types, for example, upper-deck outside versus lower-deck inside.

8.2.2 A Greedy Heuristic for Network Management—And Why It Fails

Consider a 100-room hotel facing the *unconstrained demand* pattern for some future week shown in Figure 8.5. (Unconstrained demand is the total number of room nights the hotel could sell if it accepted every booking request.) The pattern shown in Figure 8.5 is typical of a midtown business hotel—demand is low on the weekend and peaks during the middle of the week. In this example, unconstrained demand exceeds capacity on Wednesday. This means that the hotel will need to reject some bookings or it will be oversold on Wednesday (ignoring no-shows and cancellations). The network management problem faced by the hotel is to decide which bookings to accept and which to reject *considering both room rate and length of stay* in order to maximize expected contribution margin.

Let us say that the hotel offers two rates: a rack-rate of $200 per night and a discount rate of $150 per night. The hotel manager might look at the demand pattern in Figure 8.5 and conclude (correctly) that the hotel's constrained resource is Wednesday night capacity. The manager might reason that the best way to maximize operating profit is to limit the

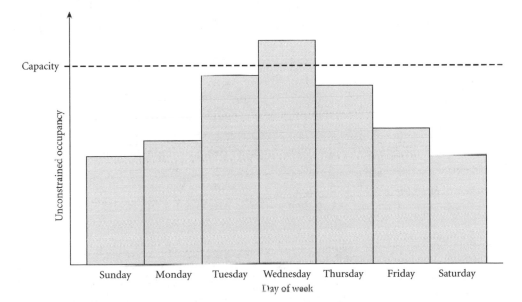

Figure 8.5 Typical unconstrained occupancy pattern for a midtown business hotel.

number of discount-rate customers booking any product that includes Wednesday night in order to protect availability for rack-rate customers. In other words, the hotel might manage bookings based strictly on fare class. This approach might improve revenue relative to a first-come, first-served policy, but it has an obvious drawback. Rack-rate customers arriving Wednesday for a one-night stay pay $200. But discount-rate customers arriving Tuesday for a three-night stay pay $450. If the hotel limits discount bookings to save room for full-fare bookings, it runs the risk of turning down a $450 customer to save room for a $200 customer—a prime revenue management sin. Clearly a more sophisticated approach is required if the hotel is to maximize expected revenue.

When there is only a single constrained resource, the manager could order all of the ODFs that use the constrained resource by total rate paid and solve the multiclass problem using EMSR or a similar heuristic. This would mean that the lowest class on Wednesday would be one-night discount Wednesday customers paying $150, the next-highest class would be one-night rack customers paying $200, followed by two-night discount stays for either Tuesday–Wednesday or Wednesday–Thursday paying $300, followed by two-night rack customers paying $400, and so on. By establishing classes in this fashion and setting the appropriate booking limits, the hotel would maximize expected operating contribution as long as unconstrained demand exceeded capacity *only on Wednesday night*.

Sorting all the ODFs on each leg in fare order and setting availabilities based on total fare is called the *greedy heuristic*[6] for network revenue management. The greedy heuristic is optimal if there is only a single constrained resource or bottleneck. It works perfectly in the hotel example if unconstrained demand for hotel rooms exceeds capacity *only* on Wednesday night. However, the greedy heuristic breaks down quickly when more than one resource is constrained. This would be the case for the hotel if unconstrained demand exceeded 100 rooms on both Wednesday and Thursday nights. In this case, it is no longer optimal for the hotel to order fare classes strictly by total revenue. The hotel should accept a two-night Wednesday–Thursday discount booking paying $300 if it believes that Thursday is not going to sell out. But if it believes that Thursday is going to sell out, it may be better off rejecting the $300 two-night booking in favor of waiting for two $200 one-night rack-rate bookings for Wednesday night and Thursday night.

When multiple resources are constrained, the right ordering of ODFs on a leg can depend on the fares and demands for all the other ODFs as well as the capacities of all the other resources in the network. In fact, as we accept bookings over time and update our forecasts of future demand, the right ordering of ODFs on each leg may change as well. In fact, there is no stable optimal ordering of ODFs when multiple resources in a network can be constrained.

The failure of the greedy heuristic can be seen with the simple network shown in Figure 8.6, where an airline offers two flights—flight 1 from San Francisco (SFO) to Denver

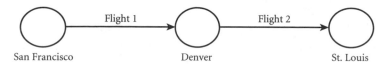

San Francisco   Denver   St. Louis

Figure 8.6   A simple hub-and-spoke network.

(DIA) and flight 2 from Denver (DIA) to St. Louis (STL)—that have been scheduled so that passengers can connect from flight 1 to flight 2 at Denver. For simplicity, let us assume that the airline offers a single fare for each product and that the San Francisco-to-Denver fare is $200, the Denver-to-St. Louis fare is $160, and the San Francisco-to-St. Louis fare is $300. Assume now that the airline has exactly one seat left on each of the two flights. The airline has a customer on the phone who wants to fly from San Francisco to St. Louis and is willing to pay the $300 fare for the privilege of doing so. Should the airline let her book? Or should the airline reject the booking in the hopes of booking local passengers on both legs? Let p_1 be the probability that the airline will receive at least one future booking request for flight 1 and p_2 be the probability that the airline will receive at least one future request for flight 2. Then the expected value of refusing the connecting customer and letting only the local customers book is $\$200p_1 + \$160p_2$. If this amount is greater than $300, then the airline is better off refusing the connecting customer and relying on local traffic to fill the last seats. If, on the other hand, $\$200p_1 + \$160p_2 < \$300$, then the airline should go ahead and allow the connecting passenger to book.

In this case, the probabilities p_1 and p_2 are the airline's forecasts of future local demand on the two flights. Whether or not the airline should accept the through passenger depends on these forecasts. This observation can be generalized to a full network: There is no unambiguous answer to the question of whether an airline should prefer connecting traffic to local traffic on a given leg. The right answer depends on the forecasts of future demand for all ODFs. Ultimately, when lots of resources are constrained, we need to optimize over the entire network in order to determine which bookings we prefer on any leg in the network.

8.3 A LINEAR PROGRAMMING APPROACH

Linear programming (LP) is a natural approach to allocating scarce resources to competing product demands. In fact, if we take the gigantic leap of assuming that future demands are known with certainty, linear programming provides an exact solution to the network management problem. Since uncertainty is a key element of revenue management decision making, it shouldn't be too surprising that a solution derived in this fashion is not wholly satisfactory. However, the linear programming formulation of the network management problem is worth studying, for three reasons. First, it solves the "capacity allocation" piece of network management and provides insight into the nature of the optimal solution. Second, the solution to the network management linear program provides a good starting point for a fully optimal solution. In many hotels and airlines, linear programming is used to determine an initial solution, which is then adjusted to account for the uncertainty in future demand. Finally, the linear program generates "marginal values" of capacity as a byproduct. These marginal values approximate the opportunity costs of the capacity and can serve as an estimate of network bid prices.

To formulate the network management problem as a linear program, assume we know the future demand for every ODF with certainty. Furthermore, assume that this demand will not be influenced by which ODFs we open and close (In other words, we have independent demands both on each flight and among flight legs). We have m resources and

n ODFs utilizing combinations of those resources. We assume each resource is used in at least one ODF, so $n \geq m$. We use the subscript i to index resources and the subscript j to index ODFs. Each resource i has a constrained capacity $c_i > 0$. Each ODF has a known demand $d_j > 0$ and a net margin $p_j > 0$. Let $x_j \geq 0$ be the amount of ODF j we will sell (our allocation). Then the *deterministic network management problem* is to find the values of x_j for $j = 1, 2, \ldots, n$ that maximize total net contribution subject to the constrained capacities of the resources.

To complete the formulation, we need to represent which resources are used to produce each ODF. To do this, we define the incidence variable a_{ij} as follows:

$$a_{ij} = \begin{cases} 1 & \text{if resource } i \text{ is used in ODF } j \\ 0 & \text{otherwise} \end{cases} \tag{8.1}$$

To illustrate the use of the incidence variables, consider the simple flight network shown in Figure 8.6. There are two resources in this network: (1) flight 1 from San Francisco to Denver and (2) flight 2 from Denver to St. Louis. With three products and two fare classes, the airline is offering six ODFs in all:

1. San Francisco to Denver full fare

2. San Francisco to Denver discount

3. Denver to St. Louis full fare

4. Denver to St. Louis discount

5. San Francisco to St. Louis full fare

6. San Francisco to St. Louis discount

Using this numbering, $a_{11} = 1$ because the San Francisco–to–Denver full-fare ODF uses flight 1, while $a_{13} = 0$ because the Denver-to–St. Louis full-fare ODF does not utilize flight 1. The values of the incidence variables for this simple example are shown in Table 8.2.

TABLE 8.2
*Values of the incidence variables (a_{ij})
for the two-flight example*

| Resource | ODF (j) | | | | | |
(i)	1	2	3	4	5	6
1	1	1	0	0	1	1
2	0	0	1	1	1	1

It is instructive to compare the incidence variables for a linear network. Consider a hotel that offers one-night, two-night, and three-night products only. The resources for the hotel are the room nights, and the products are combinations of arrival night and length of stay. Table 8.3 shows the values of the incidence variables (a_{ij}) for three different lengths of stay and a week of resources. In theory at least, the network management problem for a hotel stretches out indefinitely into the future. In practice, a hotel will only accept bookings for some limited period into the future (often a year), limiting the number of resources and products that

TABLE 8.3
Values of the incidence variables (a_{ij}) for the hotel example

| | ARRIVAL DATE | | | | | | | | | | | | | | |
| | SUNDAY | | | MONDAY | | | TUESDAY | | | WEDNESDAY | | | THURSDAY | | |
Resource	1	2	3	1	2	3	1	2	3	1	2	3	1	2	3
Sunday	1	1	1	0	0	0	0	0	0	0	0	0	0	0	0
Monday	0	1	1	1	1	1	0	0	0	0	0	0	0	0	0
Tuesday	0	0	1	0	1	1	1	1	1	0	0	0	0	0	0
Wednesday	0	0	0	0	0	1	0	1	1	1	1	1	0	0	0
Thursday	0	0	0	0	0	0	0	0	1	0	1	1	1	1	1
Friday	0	0	0	0	0	0	0	0	0	0	0	1	0	1	1
Saturday	0	0	0	0	0	0	0	0	0	0	0	0	0	0	1

need to be managed. Furthermore, in theory a hotel offers an infinite number of products, since customers can buy any length of stay. In practice, lengths of stay longer than 14 nights are extremely rare at most hotels, and hotels usually manage them as a single product.

8.3.1 The Deterministic Network Linear Program

We can now formulate the deterministic network management problem as a linear program:

$$\max_{x_j} \sum_{j=1}^{n} p_j x_j \tag{8.2}$$

subject to

$$\sum_{j=1}^{n} a_{ij} x_j \leq c_i \qquad \text{for all } i \tag{8.3}$$

$$x_j \leq d_j \qquad \text{for all } j \tag{8.4}$$

$$x_j \geq 0 \qquad \text{for all } j \tag{8.5}$$

The variables $x_1, x_2, \ldots, x_n$ are the total seats allocated to each ODF. The objective function 8.2 stipulates that the goal is to accept the demand that maximizes total net contribution. There is one constraint of the form of (8.3) for each resource. These constraints ensure that the airline can physically accommodate all the demand that it accepts. (8.4) are the demand constraints: they stipulate that sales of each ODF are limited by demand for that ODF. Finally, (8.5) ensures that all allocations are greater than or equal to zero.

Example 8.1

An airline is operating the two-flight airline network in Figure 8.6 and offering a full fare and a discount fare for each of the three itineraries. There are six ODFs using two resources, and the ODF resource mapping is as shown in Table 8.2. The airline has assigned a 100-seat aircraft on flight 1 from San Francisco to Denver and a 120-seat aircraft on flight 2 from Denver to St. Louis; demands and fares are as shown in Table 8.4. Notice that the unconstrained demand is

TABLE 8.4
Two-flight network management example fares and demands

Number	ODF		Fare	Demand
1	San Francisco to Denver full fare		$150	30
2	San Francisco to Denver discount		100	60
3	Denver to St. Louis full fare		120	20
4	Denver to St. Louis discount		80	80
5	San Francisco to St. Louis full fare		250	30
6	San Francisco to St. Louis discount		170	40

160 on the San Francisco–to-Denver flight and 170 on the Denver-to–St. Louis flight. Since these demands exceed the flight capacities for the two flights, we will need to turn some passengers away. The linear program for this example is

maximize $\quad 150x_1 \quad +100x_2 \quad +120x_3 \quad +80x_4 \quad +250x_5 \quad +170x_6$

subject to

$$
\begin{array}{rrrrrrr}
x_1 & +x_2 & & & +x_5 & +x_6 & \leq 100 \\
& & x_3 & +x_4 & +x_5 & +x_6 & \leq 120 \\
x_1 & & & & & & \leq 30 \\
& x_2 & & & & & \leq 60 \\
& & x_3 & & & & \leq 20 \\
& & & x_4 & & & \leq 80 \\
& & & & x_5 & & \leq 30 \\
& & & & & x_6 & \leq 40 \\
x_1, & x_2, & x_3, & x_4, & x_5, & x_6 & \geq 0
\end{array}
$$

which can be solved easily using Excel's SOLVER or any other LP program.

The optimal allocations for Example 8.1 and the total net contribution are shown in Table 8.5. Note that in this case, we took all of the full-fare passengers for each product. We also took *some* (but not all) of the local discount traffic in both markets and none of the San Francisco–to–St. Louis discount through traffic. At first glance, it might seem surprising that we didn't take any of the San Francisco–to–St. Louis discount traffic, since those passengers

TABLE 8.5
Two-flight network management example solution

Number	ODF	Fare	Allocation	Revenue
1	San Francisco to Denver full fare	$150	30	$4,500
2	San Francisco to Denver discount	100	40	4,000
3	Denver to St. Louis full fare	120	20	2,400
4	Denver to St. Louis discount	80	70	5,600
5	San Francisco to St. Louis full fare	250	30	7,500
6	San Francisco to St. Louis discount	170	0	0
		TOTAL REVENUE		$24,000

were paying the second-highest fare in the system—more than any of the local full-fare passengers and much more than any of the local discount passengers. But the reason we rejected them is obvious when we look at the total network: The *sum* of the fares paid by the local passengers was greater than the San Francisco–to–St. Louis discount fare. Given our demand forecasts, we gain more contribution for the system by rejecting the discount through passengers in favor of local demand.

8.3.2 Structure of the Optimal Solution

Notice that in the optimal solution shown in Table 8.5, ODFs fall into three categories:

1. ODFs for which we did not accept *any* bookings (San Francisco to St. Louis discount)
2. ODFs for which we accepted *some* but not all of the demand (Denver to St. Louis discount and San Francisco to Denver discount)
3. ODFs for which we accepted *all* of the demand (all of the full-fare ODFs)

In the optimal solution to the deterministic network management problem there will be at most one fare class for each product for which we accept some but not all demand.[7] All of the other fare classes for that product will be "all or nothing": We will either accept all of their demand or none of it. Acceptance of fare classes for a product proceeds in fare order: For each product there is a set of fare classes (possibly empty) for which we accept all of the demand and a set of fare classes (possibly empty) for which we accept none of the demand. The fares for the fully accepted classes are all higher than the fares for those classes for which we accept none of the demand. Finally, there may be one class for which we accept only some of the demand. This class will have a fare *higher* than the fares of the rejected classes but *lower* than the fully accepted classes.

Example 8.2

An airline operates on the flight network shown in Figure 8.6 with the same total demand by product as in Example 8.1, but with five classes per product, with the fares and ODF demands shown in the fourth and fifth columns of Table 8.6. This airline is offering 15 ODFs. The optimal allocations are shown in the corresponding column of Table 8.6. For the San Francisco–to–St. Louis product, it is optimal to accept all passengers who pay more than $200 and reject those who pay less. The airline should accept exactly seven of those paying exactly $200, out of a total demand of 10. Similarly, for the Denver-to–St. Louis product, the airline should accept everybody paying more than $75 and reject everybody paying less than $75 while accepting 13 out of 30 passengers willing to pay exactly $75. For the San Francisco–to-Denver product, the airline should accept everyone paying more than $130 and reject all requests whose associated fares are lower than $100.

Example 8.2 shows that we never want to be accepting bookings for a lower fare class when we are rejecting them for a higher fare class *for the same product*. For the example in Table 8.6, there is no combination of demands, capacities, or fares for which it would be optimal to accept San Francisco–to–St. Louis $170 bookings while rejecting San

TABLE 8.6
Expanded network solution

Number	Product	Class	Fare	Demand	Allocation	Revenue
1	San Francisco–Denver	A	$180	10	10	$1,800
2		B	160	20	20	3,200
3		C	140	15	15	2,100
4		D	130	18	18	2,340
5		E	100	27	0	0
6	Denver–St. Louis	A	$130	15	15	$1,950
7		B	110	20	20	2,200
8		C	90	15	15	1,350
9		D	80	20	20	1,600
10		E	75	30	13	975
11	San Francisco–St. Louis	A	$260	20	20	$5,200
12		B	240	10	10	2,400
13		C	200	10	7	1,400
14		D	190	15	0	0
15		E	170	15	0	0
					TOTAL REVENUE	$26,515

Francisco–to-Denver $180 bookings. On the other hand, it is optimal in the example to re-ject $190 San Francisco–to–St. Louis bookings that use the San Francisco–to-Denver leg while accepting $130 San Francisco–to-Denver bookings. In network management, fare classes should be nested by product but not by resource.[8]

8.3.3 Strengths and Weaknesses of the Linear Programming Approach

Efficient linear programming solution packages, such as CPLEX, have made the linear pro-gramming formulation solvable, even for many large airlines. To account for uncertainty, ex-pected demand is often used in the demand constraints (8.4), and various adjustments are made to account for overbooking and for the dynamic nature of bookings and cancellations. On the other hand, working with a large linear program is often cumbersome and produces a large number of outputs (the ODF allocations) that can be difficult to interpret and imple-ment. A large hub-and-spoke airline may have many ODFs with very low levels of demand. For example, a major hub-and-spoke airline offers connecting service between many small cities that have very small demand—say, Portland, Maine, to Chicago to San Francisco to Santa Barbara, California. This may be a perfectly valid set of connections and therefore a product that the airline wants to offer, but the expected demand for this product would likely be fewer than one passenger per day and the expected demand per fare class for this product would be even smaller. In practice, hub-and-spoke airlines can offer thousands of such ODFs with very low levels of demand—less than one expected booking per month in many cases. But these ODFs still need to be managed, and linear programming would require calculating and maintaining a booking limit for each of them. This is a tremendous amount of compu-tational and implementation overhead to manage a large number of ODFs that collectively may only represent a small fraction of total demand.

There are other issues with linear programming as a network revenue management ap-proach. One is that it is not immediately clear how to incorporate demand uncertainty. One obvious approach is to replace the deterministic demands for each ODF, d_j, with the *mean* demand for that ODF, μ_j. But analogy with the single-leg case will show that this is not right. We have shown in the single-leg case that we can make more money by explicitly allowing for uncertainty in the booking tradeoffs. Planning for mean demand does not maximize expected revenue.

Finally, the astute reader will notice that we have formulated the network linear program in terms of calculating *allotments* for different ODFs. As we saw in Section 6.5, the allotment approach breaks down when bookings do not arrive in strict fare order. This is an even more pressing issue with network management than with leg based management—it is extremely unrealistic to expect that passengers booking on different ODFs would oblige us by booking in strict order of value to the airline. In fact, passengers flying high-fare, multileg itineraries often book earlier than those flying lower-fare, single-leg itineraries. In theory at least, we could deal with the dynamics of network management by rerunning the linear program each time a booking is accepted or a cancellation takes place. However, the size and complexity of the corresponding linear program render this approach impractical. What we really need is a way to extend the concept of nesting to booking requests that utilize multiple legs. The most common way to do this is *virtual nesting*.

8.4 VIRTUAL NESTING

Virtual nesting was the earliest approach to network management. It was first applied by American Airlines,[9] and variations on the basic idea are in use at many airlines today. Virtual nesting was developed to allow an airline to adopt the preexisting, leg-based control structures in its reservation system to the network management problem with minimal changes. As the name implies, it allows ODFs to be nested. Because it is extremely flexible and can be implemented relatively easily, some variation of virtual nesting is used by practically every company that has implemented network management.

The first step in airline virtual nesting is to define a set of *buckets* on each flight leg. Each bucket represents a range of fare values. The second step is to map each ODF into a bucket on each of its legs based on an estimate of the ODF's value to the airline. The process of mapping ODFs into buckets on legs is called *indexing*. At the end of the indexing process, each bucket contains ODFs of similar value. (For the moment, we will defer the question of how we might calculate the value of an ODF.) We will use the convention that the lowest-numbered bucket on each leg contains the highest-value ODFs. The buckets are nested so that bucket 1 has access to the entire capacity of the leg, bucket 2 has access to all the inventory except that protected for bucket 1, and the lowest bucket has access only to its own allocation. Each bucket has a booking limit and a protection level that is updated every time a booking is accepted or a cancellation occurs. This means we can apply all of the mechanics for leg-based revenue management to buckets.

Example 8.3

An airline operating the simple network shown in Figure 8.6 offers a Y-Class fare and an M-Class fare for each product. This is a total of six ODFs. The airline has established three buckets on each leg. Then one possible indexing is illustrated

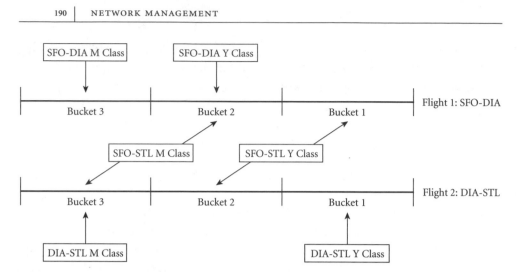

Figure 8.7 Example mappings of ODFs for a two-flight network.

in Figure 8.7. In this case the airline maps SFO-STL Y-Class passengers into bucket 1 on flight 1 but into bucket 2 on flight 2. This means that the SFO-STL Y passengers will have access to the entire capacity of flight 1, but they only have access to the bucket 2 allocation of flight 2, which is less than the capacity of the plane.[10]

A schematic diagram of a virtual nesting system is shown in Figure 8.8. The reservation system now has an additional function that maps booking requests to buckets as they arrive. Once a booking has been mapped to buckets on each leg, the reservation system checks availability of the appropriate bucket on each leg to determine whether or not the booking should be accepted. This function is closely analogous to the booking control function

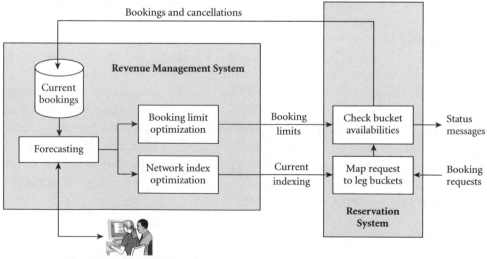

Figure 8.8 Schematic view of a virtual nesting architecture for network management.

when booking requests are managed one leg at a time, as described in Section 6.5. In fact, most network management systems utilize the fare class booking structures within the reservation systems as their buckets.

Figure 8.8 shows the conceptual architecture of a virtual nesting system. Each booking request is first mapped to buckets on its constituent resources according to some indexing scheme. Availability is then checked in each of these buckets. If there is sufficient availability in each bucket, the request is accepted; otherwise it is rejected. The function of the revenue management system is both to maintain and communicate the latest indexing and to calculate and update booking limits for each bucket on each leg.

8.4.1 Virtual Nesting Booking Control

The management of bookings under virtual nesting proceeds in a fashion closely analogous to single-leg booking control.

Virtual Nesting Booking Control

1. **Initialization**

   Establish an indexing that maps every ODF into a bucket on each leg in the ODF.

   For each leg bucket, estimate the mean and standard deviation of total forecasted demand.

   Using the mean and standard deviation of demand by bucket, average contribution by bucket, and leg capacity; use EMSR or a similar approach to determine booking limits and protection levels for each bucket on each leg.

2. **Operation**

   When a booking request for an ODF is received, check each leg in the ODF. If there is sufficient capacity in the corresponding bucket on each leg, accept the request. Otherwise reject it.

   If the booking is accepted, reduce bucket availabilities on all legs in the booked ODF.

   When cancellations occur, increase bucket availabilities for each leg in the cancelled ODF.

3. **Reoptimization**

   Periodically reforecast demand for each ODF and update expected bucket demand by leg.

   Periodically rerun EMSR or other algorithm to recalculate nested booking limits for each bucket based on the new forecasts and capacity remaining on each leg.

Note that virtual nesting could be described as *leg-based revenue management plus indexing*. This is one of its strengths—it allows airlines to use the well-established (and hard-to-change) nested fare class structures within their reservation systems.

Another strength of virtual nesting is its flexibility. As an example, simply mapping all

ODFs from the same fare class into the same bucket on each leg (i.e., mapping all M-Class bookings into an M-Class bucket on each leg and all Y-Class bookings into a higher Y-Class bucket) will give the same results as managing each leg independently. More usefully, an airline can use virtual nesting to provide preferential availability to an ODF simply by mapping it to higher buckets on its constituent legs. This can be useful, for example, if the airline is running a marketing campaign and wants to ensure that sufficient availability will be maintained for certain discount fares—even if it may not be optimal to do so from a revenue maximization point of view.

8.4.2 Indexing

Virtual nesting can be described as booking control plus indexing. We have described how booking control works within virtual nesting. This leaves the question of how ODFs should be mapped to their constituent legs—in other words, how they should be indexed. Both the indexing scheme chosen and the frequency with which it is updated strongly influence not only the additional revenue that will be achieved but also the complexity of the revenue management system. The remainder of this chapter is devoted primarily to describing different indexing approaches and discussing the implications of each.

One immediate thought might be to map an ODF into buckets on each leg based on its total fares. That is, we would map the ODFs with the highest total fare into the highest bucket, those with slightly lower total fare into the second bucket, and so on for every leg. This is equivalent to the greedy heuristic for network management. And, as we saw in Section 8.2.2, the greedy heuristic fails when multiple resources in a network are constrained. Furthermore, the reason it fails is that it ignores opportunity cost in determining how an ODF should be bucketed on one of its legs. Specifically, an ODF with a high total fare but a high opportunity cost on its other legs should potentially be bucketed below an ODF with lower total fare but no opportunity cost on its other legs. This type of bucketing can never be achieved by the greedy heuristic.

The failure of the greedy heuristic suggests that we need a way of indexing ODFs that includes their opportunity costs. As it turns out, the best way to value an ODF for bucketing on a resource is on the basis of its total fare *minus the opportunity cost (if any) on other resources it uses*. This quantity, known as the *net leg fare*, is defined as follows:

Net leg fare for ODF i on leg k = Total fare for ODF i − Sum of opportunity costs on *all resources other than* k (if any) in ODF i

The term *net leg fare* is a bit unfortunate because of its airline connotation. The same calculation holds, however, for hotels, where the resources are room nights, and for rental car companies, where the resources are rental days.

Example 8.4

A hotel has estimated that the opportunity cost for a room on Tuesday night, January 23, is $80 and the opportunity cost for Wednesday night, January 24, is $105. The hotel receives a booking request for two nights, arriving January 23 and departing January 25, with an associated total rate of $220. The net leg fare associated with that booking request is $220 − $105 = $115 for the night of January 23 and $220 − $80 = $140 for the night of January 24.

Note that the net leg fare is calculated by subtracting the opportunity cost on *other resources* from the total fare. It is a local measure of the contribution of the ODF. Only if the fare associated with the ODF exceeds the opportunity cost for all of the resources it uses should it be accepted. For this reason, it is the right value to use to map products into buckets on each leg.

Example 8.5

Consider the three-city network shown in Figure 8.6. The opportunity cost on the SFO-DIA leg is $250 and on the DIA-STL leg is $800. Each leg has three buckets, defined as follows:[11]

- Bucket 1: Net leg fares ≥ $1,000
- Bucket 2: $600 ≤ Net leg fares < $1,000
- Bucket 3: Net leg fares < $600

Table 8.7 shows how six different ODFs would be mapped into buckets in this case. Note that SFO-STL M-Class passengers are mapped into the highest bucket on flight 2 but the lowest bucket on flight 1. This means that on Flight 1 we will be protecting seats for local M-Class passengers from the SFO-STL M-Class passengers; but on flight 2 the situation is reversed.

TABLE 8.7

Net local fares and index for six ODFs in the network from Figure 8.6

		Total fare	FLIGHT 1		FLIGHT 2	
Product	Class		NLF	Bucket	NLF	Bucket
SFO-DIA	M	$400	$400	3	—	—
SFO-DIA	Y	$650	$650	2	—	—
DIA-STL	M	$550	—	—	$550	3
DIA-STL	Y	$750	—	—	$750	2
SFO-STL	M	$1,300	$500	3	$1,050	1
SFO-STL	Y	$1,800	$1,000	1	$1,550	1

The opportunity cost on flight 1 is $250, and the opportunity cost on flight 2 is $800.

8.4.3 Static Virtual Nesting

We are most of the way to a practical approach for network management. We can calculate the net local fare for each ODF on each of its legs based on its total fare minus the opportunity cost on other legs. This provides an indexing scheme that allows us to map the ODF into a bucket on each leg. If each of the buckets has sufficient availability, we accept the booking; otherwise we reject it. The remaining piece of the puzzle is how to calculate and update the opportunity cost for each leg. It is this calculation that differentiates virtual nesting approaches.

One obvious way to estimate the future opportunity cost for a product is to base it on past experience. This is, in essence, equivalent to forecasting opportunity cost.

Example 8.6

A Tuesday 2:00 flight from San Francisco to Dallas had opportunity costs of $180, $130, $190, $205, and $95 at departure. One way to estimate the opportunity cost for next Tuesday's flight would be to average the past five opportunity costs; that is, the estimate of next Tuesday's opportunity cost would be ($180 + $130 + $190 + $205 + $95)/5 = $160.

The method of using historic opportunity costs to map ODFs into buckets is called *static virtual nesting*. With static virtual nesting, an airline (or other revenue management company) estimates an opportunity cost λ_k for each resource based on the history of that resource.[12] If the resource rarely sells out (e.g., as a Tuesday night in a midtown hotel in Detroit), the opportunity cost will be small. If, on the other hand, the resource sells out with regularity, its opportunity cost will be much higher. One approach to forecasting the future opportunity cost would be to average past opportunity costs; another would be to calculate the fraction of time a resource sells out and to use the average opportunity cost of the resource when it sells out. Recall that the opportunity cost of a resource that does not sell out is $0.

Example 8.7

Flight leg 135 has historically sold out 30% of the time, and its average opportunity cost when it sold out is $750. An estimate of the expected future opportunity cost for this leg would be 0.3 × $750 = $225.

There are other approaches to static virtual nesting, but they all have one thing in common: Indexing is based entirely on past experience. This means that the indexing for a particular leg is unlikely to change during the booking period for a flight. In static virtual nesting, an airline might recalculate its indexing on a monthly or quarterly basis. In the interim, ODFs would always be mapped into the same buckets on each leg.[13] For our two-leg airline, the mapping in Table 8.7 would be used for all departures of flights 1 and 2 within this period. However, this mapping is based on the expectation that flight 2 is likely to sell out and therefore is assigned a high displacement cost. While this may be true on average, it is unlikely to be true for every departure. For example, we may be almost certain that a particular departure of flight 2 will not sell out. This means that the expected opportunity cost for this departure of flight 2 would be close to 0. But by using the mapping in Table 8.7, the airline is mapping through passengers into buckets that are too low for this departure.

Another shortcoming of static virtual nesting is implicit in the name: Since it is "static," it does not respond to changes in the course of the booking process. An airline's initial forecast of the opportunity cost for a leg might change considerably between first booking and departure. (As we have seen, there is a correspondence between opportunity cost and the boundary between open and closed classes. The assumption that a leg's opportunity cost does not change between first booking and departure is equivalent to assuming that no buckets will open or close during this period.) For the two-flight example, we could certainly have the situation where an unanticipated surge in bookings (possibly a large group) resulted in flight 1's actually closing to future bookings while flight 2 remained open in bucket 1 but closed in buckets 2 and 3. Using the mapping in Table 8.7, the only ODFs that fall in bucket 1 on flight 2 are SFO-STL through passengers. But under static virtual nesting, these booking requests will be rejected on flight 1—which is closed in all buckets. So the system is effectively closed to all bookings, even though there are seats available on flight 2 that could be profitably filled with local passengers.

It seems apparent that virtual nesting could be improved if we could update opportunity costs more often based on bookings and cancellations as they occur as well as on changing expectations of total demand for a flight. It turns out that, if we update opportunity costs often enough, they can almost serve as the only controls we need for network management. This is the idea behind bid pricing. In Section 7.3.3, we saw how bid pricing applied to a single leg. We now show how it can be applied to a network.

8.5 NETWORK BID PRICING

In Section 7.3.3, we saw that we should accept a booking request for a single resource only if the fare associated with the request exceeded the bid price for that resource. Perhaps not surprisingly, there is an equivalent condition for products consisting of multiple resources: We should only accept a multiple-resource booking if the fare exceeds the sum of the bid prices for the constituent resources. This condition can be written as follows:

> *Accept a booking for an ODF only if its fare is greater than the sum of the bid prices on the constituent resource.*

The idea behind network bid pricing is to use this condition as the basis of the revenue management system. In an airline bid-pricing system, the revenue management system calculates a bid price for each leg (later we will describe how this is done) at each time before departure. When a booking request is received, its fare is compared to the sum of the bid prices for its constituent legs. If the fare for the request is greater than or equal to the sum of the bid prices, the request is accepted; otherwise, it is rejected. That's all there is to bid pricing, at least from a booking control point of view.

In the extreme, this approach would allow us to dispense with the need for any sophisticated booking control structures and to manage bookings on bid price alone. However, we also need to allow for the fact that not all booking requests will be for a single seat. The easiest way to manage multiseat bookings is to keep track of the remaining unbooked seats on each leg and to use that number as a total booking limit.[14] Without no shows and cancellations, the total booking limit would be equal to the unbooked capacity. If we anticipate no-shows and cancellations, the total booking limit could be calculated using one of the overbooking techniques described in Chapter 9. Managing bookings in this fashion is called *network bid price control*.

Network Bid Price Control

1. Calculate an initial bid price and a total booking limit for each leg.

2. When a booking request is received, calculate the *product bid price* as the sum of the bid prices for all the legs in the product and the *product availability* as the *minimum* of the total booking limits on all the legs used by the product.

3. If the fare for the booking exceeds the product bid price *and* the number of seats requested is less than the product availability, accept the request and go to step 4. Otherwise reject the request and go to step 2.

4. Decrease the total booking limit on each resource within the product by the number of seats in the booking and go to step 2.

5. When a booking cancels, increment the total booking limits for all flights in the booking.

6. Periodically reoptimize all flight booking limits and all bid prices.

Example 8.8

Consider the solution to Example 8.2 shown in Table 8.6. If we define $75 as the bid price for the Denver-to–St. Louis leg and $125 as the bid price for the San Francisco–to-Denver leg, we will see that we have established a set of bid prices consistent with the optimal solution to the network management problem. The bid prices provide the optimal thresholds between the fare classes we want to accept for each product and those we want to reject. For the example these thresholds are $75 and $125 for the two single-leg products, plus $75 + $125 = $200 for the San Francisco–to–St. Louis through product. By using the bid prices for the two legs plus a total booking limit for each leg in the dynamic bid price control structure we could achieve a result very close to the optimal network solution in Table 8.6. And we have done so much more economically, by using just four total controls—two bid prices plus two booking limits—instead of the 15 allocations in Table 8.6.

Network bid price control is a remarkably simple approach to revenue management. It requires only two controls per leg—a bid price and a total booking limit. However, there are real-world considerations that complicate the picture substantially. First of all, we have not yet described how bid prices can be calculated. Furthermore, bid prices need to be updated (at least in theory) each time a booking is accepted or a cancellation occurs. If calculating network bid prices is time consuming or complex (as it is), the airline will require an interim control scheme to handle bookings between reoptimizations. In addition, network bid price control would require additional controls if multiple-seat booking requests are to be handled correctly. Finally, as we have stressed a number of times, any network management approach needs to be implemented within the existing CRS infrastructure, and existing reservation systems are not designed to easily enable pure bid price management.

The system shown in Figure 8.9 is known as an *availability processor* architecture. It is an implementation of a pure bid-pricing approach to network management. Booking requests

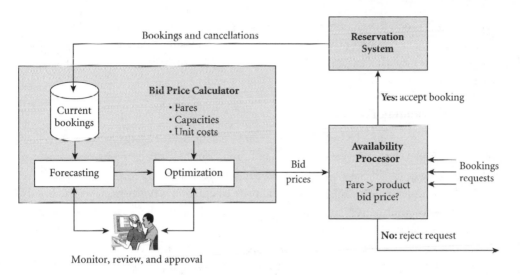

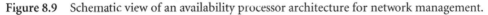

Figure 8.9 Schematic view of an availability processor architecture for network management.

arrive at an online processor known as the availability processor. The availability processor calculates the fare associated with each request and compares it to the current bid price for the requested product. If the fare is less than the bid price, the request is rejected. If the fare is greater than the bid price for the requested product, the booking is accepted and communicated to the reservation system.

8.5.1 Bid Prices and Opportunity Costs

In Section 7.3.3 we noted that the bid price for a resource was equal to the opportunity cost for that resource and could be calculated as the fare of the lowest open fare class. Not surprisingly, network bid prices are also related to the opportunity costs of the resources in the network. We can extend this observation to a network by noting that the following six quantities are (approximately) equivalent.

- *Bid price*—the minimum price we should accept for a customer on a leg
- *Opportunity cost*—the increased revenue we would see from an additional seat on a leg
- *Displacement cost*—the revenue we would lose if we had one seat less on a leg
- Marginal value of the capacity constraint in the network linear program
- Boundary between the highest closed and lowest open fare classes in a single-leg problem
- *Closed bucket boundary*—boundary between the highest closed and lowest open buckets on a leg in a virtual nest

To be sure, these six quantities will not always be exactly equal. For example, the revenue gained from an additional seat on a leg will not necessarily be the same as the revenue lost from removing a seat. The marginal value of the capacity constraint in the deterministic network linear program will not generally equal the values obtained by approaches that explicitly incorporate uncertainty. However, the near equivalence among these quantities supplies ideas for how bid prices can be calculated as well as providing insights into why bid pricing works.

8.5.2 *Calculating Bid Prices

So far, we have not specified how bid prices might be calculated for a large network. You may not be surprised to find out that calculating bid prices can be quite complex—so much so that developing faster and more accurate bid-pricing algorithms is a very active area of research. While understanding the details of bid price calculation is not critical, we will briefly describe two commonly used approaches. This section is somewhat technical and can be skimmed or skipped.

Calculating bid prices by linear programming. In section 8.3, we saw how the deterministic network management problem can be formulated as a linear program, where the outputs of the linear program are allotments for all the ODFs in the network. The value of the objective function at the optimal solution is the maximum revenue the company could achieve from its fixed stock of capacity. One way to calculate the bid price on a leg would be to solve the network linear program twice: the first time with the actual capacities and the second time with the capacity of the leg reduced by one seat. The difference in the total contribution between the two runs would be the displacement cost on the leg, which, as we have seen, is an estimate of the bid price on the leg.

Of course, this would be a cumbersome way to estimate bid prices, since it requires solving a large linear program *twice* for each leg in the network. Fortunately, this is not necessary. Deterministic displacement costs for all the legs in the network can be more practically estimated using linear programming in two different ways by using the marginal values associated with the capacity constraints as bid prices.

The marginal values associated with the capacity constraints of the deterministic network management linear program suffer from the same problem as the LP formulation itself—they ignore uncertainty. Furthermore, solving the large linear program each time that bid prices need to be updated is computationally intensive and cumbersome. Ideally we would like to find an approach to calculating bid prices that both incorporates uncertainty and is more computationally efficient.

Calculating bid prices by sequential estimation. The method of *sequential estimation* is based on the observation that the bid price on a leg should be equal to its *closed bucket boundary* in a virtual nest, where the closed bucket boundary is defined as the boundary between the lowest open bucket and the highest closed bucket on the leg. In the example in Figure 8.7, the closed bucket boundary is $500. It should be clear that the closed bucket boundary should approximate the bid price on a leg. After all, we will accept a local booking for a single seat only if its fare exceeds the closed bucket boundary, which is the definition of bid price. Furthermore, we will accept a multileg booking request for a single seat only if its net leg fare is greater than the closed bucket boundary on each leg in the ODF. You can confirm that this is the same as ensuring that its total net fare exceeds the sum of the closed bucket boundaries.

This means we can calculate bid prices for a network by finding a set of closed bucket boundaries that is consistent across the network. The challenge arises from the fact that the closed bucket boundary (bid price) on any leg depends on the closed bucket boundaries on all other legs via the net local fares of multileg ODFs. If we change the bid price on a leg we will change the net local fares for multileg ODFs on all connecting legs. This will in turn change the buckets into which those ODFs are mapped on the other legs. When we reoptimize availabilities on those legs, the new mapping may well change the bid prices on those legs, which will change the ODF mappings on the original leg. A consistent set of bid prices is one in which *the closed bucket boundaries on all legs are locally optimal given the closed bucket boundaries on all other legs.*

Sequential estimation calculates bid prices by starting with an initial estimate of all bid prices and then updating the bid price on each leg until the bucket boundaries are consistent across the entire network. To see how this works, assume we have a network consisting of two legs. We initially map all the ODFs into buckets assuming that each leg has a bid price of 0 (recall that this is equivalent to the "greedy heuristic"). Given this indexing, we can estimate the total demand by bucket on each leg. Then, for leg 1, we can use EMSR to calculate the bucket allocations on leg 1 given the current indexing. Once we have calculated the allocations on leg 1, we can reestimate the bid price on leg 1 as its closed bucket boundary. Given this new estimate of the leg 1 bid price, we can recalculate the net leg fares on leg 2 and rebucket all of the ODFs on leg 2 accordingly. We can then apply EMSR on leg 2, determine its closed bucket boundary, and use that as the new bid price for leg 2. Given this new leg 2 bid price, we can rebucket the ODFs on leg 1 and continue. Under the right conditions, this procedure will converge to a situation where the mappings and allocations on each leg are consistent with each other.

We can extend this approach to a full network as follows.

Sequential Estimation Algorithm to Calculate Bid Prices

1. Establish a set of buckets on all legs, and calculate probabilistic demand forecasts for all buckets. Set all leg bid prices to 0.

2. Loop over all legs, $k = 1, 2, \ldots, N$.

3. For the current leg k and every ODF i that includes leg k, calculate the net local fare as the net fare for ODF i minus the sum of the current bid prices for all other legs in the ODF.

4. Map all the ODFs on the current leg into buckets based on their net local fares for the ODFs. Once this is complete, use EMSR to determine allocations by bucket.

5. If all buckets are open, set the new bid price for leg k to 0. If all buckets are closed, set the new bid price for leg k to the highest bucket boundary. Otherwise, set the new bid price to the boundary between the lowest open bucket and the highest closed bucket.

6. Continue to the next leg until all legs have had new bid prices calculated.

7. When all leg bid prices have been recalculated, check the change between the new bid price and the old bid price on each leg. If the two bid prices are sufficiently close for all legs, stop—the current set of bid prices is optimal.

8. Otherwise go to step 2.

This sequential estimation algorithm will generally converge to a set of consistent bucket boundaries across a network. When bookings are accepted or forecasts change, the sequential estimation algorithm can be restarted using the previous set of bid prices. This method has been used at a number of airlines, including the Scandinavian Airlines System (SAS) and KLM Royal Dutch Airlines, as well as hotel chains, such as Omni Hotels, as part of their network revenue management systems.

8.5.3 Strengths and Weaknesses of Bid Pricing

Bid prices are more than simple tools to manage bookings. They are also useful pieces of information in themselves. As opportunity costs, they specify the value of an additional unit for each resource in the network. If a flight leg has a bid price of $250, this indicates that the airline could realize (approximately) $250 in additional revenue from adding another seat to that flight. Since the bid prices are marginal signals, this logic cannot be extended to determine the effect of adding more than one seat: A bid price of $250 on a flight leg does not mean that an airline could expect to gain $2,500 from adding 10 seats.[15] However, even with this limitation, the bid prices can provide very useful input into capacity decisions. A flight leg that consistently has a high opportunity cost at departure would be an excellent candidate to be considered for assignment to a larger aircraft, while a flight leg that consistently departs with a bid price of 0 is an excellent candidate to be considered for downsizing. A rental car company with the option to move its cars around should consider moving cars from locations with consistently low bid prices to those with consistently high bid prices.

Example 8.9

The Rent-a-Lemon rental car company rents cars at both the San Francisco airport and the San Jose airport. The two airports are 40 miles apart, and it costs $10 per car to "hike" cars from one airport to the other and back. For a date two weeks in the future, the bid price at the San Francisco airport is $73 and the bid price at the San Jose airport is $22. The expected net gain from moving a car from San Jose to San Francisco would be $73 − $22 − $10 = $41.

Bid pricing is particularly well suited to hotel applications where there is one bid price for each room type for each future night. The product bid price is the sum of the bid prices for the nights stayed. Hotel and rental car bid prices can be conveniently displayed using a calendar, as shown in Figure 8.10. The calendar shows the bid prices (labeled b) and the forecast unconstrained occupancies (labeled d) for a hotel as they might be displayed by a revenue management system for a future month. A customer wishing to rent a room for the nights of March 23, 24, and 25 would need to pay at least the sum of the bid prices for these

March						
Mon	Tue	Wed	Thur	Fri	Sat	Sun
28 $d = 85$ $b = \$84.34$	1 $d = 93$ $b = \$92.07$	2 $d = 112$ $b = \$153.12$	3 $d = 108$ $b = \$112.34$	4 $d = 99$ $b = \$92.57$	5 $d = 65$ $b = \$54.30$	6 $d = 80$ $b = \$62.33$
7 $d = 91$ $b = \$88.47$	8 $d = 102$ $b = \$122.00$	9 $d = 135$ $b = \$172.15$	10 $d = 120$ $b = \$142.34$	11 $d = 92$ $b = \$95.67$	12 $d = 53$ $b = \$42.34$	13 $d = 44$ $b = \$32.34$
14 $d = 67$ $b = \$54.37$	15 $d = 85$ $b = \$72.48$	16 $d = 110$ $b = \$122.47$	17 $d = 97$ $b = \$99.97$	18 $d = 93$ $b = \$92.34$	19 $d = 72$ $b = \$55.18$	20 $d = 66$ $b = \$54.54$
21 $d = 86$ $b = \$89.11$	22 $d = 104$ $b = \$130.02$	23 $d = 157$ $b = \$199.93$	24 $d = 140$ $b = \$178.25$	25 $d = 122$ $b = \$122.20$	26 $d = 95$ $b = \$100.69$	27 $d = 85$ $b = \$85.18$
28 $d = 84$ $b = \$84.33$	29 $d = 92$ $b = \$93.44$	30 $d = 114$ $b = \$155.67$	31 $d = 100$ $b = \$101.01$	1 $d = 82$ $b = \$78.77$	2 $d = 60$ $b = \$53.92$	3 $d = 75$ $b = \$62.74$

Figure 8.10   Bid price calendar.

nights ($199.93 + $178.25 + $122.20 = $500.38) in order to be allowed to book. On the other hand, a customer wishing to rent for March 12, 13, and 14 would be allowed to book if he were paying more than $42.34 + $32.34 + $54.37 = $129.05. The lower product bid price reflects the fact that demand is anticipated to be lower during the second period than the first. The dark shaded dates are those with a bid price greater than $150, those with medium shading have a bid price between $100 and $150, and those with no shading have a bid price less than $100. The pattern shown in Figure 8.10 is typical of a metropolitan business hotel with a midweek peak.

Bid pricing is an appealing and intuitive approach to network revenue management. However, a word of caution is in order. The product bid price is the *minimum* price we should accept for a product given remaining capacity and anticipated future demand by fare class. It does not tell us how we should actually be *pricing* the product. A hotel manager looking at the bid price calendar in Figure 8.10 should not make the mistake of thinking that he should set the rack rate on Wednesday, March 16, to $122.47. In this sense the term *bid price* is unfortunate, since, as we have seen, the bid price is better regarded as an opportunity *cost*. In the extreme case, a bid price of zero for a product tells us nothing about how we should price the product. Bid price control is a mechanism for ensuring that we do not accept any business whose margin does not exceed its opportunity cost—it does not tell us whether or not we are priced correctly in the market.

8.6 DYNAMIC VIRTUAL NESTING

Dynamic virtual nesting is the marriage of bid pricing and virtual nesting. It combines the conceptual elegance and intuitiveness of bid pricing with the practical orientation of virtual nesting. Under dynamic virtual nesting, new bid prices are frequently recalculated for all legs in the network based on current bookings and forecasts of future demands. The recalculation of bid prices could be purely periodic (e.g., nightly or weekly), it could be event driven (e.g., recalculated whenever a flight closes), or it could be ordered by a revenue analyst. In most cases, all of these can trigger a recalculation. Every time new resource bid prices are calculated, new net leg fares are calculated for each leg in the network. These net leg fares are used to define a new indexing. This indexing is put in place until the next recalculation of bid prices.

The strength of dynamic virtual nesting is that it updates bid prices to reflect the current situation on each leg—both current bookings and expected future demand—while utilizing virtual nesting to take advantage of leg-based control structures. Of course, an important determinant of the effectiveness of the approach is how often bid prices are recalculated. If bid prices are not recalculated very often, then dynamic virtual nesting is not much of an improvement over static virtual nesting. If bid prices are continually updated (say, every second), then dynamic virtual nesting will approximate network bid price control for single-seat bookings.

The first dynamic virtual nesting revenue management system was implemented in 1989 by Hertz Rent-a-Car and Decision Focus Incorporated (Carroll and Grimes 1996). The first airline dynamic virtual nesting system was developed jointly by Decision Focus Incorporated and the Scandinavian Airlines System (SAS) in 1992. In the years since, additional airlines, hotels, and rental car companies have adopted dynamic virtual nesting. It remains the state-of-the-art approach to network management in revenue management industries.

8.7 NETWORK MANAGEMENT IN ACTION

The first step taken by most airlines in revenue management was to use the approaches described in Chapter 7 to maximize expected revenue on each flight leg independently. In most cases, this approach provided tremendous benefits from not managing bookings at all—i.e., allowing customers to book on a first-come, first-served basis. However, hub-and-spoke airlines quickly realized that this approach was not capturing the full potential revenue from their systems.

Because of the need to work within existing reservation systems, the airlines generally adopted network management by instituting increasingly sophisticated forms of virtual nesting, often following the progression implied in Table 8.8. The first step was usually some form of ad hoc virtual nesting, under which a few high-value ODFs were mapped into higher buckets than their fare classes would imply. At some point, most hub-and-spoke airlines instituted some form of static virtual nesting, under which all ODFs would be mapped into buckets on each leg. These mappings would be updated quarterly or monthly based on forecasts of future demand and opportunity cost. Finally, many airlines worked to make

TABLE 8.8
Approaches to virtual nesting

Approach	Description
Greedy heuristic	Set all leg opportunity costs to 0 (not effective)
"Ad hoc" virtual nesting	Use judgment or ad hoc methods for index
Static virtual nesting	Use history to estimate leg opportunity costs
Dynamic virtual nesting	Update leg opportunity costs as bookings occur

these mappings dynamic—that is, updated frequently for each flight based on booking and cancellation activity.

The transition from leg-based revenue management to network management at the airlines involved more than just new software; the focus of revenue managers also needed to change. Under leg-based capacity control, *flight controllers* were responsible for monitoring forecasts and fare class allocations for some set of flights. For example, a flight controller for Delta Airlines might be responsible for all flights between the Atlanta hub and cities in Florida. As the name implies, flight controllers by and large took a flight-centric view of the world, looking to maximize return from their portfolio of flights. When there was a significant amount of connecting traffic, this flight-based approach could not maximize total system return.

Network management required a realignment of responsibilities. Now, there is no individual forecast for, say, M-Class bookings on a particular Atlanta-to-Orlando flight. Rather, the Atlanta-to-Orlando flight has 20 or so buckets. Each of those buckets can contain demand from hundreds of different ODFs. Thus, one bucket might include Detroit-Atlanta-Orlando Y-Class demand, Atlanta-Orlando B-Class demand, Denver-Atlanta-Orlando Y-Class demand, and so on. Furthermore, depending on demand dynamics, the mapping of ODFs to buckets might change weekly or even daily on the same flight. In essence, it is virtually impossible for a controller to manage forecasts and bucket availabilities on a flight basis. Instead, under network management the focus of the revenue management organization needs to shift from flights (or resources) to products. Instead of a flight controller focused on Atlanta-to-Florida flights, there might be a *market manager* focused on destination-Florida markets. The focus of this market manager would be on understanding the market from all domestic origins to Florida. She would be expected to ensure that all inbound forecasts to Florida incorporate the latest market intelligence. For example, each year she would be expected to know the academic schedule for colleges in the northeast to ensure that the Fort Lauderdale destination forecasts included spring break demand.

Unlike the airlines, hotels and rental car companies incorporated network management into their revenue management systems right from the start. This was not due to superior technical sophistication on their part but simply to the fact that capacity allocation on a single-resource basis simply did not work. In fact, early experiments adapting existing leg-based airline revenue management systems to work for hotels were disastrous. The first successful hotel revenue management systems, such as those for Marriott and Hyatt, and the first successful rental car system, such as those built for Hertz and National, all incorporate length-of-stay or length-of-rental control.[16]

Network management is very much on the cutting edge of pricing and revenue optimization practice. Existing systems and approaches are a compromise between what is theoretically "correct" and what is practical. The need to work with preexisting reservation systems and to respond quickly to market changes means that the use of heuristics, ad hoc solutions, and "good enough" algorithms are commonplace. Research into better algorithms and approaches to network revenue management continues.

Finally, it should be noted that the success of discount airlines means that the traditional hub-and-spoke airlines are being forced to move from a capacity control environment to a dynamic pricing environment. In this environment, the key decision is not which fare classes should be open or closed at any time, but what prices should be on offer for each product. This requires somewhat new approaches, but the basic idea that capacity should never be sold for a fare lower than its opportunity cost is still valid.

8.8 SUMMARY

- Network management is an issue for any revenue management company that sells products consisting of a combination of two or more of the resources it controls. Examples include airlines that offer connecting services, hotels renting rooms for multiple nights, and passenger trains offering tickets that include multiple legs. Network revenue management is important for hub-and-spoke airlines, hotels, rental car companies, passenger trains, and freight transportation providers. It is generally not important for cruise lines, event ticketing, and point-to-point airlines.

- A key challenge in network management is the size and complexity of the problem. A large hub-and-spoke network may have millions of product/fare class combinations it needs to manage for future departures. The size and complexity of the problem is a major consideration in implementing solutions.

- Ordering all ODFs by total fare and setting capacity limits on that basis is called the *greedy heuristic* for network management. It does not work well when more than one resource is constrained and is not used in practice.

- Linear programming can be used to determine the optimal allocation of products to buckets when demand is deterministic. In real-world applications, linear programming formulations need to be modified to account for demand uncertainty.

- Most real-world network management systems use some form of virtual nesting. Under virtual nesting, a set of buckets (analogous to fare classes) is established for each resource. When a request for an ODF is received, it is mapped into buckets on each constituent resource using a predetermined "indexing" scheme. If there is sufficient availability in each bucket, the request is accepted; otherwise it is rejected. Different ways of defining and updating the indexing will lead to different virtual nesting approaches.

- Pure bid price control is based on establishing and updating a bid price for each resource. The bid price for a resource is the minimum fare that would be accepted for selling a unit of that resource. It is equivalent to the opportunity cost for a resource.

A booking request for an ODF is accepted only if its associated fare is greater than the sum of the bid prices on all constituent resources *and* there is sufficient remaining capacity in each resource to accommodate the request.

- While pure bid price control is conceptually appealing, it is not widely used in practice since it would require very frequent reoptimization to be robust. Furthermore, it requires extensive (and expensive) modification of the reservation systems on which most revenue management companies rely.

- Dynamic virtual nesting is a combination of bid pricing with virtual nesting. Bid prices are recalculated frequently during the booking period for a product. The new bid prices are then used to define a new indexing, at which point bucket availabilities also need to be updated. Dynamic virtual nesting is the current state of the art for network management.

- Network management was incorporated into the revenue management programs for hotels and rental car companies from the beginning. Most airlines, on the other hand, initially managed capacity on a leg-by-leg basis and then introduced network management, often by way of increasingly sophisticated and dynamic virtual nesting approaches. The transition from leg-based management to network management required organizational and business process changes as well as software system changes.

8.9 EXERCISES

1. How many products can Amtrak offer on the *California Zephyr*, assuming a single fare class? (Remember that every combination of possible boarding and deboarding stations defines a different product.)

2. Consider an airline with a single hub in the Midwest. Ten flights arrive from cities in the west at the hub every day and connect with nine flights departing for cities in the east. How many products can the airline offer, assuming a single fare class? (Hint: Don't forget the nonstop products.)

3. The airline offering the flights and fares shown in Table 8.4 decides to raise the San Francisco–to–St. Louis discount fare from $170 to $225. It estimates that discount demand at this new fare will be 20. Given that all other fares and demands remain the same, what is the new optimal set of allocations and total revenue for the network?

1. This is not strictly true. The theater might still be able to gain additional revenue by considering the possibility of diversion from, say, weekend performances to weeknights in its pricing, as described in Section 5.5.

2. However, there are cruises that offer a choice of starting and ending points. And there are baseball teams that offer package deals for groups of games. In both cases, the seller is offering a product using different resources, and network management may come into play.

3. Smith, Leimkuhler, and Darrow (1992).

4. This is standard terminology. However, it can be misleading, since the real unit being managed is itinerary/fare class, not origin-destination/fare class. An M-Class passenger traveling from San Francisco to Denver on Flight 18 at 8 AM is a different ODF than an M-Class passenger traveling from San Francisco to Denver on Flight 21 at 9 AM, even though they share the same origin, destination, and fare class.

5. The highest nightly rate offered by a hotel is called the *rack rate*.

6. Recall that *heuristic* refers to a solution to an optimization problem that is not guaranteed to be optimal.

7. This requires that all of the fare classes for a product have different fares.

8. As with single-leg capacity allocation, this property holds true when demands are uncertain and independent but may not hold with dependent demands.

9. Smith, Leimkuhler, and Darrow (1992).

10. This is under the very reasonable assumption that bucket 1 on flight 2 has a protection level greater than 0.

11. Here we assume for simplicity that the buckets on each leg are the same, but this does not need to be true in general.

12. Static virtual nesting is sometimes called *displacement-adjusted virtual nesting*, or DAVN.

13. The exception is when an ODF fare changes: The airline would recalculate the net leg fares for that ODF based on the new fare and update the indexing scheme accordingly.

14. Note that multi-unit bookings are much more of an issue for airlines than for many other revenue management companies. The vast majority of car rental bookings and hotel bookings are for a single car and a single room, respectively, and the issue of managing multiunit bookings is accordingly much less important in these industries.

15. In general, additional revenue is a concave function of additional capacity—that is, the additional revenue from adding n seats will be less than n times the bid price for $n > 1$.

16. Marriott's experience is discussed in Robert Cross's book *Revenue Management* (1997). Hertz's system is described in Carroll and Grimes (1996) and National's in Geraghty and Johnson (1997).

9 | OVERBOOKING

9.1 INTRODUCTION

Overbooking occurs whenever a seller with constrained capacity sells more units than he has available (or believes he will have available). The reason that sellers engage in such a seemingly nefarious practice is to protect themselves against unanticipated no-shows and cancellations.[1] American Airlines has estimated that about 50% of its reservations resulted in either a cancellation or a no-show (Smith, Leimkuhler, and Darrow 1992). Without overbooking, many of these cancellations and every one of the no-shows would result in an empty seat—even when there are other customers willing to fly. In this situation overbooking becomes critical. Consider a flight with 100 seats that consistently faces demand much higher than 100. Assume that customers have a 13% no-show rate. If the airline never overbooks, it will, on average, leave with 13 empty seats on every flight while denying reservations to customers who want to fly. This would be an intolerable waste. The airline would be in the same situation as a manufacturer who had a plant that could only run at 87% of capacity. Without the ability to overbook, not only would the airline lose potential revenue, it would be paying to purchase, maintain, and support huge amounts of useless capacity.

The literal-minded might argue that overbooking is not really part of pricing and revenue optimization because it does not directly affect price. However, overbooking is considered part of revenue management and, in fact, is inextricably intertwined with capacity allocation. After all, to determine how many seats to offer to different booking classes on a flight we certainly need to know how many seats we will be offering in total. In this chapter, we start by giving some history of overbooking. We then characterize industries in which overbooking is used and introduce four different approaches to overbooking: a deterministic heuristic, risk-based policies, service level policies, and hybrid policies. We show how booking limits can be determined under each policy in the case of a single price and an uncertain level of no-shows. We then discuss how the simple model can be extended to a dynamic world with multiple fare classes. We finally discuss some additional complications and considerations as well as some alternatives to overbooking.

9.1.1 Historical Background

Overbooking is closely identified with the passenger airline industry (particularly by anyone who has had the experience of being denied a seat on an overbooked flight). From the
very earliest days of commercial aviation in the United States, airlines adopted the policy
that a customer with a reservation could cancel at any time before departure without paying a penalty and that a customer who had purchased a ticket for a flight would not be pe-
nalized if he did not show up for that flight. As a result, an airline ticket was "like money":
It could be used at full face value for a future flight or redeemed for cash. (This policy should
be contrasted with Broadway shows, opera, and rock concerts, where unused tickets are
generally not refundable.) This raised a problem for the airlines—how many passengers
should they allow to book on each flight? If they limited bookings to the capacity of a flight,
many fully booked flights would leave with empty seats. American Airlines estimated in
1990 that about 15% of the seats on sold-out flights would be empty if they only booked up
to capacity.[2]

By the end of the 1950s, no-shows were becoming a major problem. According to
Talluri and van Ryzin (2004), "In 1961, the Civil Aeronautics Board (CAB) reported a no-
show rate of 1 out of every 10 passengers booked among the 12 leading carriers. . . . The CAB
acknowledged that this situation created real economic problems for the airlines." As a result, the airlines were allowed to overbook. This was effective in increasing loads but, predictably, meant some passengers were refused boarding on a flight for which they held a
ticket—so-called *denied boardings* (DBs). When a flight was oversold—i.e., the number of
passengers showing up exceeded the seats on the flight—the airline would pick customers
to *bump*, that is, rebook on a later flight. If the flight was much later, the bumped passengers were provided with a meal; if it was the next day, they were provided with overnight accommodation. In addition, the airline paid a penalty to each bumped passenger. At one
point this penalty was equal to 100% of ticket value. When a passenger is bumped against
his will, it is known as an *involuntary denied boarding*. In 1966, the Civil Aeronautics Board
estimated that the involuntary denied boarding rate was about 7.7 per 10,000 boarded
passengers.[3]

Because airlines needed to overbook in order to remain financially viable, the practice became universal. The risk of being bumped from an oversold flight was seen by consumers as
yet one more irritating aspect of flying, along with delayed flights and lost luggage. However,
the airlines were reluctant to own up to overbooking. In the 1960s, flight controllers at
American Airlines recognized that overbooking was critical to financial performance. They
continued to overbook despite periodically reassuring senior management that they weren't
doing so. When denied boardings occurred, the flight controllers blamed them on "system
error."[4] Relatively unrestrained overbooking continued until 1972, when Ralph Nader was
denied a boarding on an Allegheny Airlines flight. Nader sued and won a judgment of
$25,000 based on the fact that Allegheny did not inform customers that they might be
bumped against their will. Following this judgment, the Civil Aeronautics Board ruled that
airlines must inform their customers that they engage in overbooking.

In the late 1970s, following a suggestion by economist Julian Simon, the airlines began to experiment with a *voluntary denied boarding* policy. In Simon's vision, the airlines would conduct a sealed-bid reverse auction to find enough passengers willing to be bumped at different levels of compensation. Ultimately, the airlines adopted a variant of Simon's scheme, in which an overbooked airline asks for volunteers to be bumped in return for compensation (usually a voucher for future travel). If enough volunteers are not found, the compensation level may be increased once or twice. If enough volunteers are still not found, the airline will choose which additional passengers to bump. The volunteers are termed *voluntary denied boardings* and those chosen by the airline *involuntary denied boardings*. This approach to overbooking has been successful, both from the point of view of the customers and from the point of view of airlines. Airline research shows that voluntary denied boardings are not only happy but are often eager to get bumped in return for compensation. Not only has it made customers happier, the volunteer policy has resulted in a drop in the involuntary denied boarding rate from 7.7 in 10,000 passengers to less than 1 per 10,000 passengers. The voluntary denied boarding rate for domestic U.S. airlines has hovered around 20 per 10,000 passengers since 1993.[5] Table 9.1 shows involuntary boarding rates for major U.S. domestic carriers in 2002 and 2003.

TABLE 9.1
*Involuntary denied boardings per 10,000 passengers
for major U.S. airlines in 2002 and 2003*

	2002	2003
Alaska	1.17	0.81
America West	0.20	0.40
American	0.31	0.59
Continental	0.87	1.06
Delta	1.11	1.30
Northwest	0:60	0.70
Southwest	1.09	1.02
United	0.69	0.65
US Airways	0.35	0.34
ALL	0.72	0.86

SOURCE: Bowen and Headley (2004).

Overbooking is also practiced by hotels and rental car companies, although statistics on its prevalence are harder to come by. The typical hotel practice is to find accommodations for a bumped guest at a nearby property—preferably one in the same chain. Compensation such as a discount coupon for a future stay is sometimes (but not always) offered. In many cases there is no consistent policy across a chain or group of hotels, and reimbursement policies are determined by each property manager. A rental car overbooking is usually experienced by the customer as a wait—a customer who arrives to find no car available needs to wait until a car is returned, cleaned, and refueled. In rare situations, a location may be so overbooked there is no prospect of a car for every customer. In this case, the manager will either send booked customers to competitors or move cars from another location if possible to satisfy the additional demand. Again, compensation in the form of a discount coupon may or may not be offered, depending on the situation and the company policy.

9.1.2 When Is Overbooking Applicable?

Overbooking is applicable in industries with the following characteristics.

- Capacity (or supply) is constrained and perishable, and bookings are accepted for future use.
- Customers are allowed to cancel or not show.
- The cost of denying service to a customer with a booking is *relatively* low.

It should be understood that the "cost" of denied service may include relatively intangible elements, such as customer ill will and future lost business, as well as any direct compensation. If the total denied-service cost is sufficiently high, it is not in the seller's interest to overbook, since the cost of denying service will overwhelm any potential revenue gain. For example, airlines would be unlikely to overbook at all if they had to pay a million dollars to every denied boarding.

The three characteristics just listed are the classic requirements for overbooking. Under these circumstances, companies overbook to hedge against the possibility of excessive cancellations or no-shows. However, there is another situation in which overbooking may come into play—when the amount of capacity that will be available is uncertain. Both hotels and rental car companies face this issue because of the risk of overstays and understays: Customers may stay longer or depart earlier than their reservations specify. If 10 customers depart early, then a hotel will have 10 additional empty rooms the next night. If it booked only to capacity, these rooms would go empty, even in the absence of no-shows or cancellations.

Television broadcasters also face a problem of uncertain capacity. As we saw in Section 5.6.4, broadcasters in the United States sell the vast majority of their capacity during the upfront market in May. Each buyer is sold a schedule of slots and guaranteed a certain number of impressions ("eyeballs") by the broadcaster. If the schedule sold delivers the guaranteed number of impressions (or more), then that is the end of the matter. But if the schedule does not deliver the guaranteed number of impressions, the broadcaster needs to supply the advertiser with additional slots until the guarantee is met—a practice known as *gapping*. But the broadcaster does not know in advance how many people will actually watch a particular show. A new show may be an unexpected dud or an unexpected hit.

Cruise lines and resort hotels generally avoid overbooking. In these industries, the cost of denied service is simply too high. A couple who arrives at the dock with all their luggage planning a two-week cruise is unlikely to be easily mollified when they find out they will not be able to board because the cruise is overbooked. Instead of overbooking, cruise lines and resort hotels manage the risks of cancellations and no-shows by a combination of nonrefundable deposits and higher prices.[6] Finally, most industries that sell nonrefundable bookings (or tickets) do not overbook. Theater tickets and tickets to sporting events are examples. In this case, the risks to the customer of purchasing a ticket is mitigated by the fact that bookings in these industries are transferable to others—unlike airline tickets.

Table 9.2 shows the relative importance of overbooking in some revenue management industries. Overbooking has been the most important element of passenger airline revenue

TABLE 9.2
Overbooking in different industries

Industry	Importance of overbooking	Treatment of overbooked customers
Passenger airlines	Very high	Compensation and accommodation on other flights
Business hotels	High	Reaccommodation at other hotels, usually without additional compensation
Rental cars	High	Wait or reaccommodation at other companies
Air freight	High	Reaccommodation on a later flight
Made-to-order manufacturing	Medium	Back-order or delay delivery
Cruise lines	Low	Typically do not overbook
Resort hotels	Low	Typically do not overbook
Sporting events, concerts, and shows	Low	Nonrefundable tickets with very little overbooking

management. For example, American Airlines estimated that it achieved benefits of $225 million in 1990 from overbooking (Smith, Leimkuhler, and Darrow 1992)—more than from any other element of its revenue management program, including capacity allocation and network management. Overbooking is important for hotels and rental car companies, both of which face uncertain supply (due to overstays and understays) as well as no-shows and cancellations. It is also quite important for air freight, where no-shows and cancellations are commonplace.

9.1.3 Overbooking Policies

Once a company decides it is going to overbook, it needs to decide what it wants to achieve with its overbooking policy. In other words, it needs to determine the objective function it is trying to maximize. Most companies follow one of four policies:

1. A simple *deterministic heuristic* that calculates a booking limit based only on capacity and expected no-show rate.

2. A *risk-based* policy involves explicitly estimating the costs of denied service and weighing those costs against the potential revenue to determine the booking levels that maximize expected total revenue minus expected overbooking costs.

3. A *service-level* policy involves managing to a specific target—for example, targeting no more than one instance of denied service for every 5,000 shows.

4. A *hybrid* policy is one in which risk-based limits are calculated but constrained by service-level considerations.

The different policies are closely analogous to the different replenishment policies followed by different retailers. Some stores set their replenishment levels so as to ensure that stockouts do not exceed a certain frequency: a service-level policy. Others specifically trade off the cost of a potential stockout with the cost of holding more inventory to determine the replenishment level that maximizes expected profit: a risk-based policy. Just as retailers differ in their stocking policy, so do companies differ in their overbooking policies.

For example, Hertz Rent-a-Car uses a risk-based policy to set total booking limits (Carroll and Grimes 1996) while National Car Rental uses a service-level policy (Geraghty and Johnson 1997).

9.2 A MODEL OF CUSTOMER BOOKINGS

Initially, we base our calculations of optimal booking limits on the following model.

- A supplier plans to accept bookings for a fixed capacity, C.

- The supplier sets a booking limit b before any bookings arrive.

- The supplier continues to accept bookings as long as total bookings are less than the limit b. Once the limit is reached (if it ever is), he stops accepting bookings.

- At the time of service (e.g., the departure time for a flight), customers arrive. Booked customers who arrive are called *shows*; those who fail to show are called *no-shows*.

- Each show pays a price of p.

- The supplier can accommodate up to C of the shows. If the number of shows is less than or equal to C, they are all accommodated. If the number of shows exceeds C, exactly C shows will be served and the rest will be denied service. Shows that are denied service are each paid denied-service compensation of $D > p$.[7]

The supplier's problem is to determine the total number of bookings to accept. We call this number the *booking limit* and denote it by b. Under a risk-based policy the seller sets b to balance the total revenue he will receive against the cost of denied boardings. Under a service-level policy he will set b to ensure that denied boardings do not exceed a certain fraction of total bookings or to meet some other criterion.

This model is rich enough to illustrate the fundamental tradeoffs and algorithms used to determine the total booking limit. However, it makes three heroic assumptions that we will relax in later sections.

- We have ignored cancellations by calculating the booking limit entirely based on the prospect of no-shows. This makes the booking limit much easier to calculate. Furthermore, it means that the booking limit b can be static—that is, it does not need to change over the booking period. If bookings can cancel prior to departure, then the optimal booking limit may change over time as departure approaches. We will address the calculation of dynamic booking limits in Section 9.4.1.

- We have assumed that each customer will pay the same price, p. However, as we have seen in Chapter 6, airlines, hotels, and rental car companies all offer different prices for the same unit of capacity. This can significantly complicate the calculation of the optimal total booking limit. We will address overbooking with multiple fare classes in Section 9.4.2.

- We have assumed that only those customers who arrive (i.e, the shows) pay. Bookings themselves are costless. This is the historic airline, hotel, air freight, and rental car situation, in which bookings could be cancelled without penalty and tickets were fully refundable. However, many of these industries are moving all or partway toward nonrefundable or partially refundable prices. We will address the effect of nonrefundable or partially refundable prices in Section 9.4.3.

9.3 SOLUTION APPROACHES

9.3.1 A Deterministic Heuristic

A hotel has observed that its historic show rate has averaged 85%. Furthermore, this rate has been consistent over time. A reasonable policy might be for the hotel to set its total booking limit b so that if it sells b rooms and experiences the average show rate, it will fill exactly C rooms. That is, it would set b such that $C = 0.85b$, or $b = C/0.85$.

This approach to calculating a total booking limit can be written as

$$b = C/\rho \qquad (9.1)$$

where C is capacity and ρ is the show rate. Despite its simplicity, the deterministic heuristic turns out to be a reasonable approximation to the optimal booking limit in many cases. In fact, it is still used to calculate overbooking limits by some companies.

Example 9.1

For a hotel with 250 rooms and an expected show rate of 85%, the deterministic heuristic gives a booking limit of $250/0.85 = 294$ rooms.

9.3.2 Risk-Based Policies

Under a risk-based policy the booking limit is set by balancing the expected cost of denied service with the potential additional contribution from more sales. A prerequisite to calculating a risk-based booking limit is to estimate the cost of denied service.

The cost of denied service. The cost of denied service depends upon how customers who are denied service are treated. This varies from industry to industry and from company to company within an industry. A broadcaster that cannot meet the number of impressions he has guaranteed to an advertiser needs to provide additional advertising spots until he has fulfilled the guarantee. A rental car outlet that does not have a car available when a booked customer arrives must either force the customer to wait until a car is available or provide a vehicle from a competing company.

In the passenger airline industry, denied service cost is called *denied boarding cost*. In the United States, the treatment of overbooked passengers is regulated by the Department of Transportation. As of July 2004, the DOT requires that an airline with an overbooked flight first seek customers willing to take a later flight in return for compensation. As noted before, airlines will typically increase the compensation level one or two times if they cannot find enough volunteers at the initial level. If the airline cannot find enough volunteers, it will need to bump one or more passengers. These are the rules for involuntary denied boardings.

- If you are bumped involuntarily and the airline arranges substitute transportation that is scheduled to get you to your final destination (including later connections) within one hour of your original scheduled arrival time, there is no compensation.

- If the airline arranges substitute transportation that is scheduled to arrive at your destination between one and two hours after your original arrival time (between one and four hours on international flights), the airline must pay you an amount equal to your one-way fare to your final destination, with a $200 maximum.

- If the substitute transportation is scheduled to get you to your destination more than two hours later (four hours internationally) or if the airline does not make any substitute travel arrangements for you, the compensation doubles (200% of your fare, $400 maximum).

- You always get to keep your original ticket and use it on another flight. If you choose to make your own arrangements, you can request an "involuntary refund" of your original fare. The denied-boarding compensation is essentially a payment for your inconvenience.[8]

These rules do not apply to charter flights, scheduled flights with planes that hold 60 or fewer passengers, or cases when an airline has substituted a smaller plane for the one it originally planned to use. The rules are also minimum guidelines—the airlines are free to pay additional compensation if they so choose. Usually, the only additional compensation the airlines provide are meal vouchers if the delay is more than two hours or a hotel voucher if the bumped passenger is accommodated on a flight that leaves the next day.

The airlines are unusual in that the government has mandated a procedure and compensation level for bumping passengers. Companies in other industries are generally free to deal with denied-service situations as they wish. However, denied-service cost in all cases includes one or more of four components:

- The *direct cost* of the compensation to the bumped passenger—this could be a certificate for future travel or a future hotel room night.

- The *provision cost* of meals and/or lodging provided to a bumped passenger.

- The *reaccommodation cost* of a customer denied service. For an airline, this is the cost of putting them on another flight to their destination; for a hotel it is the cost of alternative accommodation for the night.

- The *ill-will cost* from denying service. This may be hard to calculate but is usually an estimate of the lost future business from the bumped customer.

Denied-service cost will vary depending on the situation. For a passenger airline, bumping a passenger from the last flight of the day will usually incur the additional cost of lodging her overnight. Reaccommodation cost for an airline depends on whether the bumped passenger is rebooked on one of its own flights or on a competing airline's flight. Of course, the ill-will cost for a voluntary denied boarding is much less than for an involuntary denied boarding—in fact there are many cases in which a volunteer has been happy to have the opportunity to take a later flight in return for a flight voucher—perhaps even resulting in a "goodwill benefit."

The risk-based objective function. To calculate a risk-based booking limit we need to specify the objective function. Denote the number of passengers who show up at departure by s. The number of shows is a random variable that depends on both the booking limit and the total demand for bookings. Since each show pays price p, total revenue is $p \times s$. If shows exceed capacity, then the supplier must deny service to $s - C$ passengers. Each customer denied service results in a cost of D. The total denied-boarding cost is 0 if $s \leq C$ and is $D(s - C)$ if $s > C$. The *net revenue* is then

$$R = ps - D(s - C)^+ \tag{9.2}$$

(Recall that $(s - C)^+$ denotes the maximum of $s - C$ and 0.) A company pursuing a risk-based policy wants to set its booking limit so as to maximize the expected value of net revenue as defined in Equation 9.2, where the number of shows is a random variable that depends on the booking limit.

Total revenue as a function of the number of shows is plotted in Figure 9.1. Revenue increases linearly until the capacity limit is reached, at which point it begins to decrease. Two things are apparent immediately from Figure 9.1. First, since the number of shows will always be less than the booking limit, it is never optimal to set the booking limit less than the capacity. Thus, we know that $b \geq C$. Second, if the price is higher than the denied boarding cost (that is, $p > D$), net revenue would continue to increase even when shows exceed the booking limit. In this case it would be optimal to accept as many bookings as we can—we should set the booking limit $b = \infty$.

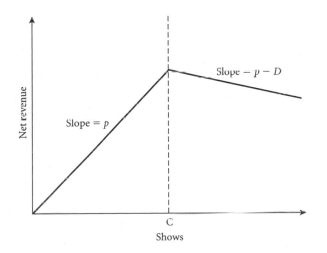

Figure 9.1 Net revenue as a function of shows.

Calculating an optimal risk-based booking limit is complicated by the fact that the number of shows is a function of three different factors:

1. The booking limit b
2. The total demand for bookings, d
3. The number of bookings that ultimately show, s

We are interested in the number of *bookings at departure*, which we denote by n. Bookings at departure is the minimum of the booking limit and the demand for bookings, that is, $n = \min(d, b)$. The total number of shows is the number of bookings at departure minus no-shows—that is, $s = \min(d, b) - x$, where x denotes the number of no-shows. We denote the *show rate*, ρ, as the fraction of bookings at departure we anticipate will show, that is, $\rho = s/n$, while the *no-show rate* is the fraction of bookings at departure we anticipate will not show, that is, $1 - \rho = x/n$. As noted before, American Airlines reported a systemwide average show rate of about 85%—that is, $\rho = 0.85$. However, the show rate can vary dramatically from case to case. In general, international and transcontinental flights have much lower no-show rates than do shorter domestic flights. Resort hotels tend to experience lower no-show rates than business hotels. Not surprisingly, the no-show rate has a major effect on the optimal overbooking policy.

A simple risk-based booking limit. The simplest interesting model is one in which the number of no-shows is independent of the number of total bookings. This is a rather gross simplification because the more bookings we take, the more no-shows we would expect. We can only justify the independence assumption by the fact that it tremendously simplifies the calculation of the optimal booking limit. Furthermore, it enables us to calculate the booking limit in a way that highlights the fundamental tradeoff in balancing the incremental price from an additional booking with the risk of an additional denied boarding.

Recall that capacity is C, the price is p, and the denied boarding cost is D, with $D > p$. Total demand for bookings d and the number of no-shows x are both uncertain and, in this model, independent. We define $F(d)$ as the probability that the total number of booking requests will be less than or equal to d and $G(x)$ as the probability that the number of no-shows will be less than or equal to x. Since these two quantities are independent, the probability that demand is less than or equal to d *and* no-shows less than or equal to x is simply $F(d)G(x)$. We want to determine the value of b that maximizes expected total revenue. For any value of b, the expected net revenue is given by the expected value of Equation 9.2; that is, $E[R|b] = pE[s] - DE[(s - C)^+]$. Substituting for s gives

$$E[R|b] = pE[\min(b, d) - x] - DE[(\min(b, d) - x - C)^+] \tag{9.3}$$

We could find the optimal booking limit by applying mathematical brute force to Equation 9.3. However, it is much more interesting to consider the structure of the problem and proceed from there. Assume we have already set a booking limit of $b > C$. What would happen if we increase the booking limit from b to $b + 1$? There are three possibilities.

1. Demand is less than $b + 1$. In this case, increasing the booking limit will not change the number of shows, and the effect of increasing the booking limit from b to $b + 1$ will be 0.

2. Demand is greater than or equal to $b + 1$ and the number of no-shows is greater than $b - C$. In this case, the airline will gain a paying customer without overbooking. The net gain is p.

3. Demand is greater than or equal to $b + 1$ and the number of no-shows is less or equal to $b - C$. In this case, the airline will gain a paying customer but will also bump another customer. The net effect is $p - D$. Since $D > p$, this is a net loss to the airline.

The decision as to whether or not to increase the booking limit is illustrated in decision tree format in Figure 9.2. The square node on the left represents the decision: namely, whether or not to increase the booking limit from its current value of b to $b + 1$. The first uncertainty is on total demand. If total demand d is less than or equal to b, then the effect of increasing the booking limit is 0—we would not have booked up to the limit. If, on the other hand, demand is greater than b, increasing the booking limit by 1 will result in an additional booking. In this case, the net effect of the additional booking will depend on the number of no-shows. If the number of no-shows is greater than $b - C$, then the additional booking will fill a seat that would have departed empty. The net effect is a gain of a price, p. If the number of no-shows is less than or equal to $b - C$, the additional booking will result in an additional denied boarding, with net effect $p - D$.

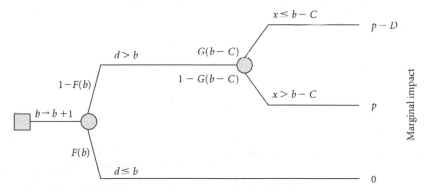

Figure 9.2 Decision tree to determine optimal booking limit in the simple risk-based model.

The change in expected net profitability is the probability-weighted sum of the quantities on the tips of the branches in Figure 9.2. If the probability-weighted sum of these quantities is greater than zero, then the supplier should increase the booking limit to $b + 1$ because he will realize more revenue (in an expected-value sense) by doing so. Once he has increased the booking limit to $b + 1$, he can use the same logic to determine whether or not he should increase it by one more seat. On the other hand, if the probability-weighted sum of the quantities in Figure 9.2 is less than zero, then the supplier should not increase the booking limit—the optimal booking limit is no larger than b (and may be smaller).

The probability that no-shows are less than or equal to $b - C$ is $G(b - C)$ and the probability that they are greater than $b - C$ is $1 - G(b - C)$. Given this, the change in expected revenue that we would anticipate from increasing the booking limit from b to $b + 1$ is

$$E[R|b + 1] - E[R|b] = [1 - F(b)]\{G(b - C)(p - D) + [1 - G(b - C)]p\}$$
$$= [1 - F(b)][p - G(b - C)D] \qquad (9.4)$$

Increasing the booking limit by 1 will lead to greater expected revenue if the quantity on the right-hand side of Equation 9.4 is greater than zero. We know that $1 - F(b)$ is always greater than or equal to zero. So as long as $p - G(b - C)D$ is greater than zero—that is, $G(b - C) < p/D$—we can keep increasing the booking limit without reducing expected revenue.[9] However, if $G(b - C) > p/D$, we should not increase the booking limit any further.

Since we know the optimal booking limit is greater than or equal to capacity, we can translate this rule of thumb into an algorithm for finding the optimal booking limit in the simple risk-based model.

A Simple Risk-Based Booking Limit Algorithm

1. Initialize $b = C$.
2. If $p/D \leq G(b - C)$, stop. The current value of b is optimal.
3. If $p/D > G(b - C)$, set $b \leftarrow b + 1$ and go to step 2.

You can confirm that this algorithm will find the smallest value of b for which $p/D \leq G(b - C)$. We can summarize this as:

> The optimal booking limit in the simple risk-based model is the smallest value of b for which $p/D \leq G(b - C)$.

Example 9.2

Consider a flight with 100 seats, a fare of $120, and a denied-boarding cost of $300. Then $p/D = 0.4$. Furthermore, assume that no-shows follow a binomial distribution with $p = 0.42$ and $n = 20$. This means that the expected number of no-shows is 8.4. $G(b - C)$ is then as shown in the third column of Table 9.3. If demand for this flight is much greater than 100 bookings, then Table 9.3 shows how passenger revenue, expected denied-boarding cost, and expected total revenue change as the booking limit is increased from 100 to 120. Following the simple risk-based booking limit algorithm, we find that $b = 108$ is the first point at which $G(b - c) \geq 0.4$ and that the optimal total booking limit is thus 108. This can be confirmed by reference to Table 9.3, which shows that the maximum expected revenue is indeed achieved at this booking limit.

The logic behind the algorithm is illustrated in Figure 9.3. For booking limits within a few seats of capacity, the probability of a denied boarding is quite low, so expected net revenue increases almost as quickly as passenger revenue. However, as the booking limit continues to increase, the expected denied-boarding cost increases faster than passenger

TABLE 9.3
Calculating booking limit for a simple risk-based model

b	$b - C$	$G(b - C)$	Passenger revenue	Expected DBs	Expected DB cost	Expected net revenue
100	0	0.00	$10,992	0.00	$0.00	$10,992
101	1	0.00	11,112	0.00	0.01	11,112
102	2	0.00	11,232	0.00	0.09	11,232
103	3	0.01	11,352	0.00	0.73	11,351
104	4	0.03	11,472	0.01	3.78	11,468
105	5	0.09	11,592	0.05	14.25	11,578
106	6	0.20	11,712	0.14	41.91	11,670
107	7	0.35	11,832	0.34	100.68	11,731
108	**8**	**0.52**	**11,952**	**0.68**	**204.52**	**11,747**
109	9	0.69	12,072	1.20	361.39	11,711
110	10	0.83	12,192	1.90	569.46	11,623

revenue until it reaches its peak at $b = 108$. At this point, we achieve the maximum expected revenue of $11,747: a 6.9% increase over the revenue of $10,992 we would achieve from not overbooking at all. Note that, if the airline never overbooked, it would observe an average show rate of $(100 - 8.4)/100 = 0.916$. Using this show rate and the deterministic heuristic in Equation 9.1 would suggest a booking limit $b = 100/0.916 = 109.17$, which can be rounded down to 109. From Table 9.3 we can see that the corresponding expected total revenue would be $11,711, or only $36 per flight less than from the optimal limit. At least in this case, the deterministic heuristic provides a good approximation to the booking limit determined by the simple risk-based policy.

The simple risk-based algorithm can be used to determine the optimal booking limit for any no-show distribution. If no-shows are normally distributed, then a standard table of the cumulative normal distribution can be used to find the optimal limit. Alternatively, Excel's

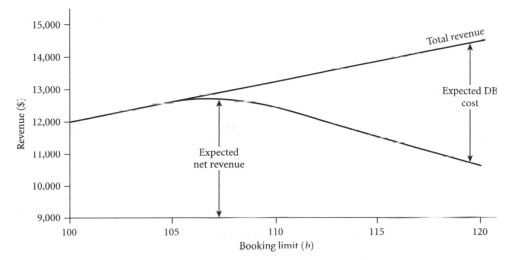

Figure 9.3 Total revenue, expected overbooking cost, and expected net revenue as a function of booking limit for the example in Table 9.3. We have assumed that total demand is greater than 110.

NORMINV function can also be used. The answer given by either of these approaches will need to be appropriately rounded in order to produce an integer answer (see Exercise 2).

Relation to the newsvendor problem. Like the two-class booking limit problem discussed in Section 7.2.4, the problem of setting a risk-based overbooking limit has a close relationship to the newsvendor problem. Recall that the solution to the newsvendor problem requires ordering an amount of inventory Y^* so that

$$\Pr\{\text{Demand is greater than equal to } Y^*\} = \frac{U}{U + O}$$

where U is the underage cost, O is the overage cost, and $U/(U + O)$ is the *critical fractile* or *critical ratio*. In setting a risk-based booking limit b, we are determining how many bookings to "order," that is, the total number of bookings to allow. The underage cost is the opportunity cost of an empty seat, that is, p, and the overage cost is the *net* denied boarding cost, that is, $D - p$. Therefore, the critical ratio is p/D. The event that triggers an overage cost is "shows exceeding capacity," which, in our simplified model is no-shows less than $b - C$. Thus, the newsvendor model would specify setting b such that the probability of no-shows less than $b - C$ is equal to the critical fraction.

How are no-shows distributed? The no-show distribution is a critical element in determining the optimal booking limit. What kind of probability distribution would no-shows follow? The simplest way to derive a no-show distribution is to assume that each booking has an identical probability, $0 < \rho \le 1$, of showing and that show decisions are independent. Then the number of shows given n bookings follows a *binomial distribution*.[10] Let $q(s|n)$ be the probability of s shows given n bookings. Then

$$q(s|n) = \binom{n}{s}\rho^s(1 - \rho)^{n-s} \quad \text{for } s = 0, 1, \ldots, n \tag{9.5}$$

with mean $E[(s|n)] = \rho n$ and variance $\text{var}[(s|n)] = \rho(1 - \rho)n$. Under these assumptions, the number of no-shows x will also follow a binomial distribution, but with parameters $1 - \rho$ and n.

The binomial density function of shows is given in Figure 9.4A for $n = 120$ bookings and show rates of 80%, 90%, and 95%. Figure 9.4B gives the corresponding cumulative distributions. Each cumulative distribution shows the probability that shows will be less than x, given 120 total bookings. This can be interpreted as the probability that a flight with x seats will be overbooked if it has 120 bookings at departure, given different no-show rates. Figure 9.4A shows that both the mean and the standard deviation of the number of shows depend upon the show rate. The mean number of shows is the show rate times the number of bookings: 96, 108, and 114 for show rates of 80%, 90%, and 95%, respectively.

Notice that the bulk of the probability on shows for any show rate between 80% and 95% lies between 80 and 110 when there are 120 bookings at departure. Thus, for a show rate of 80%, it is almost certain (a 99.97% chance, to be exact) that the number of shows will be between 80 and 110. We can use Figure 9.4B to estimate the probability we will not have an oversold flight if we have 120 bookings at departure for aircraft with different seating ca-

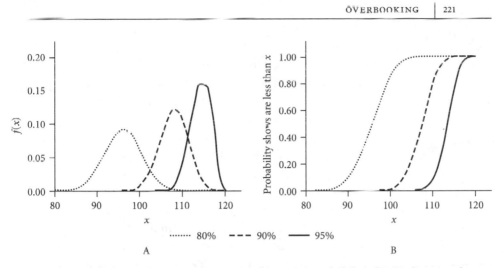

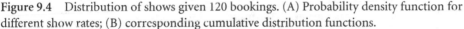

Figure 9.4 Distribution of shows given 120 bookings. (A) Probability density function for different show rates; (B) corresponding cumulative distribution functions.

pacities. As shown, if we have 120 bookings for a flight with 100 seats, we will almost certainly have at least one denied boarding if our show rate is 90% or 95%. On the other hand, we will only have about an 8% chance of being oversold if the show rate is 80%. These relationships are critical in determining the right level of total bookings to accept.

A binomial distribution of shows will result whenever the probability that any individual booking will show is independent of whether or not any other booking will show. If I have booked a flight to Chicago and I miss the flight because I was in a meeting that ran late, it is safe to say that my no-show behavior was independent of other bookings (unless, of course, there were others in the meeting who missed the same flight). On the other hand, it is quite easy to think of situations in which no-shows are not independent. For one thing, the majority of airline bookings are for more than one seat: Many bookings are either for families or for business colleagues traveling together to the same destination. One study at American Airlines found that only 45% of bookings were for a single seat, 29% of bookings were for three or more seats, and the average booking size was for slightly more than two seats (Rothstein and Stone 1967). Since it is highly likely that either the entire party will show or it will not show, the assumption that no-shows are independent does not hold. The independence assumption would also fail if there is a systematic influence on no-show behavior, for example, a snowstorm that prevented a large number of passengers from getting to the airport in time for the flight.

While the independence assumption is violated in many cases, research at several airlines has shown that a binomial distribution does fit the data reasonably well—as long as larger groups are not considered.[11] Furthermore, hotel and rental car no-shows seem to be even more independent than airlines, since many parties of two or more may still only rent one room or one car. As a result, a binomial distribution on shows is widely used in practice.

A more realistic risk-based model. The simple risk-based model in Section 9.3.2 relies on the assumption that the number of no-shows is independent of the total number of bookings. While this simplified the analysis, it is clearly a very dodgy assumption. After all, if we accept 120 bookings, we would expect to see more no-shows than if we accepted only 100 (unless, of course, the no-show rate is 0). In fact, with a no-show rate of 15%, the expected number of no-shows would be 15 with 100 bookings and 18 with 120 bookings. Ideally, we want to incorporate this effect into the calculation of our booking limit. At heart, the fundamental tradeoff remains the same—for each additional booking allowed, the airline must trade off the increased chance of a denied boarding with the decreased chance of leaving with an empty seat. However, formalizing the calculation requires a deeper level of mathematical calculation.

As before, let the random variable d represent total demand. Then the number of bookings at departure will be $n(b) = \min(d, b)$. We designate the number of passengers who show given bookings at departure $n(b)$ as $s[n(b)]$. Note that the random variable s is a function of total bookings, $n(b)$, and therefore of the booking limit b. The number of no-shows $x(b)$ is equal to the number of bookings minus the number of shows; that is, $x(b) = n(b) - s[n(b)]$. Of course, we must have $s[n(b)] \leq n(b) \leq b$. The net revenue from the flight, given $s[n(b)]$ shows, is

$$R = ps[n(b)] - D[s[n(b)] - C]^+ \tag{9.6}$$

where the first term is the total revenue received and the second term is the total denied-boarding cost. Equation 9.6 is the analog of Equation 9.2, except we have made explicit the dependence of shows on bookings at departure $n(b)$. The expected net revenue the airline will receive if it sets its booking limit at b is simply the expectation of Equation 9.6, namely,

$$E[R|b] = pE\{s[n(b)]\} - DE\{[s[n(b)] - C]^+\} \tag{9.7}$$

where $E[R|b]$ is expected net revenue.

Optimality conditions. The decision tree in Figure 9.5 illustrates the calculation of the marginal impact of increasing the booking limit. The square node represents the airline's decision: whether or not to change the booking limit from b to $b + 1$. The circular nodes represent the uncertainties it faces. The values at the tips of the branches are the impacts on expected net revenue from increasing the booking limit *relative to keeping the booking limit*

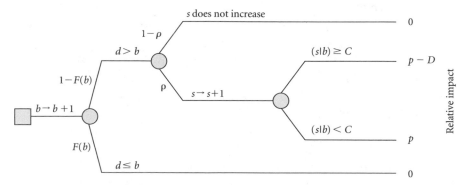

Figure 9.5 Total booking limit decision tree for risk-based material.

at b. Traversing the tree in Figure 9.5 from left to right, the first uncertainty is on total demand. If total demand is less than or equal to the current booking limit, then increasing the booking limit by one seat will have no effect—we will see the same number of bookings and, hence, of shows. This event, shown on the lowest branch in the tree, has probability $F(b)$ of occurring and a relative impact of 0.

Things get more interesting when demand exceeds the booking limit b. This will occur with probability $1 - F(b)$, and this event is represented by the upper branch coming from the first node. In this case, increasing the booking limit to $b + 1$ will result in one additional booking. We now have to consider the impact on total shows. Since we have assumed that shows are independent, the probability that the additional booking will show is ρ. If the additional booking *does not* show, which occurs with probability $1 - \rho$, then the total number of shows remains unchanged and so does total net revenue. In this case, the impact relative to keeping the booking limit at b is 0. The more interesting case is when the additional booking does show. There are then two possibilities. If the number of shows was less than capacity when the booking limit was b, then the additional show simply results in an additional price without any denied-boarding cost. This is the "good outcome" from increasing the booking limit, and its relative impact is p. However, if the number of shows was already greater than or equal to the seating capacity, then the additional show results in an additional denied boarding. This is the "bad outcome," and its relative impact is $p - D < 0$.

The change in expected net revenue from increasing the booking limit by one seat is the probability-weighted sum of the outcomes on each branch. Let $h(b)$ be the change in net revenue if we increase the booking limit from b to $b + 1$. Then $E[h(b)] = E[R|b + 1] - E[R|b]$, and, "rolling back" the tree in Figure 9.5, we can write

$$E[h(b)] = (1 - F(b))[(1 - \rho)0 + \rho \Pr\{(s|b) \geq C\}(p - D)$$
$$+ \rho \Pr\{(s|b) < C\}p] + F(b)0$$
$$= (1 - F(b))\rho[\Pr\{(s|b) \geq C\}(p - D) + \Pr\{(s|b) < C\}p]$$
$$= (1 - F(b))\rho[p - \Pr\{(s|b) \geq C\}D] \tag{9.8}$$

where $\Pr\{(s|b) \geq C\}$ is the probability that the number of shows s given the booking limit b will be greater than or equal to the capacity C. Now, we know that $\rho > 0$ and that $F(b) \leq 1$. If $F(b) = 1$, there is no gain from increasing the booking limit, since we will not receive any additional bookings. If $F(b) < 1$, the impact of increasing the booking limit will depend on the sign of $p - \Pr\{(s|b) \geq C\}D$. If this term is greater than zero, then we can increase expected net revenue by increasing the booking limit—and we should do so. If it is less than or equal to zero, we should certainly not increase the booking limit, and it is possible that a lower booking limit could lead to higher expected net revenue.

We can start at $b = C$ and increase b as long as doing so results in additional expected net revenue. As long as $E[h(b)]$ as defined by Equation 9.8 is greater than zero, we can improve expected net profit by increasing the booking limit. This is equivalent to climbing the "expected net revenue hill" in Figure 9.3. Once we reach a b such that $E[h(b)] \leq 0$, we have reached the top of the hill and the current value of b is optimal. Formally, assuming that $F(b) < 1$, the optimal booking limit is the value of b such that

$$\Pr\{(s|b) \geq C\} = \frac{p}{D} \tag{9.9}$$

Calculating the probability that shows will exceed capacity. The remaining question is how to calculate $\Pr\{(s|b) \geq C\}$: the probability that shows will exceed capacity if we set the booking limit at b. If $b = C$, we only allow bookings up to the capacity of the airplane. In this case, the only way that shows can be greater than or equal to capacity is if the demand is greater or equal to C and every single booking shows. The probability that this will occur is

$$\Pr\{(s|C) \geq C\} = [1 - F(C - 1)]\rho^C$$

If $[1 - F(C - 1)]\rho^C \geq p/D$, then we should not overbook at all. However, the probability that all passengers on a flight will show is usually very small. If we have booked 100 passengers and we have a 90% show rate, the probability that all 100 passengers will show is $0.9^{100} = 0.0000266$. In other words, an airline flying 100-seat planes with every flight booked to capacity and a no-show rate of 10% will only have about one flight in every 38,000 leave fully loaded. If the fare on the flight is \$200 and we knew that demand would exceed 100 for sure, then from Equation 9.9 an airline looking to maximize expected profitability would be willing to overbook by one seat as long as $0.0000266 D < \$200$, or $D < \$200/0.0000266 \approx \$7,500,000$. This should convince you of the strong financial incentive airlines have to overbook.

We have shown that $\Pr\{(s|C) \geq C\} = [1 - F(C - 1)]\rho^C$. In Section 9.7, we show that

$$\Pr\{(s|b + 1) \geq C\} = \Pr\{(s|b) \geq C\} + [1 - F(b + 1)] \binom{b}{C - 1} \rho^C (1 - \rho)^{b - C + 1} \tag{9.10}$$

This means we can start at $b = C$ and increase b by one seat at a time. At each step we use Equation 9.10 to update $\Pr\{(s|b) \geq C\}$ until $\Pr\{(s|b) \geq C\} \geq p/D$. At this point we have reached the optimal b^*, since increasing b further would only lead to a decrease in expected net revenue.

Example 9.3

Consider a 100-seat flight facing normally distributed demand with mean 140 and standard deviation 70 and with a show rate of 90%. For a particular ratio of price to denied boarding cost p/D, the optimal booking limit is b, for which $\Pr\{(s|b) \geq C\} = p/D$. From Table 9.4, we can see that the optimal booking limit for this flight would be 110 seats if $p/D = .25$, 113 seats if $p/D = .5$, and 116 seats if $p/D = .6$.

An algorithm for the optimal booking limit. Inspection of Table 9.4 reveals one potential problem with the hill-climbing approach. For this flight, $\Pr\{(s|b) \geq C\}$ will never rise much

TABLE 9.4

Probability that shows exceed capacity as a function of booking limit

Booking limit (b)	$1 - F(b)$	$\rho \Pr\{(s\|b) = C - 1\}$	$\Pr\{(s\|b) \geq C\}$
100	0.72	0.0003	0.0000
101	0.71	0.0013	0.0002
102	0.71	0.0046	0.0012
103	0.70	0.0117	0.0044
104	0.70	0.0244	0.0125
105	0.69	0.0427	0.0294
106	0.69	0.0647	0.0588
107	0.68	0.0866	0.1029
108	0.68	0.1039	0.1614
109	0.67	0.1132	0.2311
110	0.67	0.1132	0.3065
111	0.66	0.1047	0.3814
112	0.66	0.0902	0.4500
113	0.65	0.0728	0.5087
114	0.64	0.0554	0.5557
115	0.64	0.0398	0.5911
116	0.63	0.0272	0.6163
117	0.63	0.0176	0.6334
118	0.62	0.0110	0.6444
119	0.62	0.0065	0.6511
120	0.61	0.0037	0.6551
121	0.61	0.0020	0.6574
122	0.60	0.0011	0.6586
123	0.60	0.0006	0.6593
124	0.59	0.0003	0.6596
125	0.58	0.0001	0.6598
126	0.58	0.0001	0.6598

higher than 0.66 for any value of b: With a 90% show rate, the probability that shows will exceed capacity for this flight can never be greater than 67%, even if we set the booking limit to infinity. This means that if we have a price ratio p/D of, say, 0.75, we will never reach the point where $\Pr\{(s\|b) \geq C\} \geq p/D$ for any value of b. We could go on climbing forever, making smaller and smaller improvements each time but never reaching the top of the hill! This is the situation in Figure 9.3 when the price ratio is p/D_2.

The easiest way to avoid this situation is to set a predefined maximum booking limit $\hat{b}$ for each flight. For example, we might want to stipulate that no matter what the expected demand and no-show situation, we would never allow any flight to be overbooked twice over. In this case, we would set $\hat{b} = 3C$. We can also note that $\Pr\{(s\|b) \geq C\} \leq 1 - F(C)$; that is, for *any* booking limit, the probability that shows will exceed capacity is always less than or equal to the probability that demand will exceed capacity. (Why?) Thus, if $p/D \geq 1 - F(C)$, we know immediately that we can set b to its maximum value; that is, $b^* = \hat{b}$.

We now have all the elements for an algorithm:

Algorithm for Computing Optimal Total Booking Limit

1. If $p/D \geq 1 - F(C)$, set $b^* = \hat{b}$ and stop. Otherwise, go to step 2.

2. Set $b = C$ and $\Pr\{(s\|b) \geq C\} = [1 - F(C)]\rho^C$.

3. If $\Pr\{(s\|b) \geq C\} \geq p/D$, set $b^* = b$ and stop. Otherwise, go to step 4.

4. Set $b \leftarrow b + 1$ and $\Pr\{(s|b) \geq C\} \leftarrow \Pr\{(s|b) \geq C\} +$
$$[1 - F(b + 1)] \binom{b}{C - 1} \rho^C (1 - \rho)^{b - C + 1}.$$

5. If $b = \hat{b}$, set $b^* = \hat{b}$ and stop. Otherwise, go to step 3.

Note that the booking limit that maximizes expected net revenue can be much higher than capacity. In fact, Equation 9.9 implies that the fraction of high-demand flights on which at least one passenger would be denied boarding would be p/D. If the denied boarding cost is twice the price, this would imply that at least one passenger would be denied boarding on 50% of all high-demand flights—a fraction that some airlines might consider too high.[12] Note that for any particular flight, the probability of at least one denied boarding given we set a total booking limit of b is exactly $\Pr\{(s|b) \geq C + 1\}$. Therefore, if we wanted to set a booking limit for a particular flight such that the probability of at least one denied boarding is no greater than some factor, say, $\epsilon < 1$, then we would look to find the largest value of b such that

$$\Pr\{(s|b) \geq C + 1\} \leq \epsilon$$

We could easily formulate a "hill-climbing" algorithm that starts at $b = C$ and sequentially increases b to find the optimal booking limit under this policy. Like the previous algorithm, we would need to set a maximum booking limit ahead of time, because it might well be possible that no finite value of b would meet the criterion for a given flight.

9.3.3 Service-Level Policies

In the absence of any other considerations, properly calculated risk-based booking limits maximize expected short-run profitability. From this, it would seem to follow that risk-based booking limits would be universally used. However, this is not the case. Many airlines and other overbookers do not explicitly trade off denied-boarding costs and customer revenue to set booking limits. Rather, they try to determine the highest overbooking limit that does not cause denied-service incidents to exceed management-specified levels. Reasons that a company might prefer a service-level policy over a risk-based policy might include the following.

- Some components of denied-service cost, such as ill will, might be viewed as difficult or impossible to quantify. In view of this, management might consider a service-level policy to be "safer" than a risk-based policy.

- Risk-based booking limits can lead to wide variation in booking limits—and potential numbers of denied boardings—from flight to flight. Under a risk-based policy, an airline might set overbooking levels ranging from 10% to more than 50% of capacity for different flights departing from the same airport during the day. Instead of accepting this wide variation, the airline might be comfortable with simply setting a constant overbooking limit over all flights in order to smooth staffing needs and to ensure that no single flight ever experiences a massive overbooking situation.

- Corporate management may feel that a risk-based booking limit calculation is a "black box" that they cannot understand and do not have confidence in. On the other hand, service-level limits are easy to understand, the results are easy to measure, and they give comfort that denied-service levels will not be out of line with those experienced by competitors.

Whatever the reason, service level policies are commonplace. Examples of companies that use (or have used) service-level based policies include airlines such as American (Rothstein and Stone 1967), rental car companies such as National (Geraghty and Johnson 1997), and many hotels.

A typical service-level policy would be to limit the fraction of booked customers denied service. For example, an airline might set a policy that the fraction of bookings that result in a denied boarding should be approximately 1 in 10,000. Recalling that $(s|b)$ refers to shows given booking limit b and that C refers to capacity, this policy would be equivalent to setting b such that

$$\frac{E[((s|b) - C)^+]}{E[(s|b)]} = \frac{1}{10,000} \tag{9.11}$$

or, equivalently, $E[((s|b) - C)^+] = 0.0001E[(s|b)]$.

An alternative service-level policy would be to specify that the number of denied service incidents should be some specified fraction of *customers served* rather than of total bookings. This is the way in which airlines report denied boardings to the Department of Transportation—thus, Table 9.1 shows that Alaska Airlines experienced 0.81 involuntary denied boardings per 10,000 passengers in 2003. Under this policy, the company would set b so that

$$E[((s|b) - C)^+] = qE[\min((s|b), C)] \tag{9.12}$$

where q is the target denied-service fraction and $E[\min((s|b), C)]$ is expected sales given a booking limit of b.

It should be noted that applying the policies implied by Equations 9.11 and 9.12 on a flight-by-flight basis (or a rental-day-by-rental-day basis) will result in conservative booking limits. That is, the fraction of denied-service incidents that will actually occur will almost certainly be less than q. This is because the booking limits calculated by Equations 9.11 and 9.12 will result in an average denied-service rate of q on flights with demand sufficiently high that the booking limit is relevant. Some flights will have such low demand that they will never sell out. Including bookings on these flights will improve the denied-service statistics at a system level.

9.3.4 Hybrid Policies

Most airlines, hotels, and rental car companies are not purists when it comes to overbooking. In many cases they use a hybrid policy under which they calculate booking limits based on both risk-based and service-level policies and use the minimum of the two limits. This allows them to gain some of the economic advantage from trading off the costs and benefits of overbooking while still ensuring that metrics such as "involuntary denied boardings per 10,000 passengers" remain within acceptable bounds—however defined.

9.4 EXTENSIONS

9.4.1 Dynamic Booking Limits

Suppliers overbook in order to compensate for both cancellations and no-shows. However, so far we have only considered no-shows in our calculation of booking limits. Without cancellations, a supplier can simply calculate an optimal booking limit at the beginning of the booking period and hold it constant until departure. The supplier does not need to update the booking limit or change it over time. When cancellations are factored in, the situation becomes more complex. Specifically, the optimal booking limit for a supplier who allows bookings to cancel prior to departure will change over time. The supplier then needs to calculate a *dynamic booking limit*.

In the most general case, a supplier will face both cancellations and no-shows. This is certainly the case for most airlines, hotels, and rental car companies. American Airlines has estimated that about 35% of all bookings will cancel before departure, compared to 15% of bookings at departure that will not show. While cancellation rates are typically higher than no-show rates, cancellations are less costly than no-shows since they allow the opportunity to accept a late booking to fill the space freed up by the cancellation.

A common model of cancellations is to estimate a dynamic cancellation fraction $r(t)$, where t is the number of days until departure. Assume an airline has accepted $m(t)$ bookings at time t. Then it would expect that, on the average, $r(t)m(t)$ of those bookings will cancel while $[1 - r(t)]m(t)$ of them will convert to bookings at departure. With a show rate of ρ, the airline would expect that an average of $\rho[1 - r(t)]m(t)$ current bookings will show. One tempting (and common) approach is to use $\rho[1 - r(t)]$ as a "dynamic show rate" and to apply standard risk-based or service-based models to determine the current booking limit.

Example 9.4

An airline is using a dynamic version of the deterministic booking heuristic in Equation 9.1. The airline has an average no-show rate of 13% for a flight assigned an aircraft with 120 seats. Twenty days before departure the expected cancellation rate for this flight is 60%. The airline therefore sets a booking limit of $b = 120/[(1 - 0.6) \times 0.87] = 345$. Five days before departure the expected cancellation rate is 20%, and the corresponding booking limit is $b = 120/[(1 - 0.2) \times 0.87] = 172$.

Bookings tend to firm toward departure—the fraction of accepted bookings that will cancel decreases as t approaches 0. This means that $r(t)$, the expected cancellation rate, is typically an increasing function of t. It may not, however, be a continuous function. For example, many airlines specify that certain discount tour and group bookings cannot be cancelled later than 14 days prior to departure without penalty. This often leads to a booking "cliff," with the number of bookings crashing dramatically on the same day as all the tours and groups simultaneously cancel their unsold allocations. The booking limit needs to adjust accordingly to reflect the fact that reservations "on the books" within 14 days of departure are far more likely to convert to shows than those on the books prior to that period.

A typical dynamic booking limit is shown in Figure 9.6. Here, the heavy curve shows the total booking limit at each time before departure, while the lighter line shows actual bookings. The booking limit starts out high to allow for the possibility of a high proportion of future cancellations. As the departure date of the flight approaches, the booking limit decreases as bookings become more firm. Bookings initially start out low and increase toward departure. In Figure 9.6, total bookings hit the booking limit at time A. At that point, the airline stops accepting bookings. Note that for some period, accepted bookings can actually exceed the booking limit. In Figure 9.6, a sufficient number of cancellations occur so that bookings fall below the limit at time B. At time B the airline starts accepting bookings again, until the booking limit is reached again, at which time the flight would again be closed. In the figure, the flight closes three times and reopens twice.

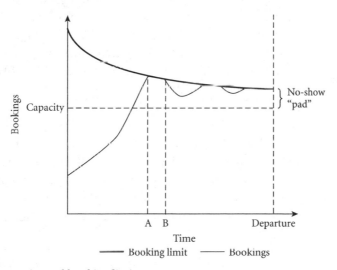

Figure 9.6 Dynamic total booking limit.

The difference between the booking limit at departure and the capacity of the aircraft is the amount the airline has overbooked specifically to accommodate no-shows. This is the booking limit that corresponds to the top of the expected revenue hill in Figure 9.3 — it is where the airline would like bookings to be just prior to observing no-shows.[13] If the airline has done a good job managing bookings over time *and* gotten a bit lucky, it will reach this point. Of course, demand may be so low that bookings never reach the limit. Or they may reach the limit at some point, but a higher or lower cancellation rate than expected may result in bookings at departure being higher or lower than the ideal. Cancellations add yet another complication to the already-dicey game of maximizing profitability.

Figure 9.6 illustrates an important aspect of dynamic booking limits — the booking limit tends to be high early on, just when actual bookings are likely to be low. Except for flights that have extraordinary levels of early-booking demand, the total booking level is not likely to be binding when there is still a long time until departure. This means that using computational resources to calculate exact total booking limits and to update them frequently months before departure is not necessary. However, as departure approaches, the optimal booking limit decreases and the number of bookings generally increases. This means it becomes more and more worthwhile to compute an exact booking limit as departure approaches. Typically an airline may only update the total booking limit for a flight monthly when it is six months or more until departure. As departure approaches, the airline will increase the frequency of recalculation. Most airlines (and rental car companies and hotels) will be recalculating the total booking limit every day during the last week before departure.

9.4.2 Overbooking with Multiple Fare Classes

The models we have studied so far have been based on the assumption of a single fare class. However, as we saw in Chapter 6, the same unit of capacity can often be sold to customers from many different fare classes. If customers are booking in reverse fare order *and* bookings can cancel or not show, then the airline faces a combined overbooking and capacity control problem. Say we have n fare classes, with $f_1 > f_2 > \cdots > f_n$ with class n booking first, followed by class $n - 1$, with class 1 booking last. The problem faced by the airline is the same in spirit as the capacity allocation problem treated in Chapter 7—that is, the airline needs to set booking limits (or, equivalently, protection levels) for each fare class. The difference is now that these booking limits need to incorporate the fact that some of the bookings from each class are likely to cancel or not show.

The problem of finding optimal booking limits for multiple fare classes—what we might call the *combined overbooking and capacity allocation problem*—is extremely difficult to solve in general. It is complicated by the fact that not only are different booking classes likely to have different fares, they are also likely to have different cancellation and no-show rates. In fact, the general problem of combining overbooking with capacity allocation is so difficult that many companies use some variant of the following approach.

Combined Overbooking and Capacity Allocation Heuristic

1. Compute a total booking limit for the entire plane using either the deterministic heuristic, a risk-based approach, or a service-level approach. Call this limit B. No matter what approach is used, B will be greater than or equal to capacity.

2. Use a capacity allocation approach such as EMSRa or EMSRb to determine protection levels. (Recall that optimal protection levels are not based on capacity.)

3. From the protection levels calculated in step 2, determine booking limits for each fare class as if the capacity were equal to B.

4. Update B and the protection levels as bookings and cancellations occur.

Example 9.5

An airline is selling three fare classes—full fare, standard coach, and discount—on a flight with 100 seats. Three weeks before departure, the airline sets a total booking limit of 115. Using EMSRb, the airline calculates protection levels of 35 for full fare and 60 for full fare and standard coach. The airline then sets booking limits of 115 − 60 = 55 for discount bookings, 115 − 35 = 80 for standard coach, and 115 for full fare.

We have left unanswered the question of how the total booking limit B should be calculated. The risk-based approaches illustrated in Figures 9.5 and 9.2 require an estimated fare that will be received if an additional seat is filled. With a single fare, this calculation is simple. When there are multiple fares, it is not so clear what the increased revenue would be from filling an additional seat. A common heuristic is to use an estimated fare that is a weighted average of the fares, where the weights are proportional to the mean demands in each fare class. In other words, the average fare is

$$\hat{p} = \sum_{i=1}^{n} \mu_i p_i$$

where μ_i is the mean demand in fare class i. Substituting $\hat{p}$ into the risk-based algorithms will enable the calculation of a booking limit.

This approach—sometimes called the *pseudo-capacity* approach—is very widely used. It has the distinct advantage of allowing the supplier to mix and match overbooking and capacity management approaches; any approach to calculating the total booking limit (e.g., risk based or service level) can be combined with any approach to calculating booking limits. Research has shown that it generally provides a good solution as long as no-show rates do not vary widely among classes—however, it is by no means "optimal."

9.4.3 Other Extensions

We have assumed that the denied-boarding cost is a constant. In reality, the denied-boarding cost per passenger is likely to be an increasing function of the number of oversales. Consider a flight that is oversold by 15 passengers. The airline might be able to persuade five people to volunteer to take another flight for $200 apiece. It might convince another seven volunteers for $250 apiece. It then may have to choose three more involuntary denied boardings, with an associated cost of $500 apiece (including ill-will cost). In this case, total denied-boarding cost is a piecewise linear function of the number of oversales, as shown in Figure 9.7.

An airline cannot know in advance exactly how many volunteers it will induce at each level of compensation for a particular flight. This means not only that the denied boarding cost is not constant, it is also a random variable. Increasing the booking limit b leads to an increase in the expected number of denied boardings $E[(s|b) − C]^+$, which in turn leads to an increased expected denied-boarding cost per passenger. Instead of a constant value of denied-boarding cost D, the airline needs to calculate an expected denied-boarding cost as a function of the booking limit. While the calculation of the booking limit can be complex in this situation, increasing denied-boarding costs tend to *reduce* the optimal booking limit relative to constant denied-boarding costs.

We have also assumed that tickets are totally refundable and that no-show customers do not pay any penalty. This was standard practice in the airline industry for many years.

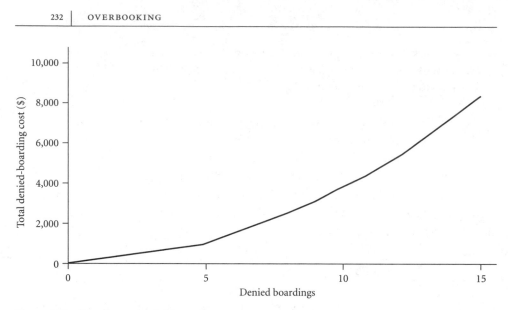

Figure 9.7 Nonlinear denied-boarding cost.

However, airlines, hotels, and rental car companies are increasingly selling partially re-fundable bookings and charging penalties for no-shows and cancellations. A partially re-fundable ticket or no-show penalty changes the underlying economic tradeoffs and there-fore also changes the optimal booking limit. Assume the airline charges a penalty of $\alpha < 1$ times the price for each no-show. Thus, if $\alpha = 0.25$, the airline would collect $25 for a pas-senger who purchased a $100 ticket but did not show. The marginal impact of changing the booking limit in the case when the airline collects αp from each no-show is shown in Fig-ure 9.8. This tree is exactly the same as the tree in Figure 9.5, with the exception that the top branch, which represents an additional no-show from increasing the booking limit by 1, now has a payoff of αp. We can use this tree to calculate the booking limit that maximizes expected net revenue using the same approach as before (see Exercise 1).

Finally, in many industries the risk of no-shows and cancellations is counterbalanced to some extent by the possibility of *walk-ups*: customers without a reservation who show up just prior to departure wanting to buy a ticket.[14] Companies sell capacity to walk-ups

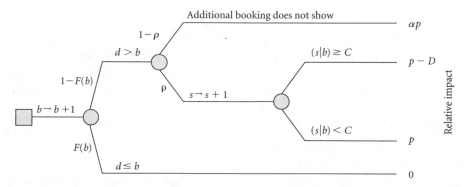

Figure 9.8 Calculating the optimal total booking limit with a no-show penalty.

only if it is available after all shows are accommodated. Since walk-up customers have not made bookings, they are not entitled to payment if they are not served. Walk-ups are highly desirable customers: not only can they be used to fill seats that would otherwise go empty, they can usually be charged high prices. Thus, hotels will often charge walk-ups the rack rate—even if the hotel is not close to being full. The theory is that a walk-up customer has a high willingness to pay since the cost of finding an alternative is relatively high.

It is easy to see that the possibility of walk-ups reduces the optimal total booking limit. If a hotel knew that it would have 10 high-paying walk-up customers arriving every day, it would set its booking limits as if it had 10 fewer rooms. Of course, like all elements of future customer demand, the number of walk-ups is uncertain at the point when the booking limit needs to be set. However, in cases where walk-ups are important, companies will forecast expected walk-up demand and incorporate its effect explicitly in calculating booking limits (see Exercise 3).

Each of these complications adds to the complexity of calculating the total booking limit. However, in any circumstances, the basic idea is the same. We want to find the booking limit such that the additional revenue we would expect from increasing the booking limit balances the additional expected denied-boarding cost we would incur.

9.5 MEASURING AND MANAGING OVERBOOKING

Prior to the deregulation of the airlines, airline management focused on *load factor* as the key performance indicator, both for individual flights and on a system level. The load factor of a flight is the ratio of the number of passengers on a flight (its load) to its capacity. A flight departing with 100 seats and 86 passengers has an 86% load factor. Load factor can be measured at any level, from a single flight to a market served by many flights to an entire airline. Up into the 1970s and even beyond, load factor was the main metric that airlines tracked. Marketing programs were evaluated based on changes in load factor—a program that increased load factors was successful, one that did not increase them was ineffective. Persistently low load factors on a flight were considered a signal that a smaller aircraft should be assigned to the route or that the flight should be rescheduled to a different time or even be dropped.

Load factor is an utter failure as a measure of overbooking policy. The booking policy that maximizes load factor is simple—accept every booking request regardless of aircraft capacity. This may result in hundreds or thousands of denied boardings, but the planes will be as full as possible.

To avoid the hordes of denied boardings that would result from an unconstrained booking policy, airline management often instructed booking controllers to "minimize denied boardings." This created a basic conflict: Any booking policy that increases load factor is likely to result in an increase in denied boardings, and policies that decrease denied boardings are likely to reduce load factors. As we have seen, an optimal risk-based booking policy neither maximizes load factors nor minimizes denied boardings. Rather, it finds the booking limit that best balances the risks of spoilage with the risk of denied boardings, to maximize expected net revenue. Therefore an airline overbooking policy needs to be evaluated based on *two* metrics:

1. *Spoilage rate*—the number of empty seats at departure for which we denied a booking, expressed as a fraction of total seat departures [15]

2. *Denied-boarding rate*—the number of denied boardings, expressed as a fraction of total seat departures (involuntary and voluntary denied boardings are usually tracked separately)

Both the spoilage rate and the denied-boarding rate need to be measured against targets. These targets can be calculated with the same forecasts used to calculate the booking limit in the first place.

Example 9.6

An airline sets a total booking limit for a flight with a 100-seat aircraft, expected demand of 110 passengers with a standard deviation of 55, a no-show rate of 10%, and a discount fare of $200 and a full fare of $350. If we are using the optimal booking limit calculated in Section 5.2, we would expect a spoilage rate of about 0.06 and a denied-boarding rate of about 0.02. Of course, the spoilage and denied-boarding rates for a specific flight will most likely be different, but the average overall flight departures with the same characteristics should be close to 0.06 and 0.02. If the rates are significantly different, we should seek the reasons why. Are our demand or no-show forecasts consistently in error? Are booking controllers intervening too often to raise or lower the booking limits?

It should be stressed that performance needs to be evaluated against targets in both directions. For example, it might seem that a denied-boarding rate of 1% would indicate better performance than 2%. After all, it meant that we had fewer denied boardings. But if the lower denied-boarding rate was achieved at the cost of a higher spoilage rate, it may mean that our overbooking policy was not sufficiently aggressive and we lost profitable opportunities to fill additional seats. If the lower denied-boarding rate did not coincide with a higher spoilage rate, we still need to understand the reason why it differed from our target. It may mean that our demand and no-show forecasts need to be adjusted for future flights.

Overbooking is only one of the pieces of the overall revenue management problem that needs to be measured. Airlines use a combination of the various metrics to measure the performance of their revenue management functions. A portfolio of metrics might include:

1. *Denied-boarding rates* to measure effectiveness of overbooking policies

2. *Spoilage rates* to measure effectiveness of overbooking and capacity allocation policies

3. *Dilution rates* to measure effectiveness of capacity allocation

4. *Revenue per available seat mile (RASM)* to measure overall effectiveness and to compare performance to that of other airlines

5. *Revenue opportunity metrics (ROMs)* to measure effectiveness of capacity allocation decisions

In each case, tracking trends are usually more important than the absolute numbers or measurement against targets, particularly when the metrics are applied at a disaggregated level. It is often difficult to say if the ROM or RASM achieved by a particular flight departure is "good" or "bad" given the multitude of market and competitive factors that can influence it either way. But a consistent downward trend in ROM or RASM is usually a signal of a situation that requires attention.

Revenue management metrics are still evolving. By using a portfolio of metrics, an RM company can get a good view of its overall performance in generating revenue from its markets relative to competition and how that performance is changing over time. It can evaluate the performance of its revenue management program and determine areas for improvement. It can evaluate individual revenue managers by measuring the number of times their interventions improved overall performance versus the times when intervention degraded performance. However, there is still a considerable amount of work to be done on developing improved revenue management metrics. A particular area of current research is developing metrics to evaluate the performance of network management. Another area is to develop metrics that separate the effects of *pricing* from those of *revenue management*.

9.6 ALTERNATIVES TO OVERBOOKING

Overbooking is not popular with customers. Customers hate arriving weary at their hotel at midnight only to be told that the hotel is overbooked and they will be bused to another hotel 10 miles away. Overbooking is also unpopular with suppliers. Not only does it create unhappy customers, it is a continual source of stress for gate agents, desk clerks, or whoever needs to deliver the news to the customer that she is going to be denied service. Airline gate agents often feel as if the sole purpose of overbooking is to make their life more difficult, and airline revenue managers spend a considerable amount of time explaining the need for overbooking and the financial benefits it brings.

In this environment, it is not surprising that companies have actively searched for alternative ways to manage the uncertainty intrinsic in allowing customers to cancel and not show.

- *Standbys.* A standby booking is one sold at a deep discount and that gives the customer access to capacity only on a "space-available" basis. Customers with standby tickets arrive at the airport and are told at the gate whether or not they will be accommodated on their flight. If they cannot be accommodated on their flight, the airline books them at no charge on some future flight (possibly also on a standby basis).

- *Bumping strategy.* If the fares for late-booking passengers are sufficiently high, an airline could pursue a bumping strategy—that is, if unexpected high-fare demand materializes, the airline would overbook with the idea that it can deny boardings to low-fare bookings in order to accommodate the high-fare passengers. For a bumping strategy to make sense, the revenue gain from boarding the full-fare passenger must outweigh the loss from "bumping" the low-fare booking, including all penalties and ill-will cost that might be incurred. Historically, airlines were reluctant to overbook with the conscious intent of bumping low-fare passengers to accommodate high-fare passengers. However, with the average full fare now equal to seven or more times the lowest discount fare on many routes, the bumping strategy is beginning to make more and more economic sense for many airlines.

- *The replane concept*, currently being offered by the company Replane, Inc. Under the replane idea, an airline that sees higher-than-anticipated demand will contact customers on the same flight (via Internet or phone, for example) and offer them some level of compensation to take a later flight. For example, a customer might be offered $100 to take a later flight to the same destination, freeing up space for a $500 passenger.

- *Last-minute discounts*. Historically, the price of airline bookings has tended to increase as departure approaches, as airlines seek to exploit the fact that later-booking customers tend to be less price sensitive than early-booking customers. However, increasingly airlines have been using last-minute deep discounts to sell capacity that would otherwise go unused. For example, the company Last-Minute Travel (www.lastminutetravel.com) specializes in selling deeply discounted capacity for flights that are nearing departure. In order to limit cannibalization, many airlines, hotels, and rental car companies only offer last-minute discounts through disguised ("opaque") channels, such as Priceline (www.priceline.com) and Hotwire (www.hotwire.com). In a similar vein, classical concerts and operas will often sell standing-room-only tickets at a deep discount once all seats have been sold.

- *Cancellation and no-show penalties*. Many airlines, hotels, and rental car companies have instituted penalties for customers who cancel or don't show. These penalties can range from 10% or less of the price all the way to 100% for a nonrefundable ticket.

Each of these approaches has drawbacks. Standby tickets usually need to be priced at extreme discounts in order to sell. Furthermore, while standbys may help reduce spoilage, they do nothing to help the situation in which the airline has accepted too many bookings and needs to deny some boardings. In fact, they make the situation worse, since both the no-shows and the standbys all need to be accommodated on some future flight to the same destination.

Cancellation and no-show penalties might seem to be an obvious answer to the overbooking problem, since such penalties should decrease the number of cancellations and no-shows as well as reduce the revenue risk to airlines. However, two points need to be made. First of all, an airline facing a cancellation penalty will still have a motivation to overbook as long as it faces a significant number of cancellations and denied boardings. An airline with nonrefundable tickets may still face a combined late cancellation and no-show rate of 10%

or more. In this case, the airline can still increase revenue by overbooking. Second, it is not always easy for an airline to institute cancellation or no-show penalties. Customers whose travel plans are somewhat unsure will value the ability to cancel or change their flight without penalty. Instituting a cancellation penalty may induce these customers to purchase from a competitor who does not penalize cancellations.

9.7 *APPENDIX: DERIVATION OF THE SHOW PROBABILITY FOR OVERBOOKING

We need to calculate how $\Pr\{(s|b) \geq C\}$ changes as we increase b from $b = C$, where $(s|b)$ is defined as the number of shows we will see given that we set a booking limit of b. We can write

$$\Pr\{(s|b + 1) \geq C\} = \sum_{x=C}^{b} f(x) \Pr\{s(x) > C\}$$
$$+ [1 - F(b)] \Pr\{s(b + 1) \geq C\} \quad (9.13)$$

$$\Pr\{(s|b) \geq C\} = \sum_{x=C}^{b} f(x) \Pr\{s(x) \geq C\}$$
$$+ [1 - F(b)] \Pr\{s(b)\} \geq C\} \quad (9.14)$$

Here, $f(x)$ is the probability that $d = x$, that is, that the demand we see is exactly x. $s(x)$ is the number of shows that we will see if we have exactly x bookings.[16]

Notice that Equations 9.13 and 9.14 express two similar probabilities in slightly different ways. Subtracting Equation 9.14 from Equation 9.13 gives

$$\Pr\{(s|b + 1) \geq C\} - \Pr\{(s|b) \geq C\} = [1 - F(b)][\Pr\{(s|b + 1) \geq C\}$$
$$- \Pr\{(s|b) \geq C\}] \quad (9.15)$$

The expression on the right-hand side of Equation 9.15 is the product of two terms. The first term, $1 - F(b)$, is the probability that demand will be greater than the booking limit b. The second term, $\Pr\{(s|b + 1) \geq C\} - \Pr\{(s|b) \geq C\}$, is the additional probability that shows will be greater than or equal to capacity as our bookings go from the old booking limit to the new booking limit. This term will always be greater than or equal to zero, since increased bookings cannot decrease the probability that shows will exceed capacity. We can simplify Equation 9.15 further by noting that the only way that the probabilities that shows will exceed capacity will increase as we change our booking limit from b to $b + 1$ is if (a) the additional booking shows, which will occur with probability ρ, and (b) shows given b bookings were exactly $C - 1$. That is,

$$\Pr\{(s|b + 1) \geq C\} = \Pr\{(s|b) \geq C\} + \rho[1 - F(b)] \Pr\{(s|b) - C - 1\}$$

Equation 9.5 gives

$$\Pr\{(s|b) = C - 1\} = \binom{b}{c-1} \rho^{C-1}(1 - \rho)^{b-C+1} \quad (9.16)$$

Substituting this into Equation 9.16 and reducing terms, we get

$$\Pr\{(s|b+1) \geq C\} = \Pr\{(s|b) \geq C\} + [1 - F(b+1)]\binom{b}{C-1}\rho^C(1-\rho)^{b-C+1}$$

9.8 EXERCISES

1. Solve the decision tree in Figure 9.8 to determine a formula for the total booking limit that maximizes expected net revenue when there is a no-show penalty of αp. Does the no-show penalty generally result in higher or lower booking limits than the case when tickets are entirely refundable?

2. A flight has 100 seats and a passenger fare of $130. The number of no-shows is independent of total bookings and is given by a normal distribution with mean of 22 and standard deviation of 15. The denied-boarding cost is $260 per denied boarding. Use a table of cumulative normal distribution values or the NORMINV function of Excel to determine the optimal booking limit in this case. Recall that the booking limit needs to be an integer.

3. Capacity, fare, denied-boarding cost, and the no-show distribution are the same as in Exercise 2. However, there is now a 0.6 probability that there will be a walk-up customer for the flight. Assuming there is a seat available on the flight after shows are accommodated, the airline will charge the walk-up customer $200. What is the optimal booking limit for this flight?

4. A flight has 100 seats and a passenger fare of $130. The denied-boarding cost is $390 per denied boarding, and the no-show rate is 0.16. Demand for this flight is extremely high; in fact, for any booking limit $b < 200$, bookings will always hit the booking limit. What is the optimal total booking limit in this case? What is the corresponding expected net revenue? How much does the airline gain from overbooking in this case?

5. A low-cost airline sells only nonrefundable tickets. Customers pay in full at the time of booking. If they cancel or miss their flight for any reason, no portion of the price is refunded, and they cannot board another flight without buying a new ticket. Despite this policy, the airline still experiences a no-show rate of 5%. That is, if it sells 100 tickets on a 100-seat aircraft, it will, on average, depart with five empty seats. Should this airline overbook? If so, what kind of policy should it adopt? If not, why not?

6. A rental car company will have 100 cars available for rent on a particular day. It expects that demand for that day will be very high, so demand is certain to be higher than 300 bookings. If it expects a 15% no-show rate, what booking level should it set if it wants to ensure that the probability that a booking will be denied service is 0.0002? (You can use the normal approximation to the binomial described in Appendix B to estimate your answer.)

1. A *cancellation* is defined as a booking that a customer terminates by notifying the seller at some point prior to the service date. A *no-show* occurs when a buyer with a booking does not cancel but simply fails to show up.

2. See Smith, Leimkuhler, and Darrow (1992).

3. Civil Aeronautics Board (1967).

4. Rothstein (1985).

5. The actual rates were 19.6 voluntary DBs and 0.9 involuntary DBs per 10,000 in 1999 and 19.6 voluntary DBs and 1.0 involuntary DBs per 10,000 in 2000 (see Talluri and van Ryzin 2004).

6. In addition, many cruise lines sell trip insurance, which will refund the price of the cruise to the buyer in case she needs to cancel.

7. We assume that all shows buy a ticket. Those that are denied service pay the price p but receive denied-service compensation of D. The *net denied-service cost* to the supplier for each denied service is then $p - D$. This represents how most airlines, hotels, and rental car companies manage denied-service situations.

8. These were the rules as of August 2004. The latest DOT rules on treatment of involuntary denied boardings are at http://airconsumer.ost.dot.gov/publications/flyrights.htm.

9. If $F(b) = 1$, further increasing the booking limit will not change expected revenue since demand is less than the booking limit.

10. Background on the binomial distribution is given in Appendix B.

11. See Thompson (1961) for an early example of such a study.

12. This is not the same as saying that the airline will experience denied boardings on 50% of its flights. Some flights will have such low demand that they essentially have no chance of being overbooked no matter how high a booking limit is set.

13. This assumes that the airline is following a risk-based policy.

14. Walk-ups are also known as *go-shows* in the passenger airlines.

15. It is important to note that only the seats on a flight for which a booking was denied were "spoiled." Seats for which there was no booking request are not considered spoiled. A flight for which we denied five booking requests that left with seven empty seats had five spoiled seats. On the other hand, a flight for which we denied three booking requests that left with one empty seat had one spoiled seat.

16. Note that $s(x)$ is different from $(s|b)$, which we have defined as the number of shows we will see given a *booking limit* of b.

10 | MARKDOWN MANAGEMENT

Nobody but a fungoid creature from another galaxy with no familiarity with earthly ways would ever pay list price for anything.

— *Dave Barry*

"Waiting for the sale" is a time-honored strategy for savvy shoppers. The fashion-conscious may splurge on spring fashions shortly after they arrive at Macy's, Nieman Marcus, Nordstroms, Bloomingdale's, or Saks; but the budget-minded know they can save by waiting. And the longer they wait, the more they save; many items will be marked down by 70% or more by the end of the season. "Waiting for the sale" is not without risk. There is always the chance that the store will sell out of a desired item before it is marked down. Nonetheless, an increasing number of customers are willing to take the risk in order to realize the savings. Dave Barry may be overstating the case, but in many categories retail list price is becoming a ceiling, with most sales taking place at a discount. More and more customers won't buy an item if it isn't on sale.

Retailers use a wide variety of mechanisms to discount their merchandise. Broadly speaking, these can be classified into promotions and markdowns. A *promotion* is a temporary reduction in price. Examples of promotions include a Memorial Day sale, a temporary two-for-one sale, an introductory low price, and a coupon for 10 cents off. The common link among these is that they are all temporary. In contrast, a *markdown* is a permanent reduction, usually to clear inventory before it becomes obsolete or needs to be removed to make way for new stock. When an item is marked down, both the seller and the buyer know that the price for that particular item will never go back up.

The difference between markdowns and sales promotions is illustrated in Figure 10.1, which shows the daily price over four months of a television set (B) and a woman's sweater (A), both expressed as a percentage of list price. The television set was promoted three times, with its price returning to list following each promotion. On the other hand, once the price of the sweater was reduced, it never returned to earlier levels. After about three weeks at list price, it was marked down 20%, followed by three further markdowns. At the end of the four-month period, the sweater was selling for about 20% of its list price, while the television was priced at list.[1]

This chapter discusses the tactics behind *markdown management*. The point of markdown management is to find the timing and magnitude of price reductions that move the

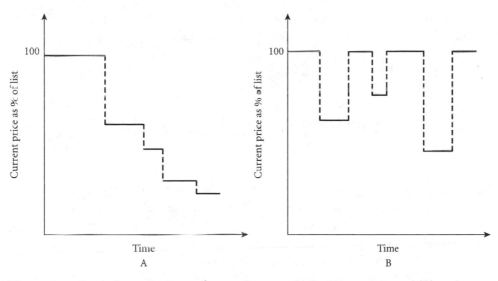

Figure 10.1 Example retail price tracks over four months for (A) a sweater and (B) a television set.

inventory while maximizing revenue. For many years, retailers relied on their judgment or simple rules of thumb to determine when and how much to mark down their goods. However, over the past decade, more and more retailers have begun to use more sophisticated analytic tools to help guide this process, and companies such as Manugistics and ProfitLogic have developed commercial markdown optimization software.[2] The current markdown management situation is reminiscent of the early days of revenue management in the airline, hotel, and rental car industries: Large retailers are increasingly using sophisticated analytical software systems to help guide their markdown management decisions. While the use of such systems is by no means universal, the fact that some early adopters have reported revenue increases of 10–15% has stimulated increasing adoption of these systems by retailers.

In this section we start by giving some background and show how, for certain goods and services, markdowns segment the market and provide a simple method by which retailers can profit from price discrimination. We outline the markdown management process that retailers follow and some of the business issues that can constrain them. We formulate the markdown problem as a constrained optimization problem and outline the most common approaches to solving the problem. Finally, we discuss the use of markdown management systems and some of the experiences of various companies in improving markdown management.

10.1 BACKGROUND

The practice of marking down distressed inventory is probably as old as commerce itself. Nonetheless, in the United States, markdowns and promotions were relatively rare prior to 1950. Sales were associated with holidays such as Christmas and Thanksgiving, or they occurred as periodic "price wars" between rivals such as Macy's and Gimbels in Manhattan.

In fact, most retailers tried hard to avoid markdowns. In the 1950s, managers at The Emporium, a leading San Francisco department store, were told:

> High markdowns benefit no one. Not the store. Not the manufacturer. Not the customer. The store loses in value of assets or inventory. The manufacturer loses in future sales and by loss of prestige of his product. The customer is getting merchandise that is not up to standard, at a low price it is true, but, remember—she would rather have fresh, new merchandise that she can be proud of and with real value at regular price than pay less for questionable merchandise.[3]

Many retailers considered markdowns to be prima facie evidence of mistakes in purchasing, pricing, or marketing. The official line at The Emporium was "Like accidents, most markdowns are a direct result of carelessness."[4] On the other hand, a few retailers have always recognized that markdowns are more than just a way to clean up after mistakes. As early as 1915, one of the leading textbooks on retailing noted that

> This method of marking up goods and making reductions as necessary seems to be the most effective way to sell some goods, especially those that are subject to changes in style. Besides bringing handsome profits to the concern directly, the spectacular cuts in prices . . . furnish excitement for readers of the store's advertising, and help to draw crowds who may buy other goods as well as those advertised.[5]

Since the 1960s, there has been a steady increase in both the size and the frequency of retail discounts. Figure 10.2 shows the growth in average discount from list price paid for items purchased at both department stores and specialty stores from 1967 through 1997. In 1967, the average price paid for all items purchased at department stores was at a 6% discount from list; by 1997, the average discount was 20%. The comparable figures for specialty stores were

Figure 10.2 Average discount from list price for goods sold at department and specialty stores from 1967 through 1997. Discounts include both markdowns and promotions. Stores with annual sales greater than $1 million to 1982 and greater than $5 million thereafter. *Source*: Data from National Retail Merchants Association (1968, 1977, 1987) and National Retail Federation (1998).

10% and 28%. Both the fraction of goods sold at a discount and the average discount inexorably increased from 1967 through 1997. Sometime in the 1970s, purchasing goods at a discount went from being an exception to being the rule. According to a Retail Service survey, more than 72% of all fashion items sold in 1998 were sold at a discount (National Retail Federation 1998).

The reasons for the steady rise in the average discount illustrated in Figure 10.2 has been much discussed. Here are some of the reasons that have been proposed.

- Increased customer mobility, leading to more intense competition among retailers.

- The rise of discount chains and outlets, many with "everyday low pricing" strategies.

- A self-reinforcing "vicious cycle" under which customers expect discounts and will not purchase unless retailers provide them, therefore creating an expectation of future discounts.

- An increasing interest by consumers in variety rather than standard items. Pashigian (1988) reports that the market share of colored and patterned sheets relative to white sheets increased from 12% in 1970 to 60% in 1990. Sales of patterned men's shirts have also increased relative to standard white and blue. Since nonstandard items have shorter shelf lives than standard items, merchants have to discount more often and more deeply in order to move old inventory and make room for new.

- The increased use of *markdown money*, by which manufacturers reimburse retailers for some portion of the discounts provided to move slow-selling items. This has made it easier and more economical for retailers to resort to more aggressive discounting. Markdown money shifts some of the risk of unsold inventory from retailers to manufacturers.

It is worth noting that a few sectors have resisted the trend toward pervasive discounting. Discounting is still relatively rare in prescription drugs, movie tickets, and various staple food and home items. As a result, for these items, even relatively small promotions can often drive dramatic sales increases. Furthermore, over the last 15 years there has been a rising number of "everyday low price" retailers, such as Wal-Mart, who discount rarely, if at all. Nonetheless, the consensus is that no matter the cause, the increase in retail discounting is likely to continue, and, for the majority of retailers, planning and executing discount programs will consume an increasing portion of their time and energy. Since retail is a notoriously thin-margin business, properly planned markdowns can play a make-or-break role in determining profitability.

10.1.1 Reasons for Markdowns

Let's return to the price histories for the sweater and the television set shown in Figure 10.1. Why was the sweater marked down but not the television set? If you asked the retailer, he would probably mention two reasons. First of all, the sweater is a fashion good—its perceived value decreases over time, and it needs to be marked down to reflect this declining value. On the other hand, the value of the television does not decline over time. The second reason is that the sweater needs to be sold in order to make room for next season's line of clothes. If it is not sold by a certain date (the so-called *out date*), it will be removed from the store and sent to an outlet store or sold to a "jobber" for 20% or less of its original price. Markdowns are necessary to move the goods and clear the space for next season's clothes. On the other hand, there is no pressing need to clear the televisions—that is, unless the current model is being discontinued or made obsolete by the imminent arrival of a new model.

As these examples show, *from the seller's point of view*, markdown products typically share two characteristics:

1. Inventory (or capacity) is fixed.

2. The inventory must be sold by a certain out date or its value drops precipitously.

These two reasons provide the *seller* with motivation to mark down.

However, there are additional reasons why the value of an item to *buyers* might decrease over time:

1. *Time of Use*. An overcoat purchased in September can be worn during the upcoming winter months, unlike the same overcoat purchased next April. Many consumers assign value to wearing the coat during the upcoming winter, with that value declining as winter progresses.

2. *Fashionability*. Some consumers place a high value on getting a fashionable item early in the season, while others may care much more about buying at the lowest price. This also applies to short-life-cycle goods such as consumer electronics and video games, where some buyers value being among the first to own the latest gadget or game.

3. *Deterioration*. The quality of a good may deteriorate over time. Day-old bread does not taste as good as fresh bread. Clothes that have been on display for months can get a pawed-over look that makes them less appealing.

4. *Obsolescence*. Consumers may believe that a better-quality version of a product will be available at some future date. As time passes, it increasingly makes sense to wait for the new product rather than buy the current version. To induce customers to buy now rather than wait may require deeper and deeper discounts. This is an especially important effect in consumer electronic goods, computer equipment, and automobiles.

Note that the first three reasons involve customer segmentation and price discrimination. *Time of use* segments the market between those customers who need an overcoat now (and are willing to pay more for it) and those who can wait. *Fashionability* segments the market into fashionistas, who place a high value on being au courant, and value-conscious customers, who are willing to wait. And deterioration allows the seller to offer an inferior product at a lower price. As we have seen, customer segmentation and price discrimination are powerful ways for a seller to increase revenue, especially when his inventory is constrained. Thus, it should be no surprise that they play a major role in the use of markdowns as a selling strategy. It seems reasonable that prices would drop for items whose quality deteriorates over time. After all, everyone's willingness to pay for day-old bread is less than that for fresh bread.

While deteriorating quality is often found in markdown products, we can use a simple model to show how markdowns can segment a market even when quality does not deteriorate.[6] Consider a seller facing the linear price-response curve $d(p) = 1,000 - 100p$, shown in Figure 10.3. Recall that this linear price-response curve is equivalent to a population of 1,000 potential buyers whose willingness to pay is uniformly distributed between $0 and $10. Assume that the good being sold has a marginal cost of zero. (As we shall see, this is often a reasonable assumption in markdown management.) Then, we know from Section 2.4 that given a single period, the price that maximizes the seller's contribution is $p^* = \$5$, with corresponding sales of 500 units and total contribution of $2,500. This contribution corresponds to the shaded area in Figure 10.3A. At this price, everyone in the population with a willingness to pay greater than or equal to $5 purchases the product, and those with a willingness to pay of less than $5 either do not purchase or purchase from a competitor.

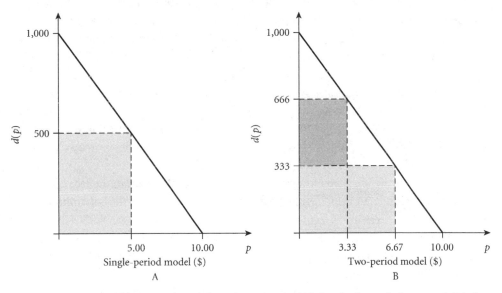

Figure 10.3 Optimal prices, sales, and total revenue in (A) the single-period case and (B) the two-period case. In the two-period case, the optimal first-period price is $6.67 and the optimal second-period price is $3.33.

So far, so simple. But what happens if, after all the buyers with w.t.p.'s higher than $5 had purchased the product, the seller had the opportunity to change the price? In this case, it should be apparent that the seller can make additional money by charging a lower price in the second period. If the seller charges a second-period price higher than $5, he won't sell anything in the second period, since all customers with w.t.p. higher than $5 have already purchased. But if he charges a lower price, say, $2.50, he can realize some additional revenue. In addition to the 500 units he sold at the first-period price of $5, he would sell an additional 250 units in the second period at a price of $2.50. His second-period buyers are those whose willingness to pay is between $2.50 and $5. By charging a lower price in the second period, the seller can increase his total revenue from $2,500 to $3,125 — a 24% increase.

In fact, the seller can do even better. If he sets his first-period price at $6.67 and his second-period price at $3.33, he can achieve total revenue of $3,333.33. This solution is shown in Figure 10.3B. He sells 333 units in the first period and 333 units in the second period, for a total contribution of $333 \times \$6.67 + 333 \times \$3.33 = \$3,330$—an increase of 33% over the single-price case! If he had more periods with more opportunities to change the price, he could make even more revenue by selling at progressively higher discounts in each period (see Exercise 1).

When the price-response curve is linear, the optimal price in the second period of the two-period model will always be one-half of the optimal price in the first period. This result depends on a number of assumptions that are unlikely to be true in practice—particularly the global linearity of the price-response curve and the fact that customers do not anticipate the markdown. However, it is interesting that there are at least two cases of products that undergo a single markdown and the discount is 50% of the full price: baked goods and Broadway tickets. Day-old bread is often sold at half off the full price. And Broadway theaters have the option to sell tickets that otherwise would not be sold through a TKTS outlet in Times Square.[7] The price of a ticket purchased at TKTS is one-half the full price.

How does a second-period markdown result in additional revenue? There was no change in market conditions between the two periods, and the pool of customers did not change. The additional revenue came entirely from *customer segmentation*. The seller has used time of purchase and decreasing prices as a way of segmenting customers between those with a high willingness to pay and those with lower willingness to pay.

However, the simple model is based on several questionable assumptions. As we have noted, it assumes a single pool of customers who are all indifferent between buying in the first period and buying in the second period. In most retail situations we would expect that at least some buyers would have a lower willingness to pay for the item in the second period, either because they benefit from having the item sooner (as in a coat at the beginning of winter rather than at the end of winter) or because the item deteriorates (as in day-old bread) or because it becomes obsolete (as in a PC). Of course, the presence of customers with decreasing willingness to pay will only increase the incentives for the seller to decrease price in the second period (see Exercise 2).

The second assumption underlying the two-period model is that customers do not anticipate the second-period markdown. If customers knew (or even suspected) that the second-period price would be lower, we would expect some (if not all) of them to wait for the sale. This is cannibalization, and cannibalization reduces and can even eliminate the benefits of segmentation. One way to add cannibalization to the two-period model is to specify a fraction of customers who will wait to buy in the second period even though their willingness to pay exceeds the first-period price. In other words, these customers would be willing to pay the first-period price, but they wait for the second period because they anticipate the markdown. Thus, a *cannibalization fraction* of 10% would mean that 10% of the customers who would be willing to pay at the first-period price wait to purchase in the second period instead.

Table 10.1 shows how optimal first- and second-period prices and total revenue change as the cannibalization fraction increases from 0 to 100%. As you might expect, increasing cannibalization results in decreased revenue. Furthermore, as cannibalization increases,

TABLE 10.1
Effect of cannibalization in the two-period model

Cannibalization fraction	First-period price	Second-period price	Total revenue
0%	$6.67	$3.33	$3,290
20	6.87	3.75	3,125
40	7.06	4.12	2,914
60	7.22	4.44	2,778
80	7.37	4.74	2,632

both the first-period price and the second-period price increase. However, as long as the cannibalization fraction is less than 100%, the retailer still benefits from marking down in the second period. In other words, in this model, the retailer can improve revenue from following a markdown policy unless he believes that all of his customers will wait for the sale.

10.1.2 Markdown Management and Demand Uncertainty

In the previous section, we saw how markdown management could improve profitability when demand is deterministic and the seller knows both the size of the total market and the distribution of customer willingness to pay. Of course, this "perfect knowledge" assumption is highly unrealistic. In fact, it is easy to see that the seller's uncertainty about demand provides an additional motivation for pursuing a markdown policy. Consider a merchant with an inventory of a particular style of sweater who is unsure if the sweater will be a top seller during the upcoming season. If the sweater is a top seller, he will be able to sell his entire inventory at $79; if it is not a top seller, then the market price will only be $59. If he has two periods in which to sell the sweaters and offers them at $59 during the first period, he will sell them all during the first period. But if he offers them at $79 during the first period, he may sell them all at the high price; if not, he can lower the price to $59 in the second period and sell the remaining stock. In this case, a markdown policy enables the seller to maximize revenue in the face of demand uncertainty.

The use of markdowns to resolve demand uncertainty is exemplified in dramatic fashion by the *Dutch auction*, a term that derives from the use of this mechanism in Dutch flower markets. The most famous of these markets is in the town of Aalsmeer, where more than 4 billion flowers are sold every year. In a Dutch auction, the seller sets a maximum and a minimum price for the product he is seeking to sell.[8] During the period of the auction (5 minutes in the case of the Aalsmeer flower auction), the price drops steadily from the maximum price to the minimum price. Each potential buyer has a button that he can press at any time during the auction. When the first buyer pushes her button, she has bought the lot at the current price and the auction is over. If the price drops to the seller's specified minimum without any takers, the lot goes unsold.

In some ways, the Dutch flower auction is like a fashion season in fast-forward. The two markets share some important similarities: Both flowers and fashion goods are perishable. In both cases, the seller is often uncertain about the value that buyers will place upon his good. For fashion goods, the uncertainty arises from the fickle tastes of customers and the inability of the seller to know whether any specific item will be "hot" during the current season. In the flower market, the uncertainty is due to the daily changing supply and demand for each type of flower. In both markets, the pattern of lowering prices over time can be seen as a way by which sellers seek to extract the highest price for their constrained and perishable supply in the face of demand uncertainty.

10.1.3 Criteria for a Markdown Management Opportunity

Given the effectiveness of falling prices at segmenting demand and resolving demand uncertainty, why are markdowns not universally used? The reason is that a markdown policy is only effective when supply is constrained and perishable and customers' w.t.p.'s do not increase over time. Constrained supply is important because it creates uncertainty in consumers' minds whether or not the good will be available in the second period. A customer may know that a Ralph Lauren jacket list-priced at $1,200 will ultimately go on sale for $700; but she cannot be sure it will be available (at least in her size) if she waits. In this case, the jacket purchased late is an "inferior" good not only because the jacket may no longer be fashionable but also because it is less likely to be available.

The Dutch auction illustrates this phenomenon in dramatic fashion—if a buyer waits too long to press his button, he will find that someone else has outbid him and purchased the lot. A customer who wants to buy a ticket to a specific Broadway play (particularly a popular one) cannot rely on finding tickets available at TKTS on the day of the performance. In the extreme case, if all customers know that a good will be cheaper later on and they are indifferent between purchase periods, they will all wait to buy at the discount. Consider the modification of the simple two-period model in which all of the customers anticipate a lower price in the second period. Recall that all of the potential customers have the same willingness to pay in the first period as in the second. This means that the product being sold does not degrade between the two periods (at least not in the customers' eyes). In this stylized case, all customers would wait for the sale—no one would purchase in the first period because they know that the price will be lower in the second period. The seller would gain no advantage from offering a lower price in the second period and would only offer a single price in both periods.

This emphasizes that the following three criteria are required for a markdown opportunity to be present.

- The item for sale must be perishable.
- The supply must be limited.
- The desirability of the item must hold constant or decrease as it approaches its perishability date.

These criteria can be used to determine the situations under which a markdown policy can be effective.

10.1.4 Markdown Management Businesses

We have seen that markdown policies are used for retail fashion goods, baked goods, Broadway theater tickets, and wholesale flower sales. Here are some other businesses in which markdowns are common.

- *Holiday items*, including Halloween candy; Christmas trees, decorations, and cards; fireworks for the Fourth of July. Such items usually begin to be marked down just before the holiday, with much deeper discounts once the holiday is over.

- *Tours*. A tour package typically includes both airline transportation and lodging. Although tours constitute less than 10% of leisure travel in North America, they represent a major portion of vacation travel in Europe and Asia. A typical tour package would be six days on the Costa del Sol (in Spain), consisting of both round-trip air transportation and hotel accommodations. Bus travel to and from the air port in Spain and meals might also be included. Tour operators start selling tours a year or so ahead. As time passes, the tour operator continually monitors the bookings for different tours. If a tour is performing worse than expected (i.e., bookings are low), the tour operator may lower the price. Since the price is always lowered (never raised) and the stock of inventory is perishable, the tour operator faces a markdown management problem.

- *Automobiles*. Like fashion goods, most automobile manufacturers operate on an annual selling season. New models arrive every September and must be sold within a year to make room for next year's model. Although some models may be "hot" and not require discounting, other models will not sell quickly enough at the list price in order to clear the lot. The manufacturer and the dealer will use a mixture of promotions and markdowns to move the inventory. In general, the average selling price of an automobile (including reduced annual percentage rate, APR) tends to decline fairly steadily over the season. This gives automobile pricing the flavor of a markdown management problem, although the markdowns are typically realized through various promotional vehicles rather than as a reduction in the list price.

- *Clearances and discontinuations*. Almost any seller can be in a situation where he has inventory he needs to clear by a certain date. When Maytag announces that it will be shipping a new and improved model of washing machine in three months, retailers have three months to sell their existing inventory before it becomes obsolete. Sequential markdowns are used to maximize revenue from this existing stock. The problem occurs at least occasionally for almost all retailers (and many wholesalers) but most frequently for those selling short-life-cycle goods such as computers and home electronics. In many cases, sellers of short-life-cycle goods mark down some portion of their total inventory every day.

Markdown management is a problem that many businesses face every day and almost all businesses face sometime. In the next section, we describe some basic methods for optimizing the timing and amounts of markdowns.

10.2 MARKDOWN OPTIMIZATION

We have seen *why* sellers might use a markdown policy. We now develop some models to determine *how* they should mark their inventory down over time. These models will be based on the following assumptions.

- A seller has a fixed inventory (or capacity) without the opportunity to reorder.

- The inventory has a fixed expiration date (the *out date*), at which point unsold inventory either perishes or is sold at a small salvage value.

- Initially, the price of the good is set at list price. The seller can reduce the list price one or more times before the expiration date.

- Only price reductions are allowed. Once the price has been reduced, it cannot be increased again.

- The seller wants to maximize total revenue—including salvage value—from his fixed inventory.

Markdown optimization typically assumes that marginal costs are zero and that the goal of the seller is to maximize total revenue. This may seem surprising since the seller obviously paid someone for the goods. However, at the point a seller is considering markdowns, his costs are sunk—his inventory has already been bought and paid for. Furthermore, since the seller cannot reorder, increased sales do not result in additional future orders. Therefore, the incremental cost of an additional sale is 0 and we can state the objective function in terms of maximizing revenue from a fixed inventory.

Let p_1 denote the initial (list) price and assume that we have T markdown opportunities before the out date. For example, a typical season for a fashion item might be 15 weeks. Assuming that the item might be marked down at most once per week, we would have p_1 as the price during the first week, p_2 as the price during the second week, and so on through the final price of p_{15}.[9] We assume a salvage value of r that is received for all unsold items following the last markdown. This would be the price a retailer would receive from a jobber for unsold clothes, for example. If inventory entirely perishes at the end of period T—as in the case of a tour operator—then $r = 0$. It should be obvious that we would never set the price during any week to be less than r, since we can always wait and sell all inventory at r.

Let x_i be the unsold inventory at the beginning of period i. Then x_1 is the initial inventory, which is given. We assume that demand in any period is a function of the price in that period, and we let $d_i(p_i)$ denote the price-response function in period i. The price-response functions $d_i(\cdot)$ satisfy all of the usual properties—i.e., they are downward sloping, continuous, etc. Sales in period i are denoted by q_i. Since sales in any period are constrained by the inventory on hand, we have $q_i = \min[d_i(p_i), x_i]$. We initially consider deterministic models, in which p_i will uniquely determine $d_i(p_i)$ and hence q_i. We then turn our attention to (more realistic) probabilistic models, in which both $d_i(p_i)$ and q_i are random variables.

The starting inventory in each period is equal to the starting inventory from the prior period minus prior-period sales; that is, $x_{i+1} = x_i - q_i$ for $i = 1, 2, \ldots, T - 1$. This process is illustrated in Figure 10.4. The retailer starts with an inventory x_1 and chooses a price p_1. He realizes sales of $q_1 = \min[d_1(p_1), x_1]$, and his inventory at the start of the second period is $x_2 = x_1 - q_1$. He chooses his second-period price p_2 and the process continues. At the end of the season he has unsold inventory $y = x_T - q_T$ for which he receives a salvage value of r per unit. Thus, his total revenue from his fixed inventory is $TR = p_1 q_1 + p_2 q_2 + \cdots + p_T q_T + yr$.

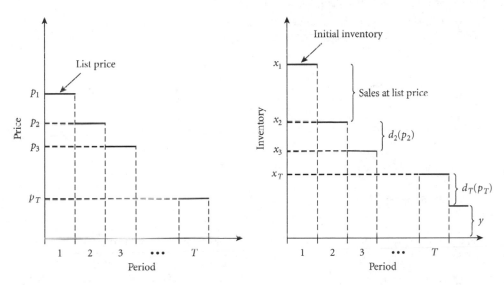

Figure 10.4 Dynamics of markdown optimization.

In a deterministic model, the seller finds the set of prices that maximize TR. In a probabilistic model, he finds the prices that maximize the expected value of TR, that is, $E[TR]$.

10.2.1 A Deterministic Model

Since we know that sales in each period need to be less than starting inventory in that period, you might think that we need a set of T constraints specifying that $q_i \leq x_i$ for $i = 1, 2, \ldots, T$. However, with a little reflection, it should be clear that we require only one constraint, namely, that the sum of sales for all periods needs to be less than or equal to the starting inventory. With this in mind, we can write the deterministic markdown optimization problem as

$$\max_{p_1, p_2, \ldots, p_T} \sum_{i=1}^{T} p_i \, d_i(p_i) + ry$$

subject to

$$\sum_{i=1}^{T} d_i(p_i) \leq x_1$$

$$y - x_1 - \sum_{i=1}^{T} d_i(p_i)$$

$$p_i \leq p_{i-1} \qquad \text{for } i = 1, 2, \ldots, T$$

$$p_T \geq r$$

We can simplify the formulation even further by substituting for y in the objective function, which gives a new objective function:

$$\max_{p_1, p_2, \ldots, p_T} \sum_{i=1}^{T} (p_i - r) \, d_i(p_i) + rx_1$$

Since rx_1 is simply a constant, we can eliminate it from the objective function and write the markdown management problem (MDOWN) as

$$\max_{p_1, p_2, \ldots, p_T} \sum_{i=1}^{T} (p_i - r)\, d_i(p_i) \tag{10.1}$$

subject to

$$\sum_{i=1}^{T} d_i(p_i) \leq x_1 \tag{10.2}$$

$$p_i \leq p_{i-1} \quad \text{for } i = 1, 2, \ldots, T \tag{10.3}$$

$$p_T \geq r \tag{10.4}$$

The interpretation of the markdown management problem (MDOWN) is straightforward. Objective function 10.1 states that the goal of the retailer is to maximize total revenue from the inventory. This is expressed as maximizing the total increment over the salvage value received for each unit sold. Constraint 10.2 states that the retailer cannot sell more than his first-period inventory. The constraints in Equation 10.3 guarantee that the markdown prices are decreasing over time, and Constraint 10.4 guarantees that the final price is greater than the salvage value.[10]

Example 10.1

A retailer has a stock of 160 men's sweaters, and he has four months to sell the sweaters before he needs to clear the shelf space. The merchant wishes to establish a list price at the beginning of the first month and then mark the sweaters down at the beginning of each of the next three months. Sweaters unsold at the end of the fourth month will be sold to an outlet store for $5 apiece. Furthermore, by dint of his long experience, the seller knows that demand in each of the four months can be represented by independent linear demand curves:

$$d_1(p_1) = (120 - 1.5p_1)^+$$
$$d_2(p_2) = (90 - 1.5p_2)^+$$
$$d_3(p_3) = (80 - 1.5p_3)^+$$
$$d_4(p_4) = (50 - 2p_4)^+$$

where p_i is the price in month i for $i = 1, 2, 3, 4$. Formulating this problem as in MDOWN (Equations 10.1 through 10.4) gives the results shown in Table 10.2. If the retailer had to maintain a single price during the entire four months, his price-response curve would be the sum of the four individual price-response curves, that is, $d(p) = d_1(p) + d_2(p) + d_3(p) + d_4(p)$, and his price optimization problem would be to find the price p that maximizes $pd(p) + \$5(160 - d(p))^+$. The optimal solution to this problem is $p = \$34.72$ with $d(p) = 133$ so the total contribution is $133 \times \$34.72 + 27 \times \$5 = \$4,752.76$. The optimal markdown policy resulted in a revenue increase of about 7% over the use of a

TABLE 10.2
Optimal solution for example deterministic markdown problem

Month	Price	Discount	Demand	Revenue
1	$42.50	0%	56	$2,380.00
2	$32.50	23.5%	41	$1,332.50
3	$29.17	31.4%	36	$1,050.12
4	$15.00	64.7%	20	$300.00
Unsold	$5.00	—	7	$35.00
TOTAL	—	—	160	$5,097.62

single price. This is a bit smaller than the level of improvement claimed by many vendors of markdown management software.

If a seller really knew the price-response curves for each week in the selling season, he could plug them into MDOWN and solve for the optimal markdown schedule at the beginning of the season, and his work would be done. Since the curves are deterministic, sales will be exactly as predicted, and there would be no need to deviate from his initial planned markdown schedule. In reality, of course, things are not so simple. Without access to the ever-elusive crystal ball, sales are likely to deviate from expectations. The most effective approach is to incorporate this uncertainty explicitly in calculating prices—an approach we take in the next section. However, the deterministic problem formulation can be used as the basis of a simple dynamic markdown algorithm.

Deterministic Markdown Pricing Algorithm

1. Solve MDOWN to determine the initial price of p_1.

2. Observe sales q_1 during the first period. Starting inventory for the second period is $x_2 = x_1 - q_1$.

3. Solve MDOWN for $p_2, p_3, \ldots, p_T$ using a starting inventory of x_2. Put p_2 in place as the price for the second period.

4. At the beginning of each subsequent period, current inventory will be the previous period's starting inventory minus last-period sales; that is, $x_i = x_{i-1} - q_i$. Solve MDOWN for $p_i, p_{i+1}, \ldots, p_T$ using a starting inventory of x_i. Use the value of p_i as the price during the upcoming period i.

Example 10.2

Consider the previous example and assume that during the first month, the retailer sells 70 sweaters instead of the 56 he anticipated. This means he has a starting inventory of only 90 sweaters at the beginning of month 2. Using $x_2 = 90$, he can use the demand curves $d_2(p_2)$, $d_3(p_3)$, and $d_4(p_4)$ to recalculate prices for months 2, 3, and 4. The new optimal prices are $p_2 = \$34.00$, $p_3 = \$30.67$, and $p_4 = \$16.50$. He therefore sets his price for month 2 at $34.00. At the end of month 2, he can observe remaining inventory and solve once more to determine the price he will charge in month 3.

This algorithm does not explicitly incorporate future uncertainty into its calculation of the current price. However, it does recalculate the price in each period, recognizing that sales to date are likely to be different from those originally anticipated. While this is less than ideal, this general approach can lead to improvements over standard practice. One study computed the results of a deterministic algorithm similar (but not identical) to this one applied to 60 fashion goods at a women's specialty apparel retail in the United States and computed the predicted results to what actually occurred when the store used its usual markdown policy. To correspond to actual practice, the algorithm only changed the discount level if the new discounted price was at least 20% lower than the previous price. Furthermore, each style had to be offered at list price for at least four weeks prior to the initial markdown. The deterministic algorithm increased total revenue by about 4.8% relative to standard store practice. Much of this increase came from taking smaller markdowns sooner than usual store policy.[11]

10.2.2 A Simple Approach to Including Uncertainty

A seller is facing his last markdown opportunity. He has a fixed inventory x and must set the price p for which it will be sold during the upcoming period. At the end of that period, any remaining unsold inventory will be sold for the salvage price r (which may be 0). If he knows the price-response curve for this period, his problem is a very simple single-period special case of MDOWN. But now we add uncertainty to the mix. Specifically, we assume that demand given price, $D(p)$, is a random variable whose distribution depends on p. What price should the seller set to maximize expected revenue? The problem faced by the seller is

$$\max_{p} E[\,TR(p)\,] = pE[\min[D(p), x]] + (x - E[\min[D(p), x]])r$$
$$= (p - r)E[\min[D(p), x]] + rx \qquad (10.5)$$

where the first term on the right-hand side is expected revenue from first-period sales and the second term is salvage revenue.

Equation 10.5 is not too difficult to solve if we can model how the expectation $E[\min[D(p), x]]$ depends on p. One simple possibility is to assume that $D(p)$ follows a uniform distribution between 0 and $a - bp$ for some a and b. Then, if $a = 200$ and $b = 10$, demand would be uniformly distributed between 0 and 180 when $p = \$2.00$ and uniformly distributed between 0 and 150 for $p = \$5.00$. Expected first-period revenue, salvage revenue, and total revenue for different prices are illustrated in Figure 10.5 for the case of $a = 200$, $b = 10$, a salvage value $r = \$5.00$, and an inventory of $x = 60$. In this case, the optimal price is $\$13.29$, with corresponding expected sales revenue of $\$440.89$, expected salvage revenue of $\$134.23$, and expected total revenue of $\$575.02$.

We can extend this formulation of the two-period markdown problem to create a simple algorithm that incorporates uncertainty. The idea is similar to the deterministic algorithm in the previous section, in which we solved the single-period deterministic problem to establish a markdown price for the next period, observed sales during that period, and then solved the same problem again at the beginning of the next period, using the new inventory value to get a new price. This time we follow a similar philosophy using the probabilistic

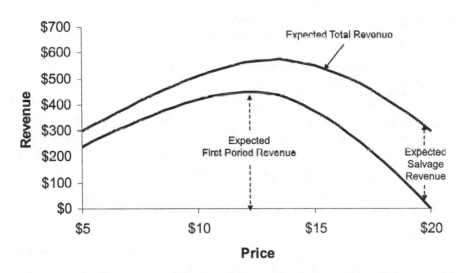

Figure 10.5 Expected revenue as a function of price in the single-period markdown model with salvage.

formulation in Equation 10.5, but with a twist. At the beginning of each period, we estimate a probability distribution on future demands as if we are *going to hold the price constant for all remaining periods.* That is, for any price in period t, we define the random variable

$$\hat{D}(p_t) = \sum_{i=t}^{T} D_i(p_t).$$

Example 10.3

A seller faces two pricing periods, with the out date occurring at the end of period 2. $D_1(\$5.00)$, the demand in period 1 given a price of $5.00, follows a normal distribution with mean of 50 and variance of 25, and $D_2(\$5.00)$ follows a normal distribution with mean of 30 and variance of 10. Then $\hat{D}(\$5.00) = D_1(\$5.00) + D_2(\$5.00)$ follows a normal distribution with mean of 80 and variance of 35.

In the simple probabilistic algorithm, we calculate the price for the upcoming period *as if* it were the final markdown period. Then we find the current price p_t by solving Equation 10.5 using $\hat{D}(p_t)$ as our probabilistic forecast of demand. This is equivalent to assuming that the price we choose for the current period will be held constant for the remainder of the selling season. This leads to the simple probabilistic algorithm.

Simple Probabilistic Markdown Pricing Algorithm

1. Set an initial price of p_1.

2. Observe sales q_1 during the first period. Starting inventory for the second period is $x_2 = x_1 - q_1$.

3. At the start of each period t, calculate the distribution of $\hat{D}_t(p_t) = D_t(p_t) + D_{t+1}(p_t) + \cdots + D_T(p_T)$.

4. Find p_t that maximizes $(p_t - r)\, E[\min[\hat{D}_t(p_t), x_t] + rx_t$. Set this value as the price for the current period.

This simple probabilistic algorithm was tested for six items in eight stores of the Chilean fashion retail chain Falabella and compared against actual sales for the 1995 autumn-winter season. The recommendations from the probabilistic algorithm generated revenue 12% higher than that obtained by the product managers.[12] This approaches the magnitude of improvement claimed by markdown optimization software vendors. It is tempting to compare the 12% improvement in this study with the 4.8% improvement reported from the deterministic approach reported in Section 10.2.1. However, this would ignore the fact that the improvements came from applications in two very different settings and that the improvements were reported based on differences from previous store practice, which may have been very different in the two situations.

10.3 ESTIMATING MARKDOWN SENSITIVITY

A key element in effective markdown optimization is estimating *markdown sensitivity*—the increase in sales we expect as a function of the additional discount we take. Any technique for measuring price sensitivity, such as price testing, can also be used to estimate markdown sensitivity. However, retailers increasingly have systems that enable them to track historic sales and discounts by item and by category. If this information is sufficiently complete, it can be used to estimate markdown sensitivity.

Sales and prices from an actual markdown schedule are illustrated in Figure 10.6.[13] This figure shows price (as a percentage of list) and weekly sales for a woman's blouse across a 30-week selling season that started in week 23 and lasted through week 52. In this case, there were three markdowns: a 30% markdown in week 32, a further 20% taken off in week 40, and another 20% reduction in week 48. The final price was 30% of the list price. Sales of the blouse grew for the first few weeks and then began to decline until the first markdown was taken, at which point sales surged. Each of the three markdowns was accompanied by a

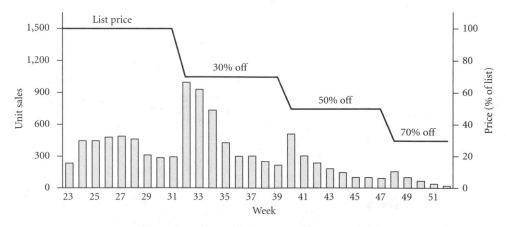

Figure 10.6 Example weekly sales and price under a markdown policy.

jump in sales followed by a decline. This pattern is typical—markdowns, like promotions, can be extremely effective in driving sales.

The first step in using the information in Figure 10.6 to estimate markdown sensitivity is to calculate a *baseline product life cycle* forecast. This is a forecast of how sales would have proceeded through the season without any markdowns whatsoever—i.e., how the item would have sold if the price remained constant at list price. The baseline product life cycle can be estimated by aggregating sales of fashion goods for periods in which no markdowns have been taken. Figure 10.7 shows the baseline product life cycle along with actual sales for the markdown schedule in Figure 10.6. One way to estimate price sensitivity is to attribute all sales in excess of the baseline product life cycle to the effect of markdowns and to fit an appropriate price-response curve. For the example in Figure 10.7, the sales in excess of the baseline for weeks 32 through 39 would be attributed to the 30% markdown taken in week 32, the sales in excess of the baseline for weeks 40 through 47 would be attributed to the 50% total discount in place during that period, and the sales in excess of the baseline for the remainder of the season would be attributed to the 70% total discount initiated in week 48.

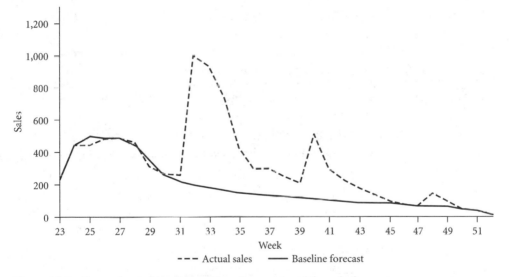

Figure 10.7 Example weekly sales and baseline product life cycle forecast.

Example 10.4

For the example in Figure 10.6, the baseline product life cycle forecast of sales and the actual sales for weeks 32 through 39 are as shown in Table 10.3. Forecast sales of 1,219 at the list price and actual sales of 4,253 at the 30% discount provide two points that can be used to establish a price-response curve.

Note from Table 10.3 that the seller experienced a $(4,253 - 1,219)/1,219 = 249\%$ increase in sales from a 30% decrease in price, corresponding to a markdown elasticity of $249/30 = 8.3$. Such unusually high levels of elasticity are often found in markdown and

TABLE 10.3
Baseline forecast and actual sales for
weeks 32 through 39 in example

Week	Baseline forecast	Actual sales
32	200	1,100
33	182	941
34	165	739
35	152	430
36	142	302
37	134	281
38	126	249
39	118	211
TOTAL	1,219	4,253

promotions situations. They do not imply that the elasticity of sales with respect to list price is anywhere near as high.

10.4 MARKDOWN MANAGEMENT IN ACTION

As of 2004, markdown managment and markdown optimization systems are still in a relatively early phase of adoption. While the basic algorithms for markdown optimization have been available for many years, there are a number of reasons why retailers did not begin to use markdown management software systems until the mid-1990s.

- Prior to the 1990s, many large retailers simply did not have the required sales and pricing data available in the format needed for markdown optimization. Retailers have only recently begun to adopt enterprise resource planning (ERP) and customer relationship management (CRM) software systems that capture this information.

- Most retailers managed promotions and markdowns using a promotions budget. A promotions budget specified the maximum amount of money a store was allowed to "give up" from list price via promotions and markdowns. For example, a store might have $100 million of inventory when valued at list price. If that store is allocated a $15 million promotions budget, then discounts from promotions and markdowns would be expected to total less than $15 million. A sweater with a list price of $80 that sells on sale for $65 would result in a $15 charge against the promotions budget. While the promotions budget approach may have given many chains the illusion of control, it did not provide an incentive for stores to find the levels of promotions and markdowns that maximized return given local market conditions. Rather, it was a hangover from the era when promotions and markdowns were considered the avenue of last resort for moving merchandise.

- In most stores, buyers were responsible for the entire lifecycle of fashion merchandise. This meant choosing what items to purchase, which colors and sizes to purchase, setting list prices, and planning promotions and markdowns. Buyers often resisted the adoption of systems that centralized markdown, promotions, and pricing decisions, arguing that local knowledge and experience were necessary for the decisions to be made correctly.

These are obstacles that vendors and advocates of markdown management systems had to overcome (and still need to overcome in many cases). However, the tide seems to have turned, and retailers are increasingly adopting such systems. One reason seems to be that the opportunties for expansion by opening new stores have largely evaporated for many chains. According to Michael Levy of ProfitLogic, "There was a huge wave of retail expansion in the mid-nineties and the number of retail square feet increased dramatically. Then, expansion slowed and retailers were forced to focus on improving operations."[14] Another reason is unquestionably the arrival of the 800-pound gorilla of retailing: Wal-Mart. With its wildly successful "everyday low pricing" policy, Wal-Mart has forced its competitors to improve every facet of their operations, from purchasing and logistics through pricing and promotions. While retailing has always been a thin-margin business, the need to wring every penny of profit from the market has never been greater.

The first widely publicized success of markdown optimization was at ShopKo. In 2000, ShopKo, which operates 141 discount stores under the ShopKo name and another 229 smaller rural discount stores under the Pamida brand, installed a markdown optimization system developed by Spotlight Solutions.[15] A pilot program run on 300 programs showed a 14% increase in revenue from using the markdown optimization software. The success of the ShopKo pilot was widely reported, including in a *Wall Street Journal* article, helping to spur interest in the potential for such solutions. In addition to ShopKo, retailers that have announced the adoption of markdown optimization systems include The Gap, JC Penney, Home Depot, Bloomingdale's, Sears, and Circuit City.

While the use of markdown optimization systems by retailers is still relatively new, there is sufficient experience to reach a few general conclusions. One observation is that markdown optimization systems consistently recommend earlier small discounts in situations where humans tend to wait and take larger markdowns later. The reason seems to be that the people making markdown decisions tend to be the same people who bought the merchandise in the first place and who are reluctant to "admit a mistake" by marking down. As the pioneering American retailer E. A. Filene put it:

> One of the few certainties in retailing is that some of the merchandise bought enthusiastically in the wholesale market, where it looks eminently saleable, will, when it reaches the store, prove stubbornly unsaleable. But despite this inevitability, *buyers, like the rest of humanity, are reluctant to admit and address their errors.* They find endless excuses for the slow sale of merchandise: the weather's still too hot; the weather's still too cold. Easter's late this year; Easter was early this year. It hasn't been advertised; the ad was lousy; the ad ran on the wrong day; the ad ran in the wrong newspaper.
>
> The danger in these rationalizations is that they usually increase markdowns. A coat that does not sell early in the fall may still tempt customers if it is marked down early by as little as 25 percent. But as the season ends, it must be marked down far more drastically to tempt a customer who, having done without a new coat for so long, may otherwise reasonably decide to wait until the next season.[16]

Markdown optimization systems have generally resulted in retailers' taking smaller discounts earlier than they used to do, usually with good results. E. A. Filene's observation, made in 1910, has been vindicated, 90 years later.

It has also become apparent that one of the most important benefits from markdown management systems has been their ability to tailor markdown schedules to the particular characteristics of individual regions or stores. In many cases, retailers had simply used the same markdown cadence for all stores in a chain: a particular style of sweater would be marked down by the same amount at the same time in Boston as in Los Angeles. Markdown management systems have been an important catalyst for enabling different markdown schedules for different stores. Canadian apparel retailer Northern Group Retail Ltd. implemented a markdown management solution from ProfitLogic that it credited for helping move the company away from chainwide discounting to an approach "more attuned to regional needs, weather patterns, and other trends."[17] A men's retail clothing chain traditionally put swimsuits on sale in September in all their stores nationwide. This made sense in northern locations such as Boston, Chicago, and New York, where the summer season was ending, but it made little sense in Orlando and Miami, where the tourist season was just beginning. The adoption of a markdown management system was the catalyst that enabled the chain to establish different markdown schedules in New York and Miami.

A final observation is that much of the difficulty in implementing markdown management systems has been the need to incorporate a wide variety of business rules, such as the following.

- The first markdown cannot occur for at least four weeks after the product is introduced and cannot be less than 15%.

- All items in a given line (e.g., Liz Claiborne sweaters) must have the same markdown cadence in a given store; that is, they must all be marked down the same percentage at the same time.

- No more than four markdowns can be taken for any item during the sales period.

- Every markdown must result in a discount at least 10% greater than the previous markdown.

- Markdown percentages must be in units of 5%; that is, markdown percentages such as 13% and 22% are not allowed.

- The final price (i.e., the price after the final markdown) must be at least 25% of the original price.

- A markdown must be in place for at least one week before it can be changed.

- All stores in a specified region (e.g., Manhattan, London, southern California) must have the same markdown cadence.

- Sufficient inventory must remain unsold to provide minimal stocking levels for outlet stores.[18]

As with any pricing and revenue optimization system, business rules are implemented as constraints on the basic optimization problem. Many of the business rules required in markdown management lead to integer-type constraints that are hard to implement in practice. The basic formulations of the markdown optimization problem we derived in this chapter can usually be solved easily and efficiently using standard techniques and software packages if the problems are not too highly constrained. However, the constraints imposed by business rules can make the problem much too complex to be solved using standard methods. Instead, custom (and often proprietary) algorithms are often needed that draw on such approaches as simulated annealing and genetic algorithms to find solutions that meet all of the business rules.

10.5 SUMMARY

- Under a markdown policy, the price of an item is sequentially decreased until either it sells or a selling period expires. It is widely used in a variety of industries, notably fashion goods and short-life-cycle products. The use of markdowns has been growing steadily in the United States, at least since World War II.

- A markdown policy is effective when the item for sale is perishable, supply is limited, and the desirability of the item decreases as it approaches its expiration date.

- A markdown policy is also a way a seller can maximize expected revenue when supply is constrained and he is uncertain about the distribution of customer willingness to pay.

- Markdown policies enable the seller to segment his customers among those who are willing to pay more in order to buy early and those who are willing to wait to purchase in order to save money.

- When price-response curves are known, the markdown optimization problem can be formulated and solved as a mathematical program.

- When price-response curves are uncertain (as is usually the case), the markdown optimization problem can be formulated and solved as a dynamic program. This requires starting in the last period and working backward in time.

- The markdown optimization problem becomes much more difficult when uncertainty, dynamics, and complex business rules need to be factored in. Many companies use commercial software systems to solve the resulting optimization problem.

- Many of the benefits of real-world markdown management implementations have come from taking smaller discounts earlier than customary practice and from the ability to derive markdown cadences tailored to the specific situations of individual stores within a chain.

10.6 EXERCISES

1. Extend the two-period markdown model in Section 10.1.1 to three periods. That is, assume that the price-response function is $d(p) = 1,000 - 100p$, marginal cost is 0, and customers purchase as soon as price falls below their willingness to pay. What

three prices, p_1, p_2, and p_3, will maximize total revenue? What if there are four periods and four prices? What is the general formula for n prices?

2. Now extend the two-period markdown model in Section 10.1.1 to the case where customers have a lower willingness to pay for the good in the second period. Specifically, assume that each customer's willingness to pay in the second period is 75% of her willingness to pay in the first period. All other assumptions remain the same.

   a. What is the optimal price and corresponding total revenue for the seller, assuming he can charge only a single price in both periods?

   b. What are the optimal prices and corresponding total revenue, assuming he can charge different prices in the two periods?

3. A department store has 700 pairs of purple Capri stretch pants that it must sell in the next four weeks. The store manager knows that demand by week for the next four weeks will be linear each week, with the following price-response functions:

   Week 1: $d_1(p_1) = 1{,}000 - 100p_1$

   Week 2: $d_2(p_2) = 800 - 100p_2$

   Week 3: $d_3(p_3) = 700 - 100p_3$

   Week 4: $d_4(p_4) = 600 - 100 p_4$

Assume that the demands in the different weeks are independent, that is, that customers who do not buy in a given week do not come back in subsequent weeks.

   a. What is the optimum price the retailer should charge per pair if she can only set one price for all four weeks? What is her corresponding revenue?

   b. Assume she can charge a different price each week. What are the optimum prices by week she should charge? What is her corresponding revenue?

1. Further examples of retail price tracks such as these can be found in Warner and Barski (1995).

2. In this section, we use the terms *markdown management* and *markdown optimization* interchangeably.

3. Emporium (1952).

4. Ibid.

5. Nystrom (1915).

6. A similar model was first proposed by Lazear (1986).

7. TKTS is a nonprofit consortium of theaters operating a discount-ticket booth. Getting tickets at the lower price requires waiting in line, and there is no guarantee that the show you want will be available when you get to the counter. Thus, TKTS creates an inferior product that can be sold at a lower price with minimal cannibalization of full-price tickets.

8. The term *Dutch auction* has also been used for a somewhat different method for selling multiple products in financial markets and on eBay, leading to some confusion.

9. There is no restriction that the periods need to be of equal length. If, for example, the retailer had a policy that all items had to be sold at list price for at least three weeks before being marked down for the first time, the first period would be three weeks long and there would be only 13 total pricing periods for the season.

10. Strictly speaking, constraint (10.4) is not required, since the optimal solution to MDOWN will never result in a markdown price that is less than the salvage value.

11. Heching, Gallego, and van Ryzin (2002).

12. Bitran, Caldentey, and Mondschein (1998).

13. This figure was adapted from Levy and Woo (1999).

14. Quoted in Hamermesh, Roberts, and Pirmohamed (2002, p. 14).

15. Spotlight Solutions was later acquired by ProfitLogic.

16. Quoted in Harris (1982, p. 132).

17. From "The Price You Pay" by John McPartlin (2004, p. 50).

18. This may seem a bit odd, since the rationale behind establishing outlet stores in the first place was to dispose of unsold mecrchandisc from retail outlets. But for some retailers, outlet stores have become significant profit centers in their own right, and they want to ensure there is sufficient unsold inventory from their retail stores to guarantee stocking.

11 | CUSTOMIZED PRICING

11.1 BACKGROUND AND BUSINESS SETTING

All of the pricing tactics we have studied so far assume that buyers and sellers interact in the same basic fashion. The seller offers a stock of goods to different customer segments through different channels. Potential customers arrive, observe a price, and decide whether or not to purchase. The seller needs to decide what price to offer for each product to each customer group through each channel. The seller monitors sales of his goods and periodically updates the prices and/or availabilities he is offering. This is the *list-pricing* model. All of the pricing settings we have covered so far, including peak load pricing, revenue management, and markdown management, are varieties of list pricing.

List pricing may seem quite general. However, there is another important class of pricing—*customized pricing*—that is of equal or greater importance in many industries. In customized pricing, potential customers approach the seller, one by one, and the seller quotes each one a price. Often (but not always) each potential buyer wants something different—either a different bundle of products or services or a different quantity or a different variation on a basic product. In customized pricing, the seller can quote a different price for each request. The price can be based on knowledge of the individual buyer, the product(s) requested by the buyer, and other factors, such as general market conditions and competitive offerings. We now describe some examples of customized pricing.

11.1.1 Telecommunication Services

A company sells telecommunications services in the North American market. The company has a list of more than 40 different services it provides, including local, long-distance, and international voice transmission as well as data communication and corporate networking services. Different customers request different combinations of these services. Services are sold on a contract basis, with customers typically agreeing to a contract under which the company provides all of their telecommunication services for the next year. The company has three major competitors who can provide the same spectrum of services it offers, as well

TABLE 11.1
Global telecommunications company sales breakdown by channel

Segment	Annual revenue	Customer size	Transaction rate	Sales organization
Global	$8 billion	Large global	20–30/month	14 corporate sales staff
Growth	$8 billion	Medium	7,000/month	4,000 regional sales staff
Metro	$3 billion	Small	50,000/day	Inbound and outbound telesales

as 10 or more smaller regional competitors who provide more limited offerings. Each new contract or contract renewal is competitive.

This company has segmented its global market into the three segments shown in Table 11.1.

- *Global customers* are those whose annual telecommunications bill is greater than $10 million. Most global customers are Fortune 1000 companies with major international operations. These accounts are large enough that winning or losing one of them can make a measurable difference to total corporate revenue, and they receive considerable attention from senior management. The bids for these customers are managed by a team of 14 senior sales staff at corporate headquarters and are almost always in competition with one or more of the three major competitors. There are usually several rounds of negotiations before a deal is closed with a global customer.

- *Growth customers* are those with annual telecommunications accounts between $10,000 and $10 million. These customers are mostly large and medium-size business, along with state and local government agencies and various nonprofits, such as universities. These accounts are handled by 4,000 quota-carrying sales staff located in 42 regional sales offices. Accounts are distributed geographically, with some vertical specialists (e.g., retail, educational, government) within each regional office. Bids are almost always competitive, usually against one or more of the three global players, although some of the smaller competitors may bid on these deals as well. Larger deals with growth customers may involve one or two rounds of negotiation.

- *Metro customers* are those whose telecommunications bills are below $10,000 per year. These tend to be small businesses, such as restaurants, dry cleaners, independent retailers, and the like. Metro sales are handled primarily through telesales. There is no negotiation with these customers. The small-customer market tends to be quite competitive, since the needs of the small customers can usually be met by one or more of the smaller competitors as well as the big four.

The telecommunications company needs to set its prices to maximize profitability in each of the three segments. Since it has the ability to set different prices for different customers, this is a customized-pricing problem.

11.1.2 Unsecured Consumer Loans

In Great Britain a common way for people to borrow money to renovate their houses, buy a used car, go on vacation, or consolidate credit card debt is by obtaining an unsecured consumer loan. Amounts for unsecured consumer loans range from £500 to £20,000, and typical terms are one to seven years, with larger loans typically having longer terms. Unsecured loans are offered not only by traditional banks, such as Barclays and NatWest, but also by retailers, such as Sainsbury's (a major grocery chain), and specialized Internet lenders, such as Egg. The market has many competitors, with more than 20 major nationwide providers in addition to many regional lenders. Typical annual percentage rates (APRs) and corresponding monthly payments for a five-year loan of £3,000 as advertised by different lenders are shown in Table 11.2.

TABLE 11.2

Interest rates (APRs), monthly payments, and total interest payments for a 5-year unsecured personal loan of £3,000 as advertised by various lenders in June 2003

Provider	APR (%)	Monthly payment (£)	Total interest (£)
Northern Rock	6.9	92.49	329.79
Nationwide	7.9	93.87	379.35
AA Loan	10.9	98.07	530.67
Egg	10.9	98.07	530.67
Sainsbury's Bank	11.5	98.93	561.41
American Express Bank	11.7	99.21	571.69
MBNA Express Loan	11.9	99.50	581.99
Lombard Direct	11.9	99.50	581.99
Woolwich	11.9	99.50	581.99
Virgin	11.9	99.50	581.99
Alliance and Leicester	12.5	100.36	612.99
Barclays	12.9	100.94	633.75
Halifax	13.9	102.39	685.94
HSBC	14.9	103.85	738.57
NatWest Bank	15.9	105.32	791.63
Lloyd's TSB	17.7	108.01	888.22

SOURCE: *Money Facts*, July 2003.

The sales process for the Bank of Albion, a typical (albeit mythical) provider of unsecured loans is shown in Figure 11.1. Potential customers enter the process through one of four channels:

- *Branch:* entering a branch and inquiring about a loan
- *Direct:* calling a toll-free number
- *Internet:* Inquiring about a loan through the bank's Web site
- *Agent:* referred by a third party, such as a real estate broker

Regardless of channel, a potential customer is asked how much she wants to borrow over what term and a brief series of questions to establish name, age, and time at current address. The bank then quotes an APR and monthly payment. About 14% of the customers drop out at this point ("lost quotes"), while the remainder go on to fill out a more extensive

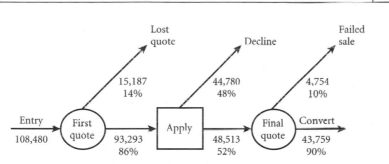

Figure 11.1 Consumer loan sales and pricing process at the Bank of Albion.

application that includes additional questions about such items as employer, income, expenses, and other loans outstanding. This information enables the bank to assign a credit score to each applicant. About 50% of applications are declined by the bank as too risky. For the accepted applications, the bank has the opportunity to adjust the APR—for example, it can offer a higher APR to high-risk customers if it chooses. About 90% of customers whose applications are accepted go on to take a loan.

The bank faces two pricing decisions: what APR to offer in the initial quote, and what adjusted APR to offer to customers whose applications have been accepted.[1] This is a customized-pricing problem because the bank can choose different APRs for different customers based on type of loan, channel, and market segment.

11.1.3 Other Customized-Pricing Services

In addition to the foregoing two examples of customized pricing—one business to business and one business to consumer—there are some others.

- Businesses purchasing trucking services usually solicit bids from a number of competing carriers, such as Roadway and Schneider. Each carrier will submit a bid detailing a price schedule at which it will carry freight for the customer for some period of time, usually a year. Each carrier faces the problem of determining what price schedule to bid.

- A metropolitan police department wishes to purchase 50 police cars. It solicits bids from Ford, General Motors, and Daimler-Chrysler. The bid solicitation describes the performance and options required. Each of the three manufacturers needs to determine what price to bid.

- A hospital has decided to purchase a magnetic resonance imaging (MRI) machine to improve its diagnostic capabilities. It sends copies of a request for proposal (RFP) to the five leading MRI manufacturing companies. The RFP specifies the required capability as well as the criteria the hospital will choose to determine the winning bidder. Each of the manufacturing companies needs to determine what price to bid.

- A customer applies to his local bank for a mortgage. Based on the customer's credit history, the amount of the loan, and the characteristics of the house he is planning to purchase, the bank must determine whether or not to offer him a mortgage and, if so, at what rate.

In each of these customized pricing situations the potential customer has approached the seller. Since the customer has already signaled his willingness to purchase, demand induction is usually not an issue. Instead, the major issue in customized pricing is usually not *if* the customer will purchase but *who* the customer will purchase from. This is one important difference between customized pricing and list pricing. Here are two others.

1. *In customized pricing, the seller can quote a different price to each customer.* The customized price can (and should) reflect the best information the seller has at that time. Of course, the seller will usually not have perfect information about the buyer's preferences or about the competition. But, as we will see, he can use statistical reasoning to improve his expected profitability.

2. *In customized pricing, the seller can track lost business.* In a customized-pricing situation, the seller will either win—i.e., get the business—or lose. In many (but not all) situations, a losing seller can find out which of his competitors won the business. However, even when this information is not available, the buyer knows that a potential customer has inquired about his product and decided not to purchase. This is in contrast to list pricing, in which the seller can only observe how many units he sold—not how many customers considered buying his product but decided against it. This *lost bid* information is important because it forms the basis for statistical estimation of customer bid-response functions.

The existence of a *bid* or a *price quote* is a common element in customized pricing. In business-to-business settings, the quote is often in response to a request for proposal (RFP) or a request for quote (RFQ) issued by a buyer. In business-to-consumer situations, such as unsecured consumer loans and mortgages, the price quote often occurs after a customer has made a phone call or filled out an application. In any case, the price quote occurs only after the seller knows something about the buyer and what she wants. This contrasts with list pricing, in which potential customers find prices by accessing a price list (online or in a catalog) or reading a label in a store and the prices need to be set before the seller knows the identity of any individual potential customer.

List pricing and customized pricing often coexist, in the sense that a seller will use a list price to set a "ceiling," while most customers are quoted a price at a discount from the list. For example, the *manufacturer's suggested retail price* (MSRP) is usually an upper limit on the price for, say, a new car, with the selling price ultimately determined by some combination of the customer's ability to negotiate and the dealer's willingness to sell at a lower price.[2] In a similar vein, shipping companies maintain voluminous tariff schedules that specify list prices for shipping different types of freight between every zip code pair in the United States. However, only a small fraction of sales (usually less than 5%) takes place at list price. The rest moves at discounted rates negotiated individually with customers.

In the remainder of this chapter, we formulate the customized-pricing decision as an optimization problem and show how that problem can be solved to maximize the expected contribution margin from each bid. A key element in the customized pricing-problem is the *bid-response curve*, which specifies the seller's expectation on how each customer will respond to his bid price. We show how price-response curves can be estimated for different customers seeking to purchase different products. We then show how the customized-pricing model can be enhanced to deal with other pricing settings as well as objectives other than maximizing expected contribution. Finally we discuss how these computations fit into a general process for customized pricing.

11.2 CALCULATING OPTIMAL CUSTOMIZED PRICES

To motivate the formulation of the customized-pricing problem, we put ourself in the place of a seller who has been asked to bid on a potential deal. By *deal* we mean a particular piece of business, which may be a single order or a contract to provide future products and services. By *bid* we mean the price we offer.[3] This is a simplified setting since it assumes the buyer has dictated all elements of the deal and that the only decision on the part of the bidder is what price to bid. In the real world, a bidder may also have to decide on other elements in his bid, such as delivery date, contract terms and conditions, and even product functionality. Furthermore, we assume initially that the bidder is submitting a single take-it-or-leave-it bid. Of course, in many situations, not only price but every element of the deal may well be on the table.

The first thing we need to determine is our goal for this bid. That is, what is our objective function? For now, we assume that we want to maximize expected contribution from the bid. For a given price, p, expected contribution can be expressed as

Expected contribution at price p = (Deal contribution at p)

$$\times \text{(Probability of winning bid at } p) \tag{11.1}$$

The first term on the right-hand side of Equation 11.1 is the *deal contribution*—the margin we will realize if we win the bid. If the bid is to purchase d units of an item with unit cost of c, then our deal contribution would be $(p - c)d$. The calculation of deal contribution would be more complicated if we were bidding to supply a complex bundle of products and services, each of which has a different unit cost, or if we were negotiating a contract for future services in which the volume and mix of services to be supplied were uncertain.

The second term on the right-hand side of Equation 11.1 is the probability that we will win the deal at a given price. Our uncertainty about winning at a given price derives from two sources.

- *Competitive uncertainty.* We do not know what our competitors will bid. In fact, in many cases we may not know the identity or even the number of competitors we face.

- *Preference uncertainty.* We do not know exactly what criteria (both conscious and unconscious) the buyer will use to evaluate competitive bids. Nor do we know for sure how the buyer values our brand and our product/service offerings relative to the competition.

In most situations both preference uncertainty and competitive uncertainty will be present: We won't know exactly what our competitors are going to bid, nor will we know exactly how the buyer will choose among competing bids. Of course, if we knew what our competitors were bidding and how the buyer would choose among bids, our problem would be relatively simple—we would submit the most profitable bid that would win. However, in the real world, bidders rarely, if ever, have access to that level of information.[4]

There is, however, one important situation in which preference uncertainty is absent—when we know that the buyer is going to choose the lowest bid. This is the case, for example, when a government agency is required by law to choose the lowest-cost bidder. In these situations, the agency often issues extremely detailed specifications for the goods to be purchased so that price is the only remaining issue on which selection is made. Preference uncertainty can also be absent in supplier auctions, either online or offline. In a supplier auction the buyer initially selects a set of acceptable suppliers and commits to purchase from the lowest bidder. In most seller auctions each supplier has the opportunity to observe the bids of other suppliers and then to submit a lower bid if he desires to do so. This ability to rebid based on the bids of other suppliers injects additional complexity into the pricing process that we will not address here.[5]

11.2.1 Single-Competitor Model

Imagine you are an auto manufacturer bidding against a single competitor to sell 50 pickup trucks to a county park district. The park district will buy all 50 trucks from a single supplier and is committed by law to pick the lowest bidder. Each supplier has been asked to submit a single sealed bid. The bids are final, and the lower of the two bids will win. Your production cost per truck is $10,000. Based on past experience, your belief about what your competitor will bid can be described by a uniform distribution between $9,000 and $14,000, as shown in Figure 11.2. What should you bid to maximize expected profitability?

Call your bid p and the competing bid q. You will win if your bid is less than the competing bid, that is, if $p < q$. (For simplicity, we ignore the possibility of a tie.) Let $\rho(p)$ be the probability that you would win if you bid a price p. Then $\rho(p) = 1 - F(p)$, where F is the cumulative distribution function of the competing bid—that is, $F(x)$ is the probability that

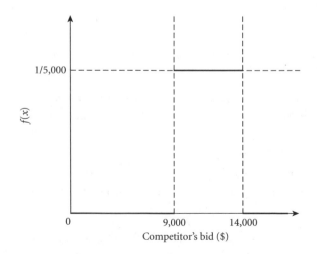

Figure 11.2   Uniform probability distribution on a competitor's bid.

the competing bid will be less than x. Your probability of winning the bid as a function of price is then as shown in Figure 11.3. If you bid below $9,000, then you will win for sure, since you know that the competitor will bid more than $9,000. Your probability of winning the bid decreases linearly between $9,000 and $14,000 and is zero if you bid above $14,000.

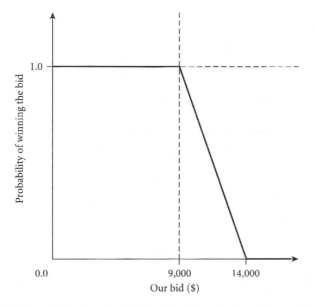

Figure 11.3 Probability of winning the bid as a function of price when our belief about the competitor's bid follows the uniform distribution in Figure 11.2.

We call $p(p)$ the *bid-response function* for this deal. For each deal, the bid-response function specifies the probability of winning the deal as a function of our bid. It is the customized-pricing analog of the price-response curve introduced in Chapter 2. Where the price-response curve specifies total expected demand as a function of list price, the bid-response curve specifies the probability of winning an individual bid as a function of price bid. Like the price-response curve, the bid-response function is downward sloping; that is, the probability of winning the bid decreases as the bid price increases. The bid-response probability is less than or equal to 1 for all prices and decreases to 0 at high bids. For the example, the bid-response curve is given by

$$p(p) = 2.8 - p/5,000 \quad \text{for } \$9,000 \leq p \leq \$14,000 \tag{11.2}$$

and the price that maximizes expected profitability can be found by solving

$$\text{Maximize} \quad 50(2.8 - p/5,000)(p - 10,000) \tag{11.3}$$

Using the techniques from Section 4.4, we find that the objective function in Equation 11.3 is maximized at $p^* = \$12,000$. At this price, the probability of winning the bid is $2.8 - 12,000/5,000 = 0.4$. The margin per unit if the deal is won is $\$12,000 - \$10,000 = \$2,000$ and expected total margin is $40\% \times 50 \times \$2,000 = \$40,000$.

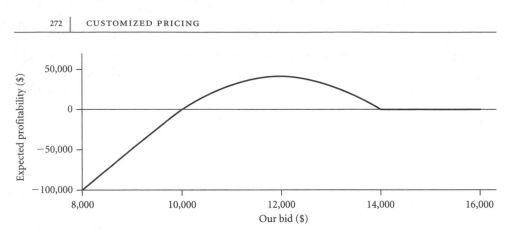

Figure 11.4   Expected profitability as a function of price bid in example.

Figure 11.4 shows how expected profit varies as a function of your bid. The expected profit function has the familiar hill shape. At a bid price below $9,000, you are certain to win the deal, but at a loss. Above $9,000, your probability of winning the bid decreases. However, you begin to gain some positive expected profit at prices above $10,000. Above $10,000, unit margin increases with increasing price, but this increase is counterbalanced by the decreasing chance of winning the deal. At $12,000, these two effects balance, and expected contribution is maximized. Above $12,000, decreasing chances of winning the deal overwhelm the increased margin. At any bid above $14,000, you are certain to lose the deal, so expected contribution is $0.

The optimization problem in Equation 11.2 is identical to the problem confronting a seller facing a deterministic price-response curve of $50(2.8 - p/5,000)^+$ and a unit cost of $10,000. In both cases, the optimal price is $12,000. However, there is an important difference between the two situations. A seller facing a deterministic price-response curve of $d(p) = 50(2.8 - p/5,000)^+$ and charging $12,000 per unit will sell exactly 20 units and will make a profit of $40,000. But in the bid-response case, by bidding $12,000 per unit, you will either win the bid and sell 50 units, for a total contribution of $100,000, or you will lose the bid and realize nothing. Changing price does not change the number of units you sell; it changes your probability of selling all the units. At the optimal price of $12,000, you have a 40% chance of winning the deal and making $100,000 and a 60% chance of losing the deal and making nothing.

11.2.2 The General Problem

We can generalize the example in a very straightforward fashion. Specifically, the *customized-pricing problem* for a particular deal is

$$\text{Maximize} \quad \tau(p) = \rho(p)m(p) \tag{11.4}$$

where $\tau(p)$ is expected contribution at price p, $\rho(p)$ is the bid-response function, and $m(p)$ is deal contribution at price p. For our purposes, $\rho(p)$ will be a continuous, downward-sloping function of p, and $m(p)$ will be a continuous, upward-sloping function of p. This means that $\tau(p)$ will be hill shaped, as shown in Figure 11.4, and there will be an optimal price p^* that maximizes expected contribution.

Assume, as in the example, that we are bidding for an order of d units and that our unit cost is c. In this case, $m(p) = d(p - c)$ and $\tau(p) = d\rho(p)(p - c)$. The value of p^* that maximizes $\tau(p)$ can be found by setting the derivative of $\tau(p)$ equal to 0. That is,

$$\tau'(p^*) = d\rho'(p^*)(p^* - c) + d\rho(p^*) = 0$$

which, after a bit of algebra, gives

$$-\frac{\rho'(p^*)p^*}{\rho(p^*)} = \frac{p^*}{p^* - c} \tag{11.5}$$

The expression on the left-hand side of Equation 11.5 is the *bid-response elasticity*, that is, the percentage change in probability of winning the bid that will result from a 1% change in price.[6] A bid-price elasticity of 2 means that a 1% *increase* in price will lead to a 2% *decrease* in the probability of winning the deal. The expression on the right-hand side of Equation 11.5 is the inverse of the contribution margin ratio. In other words, at the optimal customized price, the bid-response elasticity is equal to the inverse of the contribution margin ratio:

Bid-response elasticity at optimal price $= 1/(\text{Contribution margin ratio})$

This is the customized-pricing analog of the condition for optimal deterministic prices in Equation 3.21.

Note that using probabilities to represent our chances of winning a deal does not imply that either the buyer or our competition is making decisions by flipping a coin or using any other type of random process. Indeed, we would expect the competition to be setting the prices they will bid based on rational analysis of the opportunity—including his best information on what he believes *we* will bid. The uncertainty in the process arises entirely from our lack of information on the behavior of the other players in the bidding game: the buyer and the competition.

11.2.3 Multiple Competitors

We would naturally expect the addition of more competitors to reduce our probability of winning a deal. Otherwise, we would be willing to pay additional companies to compete against us—behavior that is rarely seen in real life. We can demonstrate the effect of multiple competitors using the simple example of the county park district. What if we faced two competitors instead of one bidding for the order of 50 pickup trucks? To simplify matters, let's assume we have identical beliefs about how both competitors will bid. That is, we believe that both competitor 1 and competitor 2 will price according to the uniform distribution shown in Figure 11.2.

We also assume that the two competing bids will be independent—that is, that information about one competitor's bid would not change our assessment of the bidding behavior of the other competitor. While the independence assumption may generally be reasonable, there are situations where it is not appropriate. One case would be when we believe that our two competitors are colluding to coordinate their bids. In that case, knowledge of how one of them is going to bid would obviously tell us quite a bit about how the other competitor planned to bid. The second case would be when the two competitors are not necessarily colluding but are basing their bids on joint information that we do not share. If both of the competitors share a common cost (say, a common supplier) that is unknown to us, learning what one of them planned to bid might enable us to estimate the common cost and therefore to come up with a better estimate of what the other competitor would bid.

We will win the deal in the example if and only if our bid is below the lower of the bids submitted by competitor 1 *and* competitor 2. For a given p, the probability that our bid will be lower than the bid from competitor 1 is $1 - F(p) = 2.8 - p/5,000$, which, by assumption, is also the probability that our bid will be lower than the bid from competitor 2. Since competitors 1 and 2 are submitting independent bids, the probability that p will be lower than both competing bids is $\rho(p) = (2.8 - p/5,000)^2$. This bid-response curve is shown in Figure 11.5. You can see that the addition of the second competitor decreases our chance of winning the bid for all realistic prices.

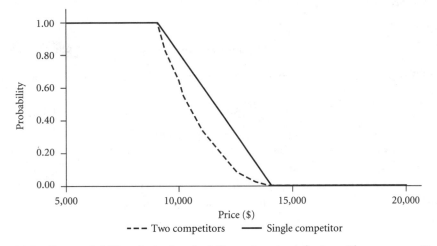

Figure 11.5   Our probability of winning the bid as a function of price with one competitor and with two identical competitors.

With two competitors, our expected contribution is given by

$$\tau(p) = 50(2.8 - p/5,000)^2(p - 10,000)$$

In this case, the price that maximizes expected revenue is $p^* = \$11,333.33$ per unit, with a corresponding probability of winning the bid of 28.4% and an expected total profit of $18,963. Note that the additional competition creates pain for us in two ways: Our optimal bid is lower, so total contribution is lower if we win the deal, *and* our probability of winning the deal is lower, even at our lower bid. The overall effect is dramatic: Our expected contribution from the deal is reduced by more than 50% from $40,000 to less than $19,000. This is a graphic illustration of the power of competition to reduce both the price and the profitability of a deal. Obviously, there is a strong incentive for the buyer to increase the number of bidders—or at least make the bidders believe there are more competitors!

As a matter of reference, the probability that a bid p is the lowest when there are n competitors submitting independent bids is given by

$$g(p) = [1 - F_1(p)] \times [1 - F_2(p)] \times \cdots \times [1 - F_n(p)] \tag{11.6}$$

where $F_i(x)$ is the cumulative distribution function on the price bid by competitor i—that is, the probability that competitor i will bid less that x.

Equation 11.6 gives the probability that our bid will be the lowest in any situation where competitors are submitting independent bids. If the buyer is choosing a winner based strictly on lowest bid, then this also gives our probability of winning at any price; that is, $\rho(p) = g(p)$. However, if the buyer is taking factors other than price into account when choosing a winner, then our probability of winning the bid will not be the same as our probability that we have submitted the lowest bid. We will treat this situation next.

11.2.4 Nonprice Factors in Bid Selection

So far, we have assumed that the buyer makes his purchasing decision based entirely on price. This is the exception rather than the rule. Price is almost always a factor in bid selection, but it is rarely the *only* factor. It is much more common for a buyer to make her choice based on a combination of factors. Sometimes the buyer will lay out her decision criteria in an RFP, for example:

- Previous experience with supplier—10%
- Quality of proposal—5%
- Technical fit of solution—25%
- Price—60%

In this case, the buyer is declaring that price will be the most important factor in her decision but that other factors will also be considered.[7] In most cases the buyer doesn't provide even that much information. From the bidders' point of view, the buyer is going to make her decision based on some combination of "objective" factors, such as price and solution fitness, and "subjective" factors, such as the brand image of the bidders, the buyer's experience (or lack of it) with the different bidders, and even the personal relationship the buyer might have with a bidder's sales representative. These elements need to be incorporated into the process of optimal customized pricing.

To make this more specific, consider the case of a large insurance company deciding to purchase 150 laptop computers for a new branch office. The IT department invites IBM and Dell to bid on this business. IBM and Dell both know they are the only suppliers invited to bid. However, both of them also know that the company has only purchased IBM computers in the past, their overall experience with IBM has been good, *and* the purchasing agent has a good relationship with the IBM sales representative. In this case, both Dell and IBM are likely to believe that IBM has an edge on this deal. In the extreme case, Dell might believe that IBM has a lock on the deal and the buyer is only going through a competitive bidding process to satisfy its own internal procedures and to keep IBM honest. If Dell truly believes this, then it is facing a bid response curve such that $\rho(p) = 0$ for any value of $p > c$;

that is, it stands no chance of winning the deal. Dell might still bid—if only to keep pressure on IBM and to signal Dell's willingness to sell to the bidder—but it would need to use these strategic considerations to determine which price to set.

In the more likely scenario, Dell might feel that IBM has an edge but that Dell has a shot at winning the business if it significantly beats IBM's price. How can this situation be addressed? One possibility is for Dell to estimate IBM's *bid premium* on this deal. The Dell sales representative might believe that Dell needs to bid at least $200 per laptop less than IBM in order to win. This bid premium reflects the "edge" that IBM has won through its strong history and good relationship with the customer.

It is easy to incorporate this type of premium into the calculation of the optimal customized price. Let us assume for a moment that Dell's cumulative distribution on IBM's bid is $F(x)$; that is, for any x, Dell believes that the probability that IBM will submit a total bid less than x is $F(x)$. If IBM and Dell were at parity—that is, neither one had a premium relative to the other—then the buyer would be choosing a supplier based strictly on price and, as described in Section 11.2.1, the bid-response curve $\rho(p)$ would be equal to $1 - F(p)$. The effect of a $200-per-unit premium for IBM is to shift this bid-response curve to the left by $150 \times$ $200 = $30,000, as shown in Figure 11.6. In other words, Dell needs to bid $30,000 lower on the deal to achieve the same probability of winning as it would without the premium. For any potential bid p, Dell's probability of winning is the probability that IBM's total bid is greater than $p + $30,000 and Dell's bid-response function is $\rho(p) = 1 - F(p + 30,000)$. As shown in Figure 11.6, the net effect is that, for any bid it might make, Dell faces a lower probability of winning the deal than if it were at parity with IBM. In this situation, Dell can calculate its optimal bid by solving 11.4 using the shifted bid-response curve (see Exercise 1).

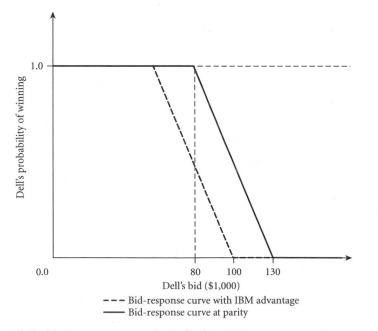

Figure 11.6 Shifted bid-response curve for Dell when IBM enjoys a premium.

We pause here to make a number of points. First of all, it is unlikely that Dell would know *exactly* IBM's bid premium. In fact, Dell might be uncertain about which seller actually enjoys a premium; that is, Dell may not know whether the buyer favors Dell or IBM or is truly neutral between the two vendors. In this case, the bid premium itself is a random variable. Second, the buyer has a strong motivation to mislead the sellers about his preferences—or at least to be selective with his communication. It is in the buyer's best interest for each bidder to *believe* that the other bidder enjoys a premium. Thus the buyer may overstate his satisfaction and loyalty to IBM when talking to the Dell sales representative and to deny any loyalty to IBM when talking to the IBM sales representative. Of course, both IBM and Dell should have savvy sales representatives who know enough to take such statements by the buyer with the requisite grain of salt.

Regardless of the posturing and misrepresentation that may take place, at the end of the day each bidder must take all the information it has available to it and craft the best bid that it can. Information is likely to be asymmetrical among bidders: As the incumbent, IBM should know much more about the buyer and her needs than Dell does. Since different bidders have different levels of information, the bid-response curves are *subjective* and specific to each bidder. In our example, IBM may submit a bid that it believes has a 70% chance of winning, while Dell submits a bid that it believes has a 45% chance of winning. Obviously, these estimates are inconsistent with each other, but that is no more unusual than the fact that two people with different beliefs or information will assess different probabilities for a given team to win a baseball game.

11.3 BID RESPONSE

By this point it should be clear that the most challenging part of optimizing customized prices is determining an appropriate bid-response function. If we had a bid-response function already in hand, finding the price that maximizes expected contribution is relatively simple—just solve the optimization problem in (11.4). This leaves us with this question: How do we estimate the bid-response function to use for a particular deal? There are at least three possibilities.

1. We could use *bottom-up modeling* to derive a bid-response function from our probability distributions on how we believe our competitors will bid and the selection process we believe the buyer will use. This is what we did in the previous section.

2. We could convene the people within the company who have knowledge of this particular deal, experience with the customer, understanding of the competition, and experience with similar bidding situations and derive a bid-response curve based on their *expert judgment*. This approach is often used when a deal is particularly large, important, or unique. Approaches for synthesizing expert information in this fashion can be found in any standard textbook on decision analysis, such as Clemen (1997).

3. We could use *statistical estimation* based on the historic patterns of wins and losses we have experienced with the same (or similar buyers) in similar past bidding situations.

Ideally, for each bid we would like to incorporate all the information we have—whether current or historical—to derive the best possible estimate of the bid-response curve. However, we are likely to be constrained by practical considerations. For example, the Bank of Albion must generate quotes for an average of 5,000 loan requests every working day. It would be impossible for the bank to convene a panel of experts to derive a bid-response curve for each one, and it would hardly be a cost-effective use of corporate resources for them to do so, even if possible. Companies require an approach that trades off the desire to incorporate the best possible information and analysis with the requirements for speed and cost effectiveness. This tradeoff may be different for different segments of business within the same company, as we next see.

11.3.1 Bid Response in a Corporate Setting

Consider again the case of the telecommunications company and its three market segments. A typical approach to setting prices in each segment is shown in Table 11.3. Customers in the global market segment are awarding contracts that can be worth tens or hundreds of millions of dollars per year. Winning one of these contracts can have measurable effects on corporate revenue and even share price. As a result, the telecom company works hard on each bid. It is not uncommon for a single salesperson to work full time for a month or more on preparing and negotiating a deal. The sales staff working the global accounts is supported by a team of analysts who help crunch the numbers. For a particularly important account, the analysts will work with the sales team to try to predict how various competitors might bid and to analyze different scenarios. Senior management will often take an active role to help close the deal. Each deal is likely to involve several rounds of negotiation. The analytical approaches to determine pricing in this segment are likely to be decision analysis and game theory.

TABLE 11.3
Telecommunications company sales breakdown by channel

Segment	Description	Annual account revenue	Pricing approach
Global	Large and highly visible	≥$10 million	Intense and detailed analysis by the "best and the brightest" applied to each bid
Growth	Medium size	$10,000–$10 million	Routine customized-pricing process to determine optimal price for each bid
Metro	Small	<$10,000	Ten standard pricing packages established

At the other extreme, the metro segment consists entirely of customers whose accounts are less than $10,000 per year. Inquiries in this segment can arrive either by telephone or Internet. Given that the majority of the metro business consists of accounts of less than $5,000 per year and that the company receives about 50,000 inquiries per day in this segment, it is clearly neither feasible nor worthwhile for the company to expend much time or resources trying to optimize the price it quotes to each potential customer. Rather, it has established a schedule of about 20 different pricing programs, with customers in different regions eligible for different programs. The problem of managing these pricing programs is not really one of customized pricing but rather of dynamic list pricing.

This leaves the growth segment, consisting of accounts in between the two extremes. Deals in this segment are significant enough to call for some analysis but not large enough to make it worthwhile to expend significant time or energy on each one. Ideally, the company would like a way to quickly estimate the bid-response curve for each customer and determine the price to bid within a few hours or days and without a major investment of personnel. This is the "sweet spot" for an automated customized-pricing process. Such a process involves analysis of historical customer response and uses of that information to optimize future bids.

The breakdown in Table 11.3 is fairly typical of many business-to-business pricing settings. Most companies selling to businesses will maintain a separate process for selling to a small number of very large, very important customers and to other customers. Often the distinction is between *national* (or *global* in the case of the telecommunications company) customers, who are handled by a centralized sales staff, and *regional* customers, who are handled by a regional sales staff. Bids to national customers will typically be larger, be viewed as more strategic, receive more senior management attention, and involve greater amounts of analysis and negotiation than bids to regional customers. Often, the national customers will represent 20% to 40% of the total revenue and, typically, will be less profitable than the other segments.

While the details will vary from company to company and industry to industry, most companies will find themselves in a variety of different bidding situations. For each situation, the company needs to establish an approach for determining the prices to bid. For large and important deals, it is a good idea for the company to spend time, effort, and resources. For small, highly standardized deals, it is usually most effective for a company to use a list-pricing approach. However, for intermediate deals, the company can improve profitability by estimating the bid-response curve for each deal and calculating the optimal price to bid. This requires the ability to estimate bid-response curves very rapidly. This is the problem we turn to next.

11.3.2 Estimation of the Bid-Response Function

In this section, we address how historical information about bids won and lost at different prices can be used to estimate a bid-response function. This approach is applicable under three general conditions.

1. The historical record includes bids for similar products to similar customers.
2. The current market conditions and products being offered are similar to those in the historic record.
3. There is a sufficient number of bids in the historic record to estimate a statistically significant bid-response curve.

Under these conditions, there are many different functions that can be (and sometimes are) used to represent bid response, and there are a number of different ways that these functions can be fit to historical data. We will not try to cover all of the different bid-response functions, nor will we cover all of the possible estimation approaches. This would involve a long detour into statistical issues that are well outside the scope of this book. Rather, we will give an overview of the most popular approach (maximum-likelihood estimation) to estimating the most commonly used bid-response function (the logit function). Along the way, we will mention some of the alternatives and provide references to more extensive discussions of the pros and cons of different approaches.

The starting point for the bid-response estimation process is a bid-history database. A simple example of a bid-history database is shown in Table 11.4, which shows the bid prices and the results of 40 bids for a hypothetical item. Note that the bids range from $9.10 to $9.80. For the first bid, the bid price was $9.20 and the outcome was a win (W). On the other hand, for the third bid, the bid was $9.70 and the outcome was a loss (L). This is the minimum information needed to estimate a bid-response function.

TABLE 11.4
Sample bid prices and results

Bid	Price	Result	Bid	Price	Result
1	$9.20	W	21	$9.70	L
2	$9.35	W	22	$9.40	W
3	$9.70	L	23	$9.30	W
4	$9.50	W	24	$9.40	L
5	$9.30	L	25	$9.35	L
6	$9.40	W	26	$9.60	L
7	$9.45	L	27	$9.20	W
8	$9.60	W	28	$9.40	W
9	$9.25	W	29	$9.25	W
10	$9.65	L	30	$9.50	W
11	$9.18	W	31	$9.32	W
12	$9.60	L	32	$9.10	W
13	$9.20	L	33	$9.80	L
14	$9.40	L	34	$9.65	W
15	$9.20	W	35	$9.70	L
16	$9.75	L	36	$9.35	W
17	$9.25	W	37	$9.30	W
18	$9.50	L	38	$9.60	L
19	$9.50	L	39	$9.40	W
20	$9.25	W	40	$9.50	W

We can visualize the relationship between price and wins and losses by assigning each win a value of 1 and each loss a value of 0. The outcomes of the 40 bids in Table 11.4 as a function of price are shown in Figure 11.7. Figure 11.7A is a scatter plot of the wins and losses as a function of price, while Figure 11.7B is the same scatter plot with the points *jittered*—that is, a small random number has been added to each point.[8] We can see that lower bids are more likely to win, but there is not a strict relationship between price and outcome: Some bids at $9.50 were won and some bids at $9.30 were lost. We want to find the bid-response function that best captures our probability of winning a bid at each price based on the results of these 40 bids—recognizing that a bid-response curve estimated on such a small amount of data is unlikely to have much significance.

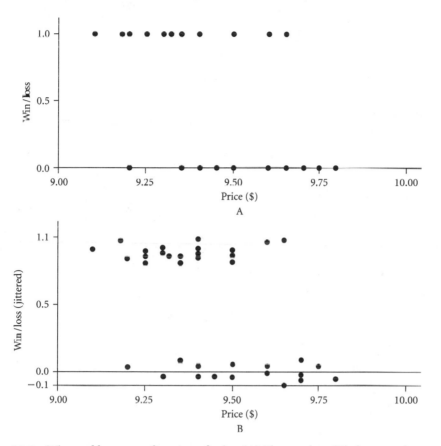

Figure 11.7 Wins and losses as a function of price. (A) The raw data; (B) the same data jittered by adding a small random number to each value.

Fitting a bid-response curve to data such as those in Table 11.4 is a problem of statistical estimation. The independent variable in the estimation is the price, and the dependent variable is the won/loss indicator. This problem is an example of binary estimation, since the dependent variable can only take the value 0 or 1. (Dependent variables that can only take the value 0 or 1 are called *dichotomous variables* or *Bernoulli variables*.) The first question we need to answer is: What kind of function do we want to fit to these data? One possibility is a straight line. We can fit a line to the data very simply using the regression capability in Excel or other statistical software package. The linear bid-response function that best fits the data in Table 11.4 (in terms of minimizing the sum of squared errors) is $\rho(p) = 14.8 - 1.509p$, shown in Figure 11.8A along with the jittered win/loss data.

The linear price-response function in Figure 11.8A is not too unreasonable. It is continuous and downward sloping. Since it has a constant slope of -1.509, this price-response function implies that each increase of $0.01 in price would result in a decreased probability of winning the bid of 0.015. However, there are problems with a linear bid-response function. First of all, for prices above $9.81 it predicts that the probability of winning is less than 0, and for prices less than about $9.14 it predicts win probabilities greater than 1. Since

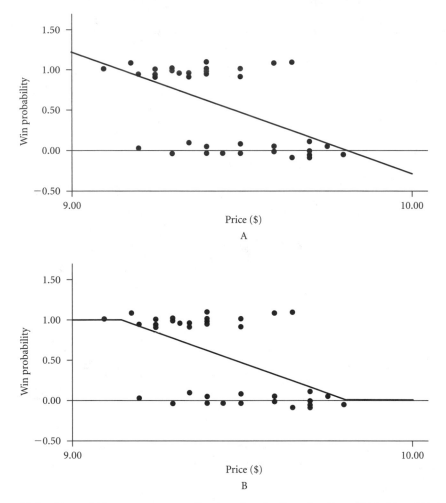

Figure 11.8   Linear bid-response curves fitted to the win/loss data from Table 11.4. (A) A pure linear bid-response curve; (B) the same curve capped at 0 and 1. The jittered win/loss values are also shown.

probabilities must be between 0 and 1, the linear bid-response function at least would need to be capped as shown in Figure 11.8B.

Even when capped, however, a linear price-response function is unrealistic in most cases. Inspection of Figure 11.8 indicates that the linear model (capped or uncapped) is simply not a very good fit to the data. For one thing, the linear model specifies that the change in probability from a $0.01 price is the same for any price between $9.14 and $9.81. However, we would usually expect the effect of changing our price is greater when our probability of winning the bid is around 50% than when it is very high or very low. This would imply that we consider an alternative form for the bid-response curve.

Another way to think about this is to consider the *bid-reservation price*—the maximum price at which the buyer would accept our bid. If the bid-reservation price is $9.50, then we will win the deal if we bid at any price of $9.50 or less, and we will lose the deal if we bid above

$9.50. Of course, as a seller we do not know the buyer's bid-reservation price—if we did, we would simply bid at that price (assuming, of course, that it is above our variable cost). This means we need to treat the bid-reservation price as a random variable, say, x, with a corresponding distribution $f(x)$ and cumulative distribution function $F(x)$. At any price p, our probability of winning the bid is simply the probability that $p \leq x$; that is, $\rho(p) = 1 - F(p)$. Note that the cumulative distribution function incorporates both our preference uncertainty and our competitive uncertainty about the deal. That is, our uncertainty about the buyer's bid-reservation price is due to the fact that we do not know exactly what our competitors are going to bid or exactly how the bidder will choose among them.

The logit bid-response function. What form would we expect the bid-response function, $\rho(p)$, to have? We have seen that if $f(x)$ is uniform, then $\rho(p)$ will be linear. But in most cases, we would expect $f(x)$ not to be uniform but to be more or less bell shaped. When $f(x)$ is bell shaped, the corresponding bid-response curve $\rho(p)$ has a reverse S shape—similar to the price-response curve shown in Figure 3.8. When our bid price is very high or very low (relatively speaking), the effect of a small price change on our chance of winning the bid will be relatively small. However, when our price is in the more competitive intermediate range, we would expect that small changes in our price would have a larger effect on our chances of winning. Other advantages of these types of function for representing binary response are given in Pampel (2000).

There are a number of different functional forms that can be used for an S-shaped bid-response function. These include the probit and power functions. You may run across other models, such as the Gompertz, Burr, or Urban models.[9] Each of these models gives a reverse S-shaped response function and may be useful under certain circumstances; however, the *logit* model is most commonly used. For each bid, the logit model has the form shown in Equation 11.7, where a and b are parameters of the model and p is price:

$$\rho(p) = \frac{1}{1 + e^{(a+bp)}} \tag{11.7}$$

For the logit bid-response function to be sensible, the parameters a and b need to be within certain ranges. Specifically, we must have $b > 0$ for the win probability to be a decreasing function of price. Higher values of b correspond to higher levels of price responsiveness—a value of $b = 0$ corresponds to no price response whatsoever (that is, the probability of winning does not depend on price). As price approaches infinity, the logit bid-response function predicts that our probability of winning the bid approaches 0, which is reasonable. However, as our bid approaches 0, the logit bid-response function predicts that our probability of winning the bid approaches $1/(1 + e^a) < 1$.

To add a little meaning to the parameters a and b, we note that Equation 11.7 implies that our probability of winning a bid will be exactly 50% when $p = -a/b$. Define $\hat{p} = -a/b$. Then we know that $\rho(\hat{p}) = 0.5$. Furthermore, we can rewrite Equation 11.7 in terms of $\hat{p}$ and b alone as

$$\rho(p) = \frac{1}{1 + e^{b(p-\hat{p})}}$$

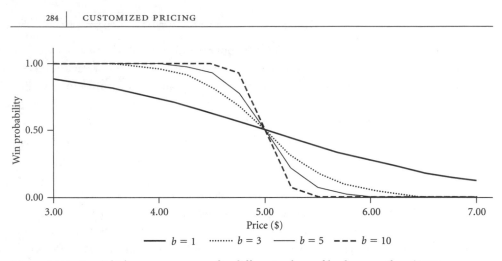

Figure 11.9 Logit bid-response curves for different values of b when $-a/b = \$5.00$.

This is a more intuitive formulation of the bid-response curve. In this formulation, $\hat{p}$ orients the curve by defining the price at which we have a 50% chance of winning the bid. Higher values of b then correspond to higher levels of price sensitivity. This is illustrated for different values of b when $\hat{p} = \$5.00$ in Figure 11.9.

The slope $\rho'(p)$ and elasticity $\varepsilon(p)$ for the logit bid-response function are:

$$\rho'(p) = \frac{-be^{a+bp}}{(1 + e^{a+bp})^2}$$

$$= -b\rho(p)(1 - \rho(p))$$

$$\epsilon(p) = -\rho'(p)p/\rho(p)$$

$$= \frac{bpe^{a+bp}}{1 + e^{a+bp}}$$

$$= bp(1 - \rho(p))$$

where $\rho'(p)$ is the slope of the bid-response function and $\epsilon(p)$ is its elasticity. Note that both the slope and the elasticity depend on the price as well as the parameters a and b.

Estimation by minimizing squared errors. We now have a functional form—the logit function—and the bid history shown in Table 11.4. The estimation problem is to find the values of the parameters a and b that generate the logit function that best fits the data. Just as there are alternative forms that can be used for the bid-response function, there are different approaches to estimating the underlying parameters. These different approaches arise from different meanings of the term *best fit*. Let i refer to one of the historic bids and p_i to the corresponding bid price. For each observation i, let $W_i = 1$ if we won the bid and $W_i = 0$ if we lost. Then, for any value of a and b, $\rho(p_i) = 1/(1 + e^{a+bp_i})$ is the probability we would have assigned to winning the bid. Obviously, we would like to choose a and b so that $\rho(p_i)$ is large for the bids we won ($W_i = 1$) and low for the bids we lost ($W_i = 0$). In fact, we would like $\rho(p_i)$ to be as close to W_i as possible. One way to do this is to minimize the sum of squared errors.

Assume that we have chosen values for the parameters a and b. Then the corresponding probability that we would win bid i is $\rho(p_i; a, b) = 1/(1 + e^{a+bp_i})$. Here, we have included *a* and *b* in the specification of the bid-response function to emphasize that our estimate of the win probability will depend on the values chosen for these parameters. For each bid, the squared error is

$$s_i(a, b) = [p(p_i; a, b) - W_i]^2 \tag{11.8}$$

$$= [1/(1 + e^{a+bp_i}) - W_i]^2 \tag{11.9}$$

Note that the squared error for a bid can range in theory from 0 (if we have assigned a win a probability of 1 or a loss a probability of 0) to 1 (if we have assigned a win a probability of 0 or a loss a probability of 1). Since the logit function is always between 0 and 1, the squared error will be between 0 and 1 for every observation. Ideally, however, we would like the squared error for each bid to be small, which will happen if we are assigning high probabilities to the wins and low probabilities to the losses. One obvious way to accomplish this is to find the values of *a* and *b* that minimize the sum of the squared errors over all of the observations. More formally, we solve the unconstrained optimization problem in Equation 11.10:

$$\min_{a,b} \sum_i [1/(1 + e^{a+bp_i}) - W_i]^2 \tag{11.10}$$

Solving Equation 11.10 using the data from Table 11.4 gives the values $a = -75.536$ and $b = 7.973$. These values are reasonable, in the sense that they predict that the fraction of bids we will win goes down as our price goes up (because $b > 0$) and that we would win the vast majority of our bids if we bid close to zero (because $a \ll 0$). Note that these parameter values mean we would expect our chance of winning the deal to be 50% when we set our bid price to $\hat{p} = 75.536/7.973 = \$9.47$.

How well does the estimated curve fit the underlying data? As in most cases of statistical estimation, there are a number of goodness-of-fit statistics we could use. One that is particularly appropriate in this case is the sum of squared errors (SSE) itself; that is,

$$SSE = \sum_i [1/(1 + e^{a+bp_i}) - W_i]^2 \tag{11.11}$$

For the estimated values of *a* and *b*, the estimated SSE is 6.528, or an average of 6.528/40 = 0.163 per observation. To see if this is any good, we can compare this value to the SSE that would be obtained if we assumed that our chance of winning each bid were a constant, independent of price. Since we won 23 out of 40 bids, our estimate of winning each bid under this assumption would be 23/40 = 57.5%. The SSE that would result from simply assuming we had a 57.5% chance of winning each bid would be 9.775, or 0.244 per observation. Using the logit model has reduced the average squared error by about one-third. This, combined with the fact that the parameter values for the model are quite sensible, would help give us confidence that we had a reasonable model—although, it should be stressed again that 40 observations are not sufficient to estimate this type of model in a statistically reliable fashion.

Maximum-likelihood estimation. While minimizing the sum of squared errors is a perfectly reasonable way to estimate the parameters of a price-response function, it is usually not the favored approach. Rather, most statisticians tend to choose *maximum-likelihood estimation* as their favored approach to estimating *a* and *b*. The reasons why one approach would be favored over another need not concern us here; in most cases, the two approaches give values of the underlying parameters that are very close to each other (especially when the underlying data set is large). However, for completeness, we will briefly discuss the method of maximum-likelihood estimation as it applies to the logit bid-response function.

The basic idea behind the maximum-likelihood function is to *find the values of a and b that maximize the estimated probability of achieving the pattern of wins and losses that were actually observed*. For any values of the parameters *a* and *b*, the probability of winning bid *i* would be $\rho(p_i) = 1/(1 + e^{a+bp_i})$ and the probability of losing bid *i* would be $1 - \rho(p_i) = e^{a+bp_i}/(1+e^{a+bp_i})$. We can combine these two expressions and write the probability of realizing the outcome that we actually saw for bid *i*, given the parameters *a* and *b* and the price p_i, as

$$L_i(a, b) = \rho(p_i)W_i + [1 - \rho(p_i)](1 - W_i) \tag{11.12}$$

$$= \left[\frac{W_i}{1 + e^{a+bp_i}} + \frac{(1 - W_i)e^{a+bp_i}}{1 + e^{a+bp_i}}\right] \tag{11.13}$$

Note that $L_i(a, b) = \rho(p_i)$ if we won the bid, and $L_i = 1 - \rho(p_i)$ if we lost the bid. Now, assume that we have a set of *n* bids and their outcomes. Assuming that all of the bids are independent, the *likelihood* of observing the particular pattern of wins and losses that we actually achieved for bids $i = 1, 2, \ldots, n$ is given by

$$L(a, b) = \prod_{i=1}^{n} L_i(a, b)$$

$$= \prod_{i=1}^{n}\left[\frac{W_i}{1 + e^{a+bp_i}} + \frac{(1 - W_i)e^{a+bp_i}}{1 + e^{a+bp_i}}\right] \tag{11.14}$$

where the symbol $\prod_{i=1}^{n}$ means that we multiply the *n* individual elements together. Maximum-likelihood estimation (MLE) finds the values of *a* and *b* that maximize the likelihood of the actual observation. That is, MLE solves the optimization problem $\max_{a,b} L(a, b)$, where $L(a, b)$ is given by Equation 11.14.

With a large number of observations, the likelihood of even a very good predictor will be very low. For example, assume we had a model that could predict, with 90% accuracy, whether or not we would win a bid—far higher than we will usually be able to achieve. For a sample of 1,000 bids, the expected likelihood for such an estimator would be $0.9^{1,000} = 1.79 \times 10^{-46}$. Working with such tiny numbers presents all sorts of numerical problems. Therefore, the usual approach is to maximize the natural logarithm of the likelihood. Since the logarithm is an increasing function of the probability, the values of *a* and *b* that maximize likelihood will also maximize the logarithm of likelihood (and vice versa). That is, we find the values of *a* and *b* that solve this optimization problem:

$$\max_{a,b} \ln(L(a, b)) = \sum_{i=1,n} \ln\left[\frac{W_i}{1 + e^{a+bp_i}} + \frac{(1 - W_i)e^{a+bp_i}}{1 + e^{a+bp_i}}\right] \tag{11.15}$$

This is a much easier problem to work with than maximizing the likelihood function itself. Not only does it enable us to work with much more reasonable numeric values, it is additive, which makes it easier to work with in general. Note that, since the likelihood is always less than 1, the log likelihood will always be less than zero. Maximizing the log likelihood means finding the values that bring the value of Equation 11.15 as close to zero—the "least negative"—as possible.

Solving Equation 11.15 for the data in Table 11.4 gives us the values of $a = -80.576$ and $b = 8.506$ as the maximum-likelihood estimators for the logit parameters. The corresponding logit bid-response curve is shown in Figure 11.10. Note that these parameter values imply that we would expect to win 50% of our bids if we set a price of $80.567/8.506 = \$9.47$—the same value obtained when we estimated a and b by minimizing the sum of squared errors. The corresponding total log likelihood is -19.752. We can compare this to the log likelihood that would be obtained using an estimator independent of price—that is, $p(p_i) = .575$ for all values of i. The log likelihood for the constant estimator is -27.274. Using the logit response model has resulted in an improvement in log likelihood of about 30% over a constant estimator. In case this doesn't seem sufficiently impressive, we should note that it improves the likelihood by a factor of 1,808!

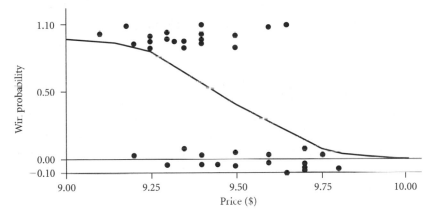

Figure 11.10 Logit bid-response curve fit to the values in Table 11.4 by maximizing log likelihood. The parameters of the curve are $a = -80.576$ and $b = 8.506$.

11.3.3 Extension to Multiple Dimensions

We have shown how the parameters of the logit bid-response function can be estimated in the case of a single product being sold to a single customer segment through a single channel. In this case we only need to estimate values for two parameters a and b. However, in most cases we would expect there to be differences in customers, channels, and products. Some of the differences that can occur include the following.

Channel Variation

- Internet vs. call center
- Retail vs. wholesale
- Direct vs. indirect

Product Variation

- Size of order
- Products ordered
- Configuration of products
- Ancillary services (e.g., extended warranty)

Customer Variation

- Size of customer
- Location
- Size of account
- Business
- New or repeat

To maximize profitability, a company would like to use as many of these variables as possible in setting its prices. A new, small customer with a large order entering through the Internet should get a different price from a repeat large customer with a small order through a direct channel, and so on. In the extreme, we would like to estimate different bid-response functions—and hence different optimal prices—for every element of the pricing and revenue optimization cube in Figure 2.4.

As an example, the Bank of Albion needs to determine what APR it should charge for a new customer requesting a £1,000 24-month loan via the Internet as well as what APR it should charge for a repeat customer requesting a £10,000 60-month loan through a branch. These two requests differ in all three dimensions: customer segment (new vs. repeat), channel (Internet vs. branch), and product (size and term of loan). To the extent that the Bank of Albion is willing to price differently based on all three of these dimensions, it should understand the influence of each one on price sensitivity.

To understand the influence of these different factors, we need more information in our bid-history database than simply prices and wins versus losses. Specifically, for each bid, we need to have information about the customer segment, channel, and product(s) associated with that bid as well as the price and whether or not we won the bid. This richer set of information is illustrated in Figure 11.11.

W/L	Price	Customer characteristics	Product characteristics	Market characteristics
0				
1				
1				
1				
0				
1				
0				
1				
1				
0				
0				
1				

Figure 11.11 Typical bid-history table template.

We can incorporate additional dimensions in the bid-response function by using a multivariate logit function of the type shown in Equation 11.16. Here, p_{ijk} is the price we offer to a customer of type i, purchasing a product of type j, through channel k, and a_{ijk} and b_{ijk} are the parameters of the corresponding logit function. This approach would indeed give us a separate bid-response curve for each cell in the PRO cube. We could then determine the optimal price for each cell by solving Equation 11.4 for each cell. These prices would be stored in a database, and, when a bid request arrives, we would simply need to access the price in the corresponding cell in the PRO cube:

$$\rho(p_{ijk}) = \frac{1}{1 + e^{a_{ijk} + b_{ijk} p_{ijk}}} \tag{11.16}$$

The bid-response function specification in Equation 11.16 has a major drawback. Estimating all the values of a_{ijk} and b_{ijk} would require performing a separate logit regression for each cell in the PRO cube. However, reliable estimation of the parameters of the logit bid-response function requires at least 200 historical observations. In general, we cannot expect to have this many observations for *every* cell in the PRO cube. If we had 50 different products, being sold to 10 different customer types through five channels, then our PRO cube would have $50 \times 10 \times 5 = 2,500$ cells. For each cell to have 200 historical observations, we would need a historic-bid database with *at least* $2,500 \times 200 = 500,000$ entries.[10] Most companies do not have anywhere near this much historic-bid data.

There are several possibilities for reducing the dimensionality of the problem to a more reasonable level. One of the simplest is to define a single value of a and a single value of b for each product, customer, and channel value—rather than for each combination. In this case, changing our notation slightly, we would calculate

$$\rho(p_{ijk}) = \frac{1}{1 + e^{a_i + a_j + a_k + (b_i + b_j + b_k)*p_{ijk}}}$$

where a_i and b_i are the parameter values estimated for customer type i, a_j and b_j are those estimated for a product of type j, and a_k and b_k are those estimated for channel type k. This reduces the number of parameters required for the 50-product, 10-customer-type, 5-channel case from 5,000 to $2 \times (50 + 10 + 5) = 130$. The historical data required to derive a statistically reliable estimate of this smaller parameter set is thereby much reduced.

11.3.4 Summary

This section has given an overview of the most important issues involved in estimating a bid-response function from historic win/loss data. Although a variety of approaches can be used, we focused on fitting a logit bid-response curve to historic data by minimizing squared errors or maximizing the (log) likelihood. This approach has much to recommend it: The logit function is most often used in these applications, and the method of maximizing log likelihood is easy to understand and apply. It is also easy to incorporate multiple dimensions and both customer and product segmentations into the estimation. However, we should stress that many practical applications require more sophisticated statistical estimation techniques. These include methodologies such as CART (classification and regression trees) and

CHAID for inferring market segments from raw data. More information on these approaches can be found in Breiman (1984) or, at a more technical (and comprehensive) level, Hastie, Tibsharani, and Friedman (2001). The estimation and application of alternative models to the logit and some of the issues that arise in practical applications can be found in Train (2003). Finally, a good technical overview of the area of customer behavior models and their application in marketing is given in Anderson, de Palma, and Thisse (1992).

11.4 EXTENSIONS AND VARIATIONS

We have shown how a bidder can find the customized price that will maximize expected contribution from a prospective deal in a simple bidding situation, assuming that the bidder faces no constraints on the price he can bid. There are two obvious variations on this basic model:

- The seller might want to do something other than maximize expected contribution.
- The seller might be constrained in the price he can offer for this deal.

In the first case, the seller is pursuing a *strategic goal* that involves something other than maximizing expected deal contribution. In the second case, the seller is subject to one or more *business rules* that limit his choice of potential prices. These business rules could arise externally (it may be illegal to charge different prices to certain groups of customers) or internally (the company may wish to keep prices through one channel lower than prices through another channel, for example). In both cases, the effect is to change the form of the basic customized-pricing problem to something other than the form given in Equation 11.4.

There is another way in which the determination of the optimal customized price would differ from solving Equation 11.4, when the bid setting itself is more complex than just a single bid for a known quantity of goods. In many cases, the bid setting itself is much more complicated—bids may involve many different bundled products and services and may involve several rounds of negotiation. These variations require extensions to the simple model, which we discuss in Section 11.4.2.

11.4.1 Strategic Goals and Business Rules

Consider the following situations.

> A package express company responds to 100,000 bid requests per year. Each request is for a contract to supply package express services for the next 12 months. The company currently seeks to maximize expected contribution for each bid, and it wins approximately 40% of the time. In 1995, senior management for the company declares that the company has an important new initiative with the goal "to become the dominant provider of shipping services to online retailers." As part of this initiative, the CEO tells the executive vice president of sales that he now wants the sales force to win at least 75% of its bids to online retailers while maintaining a reasonable level of profitability.

Gammatek is a distributor that purchases various types of electronic equipment that it sells to corporate, government, educational, and retail customers throughout North America. Gammatek has five divisions: CPUs, printers, storage devices, peripherals, and consumer electronics. It has about 23,000 customers and bids on about 400,000 pieces of business a year, with about 75% of the bid requests coming in to the call center and the remainder via Internet. Since Gammatek can set a different price for each bid, it has adopted a customized-pricing process. At the beginning of the 2003 fiscal year, Gammatek's president announces that each division will have a minimum average margin target it will be expected to meet for the coming year. These targets were adopted because of the perception that stock analysts will be watching margins particularly closely in the coming year due to a soft economy and are likely to reduce the rating of any company with eroding margins.

The Bank of Albion receives about 1 million requests per year for consumer loans. For each loan, the bank quotes an APR based on the size and term of the loan, customer credit score, and channel through which the request was received. Its newest marketing campaign advertises that a "typical" £5,000 loan has an APR of 12.9%. This means that, by British law, the average APR for £5,000 loans issued by the bank must be less than or equal to 12.9%.

In each of these three cases, the bidder needs to do something other than simply determine the prices that maximize expected contribution. The package express company needs to calculate prices that enable it to hit its market-share target for the online retail market. As we shall see, it can meet this *strategic goal* by solving the customized price optimization problem with a different objective function. Gammatek and the Bank of Albion want to maximize expected contribution, but they now face business rules that constrain the prices they can charge. In the case of Gammatek, the constraints arise from the internally imposed margin targets; in the Bank of Albion's case, the constraint is an externally imposed legal requirement. In both cases, the business rules can be addressed by constraining the basic customized pricing problem.

Let $\rho_i(p)$ and $f_i(p)$ be the bid-response functions and the deal-contribution function, respectively, for a particular deal, i. One way for the package express company to meet its market-share target would be to solve the constrained optimization problem:

$$\max_p \rho_i(p)f(p)$$

subject to

$$\rho_i(p) \geq 0.75 \tag{11.17}$$

whenever it is bidding to an online retailer. (Bids to all other customers would still be unconstrained.) Constraint 11.17 guarantees that the company will have *at least* a 75% probability of winning each bid to an online retailer. If the unconstrained optimal price would result in a probability of winning the bid that was greater than 75%, the constraint will not make any difference — the optimal price will be the same. On the other hand, if the unconstrained optimal price would have resulted in a probability of winning of less than 75%, Constraint 11.17 will ensure that the calculated price yields a win probability of 75%. In this case, the constrained price will be *lower* than the unconstrained price.

Figure 11.12 shows expected contribution as a function of the probability of winning the bid in a typical bid-response situation. The unconstrained optimum contribution is, of course, at the top of the hill. The win probability corresponding to the unconstrained optimum price is denoted by ρ, which is equal to about 0.55 in the figure. If the market-share target is less than ρ^*, then the constrained optimum price is the same as the unconstrained optimum price. If the market-share target is greater than ρ^*, then the constrained optimum price will be lower than the unconstrained optimum. As shown in Figure 11.12, the expected contribution from this bid will also be lower—we are "buying market share" by pricing lower than the contribution-maximizing price. Figure 11.12 shows the amount of lost contribution if the bidder enforces a target win probability of 0.75 for this bid. This difference is, in fact, the opportunity cost associated with the constraint that enforces the business rule.

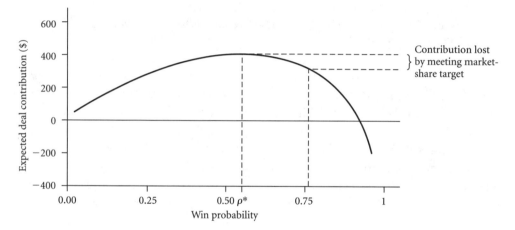

Figure 11.12 Applying a minimum market-share constraint.

To meet its minimum margin targets, Gammatek will also need to constrain its prices. Since Gammatek is a distributor, its contribution for each deal is the price minus the cost. This means we can write its unit margin as $m = (p - c)/p$. Let m^* be the minimum margin required for a particular line of business. (There would be a different value of m^* for each line of business.) Then one way to meet the minimum margin requirement is to ensure that $(p - c)/p \geq m^*$ for every bid, or, equivalently, that $p \geq c/(1 - m^*)$ for every bid. This constraint can be incorporated directly into the customized pricing problem:

$$\max_{p} \rho(p)f(p)$$

subject to

$$p \geq c/(1 - m^*) \tag{11.18}$$

Note that the minimum margin target has an effect opposite to that of the minimum market-share target: For each bid it will result in prices that are greater than or equal to the unconstrained optimal prices. However, like any constraint, if it is binding, it will result in a lower expected contribution than the unconstrained case.

Portfolio constraints. You may have noticed that we fudged in applying the minimum margin constraint at Gammatek. The corporate goal was for each division to meet a margin target. This target would logically be applied to the total margin achieved by the business—the total contribution for the division divided by the total revenue for the division. However, we applied Constraint 11.18 to every deal. This is too restrictive! The division could accept a lower-than-target margin on some deals as long as there are sufficient higher-margin deals so that the division average exceeds the target. Specifically, the division could possibly make additional money by pricing below the margin target to some very price-sensitive customers while pricing higher to some other customers who are less price sensitive.

It is clear that the package express company is in a similar situation—it does not need to have a win probability of 75% or higher on every bid in order to win 75% of its bids, anymore than every person in a group needs to be above six feet tall for the average height of the group to be six feet. It could well be optimal for the package express company to accept a 50% probability of winning a particularly competitive bid if it anticipates that it will be bidding on a less competitive bid in the future that it will have a 70% chance of winning. Finally, it is not clear at all how to incorporate the "mean APR" constraint into the customized pricing problem at the Bank of Albion, other than forcing every bid to take place at the mean, which would hardly seem to qualify as price and revenue optimization at all.

The upshot is that there are certain business rules that cannot be applied independently to each bid as it arrives. Rather, they need to be treated as *portfolio constraints* in order for expected profit to be maximized over all bids. That is, these rules cannot be applied one bid at a time; they must be applied across the portfolio of all bids. This requires that the bidder maintain a forecast of expected business for each combination of customer, product, and channel—in effect, for each cell in the pricing and revenue optimization cube. To see this, let d_i be the number of bids we anticipate from cell i in the PRO cube and p_i be the corresponding optimal price. (In other words, each index i corresponds to a different combination of product, customer type, and channel.) Then the pricing problem faced by the Bank of Albion can be formulated as

$$\max \sum_i \rho_i(p_i) f_i(p_i) d_i$$

subject to

$$\frac{\sum_i \rho_i(p_i) d_i p_i}{\sum_i \rho_i(p_i) d_i} \leq p^*$$

where p^* is the advertised "typical" rate. The constraint guarantees that the average price over all bids will be less than or equal to p^*, but it does not constrain every price to be less than or equal to p^*.

From a practical point of view, the existence of one or more portfolio constraints significantly complicates the customized pricing process. Instead of being able to calculate bid prices for deals one by one as they arrive, prices need to be precalculated for the entire PRO cube. Precise treatment of portfolio constraints also requires the forecasting of anticipated demand for each combination of product, customer type, and channel (the d_i in the earlier example). For these reasons, it is important to carefully consider whether it is important to fully incorporate portfolio constraints into the estimation of customized prices, or whether bid-by-bid approximations will suffice.

Infeasibility. Business rules are usually applied for good reasons. However, there can be a dangerous tendency for business rules to accrue over time, particularly if obsolete rules are never removed. If unchecked, the accumulation of business rules can lead to the customized pricing problem becoming overconstrained or even infeasible. For example, a computer equipment wholesaler may want to impose two business rules:

1. "We need to win at least 40% of our bids in the small-business segment."

2. "We need to maintain a margin of at least 12% on sales in our printer division."

Taken individually, each goal might be quite reasonable. However, if printers represent a large fraction of the company's sales to the small-business segment, the two goals might be mutually incompatible—namely, it might be impossible for the company to win 40% of its bids in the segment while maintaining a margin of 12% or more on its printer sales. This is the problem of infeasibility. The likelihood of infeasibility rises as the number and variety of business rules in place at one time increases.

The problem of infeasibility is often dealt with in customized pricing software by forcing the user to rank the business rules in the order of importance. In case of an infeasibility, the software will start by relaxing the least important rule first and continue to relax rules until it can find a solution. This is a standard *technical solution*. However, the larger issue is that any company utilizing customized pricing needs to actively manage business rules to keep them from being overapplied and accruing over time. As we have seen, adding business rules can never improve expected contribution. Therefore, they should be added only when necessary. In particular, it is important that a process be in place for periodically reviewing the rules that are in place and replacing those that are obsolete or no longer applicable.

11.4.2 Variations to the Basic Bidding Model

So far, we have looked at customized pricing in its simplest setting—when sellers submit a single bid for a known product to a buyer. Although this setting is realistic in some markets, in many others there are significant variations from this simple setting that have implications for how the bidders should set their prices. In this section we touch on a few of the most important examples.

Contract versus single purchase. In many cases, a buyer will request bids for a contract for future goods or services, typically for a fixed period, such as the next six months or a year. This is very popular for many freight, telecommunications, and other service companies.

A five-year IT outsourcing deal would also fall into this category. The particular twist it adds to customized pricing is this: A seller must make its bid without precisely knowing the level or mix of business he will actually realize if he wins the bid.

Consider a video game manufacturer soliciting bids from a trucking company to distribute its video games nationwide for the next 12 months. The trucking company needs to decide what discount from its basic tariff it should offer. If the manufacturer's newest game is a hit, then the trucker may ship a huge volume of games over the next few months—so much so that it might require additional trucks to be added to the fleet to accommodate the increased business. If, on the other hand, the game is a bust, the additional business from this customer would be simply incremental and not require any additional investment. Each trucking company needs to account for this uncertainty in its bid.

In this case—when the level or mix of demand from a potential customer is uncertain *and* the profitability of an account depends on the level or mix of demand—the bidder needs to forecast the demand he anticipates from that customer and use that information in calculating the price to bid. Furthermore, if there is a wide range of possible outcomes, he may need to explicitly incorporate the uncertainty in the business level in his bid.

Multiple line items. It is extremely common that a bid includes more than item. As a very simple example, the park district may submit an RFQ that asks for a bid on 10 medium-size automobiles and 10 pickup trucks as part of the same bid. At the more complex end of the spectrum, a bid to construct a power plant may include thousands of individual line items. As an intermediate example, a large "Class 8" truck built by Freightliner or Peterbilt comes with several hundred options a customer can choose, ranging from the configuration and type of transmission and engine to the size of the mud flaps. For each option (e.g., engine type), there are two or more alternatives, each with a different list price. A customer configures the truck by choosing the options he wants, and the manufacturer must determine the overall discount to offer based on the fully configured truck.

When multiple line items are involved in a bid, the tactic a bidder should use to determine his price depends on how the buyer is going to select a supplier. Here are the three broad possibilities.

- *Single bundled price.* The buyer may commit ahead of time to purchase from a single bidder and require only a single "all in" price from each bidder. This is the case with the configurable Class 8 truck purchase, for example. In this case, the price for the entire bundle can be determined using the standard optimal customized-pricing approach.

- *Itemized prices with single supplier.* In this case, the purchaser commits to purchase from a single bidder but requires itemized prices. This may seem identical to the previous case, but there are a number of potential pitfalls. First of all, even though the purchaser will only be paying a single price, his choice of supplier may be influenced by some of the itemized prices. For example, automobile purchase decisions are often more influenced by the base price of the car than by the cost of the options. Some purchasers are more likely to purchase the same car if it is presented as a $19,000 car with $5,000 worth of options than if it is presented as a $20,000 car with $3,800 worth of options. This is an issue of *price presentation*, which is treated in some detail in Chapter 12.

A more important issue with itemized prices is that they give the purchaser more scope and leverage for negotiation, particularly in a competitive bid. When there is only a single price, there is only one dimension for negotiation. When there are many line-item prices, a savvy buyer will negotiate each one along with the total discount. For this reason, sellers prefer to offer a single bundled price, while buyers almost always prefer line-item prices, even when they will only be purchasing from a single supplier.

- *Itemized prices and multiple suppliers.* In this case, the purchaser requests itemized prices and reserves the right to purchase different items from different bidders. For example, the park district might reserve the right to purchase the cars from one company and the trucks from the other. Obviously, the motivation for the purchaser is to select the cheapest supplier for each item (*cherry picking*). In this case, the strategy for the seller is to treat each item as an individual bid and to calculate the optimal price for each line item independent of the others. Of course, a supplier might want to provide an extra discount if the purchaser will purchase everything from him.

The tactics for dealing with these different settings are fairly clear: What is most important for a bidder is to understand what game he is playing before he submits his bid. That is, if itemized prices are requested, it is critical to know whether or not the purchaser is committed to a single supplier or whether he is reserving the option to purchase from more than one bidder.

Negotiation. In many customized-pricing situations there is an element of negotiation—the first deal proposed is not necessarily the final one. Negotiation may take place on price ("Cut the total price by 1% and I'll sign right now"), on product bundle ("Throw in the extended warranty and we have a deal"), or both. Clearly, this is a different setting from the single-bid process that we have considered, and recommended prices need to be modified accordingly.

There is a substantial literature on the art and science of negotiation, not to mention a small industry devoted to helping people become better negotiators. However, from the point of view of pricing and revenue optimization, the critical consideration is that the initial bid be high enough to leave room to lower prices through the process while still maintaining acceptable profitability. Of course, the initial price cannot be too high or the bid might be rejected out of hand. One way to incorporate negotiation into the process is to give the salesperson a range within which to bid. This is illustrated in Figure 11.13 for the example of the park service vehicle bid. Expected contribution is within 4% of the optimal for any amount bid between $11,600 and $12,400. The salesperson negotiating the deal might be provided with this range of prices and expected to use his negotiating skill to obtain a price as high as possible within the range. The savvy salesperson will choose an initial bid at the high end of the range to give himself room to bargain. This allows the company to provide guidance to a salesperson in the negotiation process while ensuring that the final price achieved is sufficiently close to optimal.

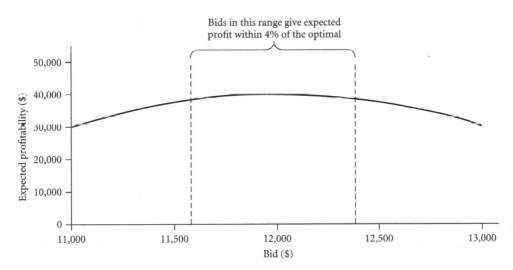

Figure 11.13 Price range within which expected contribution is within 4% of the optimum for the example with the profitability curve shown in Figure 11.4.

Fulfillment. In many contract bidding situations a buyer may not wish to commit *all* of his business to a single supplier. For example, a shipper may not want to commit all of his business for the next year to a single trucking company. Instead, the shipper may want to have contracts with two different trucking companies in order to provide himself with flexibility in case of a dispute with one of the trucking companies or in case one is shut down temporarily by a strike. Furthermore, having contracts with two different trucking companies may save the shipper money if he picks the cheaper trucker for each shipment. In other business-to-business relationships, a purchaser will choose two or more competitors as *preferred suppliers*. As specific needs arise during the year, the purchaser will choose among the preferred suppliers for each order.

In this case, the determination of the price to bid needs to consider not only the probability of "winning"—that is, becoming a preferred supplier—it must also consider the amount (and mix) of business that will come his way during the term of the contract. Generally, both the bidder's probability of becoming a preferred supplier and the amount of business he will receive from the contract will increase as he decreases his price. Both considerations need to be incorporated into the estimated contribution.

11.5 CUSTOMIZED PRICING IN ACTION

Effective customized pricing requires a disciplined business process both to calculate and administer prices and to ensure that the parameters of the bid-response functions are updated to capture changes in the market. A high-level sketch of such a process is shown in Figure 11.14. There are three core steps in the customized pricing process.

1. *Calculate bid-response function.* Based on available information about the customer, the product (or products) she wishes to purchase, and the channel through which

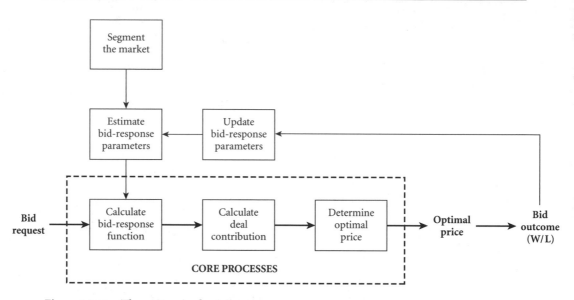

Figure 11.14   The customized pricing process.

the request was received, the bidder estimates how the probability of winning this customer's business varies as a function of price. This requires retrieving (or calculating) the parameters of the bid-response function that apply to this particular combination of segment, channel, and product.

2. *Calculate deal contribution*. The bidder estimates the deal contribution function relating contribution from this deal to its price.

3. *Determine optimal price*. Combining the bid-response function and the deal-contribution function, the bidder calculates the price that maximizes expected contribution (or other goal) subject to applicable business rules.

These three core steps may be executed each time a bid request is received and a price needs to be calculated. Alternatively, the PRO cube might be populated ahead of time with optimal prices that are accessed whenever a bid request is received. This requires executing the three core steps in "batch mode" prior to processing any bids. Which approach is better depends on the volume of bids to be processed and the time available to respond to each one. A lending company that needs to respond rapidly to thousands of customer inquiries about consumer loans every day is more likely to prepopulate a database with prices. On the other hand, a heavy equipment manufacturer who responds to 40 or 50 RFPs per week, with several days available to respond to each, is more likely to optimize the price for each bid independently.

Whichever approach is used, the core steps need to be supported by three additional steps that are executed less frequently.

1. *Segment the market*. The bidder determines the market segments he will use to differentiate his prices. This establishes the structure of the PRO cube and needs to be done prior to estimating any bid-response parameters. Typically, the market segmentation

does not need to be updated very often—perhaps annually or semiannually. The exception is when the bidder seeks to serve a new market or type of customer.

2. *Estimate bid-response parameters.* The bidder estimates the parameters of the bid-response function when the market is initially segmented. The bid-response parameters need to be reestimated whenever the segmentation itself is changed.

3. *Update bid-response parameters.* The bidder updates the parameters of the bid-response function on a routine basis—usually weekly or monthly—to ensure that changes in the underlying market are captured. Updating the bid-response parameters is not much different from estimating them in the first place. In the simplest approach the results of the most recent bids (i.e., those since the last update) are appended to the bid-history file in Figure 11.11, and the same approach is used to estimate the updated parameters using the new, larger database of bids. However, this approach would give increasingly old bid results the same weight as much newer bids in estimating the parameters. For this reason, most companies drop old bids from their bid-history file—where old bids may be defined as those over a year old. Alternatively, other companies use Bayesian updating approaches that utilize all bid information but weight newer bids more than older bids.

11.6 EXERCISE

1. Dell is bidding against IBM for an order of 150 laptops. Dell's unit cost is $1,000 per laptop, and, based on previous experience, Dell's belief is that IBM's bid will be uniformly distributed between $1,200 and $1,500 per unit.

   a. Assuming that Dell and IBM are at parity (e.g., neither supplier enjoys a premium on this deal), what is Dell's optimal price per unit to bid? What is Dell's corresponding probability of winning the bid and expected contribution?

   b. Assume that IBM is an incumbent supplier to this customer and, as a result, Dell believes that IBM enjoys a $200 per unit premium for this deal. Assuming that Dell has the same distribution on IBM's bid as previously stated, what is Dell's optimal price per unit to bid? What is Dell's corresponding probability of winning the bid and its expected contribution?

1. In addition, it faces the related question of which applications to decline, although this is not, strictly speaking, a pricing issue.

2. The exception is the rare case when a hot new model (such as the Porsche Boxster) is first introduced and production cannot meet demand. In this case, dealers may charge above the MSRP to capture the opportunity cost created by the constrained supply. Judging from online chat room comments, pricing above MSRP is extremely unpopular with customers. See Section 12.2.1 for a discussion of why this might be so and its implications for pricing.

3. In this section we will occasionally talk about the *bid price*, by which we simply mean the price associated with the bid. This should not be confused with the *bid price* used in revenue management as defined in Section 7.3.3.

4. At least legally.

5. For more details on the operation of online supplier auctions see Elmagrabhy and Keskinocak (2003).

6. As in the definition of price elasticity in Equation 3.5, the minus sign guarantees that the elasticity will be positive, since $\rho'(p)$, the derivative of the price response function, is less than zero.

7. How these factors might actually translate into a decision between competing suppliers and the extent to which the buyer is being truthful about her selection criteria are separate issues.

8. The sole reason for jittering the data is to provide some dispersion so that it is easier to visualize the patterns of wins and losses. Only the original, unjittered values are used in any analysis.

9. These and other models are described in Aldrich and Nelson (1984).

10. In reality, even more historical data would be required, since we need a *minimum* of 200 observations in each cell.

12 | PRICING AND REVENUE OPTIMIZATION AND CUSTOMER ACCEPTANCE

The tactics we studied in previous chapters assume that the seller is seeking to maximize expected contribution (or some other objective) subject to constraints reflecting the technical limitations of price administration systems (such as airline booking systems) or self-imposed business rules (such as a minimum margin requirement). We have implicitly assumed that the prices we charge now will not influence future consumer behavior—or at least that we can ignore any such influence when we determine the price to offer now. There are (at least) two ways in which this assumption can fail. The first is when a buyer updates her expectations of our future prices based on the price we offer now and changes her future behavior as a result. A customer who gets a bargain from us today is presumably more likely at least to check our prices when shopping in the future. And a customer who finds our prices high today may be more likely to consider alternative sellers in the future, even if he purchases from us today.

The fact that buyers use our current prices to update their expectations of our future prices can be mathematically modeled and incorporated into pricing and revenue optimization calculations. One approach is to use long-run rather than short-run price-response curves in determining prices. Another approach is to impute an additional value to winning a customer in addition to the immediate contribution gained from the purchase. In either case, incorporating buyer updating of price expectations in our current pricing decision is generally a straightforward extension of the standard PRO techniques.

A second, more pernicious, influence of current pricing on future behavior occurs when a pricing tactic makes buyers angry because it is perceived as "unfair." In this case, there is the chance that buyers may decline to purchase from a seller either now or in the future for reasons that might be totally unrelated to the absolute price we charge. A buyer can be influenced by the manner in which a seller presents a price (or price change), how the current price compares to past prices, and how the price quoted to that buyer compares to prices quoted to other buyers. In extreme cases buyers can become so offended that they force the abandonment of what seems to a seller like a perfectly reasonable pricing scheme. These reactions often violate economic principles of rationality and are therefore hard to incorporate into the types of mathematical optimization models we have discussed. Nonetheless, these reactions must be considered when planning and setting up a dynamic or differentiated pricing strategy. We have touched on these reactions briefly in Chapter 4, but we explore them more fully here, starting with two examples.

Coca-Cola Makes Customers Hot

In a 1999 interview with the Brazilian magazine *Veja*, Douglas Ivester, chairman and chief executive officer of the Coca-Cola Corporation, announced that his company was testing a new vending machine that would change the price of soft drinks in response to outside temperature. When it was hot outside, a cold can of Coke would cost more than when it was cold outside. As he explained:

> Coca-Cola is a product whose utility varies from moment to moment. In a final summer championship, when people meet in a stadium to enjoy themselves, the utility of a chilled Coca-Cola is very high.[1] So it is fair it should be more expensive. The machine will simply make this process automatic.

While Douglas Ivester might have thought this was fair, others emphatically did not agree. The *San Francisco Chronicle* called the idea "a cynical ploy to exploit the thirst of faithful customers," the *Honolulu Star-Bulletin* labeled it "a lunk-head idea," and the *Miami Herald* referred to Coca-Cola management as a bunch of "soda jerks."

Coke began to backpedal immediately. "We have no plans to introduce technology that would increase prices in hot weather," said spokesperson Ben Deutsch. Although Coca-Cola is rumored to have tested weather-sensitive machines in Japan, it has never employed them in the United States. And the temperature-sensitive vending machine gaffe is widely considered to be one of the factors contributing to Ivester's losing his job.

Amazon Flubs DVD Pricing

One night in August 2000, a customer ordered from Amazon the DVD of Julie Taymor's movie *Titus*, paying $24.49. Browsing on Amazon a few nights later he found that the price had jumped to $26.24. As an experiment, he deleted the cookies on his computer that identified him to Amazon as a regular customer. Revisiting the Amazon Web site, he was quoted a price of $22.74 for the same DVD.[2]

This customer happened to be a regular purchaser of DVDs from Amazon, and he came to the reasonable conclusion that Amazon was charging higher prices to its most loyal customers. When he recounted his experience with Amazon on the Web site DVDTalk.com, the reaction was immediate and overwhelmingly negative. Comments posted on DVDTalk.com over the next weeks included:

- "Amazon is over in my book."
- "I will never buy another thing from those guys!"

- "I am so offended by what they did that I'll never buy another DVD from them again."
- "Amazon is suck (sic)."

The tale spread via e-mail and chat rooms, and *Computerworld* published a story about Amazon's pricing policies. The national press picked up the story. Press coverage generally jumped to the conclusion that Amazon was experimenting with "dynamic pricing," by which they would charge different customers different prices. As one reporter defined it, "dynamic pricing... involves putting customers into groups based on how price sensitive they appear to be. If someone accepts the $10-higher price, say, three times in a row, maybe that's all they will ever get in the future," one commentator speculated.[3] While a few reporters noted that dynamic pricing was hardly unknown in the offline world, their response to Amazon's action was almost universally negative.

In response to the negative publicity, Amazon apologized and claimed that it was merely running a price-sensitivity test: "It was done to determine consumer responses to different discount levels," said Amazon spokesman Bill Curry. "This was a pure and simple price test. This was not dynamic pricing. We don't do that and have no plans ever to do that."

What happened? In both cases, consumer reaction did not follow the standard model of rational economic decision making. After all, a "rational" consumer should care only about her price—not the prices charged to other customers or what the company might have charged in the past or might charge in the future. In the cases of Amazon and Coke, apparently sensible pricing schemes were abandoned due to consumer reaction. Clearly, these stories do not reflect shopping automatons comparing prices to their willingness to pay and dispassionately deciding whether or not to buy. Rather, they show human beings reacting emotionally to such seemingly irrelevant issues as the prices other people might be offered or how prices might change over time.

The topic of this chapter is how consumers react to prices in ways that go beyond the predictions of simple economic decision models and the implications of these reactions for pricing and revenue optimization. Our analysis of customer behavior has assumed that a rational consumer surveys her available buying options and chooses the one that maximizes her surplus—defined as the difference between her willingness to pay and the price. If none of her options has a positive surplus, she doesn't buy. This simple model is quite robust and can accommodate a wide range of behaviors. For example, it says nothing about what factors determine her willingness to pay and how they enter into her calculation. Some buyers may have a much higher willingness to pay for a particular brand (e.g., Coca-Cola or Mercedes), while others might be utterly indifferent to brand. Consumer preferences certainly change over time, so the willingness to pay for a new car may increase after a raise, and the willingness to pay for a hamburger may increase as dinnertime approaches. We could imagine all sorts of bizarre willingness-to-pay distributions changing in different ways over time across a population. But no matter how bizarre they might be, the same analytical tools would still apply.

Although the basic model of customer price response is quite robust, there are many types of behavior that it cannot represent. In particular, customers do not view buying and selling unemotionally as simple transactions among consenting adults. Rather, they often react to prices in ways that economists consider "irrational."[4] Customer response to price is not always based only on the price and product being offered. Instead, a number of other, seemingly irrelevant, factors can influence buying behavior, including:

- How the price is presented and packaged
- How much profit the customer believes the merchant will realize
- How this price compares to past prices and anticipated future prices
- Prices the customer believes are being charged to other customers

All of these factors can influence consumer behavior, but none of them can be easily accommodated within the willingness-to-pay model.

Broadly speaking, we will consider two categories of "irrationality" influencing the psychology of purchase. The first category consists of reactions to the way a price is presented, so-called *presentation issues*. One well-known example of a price presentation issue is the *digit-ending* phenomenon—buyers tend to overweight the leading digits when comparing prices so that, in immediate valuation, $19.99 seems to be a greater savings from $20.00 than $19.93 from $19.99. Another, more important example, is the fact that customers will respond differently to the same price for an item if it is presented as a sale price rather than a list price or a surcharge. The second category of irrational price response involves the issue of fairness. The belief that one is entitled to "fair treatment" is deeply ingrained in most people. Perceptions of "unfair treatment" can trigger strong emotional responses such as those expressed in the DVDtalk.com postings about Amazon.

The two categories of irrationality both influence consumer decisions, but they manifest themselves in different ways. A company that is doing a poor job at price presentation will simply sell less than it might, but it is unlikely to hear anything from its customers. After all, customers are unlikely to complain if a merchant's prices end in $.88 rather than $.99. In contrast, customers are likely to complain—and loudly—if their sense of fairness is violated. Poor price presentation will not land you on the front page of the newspaper, but "unfair pricing" just might—just ask Coca-Cola and Amazon.

12.1 PRICE PRESENTATION AND FRAMING

As we saw in Chapter 11, unsecured loans are a popular form of consumer credit in Great Britain. Table 11.2 shows three ways a bank could advertise the price of a £3,000 loan. The APR (annual percentage rate) offered by different lenders ranges from 6.9% to 17.7%. The corresponding monthly payment ranges from £92.99 to £108.11—perceptually a much smaller range. Finally, the total interest the customer would pay for the different loans ranges from £329.79 to £888.22.

What is the "price" of a loan? There is no single answer, since any one of the three quantities shown in Table 11.2—APR, monthly payment, or total interest—could be considered the price. Given the amount borrowed, the term, and any one of the three quantities shown, the other two figures can be readily calculated. However, you probably won't be surprised to learn that banks in the United Kingdom choose to advertise the "price" that both makes the idea of taking out the loan most appealing to the potential borrower *and* makes the lender appear most competitive. In its advertising, Egg, an Internet lender, emphasizes its low APR of 10.9%. On the other hand, NatWest advertises that its loans will cost only £105.32 per month. None of the banks advertise the total interest the customer will ultimately pay, since this would make the loan appear more expensive in total and possibly dissuade potential lenders.

The consumer loan example illustrates that customer purchasing behavior can be influenced by how price is presented and that companies decide how to present their prices accordingly. Perfectly rational consumers would be able to calculate that a three-year, £3,000 loan at an APR of 11.9% would result in monthly charges of £99.50 and total interest payments of £581.99 and that one at an APR of 14.9% would result in monthly payments of £103.85 and total interest payments of £738.57 and not be influenced by how the bank presented its pricing. But, since we do not live in a world of rational consumers, companies need to understand how buyers can be swayed by the presentation of prices and incorporate this understanding into their pricing and revenue optimization programs.

The realization that consumer behavior is not always consistent with economic theory dates from at least 1958, when Herbert Simon introduced the concept of *bounded rationality*. According to Simon, people (and firms) do not always make decisions in accordance with the principles of economic rationality. Rather, they often use mental shortcuts, rules of thumb, or simple heuristics to make decisions in a complex, rapidly changing, and often-confusing world. Over the past 45 years, researchers have continued to investigate the ways in which the real world of buying and selling differs from the idealized models used by economists. In this chapter, we discuss the implication of their findings for pricing and revenue optimization.

12.1.1 Prospect Theory

Prospect theory was introduced by Daniel Kahneman and Amos Tversky in 1979. The observation underlying prospect theory was that people do not evaluate opportunities based on a strict evaluation of expected costs and benefits. Rather, they use various mental shortcuts and rules of thumb to make decisions. This can lead to outcomes that are inconsistent with ideas of economic "rationality." Much of prospect theory relates to the way that people evaluate uncertainty and is not directly relevant to pricing and revenue optimization.[5] But the prospect theory principle of *asymmetrical gains and losses* is relevant. The principle of asymmetrical gains and losses says that people tend to experience losses much more intensely than they value gains. This idea is illustrated in Figure 12.1. Customers value a gain of Δ much less than they feel the pain of a loss of equal value. Since paying a price is viewed as a loss, this means that a surcharge (or price rise) of $5.00 is viewed much more negatively than a discount (or price drop) of $5.00 is viewed positively. In short: Price rises are felt more intensely than price drops.

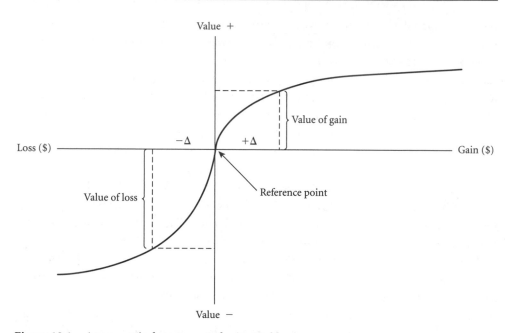

Figure 12.1 Asymmetrical treatment of gains and losses.

As an example, consider the following scenario.

- *Station A* sells gasoline for $1.60 per gallon but gives a discount of $0.10 per gallon if you pay with cash.

- *Station B* sells gasoline for $1.50 per gallon but charges a surcharge of $0.10 per gallon if you pay with a credit card.

The two approaches are identical in terms of what any particular buyer will pay. Yet, Station B's approach is never seen. Why? According to prospect theory, the reason is immediate from Figure 12.1. For each station, the list price establishes the reference price in the buyer's mind. For Station A the $0.10 discount ($+\Delta$) is viewed as a gain relative to the reference price of $1.60, while for Station B the $0.10 surcharge ($-\Delta$) is viewed as a loss relative to the reference price of $1.50. Prospect theory predicts that a buyer using a credit card would be more likely to patronize Station A than accept the surcharge associated with Station B.

Asymmetrical treatment of gains and losses has implications for how prices should be presented. Customer reaction to a $65 shirt will depend not only on the price itself but also on how it is presented:

- "List Price is $60 with a $5 surcharge" will be viewed very negatively.

- "List Price is $65" is neutral.

- "List Price is $70, on sale for $65" will be viewed more positively.

Every merchant knows that the last approach will sell more shirts.

The other aspect of customer valuation illustrated in Figure 12.1 is that the valuation of gains seems to demonstrate diminishing returns. That is, small discounts can have disproportionate effects, while larger discounts have proportionally smaller effects. Thus, offering (or seeming to offer) any discount at all seems to drive additional business.

Asymmetrical treatment of losses and gains may explain some of the negative reaction to Coca-Cola's announcement of temperature-dependent vending machine pricing. Note the wording of Douglas Ivester's announcement: "In a final summer championship, when people meet in a stadium to enjoy themselves, the utility of a chilled Coca-Cola is very high. *So it is fair that it should be more expensive.*" From a prospect theory point of view, he chose the very worst price presentation possible—he framed the scheme in terms of a surcharge. He focused attention on the high-price scenario and triggered an immediate negative reaction. Coca-Cola would probably have fared better if Ivester had said something like: "On a cold day, the utility of a chilled Coca-Cola is not as high as on a hot day. So it is only fair that it should cost less—our customers deserve a price break in that situation."

Prospect theory provides one explanation of a nearly universal phenomenon in pricing—discounts are common, surcharges are rare. As we saw in Chapter 10, more than 70% of the retail sales of fashion goods in the United States in 2000 were sold at some discount from list price. It is safe to assume that only a tiny fraction (if any) of retail sales took place at a surcharge from list price.[6] Clearly, sellers believe that promotions and markdowns stimulate sales more than is explainable simply by the lower price. If the absolute price was all that mattered, sellers would be indifferent between running a sale and lowering list price. Rational consumers would simply compare their willingness-to-pay against the current price and decide whether or not to purchase. They would be indifferent between buying at list price and buying at sale price.

But this is clearly not the case. Consumers like promotions and markdowns. In fact, they like them so much that some retailers have set artificially high list prices in order to hold perpetual "virtual sales." A 1989 lawsuit held that the May Company "deceived customers by artificially inflating its so-called 'original' or 'regular' (reference) prices and then promoting discounts from these prices as bargains. This practice has become so rife in the U.S. retail environment that many consumers will only buy 'on sale' and then are skeptical about whether they have really bought at a fair price."[7] Prospect theory explains this as an attempt by the seller to keep the reference price of the buyer high so that the buyer focuses on the "gain" from the discount rather than on the price itself.

12.1.2 Reference Prices

Prospect theory predicts that people evaluate gains and losses relative to a reference point, with losses felt more intensely than gains. How is this reference point determined? Winer (1986) introduced the idea that many buyers shop with a "reference price" in mind that they consider fair. This reference price then becomes an element in their purchase decision, with customers less likely to buy if the actual price is higher than the reference price.

The reference price needs to be distinguished from willingness to pay. Willingness to pay is theoretically a property only of the buyer's "utility" for the item under consideration, which should be independent of current or past prices. On the other hand, reference price is a function of observed prices, past and present. In the example of the gasoline station discussed earlier, we assumed that the reference price was the list price. However, research has shown that many buyers use other information instead of (or in addition to) the current list price to form their reference prices. This information can include past prices for the same or similar items and current prices for competing items. Past prices are more likely to be used in forming reference prices for repetitive-buy items (such as groceries and toiletries) than for large or unique purchases (large appliances or artwork). While reference price effects appear to be common for repetitive-buy items, the way that reference prices are formed can vary by consumer. A study of 247 families suggested that about 67% primarily used historic price information for the same brand to set the reference price, 23% primarily used the prices of competing brands, and 10% apparently didn't use reference pricing at all.[8]

While there are different views on the psychological mechanisms by which reference prices are formed, numerous studies have confirmed that reference prices and the asymmetrical perception of losses and gains predicted by prospect theory do seem to influence buying behavior. Given this, the reason that reference prices are important from the point of view of pricing and revenue optimization is that they are influenced by a customer's past shopping and buying history. If a customer becomes used to seeing an item at a low price, he will expect the price to be low in the future and will be less likely to purchase if it is high. This can create a dilemma for the seller. Dropping the price on an item now may be optimal from a tactical point of view (that is, it may maximize short-run contribution), but it may have future repercussions if it lowers the reference prices of potential future customers.

12.1.3 Mental Budgeting

You are planning to go to a play by yourself one Sunday afternoon. Consider the following two scenarios.

- *Scenario 1:* You have already bought a $20 ticket for the play. Just after leaving your apartment, you open your wallet, the ticket slides out and slips down the storm drain, where it is lost.

- *Scenario 2:* You don't have a ticket but plan to buy one at the box office. Just after leaving your apartment, you open your wallet and a $20 bill slips out of your wallet and is lost down the storm drain.

The question under both scenarios is: Would you go to the play and buy a $20 ticket at the box office? (We assume you know that tickets are still available at the box office for $20.) Kahneman and Tversky (1979) found that the percentage of people who would go to the box office and buy a ticket is much higher under the second scenario than the first. One hundred and eighty-seven of 250 college students presented with the second scenario said they would buy a ticket while only 120 of 250 said they would in the first scenario. This contradicts the definition of economic rationality. The wealth effect of losing a $20 bill and a $20 ticket are exactly the same. Why would someone be willing to purchase a ticket in one case and not the other? The explanation, which has been supported by experiments, is that people maintain mental "budgets" and evaluate expenditures against these budgets. Thus, someone might have a mental budget of $20 (or $30) for the day's entertainment. The initial purchase of a $20 ticket is counted against this budget, so the purchase of a second ticket would exceed the mental budget. On the other hand, the loss of a $20 bill is not counted against the day's entertainment budget (perhaps it is counted as a loss against general funds), so there is still sufficient mental budget to purchase a ticket.

Mental budgeting can have implications for how (and if) products and services should be bundled. If certain options, say, a top-of-the-line car stereo, are viewed as counting against a separate mental budget than the base product (the car itself), then it will generally be more effective to sell them separately.

12.1.4 Other Presentation Issues

There are a number of other price presentation issues that have been found to affect customer behavior. For example, Gourville and Soman (2002) compared health club users who were billed once at the beginning of the year versus those who were billed monthly. Those who were billed once a year tended to use the club more during the first part of the year, with usage tailing off as the year progressed, while those who were billed monthly used the club more regularly throughout the year. More importantly, customers who were billed monthly were more likely to sign up again at the end of the year. The mode of payment apparently influenced the pattern of usage, which in turn influenced the pattern of repurchase.

A similar effect has been found for time of purchase and bundled purchases. People who have purchased a ticket six months prior to an event (say, a concert) are much more likely not to show than those who bought a ticket one day prior. Furthermore, season ticket holders are more likely to miss a given game than those who have purchased a single ticket for that game. In most settings, this effect is unlikely to be important. But if attendance or consumption encourages repurchasing, then it may be a factor to consider.

12.2 FAIRNESS

The Amazon case illustrates the emotional response that differential pricing can evoke. (In this case, much of the emotion was displaced, since Amazon was not planning to systematically charge loyal customers more — it was actually running a short-term experiment to estimate price elasticities.) The company learned the hard way that discrimination can be the third rail of pricing. A reputation for unfair pricing may alienate current and future customers. On the other hand, as we have seen, the revenue effects of differential prices are great enough that companies that can find acceptable ways to segment their customers and charge differential prices have tremendous incentive to do so.

In this section, we address the issue of *fairness* as it applies to customer reactions to pricing. Fairness in the sense we will be discussing it — and the way that most people mean it when they cry, "That's not fair!" — was not considered part of classical economics. In the last 10 years or so, economists have given much more attention to the issue of perceived fairness and how it might influence customer behavior. This is still an active and somewhat controversial area of research, and there are many aspects of pricing acceptance that are not fully understood. However, it does appear that there are at least two ways in which customers evaluate the fairness of a price. The first is relative to the perceived profit being earned by the seller. The second is relative to the prices the customer believes other buyers are paying. We treat these two in order.

12.2.1 Dual Entitlement

The first place that fairness can enter into pricing is via the buyer's perception of the seller's profit. There is a common perception that "greedy" companies should not generate "obscene" profits by "gouging" customers. Most people could probably give examples of pricing they believe violated this principle—although they might be harder pressed to give an objective criterion of when profits become "obscene" or a high price becomes "gouging." However, it does appear that most customers hold a belief that it is unfair for companies to charge too much for their goods and services—even if customers are willing to pay the high price. This idea was formalized by Kahneman, Knetsch, and Thaler (1986) under the name *dual entitlement*. Dual entitlement postulates that consumers believe they are entitled to a "reasonable" price and firms are entitled to a "reasonable" profit. Pricing that seems solely aimed to increase profit beyond what is viewed as reasonable is likely to be viewed as unfair. Specific implications of the principle of dual entitlement include the following.

- Raising prices to recoup increased costs is usually viewed as *fair* by most consumers.
- Raising prices just to increase profits is often viewed as *unfair*.
- Deviations from customary practices are often viewed with suspicion as attempts to raise price.
- Information about the reason for price changes can often help acceptance.

One of the predictions of the theory of dual entitlement is that customers would be more accepting of price rises resulting from cost rises than they would be of price rises resulting from supply shortages. This does, in fact, appear to be the case—charging more for vital supplies immediately before or after the arrival of a hurricane is viewed as very unfair by consumers. In fact, in the face of widespread consumer outrage after many suppliers hiked prices in the wake of hurricane Andrew in 1992, Florida passed a law against such price gouging. Further evidence of dual entitlement was gathered by Kahneman, Knetsch, and Thaler, who posed the following scenario to a sample of consumers:

> A hardware store has been selling snow shovels for $15. The morning after a large snowstorm, the store raises the price to $20. Rate this action as: completely fair, acceptable, somewhat unfair, or very unfair.

Of 107 respondents, 18% rated the pricing action as "acceptable or completely fair" while 82% rated it as "somewhat unfair or very unfair." In a similar vein, Kahneman, Knetsch, and Thaler asked what a store should do if it found it had exactly one item left in stock of that year's most popular toy, assuming that all other stores were sold out of it (in their 1986 paper it was a Cabbage Patch Doll). A vast majority of those surveyed thought that it would be "very unfair" for the store simply to sell the toy to the highest bidder.

One problem created by dual entitlement is due to the fact that customers do not have a very good idea of sellers' costs or profits. A 2001 phone survey of price and profit perceptions produced the results shown in Table 12.1. Each of the numbers in Table 12.1 is a gross

TABLE 12.1

Responses to consumer survey questions regarding perceived profit

Question	Mean response
If a fancy department store pays $40 to a manufacturer for a woman's blouse, what would be a fair price for the store to charge you?	$58.16
If a fancy department store pays $40 to a manufacturer for a woman's blouse, what would be a fair price for the store to charge you, keeping in mind the store must cover such costs as rent and payroll?	$62.94
If a fancy department store pays $40 to a manufacturer for a woman's blouse, how much do you think the store charges you for the blouse when it is not on sale?	$76.58
For each $100 a fancy department store makes in sales, how many dollars do you think are left over in pure profit after the store has covered all its costs?	$33.09
. . . for a discount store?	$30.24
. . . for a grocery store?	$27.52

SOURCE: Bolton, Warlop, and Alba (2001).

overestimate. A discount store might realize a net margin of 4% and a grocery store 2%—not the 30% and 27.5%, respectively, that customers apparently believe. Part of the discrepancy may be explained by reference pricing, since consumers tend to set their reference prices based on the lowest prices they see for an item, assuming these prices are still profitable for the seller. Since merchants often sell markdown items below cost, consumers tend to assume that the original list price included a vast profit for the seller. This creates a potential problem. As we saw in Chapter 10, markdown pricing is often the optimal tactical policy for a merchant selling a stock of perishable goods. However, the short-term gain in profitability from the markdowns must be compared with the longer-term effect of creating the perception in consumers' minds that the cost of the item is low and that the merchant is reaping exorbitant profits at list price.

The principle of dual entitlement seems to be closely entwined with reference prices in the minds of customers. Consider the following two scenarios, studied by Kahneman, Knecht, and Tversky.

- A shortage has developed for a popular model of automobile, and customers must now wait two months for delivery. A dealer has been selling these cars at list price. Now the dealer prices this model at $200 above list price.

- A shortage has developed for a popular model of automobile, and customers must now wait two months for delivery. *A dealer has been selling these cars at a discount of $200 below list price. Now the dealer sells this model only at list price.*

In the first case, 71% of those surveyed thought the dealer's action was unfair, while only 42% thought it was unfair in the second case. What is going on here? It appears that respondents are using the (unspecified) list price as the reference price at which the dealer is making a "fair return." Pricing at this reference price is viewed as intrinsically more fair than pricing above it, independent of the absolute price being charged or the historic pricing practices of the seller.

Some popular music concerts apparently set prices below market based on the desire of the artist and/or promoter not to be perceived as "gouging" the fan base. As Tom Petty put it:

> My top price is about $65, and I turn a very healthy profit on that; I make millions on the road. I see no reason to bring the price up, even though I have heard many an anxious promoter say, 'We could charge 150 bucks for this." . . . It's so wrong to say, "OK, we've got them on the ticket and we've got them on the beer and we've got them on everything else, let's get them on the damn parking."[9]

By one estimate, Bruce Springsteen gave away about $3 million in surplus to his fans at a Philadelphia concert by setting a single ticket price below the market price. Since the concert only grossed about $1.5 million, this is evidence of a serious desire to avoid perceptions of "unfair" pricing.[10]

Dual entitlement helps explain some of the negative reaction to Coke's temperature-sensitive pricing scheme. Raising the price on a hot day is viewed as the analogy of raising snow shovel prices after a snowstorm: a violation of dual entitlement. The situation was compounded by the fact that the announcement focused on the increased price scenario, causing consumers to focus on the cold-weather price as the reference price.

12.2.2 Interpersonal Fairness

As the Amazon case shows, price discrimination can be an extremely sensitive issue. From the seller's point of view, one of the most annoying aspects of interpersonal comparison is that it can turn a happy customer into an unhappy customer, for reasons totally unrelated to customer service. The disgruntled Amazon customer who complained to DVDtalk.com was not unhappy with his purchase or with Amazon's service; he was unhappy because of the idea that someone may have been quoted a lower price. As one of the reporters covering the Amazon story wrote, "I don't like the idea that someone is paying less than I am for the same product, *at the exact same instant*" (Coursey 2000). In other words, I may be happy with my purchase until I find out that someone paid less. This ex post facto effect will be familiar to anyone who has ever been responsible for setting salaries: Someone who has been perfectly happy with a raise may become thoroughly enraged on hearing that someone considered less worthy received a larger raise. Similarly, learning that someone else received (or was offered) a better price for the same good can instantly convert a happy customer to an unhappy one. This is irrational, at least in the narrow economic sense. My consumer surplus depends only on the price I paid, not on what others paid. Despite this, as the Amazon DVD pricing example shows, discriminatory pricing that is perceived as "unfair" can generate a tremendous amount of negative emotion and ill will.

Despite some cultural differences, it seems that concern with transactional fairness is almost universal. Some psychologists believe the phenomenon has deep roots. Researchers at the Yerkes Primate Lab performed a set of experiments in which capuchin monkeys could "buy" treats using stone tokens. The monkeys preferred grapes to cucumbers as treats. Monkeys who received a cucumber in return for a token seemed happy enough until they saw that other monkeys were getting a grape in return for a token. When this happened, their behavior changed abruptly—they began throwing the tokens back at the researchers and refusing to eat the inferior cucumber rewards, both highly unusual responses under normal circumstances. The researchers concluded: "Capuchin monkeys . . . react negatively to previously acceptable awards if a partner gets a better deal" (Brosnan and de Waal 2003, p. 299).

As with capuchin monkeys, so with cruise line passengers. Since cruise lines meet all of the criteria for revenue management described in Chapter 6, there is a strong motivation for cruise lines to offer a wide range of prices and then to manage their availabilities so as to maximize profitability. However, the realities of the cruise business make it unlikely that they can do this in a way that will escape detection by their customers. People on a cruise dine together every evening. On the second or third night, the conversation will almost inevitably turn to prices. Mr. Smith mentions that his travel agent got a great deal for him and Mrs. Smith—an upper-deck oceanview stateroom for only $1,200. Mr. Jones responds that his travel agent got him an upper-deck oceanview stateroom for $1,000. Mr. Smith's face falls and his cruise experience is suddenly ruined.

The cruise line industry has tried various mechanisms to avoid this scenario. Princess Cruises uses its revenue management system to monitor how demand is building for different types of berth on all of its sailings. If a berth type on a particular sailing is selling below expectations, Princess will lower the price to stimulate demand. However, to avoid the Smith/Jones scenario, Princess will give rebates to all customers who paid the higher price. At the time of sailing, all customers who purchased the same berth type on the same sailing will have paid the same price. As a result of this policy, Princess Cruises has eliminated much of the negative customer reactions associated with unfair pricing.

By this point, you might be forgiven for believing that any form of price discrimination (or dynamic pricing) will immediately be branded as unfair by some consumers. However, this is not the case. We have already seen that both price discrimination and dynamic pricing are ubiquitous in many industries through such practices as couponing, sales promotions, markdowns, regional pricing, and peak-load pricing. In addition, there are examples of blatant, customer-based price discrimination being widely practiced and generally accepted without complaint, including:

- Senior citizen discounts
- Student discounts
- Ladies' night specials at bars
- "Kids ride free"
- Family specials
- Lower tuition for state students than for out-of-state students at state universities
- College scholarships for low-income students, athletes, or those who score higher on tests

These examples are all "pure" price discrimination (*group pricing* in the terminology of Chapter 4), in the sense that they are based entirely on the customer and do not reflect any product or cost-of-service differences among the groups. Based on this, we would expect them to be highly controversial. Yet there is little apparent resistance to these practices.

Why? To inspire some further thought, consider the following article, excerpted from the *Cape Cod Times* of July 1997.

State Survey Finds Women Get Clipped:
Costs for haircuts, dry cleaning said to be excessive, discriminatory

Massachusetts women typically pay more than men for haircuts and dry cleaning because of discriminatory pricing practices by salons and dry cleaners, a consumer advocacy group claimed yesterday.

A woman can pay as much as $548 more than a man each year for the same dry-cleaning and haircutting services, according to the Massachusetts Public Interest Research Group.

A statewide survey by MassPIRG, including some Cape Cod salons and dry cleaners, uncovered "rampant price discrimination" in violation of state law, the advocacy group announced yesterday.

The owners of a West Barnstable salon and a Centerville dry cleaner listed in MassPIRG's report defended their pricing practices. They said that the prices are based on the time and work involved, not the customer's gender. MassPIRG claimed that 88% of the dry cleaners surveyed charge women more than men. Among the dry cleaners that discriminate, women paid an average of $1.76 more to have a shirt laundered and $1.84 more to have a shirt dry-cleaned, the group claimed.

Fifty-six percent of the hair salons surveyed charge women an average of $8.05 more than men for a basic shampoo, haircut, and blow dry, the group said.

"Despite warnings from the attorney general and the state Division of Registration, both of these industries continue to break the law and rip off consumers," said Deirdre Cummings, consumer program director for MassPIRG. . . .

Despite MassPIRG's claim, Centerville Cleaners does not charge women higher prices based on gender, owner Emilio Rigas said yesterday. MassPIRG is wrong in claiming that Rigas charges $3.75 to dry-clean a woman's shirt and $1.25 to dry-clean a man's shirt, he said.

Rigas called MassPIRG's report unfair and said no one from the agency ever spoke to him.

Shirts cost $1.25 if they can be machine-pressed and $3.75 if they require hand-pressing, regardless of who wears them, Rigas said. The cost is higher for hand-pressing, because Rigas can machine-press 100 shirts in an hour, but he can hand-press just 10 shirts in an hour, he said.

Women's shirts often require hand-pressing because of fine fabric, shoulder pads, and raised patterns, Rigas said. If a woman's shirt can be machine-pressed, Rigas said he charges the lower price.

To support his argument, Rigas displayed a price list. The list did not categorize men's and women's clothing, but it did list $3.75 for a plain blouse and $1.25 for a shirt on a hanger.

MassPIRG also claimed that Village Laundromat and Dry Cleaners on Route 6A, Barnstable, charges $4 to dry clean a woman's shirt and $3.50 for a man's shirt. A man who answered the telephone at Village Laundromat declined to discuss the report.

A woman who identified herself as the owner of Gina's Salon in West Barn-stable defended her pricing policy. She charges women $24 for a haircut and men $15 because women usually have longer hair and require more styling, she said. It takes about twice as long to cut a woman's hair, she said. (MassPIRG reported prices of $22 for women and $13 for men at the store.)

"I would like to charge men more, but you can't get men to pay it," she said. The woman would not give her last name, saying she did not want it to appear in the newspaper. . . .

William G. Wood, director of the state Division of Registration, has just three investigators for the 9,000 salons across the state. . . . Despite the MassPIRG report, Wood's office has not received a complaint about gender bias in pricing since 1993.

— Jack Perry, Staff Writer [11]

This story neatly illustrates some of the conflicting reactions raised by price differentiation. MassPIRG claims that dry cleaners and salons are practicing pure customer discrimination, but both the Centreville Cleaners and Gina's Salon claim that any price differential is based on cost differences. However, the anonymous spokesperson for Gina's Salon undercuts this argument a bit by claiming that they would like to charge men more, but men won't pay the higher price—which would certainly suggest gender-based group pricing. Finally, customer reaction to the situation seems decidedly mixed. While Deirdre Cummings of MassPIRG is outraged that consumers are being ripped off, the consumers themselves seem considerably less perturbed, since the Division of Registration has not received a single complaint in the last five years.

You may realize by now that there is no generally accepted acid test to determine what types of pricing will be widely accepted by consumers and what will raise complaints. Cultural, social, and educational factors all seem to play a role—what is acceptable to one group (or one consumer) may not be to others. Policies that favor groups perceived as disadvantaged, such as the elderly, seem to be more acceptable than those that appear more arbitrary, despite the fact that senior discounts are often a pricing tactic based on the fact that seniors tend to be more price sensitive. Furthermore, surveys have shown that business and economics students tend to accept discriminatory and dynamic pricing tactics more readily than the general public. For example, in the snow shovel scenario, 76% of University of Chicago economics students said that raising the price of snow shovels after a snowstorm was acceptable, compared to 18% of the general public. This disparity would suggest that the prospect for future pricing debacles is good, since it is the business and economic students who are likely to be formulating the pricing schemes of tomorrow and, as a group, they may be oblivious to presentation and fairness issues.

12.3 IMPLICATIONS FOR PRICING AND REVENUE OPTIMIZATION

The topic of irrational consumer behavior and its influence on real-world pricing is relatively new and not perfectly understood—especially when it comes to judgments of fairness. As one researcher put it, "Fairness, it seems, is a complex and dynamic concept with many varied inputs." [12] Given this, you would be forgiven for concluding that the current state of knowledge is that consumers act rationally except when they don't. To some extent this is a fair judgment. Nonetheless, there is enough known that we can make specific recommendations that will increase the effectiveness of pricing and revenue optimization and increase its chances for consumer acceptance. We start by summarizing the factors that make tactical pricing schemes more acceptable. We then discuss the implications of these for implementing pricing and revenue optimization. Finally, we return to the concept of fairness and discuss two cases in which unfair pricing may have won out over fair pricing despite consumer reactions.

TABLE 12.2
Pricing acceptance factors

More acceptable	Less acceptable
Product based	Customer based
Open	Hidden
Discounts and promotions	Surcharges
Rewards	Penalties
Easy to understand	Hard to understand
Available to me	Unavailable to me
Familiar	Unfamiliar

Key elements that influence the acceptability of pricing and revenue optimization programs are shown in Table 12.2. The impact of these can be summarized as follows.

- *Product-based.* Product-based pricing differences are much more readily accepted than group pricing. As we saw in Chapter 4, there is no clear distinction between product-based differentiation and customer-based differentiation. To the extent that a pricing difference can be presented as product based rather than customer based, it is much more likely to be readily accepted.

- *Openness.* Customers certainly claim to prefer pricing schemes that are open. Some of the negative press that Amazon received dwelt on the fact that Amazon was doing something "in secret." Furthermore, one of the lessons of the Amazon case is that any attempt to implement differential or dynamic pricing on the Internet will likely be discovered.

- *Discounts and promotions* are much more readily accepted than surcharges. Prospect theory predicts that the same price will be viewed more positively if it is the result of a discount rather than a surcharge. Furthermore, finding that another customer received a discount is much more likely to be received with equanimity than finding that one has been charged a surcharge—even when the net result is the same. As a result, list prices tend to be high, with discounts and promotions commonplace.

- *Rewards.* In a similar vein, a reward for loyalty or volume purchases is much more likely to be acceptable than any kind of penalty. Airlines do much better offering frequent-flyer rewards than they would offering infrequent-flyer penalties.

- *Easy to understand.* Programs viewed as easy to understand are generally more accepted. Programs that are difficult to understand will create customer concern that they are not getting a good deal simply because they do not know how to "play the game." One study has shown that in some cases customers may actually prefer suppliers who offer them fewer options—even if their resulting price is higher.[13]

- *Available.* There seems to be a critical distinction in a buyer's mind between a deal that is potentially available to him and one that is not—a distinction closely related to the difference between product-based and customer-based segmentation. Customers are much more likely to be accepting of a discount that was (at least in theory) available to them than one that was not available to them under any circumstance. Thus, the acceptance of early-booking discounts in the airline industry was helped by the fact that any customer could take advantage of them, if only they had been able to make their travel plans earlier. In the same vein, the wide acceptance of discount coupons seems to stem in part from the fact that those who don't take advantage of the coupons realize that they could have done so. We might call these *behavior-based* differentiation strategies and note that they seem to be broadly acceptable to customers.

- *Familiar.* Customers are naturally conservative—they prefer traditional ways of doing business and distrust innovations. Virtually any change in the way that prices are calculated, billed, or presented is likely to be viewed with suspicion as an attempt to raise prices. Note, for example, the widespread belief in Europe that merchants would take advantage of the introduction of the euro as an opportunity to raise prices. You should anticipate some reaction to virtually any deviation from traditional pricing practice. The least disruptive way to introduce pricing and revenue optimization is within the context of an existing tactical pricing practice, e.g., markdowns, promotion pricing, or customized pricing.

It is important to be sensitive to customer price perceptions, but it is equally important not to allow anticipated customer reactions to trump any possibility of pricing innovation. First of all, many of the key findings on price perception, prospect theory, and fairness have been based on surveys, and, as any marketing professional knows, survey responses don't necessarily reflect how people will react in real life. For example, a majority of golfers stated that charging different prices depending on when they booked a tee time (e.g., two weeks in advance versus two days in advance) would be unacceptable.[14] Nonetheless, several golf courses and online golf booking services have implemented time-of-booking pricing, with few or no customer complaints.

The second key point is that some level of customer complaints and even negative press does not *necessarily* mean that a pricing program is a failure. Consider the case of the First National Bank of Chicago.

First National Bank of Chicago Charges for Checking

In the first quarter of 1992, the First National Bank of Chicago (usually called First Chicago) realized that it had a problem with its retail banking operations. It calculated that 67% of its retail customers were not achieving "adequate profitability." A primary reason—whereas many customers used tellers rarely if it all, a small number were "transaction hounds," using tellers more than four times a month while maintaining less than $2,500 in their accounts. Since teller salaries and benefits were a major part of the bank's variable cost, it seemed only fair to charge customers for the service. As Jerry Jurgensen, First Chicago's executive vice president in charge of branches put it: "If nobody changed their behavior, 80% of my customers would never see the $3.00 charge. For the other 20%, I want one of three things to happen: I need for them to change their behavior; I need for them to be willing to pay more, or I need for them to find another bank."

First Chicago held a breakfast press conference to announce the new plan. It was not well received. The headline in the Chicago Tribune read: "First Chicago Loses Touch with Humans." Competing banks leapt at the chance to tout their free checking services. The story hit the national papers and was even featured in a joke on the Jay Leno show.

First Chicago was baffled by the reaction to their new pricing scheme. They had tested it for 18 months on different focus groups. They had gone out of their way (perhaps too far out of their way) to be open, announcing the new scheme at a press conference. And, after all, the $3.00 teller fee was based on passing a real cost through to the customer, just the type of price change that the principle of dual entitlement would predict would be acceptable.

This would seem like a classic case of a pricing fiasco—and it is often presented as such. A clueless marketing department instituted a bonehead pricing program that ignored customer sensitivities and reaped a whirlwind of criticism. Another disaster, to be put alongside Amazon and Coca-Cola in the annals of pricing infamy. However, there is a twist to the story. From a financial point of view, the First Chicago program was a success! According to an article in the *American Banking Association Journal*:

> Banks are uniform in disassociating their profitability-probing behavior from First Chicago's, which some consider to have been "PR suicide." "They fired their marketing people the next day [after the teller-fee story broke]," said a source who preferred not to be named. However, it is widely conceded that First Chicago has had material success. It reportedly lost less than 1% of customers, not the 10% predicted—despite some other Chicago-area banks advertising against it—while branch staff decreased 30% and ATM activity "skyrocketed" (ATM deposits grew 100% in three months). Speaking seven months after the restructuring, [former First Chicago senior vice president Marion Foote] said the bank was making an "adequate return" on 44% of customers, versus 33% beforehand, and customer satisfaction scores were higher than ever.[15]

Was teller surcharging a success or a failure at First Chicago? It depends upon whom you ask. The marketing and PR staff who lost their jobs would probably agree that it was PR suicide. Anecdotal evidence seemed to indicate that some potential new customers were lost because of the negative publicity. But from the cold numbers it would appear that the teller fees were successful at achieving the announced goals: increasing customer profitability. It is suggestive that, despite the overwhelmingly negative publicity, First Chicago retained the fees for more than seven years, until it became part of BankOne. And since 1995, more and more banks have begun to charge teller fees (often as part of bundled pricing packages).

However, they learned from First Chicago not to call a press conference to announce their plans in advance.

Finally, competitive and market forces may not allow a company to simplify its pricing, even if it wants to. Consider the case of American Airlines.

American Airlines Abandons Revenue Management

By spring of 1992, Robert Crandall, chairman and C.E.O. of American Airlines, decided that airline fares had gotten too complex. While American's revenue management system had originally given it an advantage over its rivals, United and Continental had developed systems of their own and it was not clear that American retained any advantage. Furthermore, customers continued to complain about a system where business travelers paid substantially more money than leisure travelers for substantially the same service. Simplifying fares seemed to be a logical choice—it would allow all of the carriers to jettison the increasingly complex fare structures, eliminate much discounting, and improve customer satisfaction, all at the same time. American had led the majors into this swamp, so, as the world's largest carrier, why shouldn't American be the airline to lead them out?

On April 9, 1992, American Airlines called a press conference to announce its "value pricing" program. Crandall explained the rationale for change:

> We have said for some time that our yields are too low, yet the conventional solution, higher and higher full fares and an ever-growing array of discount fares surrounded by an ever-changing plethora of restrictions, simply does not work. . . . In our unsuccessful pursuit of profits, we have made our pricing so complex that our customers neither understand it nor think it is fair.[16]

Under value pricing, American sold only four fares in every market: first class, regular coach, 7-day advance purchase booking discount coach, and 21-day advance purchase booking discount coach. This simple structure was to replace the previous situation, in which American often offered 10 or even 20 different fares in a market, with different booking restrictions in different markets. Value pricing would reduce the total number of fares in the network from 500,000 to 70,000.[17] As part of the plan, American also lowered its fares—first-class fares were reduced by 20–50% and regular coach fares were cut by about 40%. However, a myriad of other promotions and discount programs for groups and corporate customers were eliminated. Crandall's plan was that the new and simpler fares would induce enough additional traffic to outweigh the fare reductions.

American expected other carriers to follow its lead. After all, the complex fares associated with traditional revenue management were just as unpopular elsewhere, and the cost savings from fare simplification would be significant across the industry. American announced its intentions well ahead of time and did everything it could to signal to the other airlines that its new fare structure was about simplification, not starting a new fare war, and that simplification would be good for the entire industry. And the initial response was promising. Within a week, most major carriers, including United, Delta, Continental, and Northwest, adopted the value pricing fare structure, either in part or in whole.

Initially, it looked like American had been able to lead the airlines successfully to a new, simpler structure without touching off a fare war.

Unfortunately, the hope was premature. TWA touched off a fare war in the second week of April. Initially, American stood by its new pricing scheme. However, in late May, Northwest issued a more serious challenge. It announced a special fare promotion called "Grownups Fly Free" that offered free tickets to an adult when accompanied by a paying passenger between 2 and 17. The other airlines, including American, matched the promotions with 50% discounts of their own. These discounts were certainly effective in stimulating demand, and aircraft were flying with record loads—in many markets load factors approached 100%. However, the demand stimulation from the discounts did not outweigh the cannibalization, and many of the airlines suffered record losses along with their record load factors.

Increasingly, it became clear that value pricing was doomed. With an increasing variety of discounts and promotions being offered, things were reverting to the "bad old days." American's rivals were setting up fare structures that bracketed American's three coach fares and then using their revenue management systems to feast on American, just as American had used its system to feast on PeopleExpress. By October 1992, it was evident that value pricing was through. In an interview with the BBC, Crandall said that value pricing was "dying a slow death" and that the plan had "clearly failed." By November, American had jettisoned value pricing completely and was back to setting and manipulating thousands of fares throughout its system.

Value pricing is often presented as a failed attempt at price leadership—which it was. Competitors found that by offering more complex fare structures, they could outcompete American in key markets, and the lure of doing so proved irresistible. Ultimately, complex fare structures backed up by sophisticated revenue management beat out the simplicity of value pricing.

But there is another lesson from the value pricing failure that is less often appreciated: Customers may have preferred simple pricing to complex pricing, but they are not willing to pay for it. Customers praised the simplicity of value pricing, but they weren't willing to pay for it. When the time came to purchase a ticket, they bought from the airline that was offering the cheapest seat—not from the one offering the simplest fare structure. The customers who flocked to take advantage of "adults fly free" tickets from Northwest didn't care that they were destroying value pricing—they were simply looking for a bargain. One of the lessons is that the success of *everyday low pricing* is due primarily to the *low*, not to the *everyday*.

The most successful pricing and revenue optimization tends to be the most invisible. Systems that simply do a better job of setting prices within the context of an existing and accepted tactical pricing structure have the highest chance of success and acceptance. Nonetheless, capturing the full benefits of pricing and revenue optimization may require new pricing practices. You can increase the chance of success by paying close attention to issues of price presentation and fairness in implementation. However, you should also expect that virtually any pricing innovation will be met with skepticism (at best). Part of the art of pricing and revenue optimization is knowing when to change in response to consumer resistance and when to persevere.

12.4 SUMMARY

The topic of this chapter has been the ways in which customers may react negatively to a dynamic differentiated pricing strategy. It should be clear that pricing can elicit surprisingly emotional responses in customers. Specifically, customer response can go well beyond a mechanistic comparison of the current price to a hypothetical willingness to pay to encompass deep (and sometimes difficult-to-define) notions of fairness. The standard of fairness can be violated by a dynamic pricing policy perceived as unfair (as in the case of Coke's temperature sensitive vending machines), a differentiated pricing policy perceived as unfair (as in the case of Amazon's experiment), or simply a price perceived as providing "unfair" profits to the seller (as in the case of snow shovels). In extreme cases, a poorly thought-out pricing tactic can lead to actual consumer rebellion and, ultimately, the potential of mass defection. Here, though, it is good to remember the First Chicago example to stress that widespread negative reaction to a price tactic doesn't necessarily mean it should be abandoned.

While prospect theory, dual entitlement, reference prices, and related concepts can help explain the psychological bases of these reactions, they do not provide a complete approach. There is no systematic way yet known to incorporate these phenomena consistently within a constrained optimization problem to generate optimal prices.

If the desired action is to raise overall revenue, then the least controversial way to do so is by eliminating or restricting discounts. This is the concept behind revenue management. To raise prices for some segments, it is best to do so via product versioning (as opposed to group pricing) to the greatest extent possible. To lower prices across all customer segments, it is usually best to use temporary promotions, schedule markdowns, or open discount classes. These actions minimize (but don't necessarily eliminate) the effect on consumer reference prices and the customer resistance associated with raising prices. To lower prices for some segments but not others, it is best to do so via target price promotions (such as couponing), product versioning (specifically creating inferior products), and channel-specific discounts.

12.5 EXERCISE

1. Consider the First National Bank of Chicago case again. Which (if any) of the pricing acceptance issues discussed in this chapter did First National violate or ignore? How could First Chicago have structured or positioned its teller fees to achieve its financial goals while reducing (or eliminating) negative customer reactions?

1. Since it was Brazil, he was referring to a soccer match.

2. These details are from the story by David Streitfeld in the *Washington Post* (Streitfeld 2000).

3. Coursey (2000). It is interesting that the label *dynamic pricing* was almost universally applied to what was actually a case of price discrimination.

4. *Irrational* is not meant to be pejorative in this context—it simply refers to behavior that does not accord with the classical economic model of rational decision making.

5. However, this part of prospect theory is used to price financial instruments such as options.

6. One possible exception is popular new-model cars that dealers might be able to sell above the manufacturer's suggested retail price.

7. Kaufmann, Ortmeyer, and Smith (1991, p. 138).

8. Moon and Russell (2002).

9. Quoted in Wild (2002, p. 23).

10. Krueger (2004).

11. Perry (1997).

12. Andreoni, Brown, and Vesterlund (2003, p. 22).

13. Iyengar and Lepper (2000).

14. Kimes and Wirtz (2002).

15. O'Sullivan (1997).

16. Quoted in Silk and Michael (1993, p. 5).

17. Silk and Michael (1993).

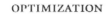

OPTIMIZATION

Optimization refers to the process of finding the maximum or minimum of a function over some region, which could be either finite or infinite in extent. We will concern ourselves with finding the maximum of a function, since that is the most relevant for pricing and revenue optimization, where sellers are usually seeking to maximize profitability or revenue.

A.1 CONTINUOUS OPTIMIZATION

We are concerned with maximizing a continuous, differentiable function $f(x)$ over a certain region—say, $x \geq 0$. x may be either a single number—a *scalar*—or a vector $x = (x_1, x_2, \ldots, x_n)$. We seek the value of x, for which $f(x)$ is maximized. This general problem can be very complex and subtle. In particular, a function may have many different local maxima within the region. If so, the problem of finding the global maximum among all the local maxima may be very difficult and may require the use of such approaches as genetic algorithms. Fortunately, the problems we treat in this book are all well behaved, in the sense that they are *unimodal*; that is, any local maximum will also be a global maximum. The problems we consider also all have convex feasible regions. This means that "hill-climbing" approaches will work well. Starting at any point, we can find an improving direction and move in that direction to a point with a higher objective function value. From that point we can find a new improving direction and repeat the process until we get to a point where no further improvement is possible. This point is the global maximizer.

There are three general possibilities that we might encounter.

- The function may have no maximum. For example, we show in Chapter 3 that a supplier facing a constant-elasticity price-response curve with elasticity greater than 1 can always increase revenue by increasing his price. In this case, there is no price that maximizes revenue.

- The function may attain its maximum value within the interior of the region.

- The function may attain its maximum value on the boundary of the region.

Given the restrictions we have put on the underlying function and the feasible region, an intelligent hill-climbing approach will find the optimal solution in the second and third cases. The first case needs to be eliminated, or a hill-climbing approach will never terminate, but continue forever.

For an interior point x^* to be a maximizer, it must be the case that all of the derivatives $\partial f(x^*)/\partial x_i^* = 0$ for all i. (If x is a scalar, this is equivalent to the requirement that $f'(x^*) = 0$.) If $\partial f(x)/\partial x_i > 0$ for some i, then $f(x)$ could be increased by increasing x_i^* by a small amount. If $\partial f(x)/\partial x_i < 0$ for some i, then $f(x)$ could be increased by decreasing x_i^* by a small amount. In either case, x^* was not a maximizer.

Thus, $\partial f(x^*)/\partial x_i^* = 0$ for all i is a *necessary* condition for x to be an interior maximizer of f. It is not, however, a sufficient condition. There are two other possibilities: x^* could be a *minimizer* of $f(x)$. Or, more rarely, x^* could be a so-called *inflection point* of $f(x)$. In the case when x is a scalar, the most common test to ensure that x^* is a maximizer of $f(x)$ is that the second derivative $f''(x) < 0$. If this condition is satisfied, then x^* will be a local maximizer of f. And if f is unimodal, it must be a global maximizer as well.

This is a very cursory treatment of a very deep topic. There are many exceptions, caveats, and subtleties to continuous optimization that we did not deal with. However, for the purpose of basic pricing and revenue optimization, a simple approach to optimization will often suffice. Most pricing and revenue optimization problems have a simple structure: Increasing a decision variable (price or capacity allotment) initially improves profit, but, at some point, further increases lead to lower profit. The maximum occurs at the point just before profit begins to degrade. With this structure, we can use simple approaches and not worry about some of the more subtle issues. This does not mean that these subtleties can always be ignored in practice. For example, in optimizing list prices, some products can be complements (like hot dogs and hot dog buns), while others are substitutes (like Coke and Pepsi). In this situation, the problem of finding the price that maximizes total expected contribution can have many local maxima, and a point that satisfies all of the first- and second-order conditions may not be the global maximum. This means that genetic algorithms or related approaches may need to be used to find the global maximum.

A.2 LINEAR PROGRAMMING

Linear programming is a well-established approach to optimization in the case where a linear objective function is being maximized subject to linear constraints. The *simplex algorithm* for solving such problems was initially developed by George Dantzig in the 1960s and has been extended and refined many times since. The simplex algorithm, like all other commercially used algorithms for solving linear programs, is a hill-climbing approach, in the sense that it moves from point to point within the feasible region, increasing the objective function at every move, until no improving direction can be found.

The standard form of a linear program is

$$\max_{x} \sum_{i=1}^{n} c_i x_i$$

subject to

$$\sum_{i=1}^{n} a_{ij} x_i \leq b_j \qquad \text{for } j = 1, 2, \ldots, m$$

$$x_i \geq 0 \qquad \text{for } i = 1, 2, \ldots, n$$

The *objective function coefficients* c_i and the *constraint coefficients* a_{ij} can each be either positive, negative, or zero. The constraints have been specified as "less than or equal to," but "greater than or equal to" constraints can also be incorporated by simply multiplying both sides by 1. Equality constraints can be incorporated by including simultaneous "less than or equal to" and "greater than or equal to" constraints. The standard form has specified that each x_i is zero or greater, but it is also possible to constrain any or all of them to be zero or less or to take either positive or negative values. Thus, the standard form is quite flexible in representing any linear objective function subject to any set of linear constraints.

The standard form can also be written as

$$\max_{x} c^{\top} x \tag{A.1}$$

subject to

$$Ax \leq b$$

$$x \geq 0$$

where $c = (c_1, c_2, \ldots, c_n)$, $x = (x_1, x_2, \ldots, x_n)$, $b = (b_1, b_2, \ldots, b_m)$, and the matrix A consists of the elements a_{ij}.

An optimization problem that can be specified in this form can be solved efficiently by a number of commercial software packages. Microsoft Excel includes a linear programming capability within its SOLVER function.

A.3 DUALITY AND COMPLEMENTARY SLACKNESS

Every linear program of the form of Equation A.1 has an associated *dual* linear program of the form

$$\min_{\lambda} b^{\top} \lambda \tag{A.2}$$

subject to

$$A^{\top} \lambda \geq c$$

$$\lambda \geq 0$$

where $\lambda = (\lambda_1, \lambda_2, \ldots, \lambda_m)$ is a vector of dual variables, one corresponding to each of the constraints in the original formulation in Equation A.1. The importance of the dual arises partly from the so-called *complementary slackness* principle:

> *The incremental change in the objective function from an incremental change in constraint j in Formula A.1 will be (approximately) λ_j. If constraint j in Formula A.1 is not binding, then $\lambda_j = 0$ and relaxing the constraint will not change the value of the objective function. If $\lambda_j > 0$, then constraint j in Formula A.1 is binding.*

In particular, if a constraint in a linear program is associated with a capacity or inventory limitation, the complementary slackness principle means that the corresponding dual variable will be the opportunity cost associated with that constraint.

A.4 DISCRETE OPTIMIZATION

Discrete optimization is generally more applicable to pricing and revenue optimization than is continuous optimization, since most of the entities of interest (demand, bookings, no-shows, prices, etc.) are discrete rather than continuous. Unfortunately, discrete optimization is more computationally difficult, in general, than continuous optimization. In continuous optimization we are navigating a smooth surface, looking for the highest point. If the continuous function is differentiable (as we have assumed), either we are at a maximum or the local derivatives give us a clear direction to move. In contrast, discrete optimization is like hopping from island to island in an archipelago, looking for the island with the highest peak. When we are on a particular island there may be no indicator to tell us which island to jump to next.

As a result, *integer linear programming*—finding the vector of integers x that solves Equation A.1—is much more difficult than standard linear programming, in which the answers do not need to be integers. In principle, the optimal integer solution to a linear program could be very far from the optimal continuous solution found by standard linear programming software. Since we are usually interested in integer solutions, this would seem to present a problem. Fortunately for most pricing and revenue optimization problems, however, rounding the continuous solution to a linear program to the nearest feasible integer solution usually turns out to give a very good answer.

The other case we are interested in is the situation in which we need to find the integer $i \geq 0$ that maximizes $R(i)$, where $R(i)$ is known to be unimodal. This is the problem faced, for example, in setting a total booking limit for a flight or setting prices with constrained capacity. In this case, we can use the *principle of marginality*, which states that *the value i^* that maximizes $R(i)$ is the smallest value of i such that $R(i + 1) \leq R(i)$*. This means that we can start at $i = 0$, calculate $R(i)$ and $R(i + 1)$, and stop whenever $R(i + 1) \leq R(i)$. As long as we know in advance that $R(i)$ is unimodal, this approach will always terminate at the optimal value of i.

This appendix provides a brief review of the concepts and formulas from probability theory that are used in basic pricing and revenue optimization. A fuller treatment can be found in any text on the subject, such as Feller (1968), Mood, Graybill, and Boes (1974), or Jaynes (2003).

We use the notation $\Pr\{X\}$ to refer to the probability that event X will occur. X can be any event, e.g., "Total demand during the week for a product will be greater than 100" or "No-shows will be exactly equal to 10 and shows will be equal to 95." However, no matter what event X represents, its probability of occurrence will always be between 0 and 1, so $0 \leq \Pr\{X\} \leq 1$. $1 - \Pr\{X\}$ is the probability that event X does not occur.

If X takes on numeric values—e.g., the number of heads when a fair coin is flipped 100 times, the number of sweaters that will be sold in a month—then X is termed a *random variable*. By convention, random variables are denoted with capital letters.

For any two events, X and Y, we use $\Pr\{X, Y\}$ (or sometimes $\Pr\{XY\}$) to refer to the probability that both X and Y occur. Thus, $\Pr\{$Shows are greater than 80, Demand is equal to 100$\}$ means "The probability that shows are greater than 80 *and* demand is equal to 100." This should be contrasted with the notation $\Pr\{X|Y\}$, which denotes the *conditional probability* of event X *given* that event Y occurs. Thus $\Pr\{$Shows are greater than 80 | Demand is equal to 100$\}$ means "the probability that shows are greater than 80 *given* that demand is equal to 100." The two concepts are linked by the formula

$$\Pr\{X|Y\} = \Pr\{XY\}/\Pr\{Y\}$$

for $\Pr\{Y\} > 0$. Note that since $\Pr\{Y\} \leq 1$, $\Pr\{X|Y\} \geq \Pr\{XY\}$.

Two events X and Y are called *independent* if $\Pr\{X|Y\} = \Pr\{X\}$. Intuitively independence refers to the case in which the probability that event X will occur is unaffected by knowledge of whether Y will occur. Independence is always mutual; X independent of Y means that Y is independent of X, and vice versa. If X and Y are independent, then $\Pr\{XY\} = \Pr\{X\}\Pr\{Y\}$.

B.1 PROBABILITY DISTRIBUTIONS

A *probability distribution* is an assignment of probabilities to a set of events that are "mutually exclusive and collectively exhaustive." *Mutually exclusive* means that, at most, one of the events will occur. *Collectively exhaustive* means that one of the events must occur. Together they guarantee that the sum of the probabilities of all events equals 1.

For a discrete distribution, $f(i)$ is the probability that event i will occur. We consider only discrete distributions defined on the nonnegative integers, that is, on $i = 1, 2, \ldots, \infty$.[1] By the *mutually exclusive and collectively exhaustive property*, we must have

$$\sum_{i=0}^{\infty} f(i) = 1$$

The function $f(i)$ is known as a *probability density function*, or p.d.f. Given a discrete probability density function, we define the *cumulative distribution function*, or c.d.f., by

$$F(i) = \sum_{j=0}^{i} f(j)$$

If $f(\cdot)$ is the p.d.f. on sales demand in a particular week, then $F(i)$ is the probability that sales demand will be less than or equal to i. Note that $F(i)$ is increasing in i, $f(0) = F(0)$, and $\lim_{i \to \infty} F(i) = 1$.

Although discrete distributions are by far the most relevant for pricing and revenue optimization, we will use continuous distributions in some cases. For a continuous distribution, the cumulative distribution function $F(X)$ denotes the probability that the random variable x will take a value less than or equal to X. The corresponding probability density function can be computed as $f(x) = dF(x)/dx$.[2] Then

$$F(x) = \int_{-\infty}^{x} f(y)\, dy$$

For a continuous distribution, the probability that a random variable will be between a and b, with $a < b$, is $F(b) - F(a)$. The c.d.f. $F(x)$ is increasing in x and $\lim_{x \to \infty} F(x) = 1$.

B.1.1 Expectation

Let the random variable X be distributed according to $f(\cdot)$. Then, the *expectation* or *mean* of X is defined by

$$E[X] = \sum_{i=0}^{\infty} i f(i)$$

when $f(\cdot)$ is a discrete distribution and by

$$E[X] = \int_{-\infty}^{\infty} x f(x)$$

when $f(\cdot)$ is continuous.

The average of a large number of samples from a distribution will approach the mean of that distribution. The mean of a distribution should not be confused with the *mode* of the distribution, which is the most likely observation given a single sample. Nor should it be confused with the *median* of the distribution, which is the value such that the probability that a single observation will exceed that value is the same as the probability that it will be less than the value.

An alternative formula for calculating the mean of a discrete distribution defined over the nonnegative numbers is

$$E[X] = \sum_{i=1}^{\infty} (1 - F(i)) \tag{B.1}$$

The concept of expectation can be extended to any function. Thus, if $g(i)$ is a function of i, the expectation of $g(i)$ is defined as

$$E[g(i)] = \sum_{i=0}^{\infty} g(i)f(i)$$

Note that, in general, $E[g(i)] \neq g[E[i]]$, with equality holding only if the function $g(\cdot)$ is linear.

For any random variable X and any number a, $E[aX] = aE[X]$. Furthermore, for random variables, $X_1, X_2, \ldots, X_n$,

$$E\left[\sum_{i=1}^{n} X_i\right] = \sum_{i=1}^{n} E[X_i] \quad \text{and} \quad E[X_i - X_j] = E[X_i] - E[X_j] \quad \text{for any } i \text{ and } j$$

This property does not apply to any function of random variables, for example, $E[X/Y] \neq E[X]/E[Y]$ in general.

For purposes of pricing and revenue optimization, the expectation of the minimum of a random variable and a fixed capacity is often important. In other words, we want to calculate $E[\min(i, C)]$, where C is a fixed capacity and i follows some distribution $f(i)$. The following formula is often useful in this case:

$$E[\min(i, C)] = \sum_{i=1}^{C} (1 - F(i)) = C - \sum_{i-1}^{C} F(i) \tag{B.2}$$

We are also often interested in $E[(i - C)^+] = E[\max(i \quad C, 0)]$. If $f(i)$ is a p.d.f. on total demand and C is capacity, then $E[(i - C)^+]$ is the expected number of customers in excess of capacity—i.e., the expected number of customers turned away. Since the expected number of customers served plus the expected number turned away must equal expected demand, we can combine Equations B.1 and B.2 to derive

$$E[(i - C)^+] = E[i] - E[\min(i, C)]$$

$$= \sum_{1}^{\infty} (1 - F(i)) - \sum_{i=1}^{C} (1 - F(i))$$

$$= \sum_{i=C+1}^{\infty} (1 - F(i)) \tag{B.3}$$

B.1.2 Variance and Standard Deviation

Two other important properties of probability distributions are the *variance* and the *standard deviation*, both of which measure the *spread* of the distribution. The variance of a distribution is the expected square of the distance between a sample from the distribution and the mean. That is,

$$\text{var}[X] = E[(X - E[X])^2] = E[X^2] - (E[X])^2$$

The variance of a distribution is always greater than or equal to 0; the higher the variance, the broader the spread of the distribution. For *independent* random variables, the variance of the sum is equal to the sum of the variances; that is,

$$\text{var}\left[\sum_{i=1}^{n} X_i\right] = \sum_{i=1}^{n} \text{var}[X_i] \tag{B.4}$$

The *standard deviation*, denoted by σ, is equal to the square root of the variance: $\sigma = \sqrt{\text{var}[X]}$. Like the variance, $\sigma \geq 0$ for any distribution. Let $\sigma[X_i]$ be the standard deviation associated with random variable X_i. Then, from Equation B.4, we can derive the formula for the standard deviation of the sum of independent random variables:

$$\sigma\left[\sum_{i=1}^{n} X_i\right] = \sqrt{\sum_{i=1}^{n} (\sigma[X_i])^2} \tag{B.5}$$

Note that Equations B.4 and B.5 hold only when $X_1, X_2, \ldots, X_n$ are independent.

The ratio of the standard deviation to the mean of a distribution is sometimes called the *coefficient of variation*, $\text{CV}[X] = \sigma/E[X]$.

B.2 CONTINUOUS DISTRIBUTIONS

B.2.1 The Exponential Distribution

The exponential distribution has a single parameter, $\lambda > 0$, and probability density function,

$$f(x) = \lambda e^{-\lambda x}$$

for $x \geq 0$. The mean of the exponential distribution is $E[X] = 1/\lambda$, and the standard deviation is the same as the mean: $\sigma = 1/\lambda$.

B.2.2 The Normal Distribution

The normal (or Gaussian) distribution is the famous bell-shaped curve, the most widely used distribution in statistics and mathematical modeling. There are two reasons for its popularity. The first is that theory has shown that the normal distribution is, in many situations, a reasonable distribution to use when the actual underlying distribution is unknown or when the underlying distribution is the result of many different random influences. The second reason is that many practical techniques have been developed for making calculations with the normal distribution. Such techniques are easily accessible in most software and spreadsheet packages, such as Excel.

The p.d.f. for the normal distribution is

$$f(x) = \frac{1}{\sqrt{2\pi}\sigma} e^{-(x-\mu)^2/2\sigma^2}$$

where μ is the mean and σ is the standard deviation.

The normal distribution with mean 0 and standard deviation 1 is so important that it has its own notation:

$$\phi(x) = \frac{1}{\sqrt{2\pi}} e^{-(x^2/2)}$$

where $\phi(x)$ denotes the normal distribution with mean 0 and standard deviation 1. The cumulative distribution function of the normal distribution with mean 0 and standard deviation 1 is denoted by $\Phi(x)$. Both $\phi(x)$ and $\Phi(x)$ are included in all statistical and spreadsheet packages. This is useful because they can be used to calculate $f(x)$ and $F(x)$ for any normal distribution, by means of the following transformations:

$$f(x) = \phi[(x - \mu)/\sigma] \qquad F(x) = \Phi[(x - \mu)/\sigma] \tag{B.6}$$

where $f(x)$ is the normal density function with mean μ and standard deviation σ and $F(x)$ is the corresponding cumulative distribution function.

Example B.1

Monthly demand for a product has been observed to follow a normal distribution with mean of 10,000 and standard deviation of 8,000. The probability that demand will be less than 12,000 units is then given by

$$\Pr\{\text{Demand less than 12,000 units in a month}\}$$
$$= \Phi[(12,000 - 10,000)/8,000] = \Phi(0.25) = 0.60$$

The normal distribution is widely used. However, a few words of caution are in order. First of all, the normal distribution is continuous, so care needs to be used in applying it to situations where outcomes are discrete. We address these issues in the section on the discrete normal distribution. It is also good to bear in mind that the normal distribution puts positive probabilities on all outcomes from $-\infty$ to ∞. This can become a problem in situations where outcomes less than zero are not physically meaningful (e.g., demand, sales, no-shows, prices). You need to be particularly cautious when using the normal distribution in a situation where the standard deviation is large relative to the mean. For example, when the mean is equal to the standard deviation (e.g., the coefficient of variation is 1), the normal distribution places about a 16% probability on the outcome's being less than zero. In cases where the coefficient of variation is high, it may be necessary to use another distribution in order to obtain reasonable results.

B.3 DISCRETE DISTRIBUTIONS

B.3.1 The Bernoulli Distribution

The Bernoulli distribution is the simplest interesting discrete distribution. It is defined as

$$f(x) = \begin{cases} 1 - p & \text{for } x = 0 \\ p & \text{for } x = 1 \\ 0 & \text{otherwise} \end{cases}$$

The Bernoulli distribution applies to the situation in which a particular event has a probability p of occurring and, thus, a probability $1 - p$ of not occurring. In this case, the outcome of the event's occurring can be arbitrarily labeled 1 and the outcome where the event does not occur can be labeled 0. The probability $1 - p$ of the event's not occurring is often denoted by q.

Example B.2

A fair coin is to be flipped once. Let 0 denote heads and 1 denote tails. Then the outcome of the flip follows a Bernoulli distribution with $p = 0.5$.

The mean of the Bernoulli distribution is p and its variance is $p(1 - p) = pq$.

B.3.2 The Uniform Distribution

The discrete uniform distribution is appropriate whenever a number of mutually exclusive events all have equal probability of occurring. Then, if there are n events, the possibility that any one of them will occur is $1/n$. We will always consider the case in which the events are indexed by consecutive integers $i = a, a + 1, a + 2, \ldots, b$, where $a \geq 0$ and $b > a$. In this case, we can write the uniform p.d.f. as

$$f(x) = \begin{cases} 0 & \text{for } i < a \\ 1/(b - a + 1) & \text{for } i = a, a + 1, \ldots, b \\ 0 & \text{for } i > b \end{cases}$$

The cumulative distribution function for the uniform distribution is

$$F(x) = \begin{cases} 0 & \text{for } i < a \\ (i - a + 1)/(b - a + 1) & \text{for } i = a, a + 1, \ldots, b \\ 1 & \text{for } i > b \end{cases}$$

Note that the c.d.f. for the uniform distribution function is linear between a and b. This leads to the connection between a uniform willingness-to-pay distribution and the linear demand function noted in Chapter 3.

The mean of the uniform distribution is $(b + a)/2$, and its standard deviation is $\sqrt{(b - a)(b - a + 2)}/\sqrt{12}$.

Example B.3

A seller believes that if he prices a new shirt at \$79.00, then total demand for the shirt will have equal probability of being any amount between 10,000 and 20,000 units. This corresponds to a uniform distribution with $a = 10{,}000$ and $b = 20{,}000$. This means the probability that demand will be less than or equal to 18,000 will be $F(18{,}000) = (18{,}000 - 10{,}000 + 1)/(20{,}000 - 10{,}000 + 1) \approx 0.8$. Mean demand is $(20{,}000 + 10{,}000)/2 = 15{,}000$ shirts, with a standard deviation of $\sqrt{(10{,}000 \times 10{,}002)}/\sqrt{12} = 2{,}887$.

B.3.3 The Binomial Distribution

The binomial distribution arises whenever each of a known number of people makes a decision between two mutually exclusive alternatives when each person has the same probability of choosing the first alternative and the decisions are all made independently (in the probabilistic sense). If the number of people choosing between the alternatives is n and the probability that any individual will choose the first alternative is p, then the total number choosing the first alternative will follow a binomial distribution with parameters n and p. In addition, the total number choosing alternative 2 will follow a binomial distribution with parameters n and q where $q = 1 - p$.

Example B.4

One hundred passengers have booked the same flight. Each passenger has probability of 0.8 of showing, and passengers will make independent decisions whether or not to show. In this case, the number of shows will follow a binomial distribution with $p = 0.8$ and $n = 100$. Furthermore, no-shows will follow a binomial distribution with $p = 0.2$ and $n = 100$.

Example B.5

Ten thousand shoppers will log on to the Web site of a car loan provider. With an APR of 6.9%, the supplier believes that each shopper will have a 0.05 probability of filling out an application for a loan. The distribution of applications filled out would then be binomial with $p = 0.05$ and $n = 10,000$.

The classic example of a binomial distribution is drawing balls from a large urn with replacement. If an urn contains a large number of black and white balls such that p is the fraction of black balls and n balls are drawn from the urn with the drawn balls replaced, then the number of black balls drawn will be binomial with parameters n and p. Similarly, if a fair coin is tossed n times, the number of heads tossed will be binomial with parameters n and $p = 0.5$.

The p.d.f. for the binomial distribution is

$$f(x) = \binom{n}{x} p^x (1 - p)^{n-x} \qquad \text{for } x = 0, 1, \ldots, n \tag{B.7}$$

where

$$\binom{n}{x} = \frac{n!}{(n - x)! x!}$$

$$= \frac{n \times (n - 1) \times (n - 2) \times \cdots}{[(n - x) \times (n - x - 1) \times (n - x - 2) \times \cdots][x \times (x - 1) \times (x - 2) \times \cdots]}$$

The mean of the binomial distribution is pn, the variance is $p(1 - p)n$, and the standard deviation is $\sqrt{p(1 - p)n}$.

Because of the terms of the form in Equation B.7, the binomial distribution can be very difficult to work with in practice. In particular, there is no easy way to calculate the c.d.f. $F(x)$ for a binomial distribution. Fortunately, for large n, the binomial distribution is well approximated by the normal distribution with mean $\mu = pn$ and standard deviation $\sigma = \sqrt{pqn}$. This approximation is quite useful; however, it is subject to some of the same cautions as the use of the discrete normal distribution.

Example B.6

An online tour broker believes that 30,000 people will visit his Web site in the next week, with each visitor having a 2% chance of purchasing a tour. The number of tours sold would then follow a binomial distribution with $p = 0.02$ and $n = 30,000$. His p.d.f. on demand can be approximated by a normal distribution with mean $0.02 \times 30,000 = 600$ and $\sigma = \sqrt{0.02 \times 0.98 \times 30,000} = 24.25$. The tour operator wants to know the probability that more than 580 customers will seek to purchase a tour. He can estimate this as $1 - \Phi[(580 - 600)/24.25] = 1 - \Phi(-0.8025) = 0.788$. Therefore, there is about a 79% chance that demand will be greater than 580.

B.3.4 The Discrete Normal Distribution

The normal distribution is a continuous distribution. However, there are cases in which we would like to apply it to situations in which outcomes are discrete. For example, we might want to model demand for one-night arrivals at a hotel as "normal with mean 200 and standard deviation 100." Furthermore, in most of these cases only nonnegative values will be meaningful—therefore we need to restrict the distribution to the nonnegative numbers. We do this by defining

$$F(i) = \Phi((i - \mu)/\sigma) \qquad \text{for } i = 0, 1, 2, \ldots, \infty$$

and

$$f(i) = \begin{cases} \Phi(-\mu/\sigma) & \text{for } i = 0 \\ \Phi[(i - \mu)/\sigma] - \Phi[(i - \mu - 1)/\sigma] & \text{for } i = 1, 2, 3, \ldots, \infty \end{cases}$$

Defining the normal distribution in this fashion makes it easy to use standard statistical functions in Excel, for example, for computations. However, we should caution that this comes with a cost: The discrete normal distribution as we have defined it will now have a mean that is different (generally higher) than μ and a standard deviation that is somewhat lower than σ. Whether this is important or not depends on the application.

1. Discrete distributions can also be defined that include negative integers. However, we only need to consider distributions over nonnegative integers.

2. We assume that $F(x)$ is continuous and differentiable.

BIBLIOGRAPHY

Aldrich, J., and F. D. Nelson. 1984. *Linear Probability, Logit, and Probit Models*. Thousand Oaks, CA: Sage.

Anderson, C. K., P. Bell, and S. P. Kaiser. 2003. Strategic operations research and the Edelman Prize finalist applications 1989–1998. *Operations Research* 52: 1–13.

Anderson, S. P., A. de Palma, and J.-F. Thisse. 1992. *Discrete Choice Theory of Product Differentiation*. Cambridge, MA: MIT Press.

Andreoni, J., P. M. Brown, and L. Vesterlund. 2002. What makes an allocation fair? Some experimental evidence. *Games and Economic Behavior* 40: 1–24.

Baker, T., N. Murthy, and V. Jayaraman. 2002. Service package switching in hotel revenue management systems. *Decision Sciences* 33: 109–131.

Baker, W., M. Marn, and C. Zawada. 2001. Price smarter on the Net. *Harvard Business Review* 79: 122–127.

Bell, P. C. 2004. Revenue Management for MBA's. *ORMS Today* 31: 22–27.

Belobaba, P. 1987. Air travel demand and airline seat inventory management. PhD dissertation. Flight Transportation Laboratory, Massachusetts Institute of Technology, Cambridge, MA.

———. 1989. Application of a probabilistic decision model to airline seat inventory control. *Operations Research* 37: 183–197.

———. 1992. Optimal versus heuristic methods for nested seat allocation. Presentation at ORSA/TIMS Joint National Meeting, Nov. 1992.

——— and L. Weatherford, 1996. Comparing decision rules that incorporate customer diversion in perishable asset revenue management situations. *Decision Sciences* 27: 343–354.

Bertsimas, D., and J. Tsitsiklis, 1997. *Introduction to Linear Optimization*. Belmont, MA: Belmont Academic Press.

Binkley, C. 2004. Taking retailers' cues, Harrah's taps into science of gambling. *Wall Street Journal* (Nov. 22): 14.

Birnbaum, J. 1986. Pricing of products is still an art, often having little relationship to costs. In *Marketing Management Readings: From Theory to Practice, Volume III*, ed. B. Shapiro, R. Dolan, and J. Quelch. Homewood, IL: Irwin, pp. 174–177.

Bitran, G., R. Caldentey, and S. Mondschein. 1998. Coordinating clearance markdown sales of seasonal products in retail chains. *Operations Research* 46: 609–624.

Bitran, G., and S. Mondschein. 1997. Periodic pricing of seasonal products in retailing. *Management Science* 43: 64–79.

Bollapragada, S., H. Cheng, M. Phillips, M. Garbiras, M. Scholes, T. Gibbs, and M. Humphreville. 2002. NBC's optimization systems increase revenues and profitability. *Interfaces* 32: 47–60.

Bolton, L., L. Warlop, and J. Alba. 2003. Explorations in price (un)fairness. *Journal of Consumer Research* 29: 474–491.

Bowen, B. D., and D. E. Headley. 2004. *Airline Quality Rating 2004*. Wichita, KS: W. Frank Barton School of Business.

Boyd, E. A., and I. C. Bilegan. 2003. Revenue management and e-commerce. *Management Science* 49: 1363–1386.

Breiman, L. 1984. *Classification and Regression Trees*. New York: Kluwer.

Brosnan, S. F., and B. M. de Waal. 2003. Monkeys reject unequal pay. *Nature* 425: 297–299.

Brumelle, S. L., and McGill, J. 1993. Airline seat allocation with multiple nested fare classes. *Operations Research* 41: 127–137.

Carroll, W., and R. Grimes. 1996. Evolutionary change in product management experiences in the rental car industry. *Interfaces* 25: 84–104.

Carswell, J. 2001. *The South Sea Bubble*. Thrupp, UK: Sutton Press.

Chase, R. B., and N. J. Aquilano. 1995. *Production and Ops Management*, 7th ed. Chicago: Irwin.

Civil Aeronautics Board. 1967. *Civil Aeronautics Board Economic Regulations Docket 16563*. Washington, DC.

Clemen, R. T. 1997. *Making Hard Decisions: An Introduction to Decision Analysis*, 2nd ed. Boston: Duxbury Press.

Cooper, R., and Kaplan, R. S. 1987. How cost accounting systematically distorts product costs. In *Accounting and Management: Field Study Perspectives*, ed. W. J. Bruns, Jr., and R. S. Kaplan. Cambridge, MA: Harvard Business School Press.

Corey, E. R. 1962. *Industrial Marketing: Cases and Concepts*. Englewood Cliffs, NJ: Prentice Hall.

Coursey, D. 2000. Behind Amazon's preferential pricing, *ZDNet News* (Sept. 10).

Cramer, J. S. 2003. *Logit Models from Economics and Other Fields*. Cambridge, UK: Cambridge University Press.

Cross, R. A. 1997. *Revenue Management: Hard-Core Tactics for Market Domination*. New York: Broadway Books.

Curry, R. E. 1990. Optimal airline seat allocation with multiple nested fare classes. *Transportation Science* 24: 193–204.

Dash, M. 1999. *Tulipomania*. New York: Three Rivers Press.

Debreu, G. 1972. *Theory of Value: An Axiomatic Analysis of Economic Equilibrium*, rev. ed. New Haven, CT: Yale University Press.

Deneckere, R. J., and R. P. McAfee. 1996. Damaged goods. *Journal of Economics and Management Strategy* 5: 149–174.

De Quincey, T. 1844. *Logic of Political Economy*. London: Palgrave Press.

Docters, R. G., M. R. Reopel, J.-M. Sun, and S. M. Tanny. 2004. *Winning the Profit Game: Smarter Branding, Smarter Pricing*. New York: McGraw-Hill.

Dolan, R. J., and H. Simon. 1996. *Power Pricing: How Managing Price Transforms the Bottom Line*. New York: Free Press.

Donofrio, S. 2002. Financial condition of the U.S. airline industry. *Testimony before the United States Senate Committee on Commerce, Science, and Transportation*. October 2, 2002.

Downey, K. 2003. Bring a fat wallet to cable scatter market. *Media Life* (July 3).

The Economist. 2001. The Big Mac Index (Dec. 14).

Electric Power Research Institute. 2002. *New Principles for Demand Response Planning*. Palo Alto, CA: EPRI.

Eliashberg, J., and Lilien, G. L., eds. 1993. *Marketing. Handbooks in Operations Research and Management Science, Vol. 5*. New York: North-Holland.

Elmaghraby, J., and P. Keskinocak. 2003. Dynamic pricing in the presence of inventory considerations: Research overview, current practices, and future directions. *Management Science* 49: 1287–1309.

Emporium. 1952. *How to Avoid Wasteful Markdowns*. San Francisco: Author.

Fahey, J. 2002. Dealers 1, Internet 0. *Forbes* (April 24).

Fatsis, S. 2002. The Barry Bonds tax: Teams raise prices for good games. *Wall Street Journal* (Dec. 3), p. 82.

Feller, W. 1968. *An Introduction to Probability Theory and Its Applications*, 3rd ed. New York: Wiley.

Friend, S., and S. Walker. 2001. Welcome to the new world of merchandising. *Harvard Business Review* (November): 133–141.

Gates, W. 2000. *Business @ the Speed of Thought: Succeeding in the Digital Economy*. New York: Warner Business Books.

Geraghty, M. K., and E. Johnson. 1997. Revenue management saves National Car Rental. *Interfaces* 27: 107–127.

Gibbons, R. 1992. *Game Theory for Applied Economists*. Princeton, NJ: Princeton University Press.

Godin, S., and C. Conley. 1987. *Business Rules of Thumb*. New York: Warner Books.

Gourville, J., and D. Soman. 2002. Pricing and the psychology of consumption. *Harvard Business Review* (September): 90–96.

Grossman, D. 2004. The airline industry goes direct. *USA Today* (November 22).

Hakim, D., with A. Berryman. 2003. Backup of Ford plant finds efficiency is no protector. *New York Times* (Aug. 19): C1.

Hamermesh, R. C., M. J. Roberts, and T. Pirmohamed. 2003. ProfitLogic. *Harvard Business School Case Study* 9-802-110.

Hammer, M. 1990. Reengineering work: Don't automate, obliterate. *Harvard Business Review* 68: 104–113.

——— and P. Champy. 1993. *Reengineering the Corporation*.

Harris, L. 1982. *Merchant Princes*. New York: HarperCollins.

Hastie, T., R. Tibshirani, and J. Friedman. 2001. *The Elements of Statistical Learning*. New York: Springer-Verlag.

Hayes, C. L. 1999. Variable-price Coke machine being tested. *New York Times* (Oct. 28): C1.

Heching, A., G. Gallego, and G. van Ryzin. 2002. Mark-down pricing: An empirical analysis of policies and revenue potential at one apparel retailer. *Journal of Revenue and Pricing Management* 1: 139–160.

Heilbroner, R. 1999. *The Worldly Philosophers*, rev. 7th ed. New York: Touchstone Press.

Hirst, E., and B. Kirby. 2001. *Retail-Load Participation in Competitive Wholesale Electricity Markets*. Washington, DC: Edison Electric Institute.

Huge, E. C. 1990. Quality of conformance to design. In *Total Quality: An Executive's Guide for the 1990's*. Ernst & Young Quality Consulting Group. Homewood, IL: Business One Irwin.

Iyengar, S., and M. Lepper. 2002. When choice is demotivating: Can one desire too much of a good thing? *Journal of Personality and Social Psychology* 79: 995–1006.

Jaynes, E. T. 2003. *Probability Theory: The Logic of Science*. Cambridge, UK: Cambridge University Press.

Johnson, C., with L. Allen and A. Dash. 2001. *Retail Revenue Management*. Forrester Research Report (December).

Johnson, H., and R. S. Kaplan. 1987. *Relevance Lost: The Rise and Fall of Management Accounting*. Cambridge, MA: Harvard Business School Press.

Kahneman, D., J. Knetsch, and R. Thaler. 1986. Fairness and the assumptions of economics. *Journal of Business* 59: 285–300.

Kahneman, D., and A. Tversky. 1979. Prospect theory: An analysis of decisions under risk. *Econometrica* 47: 313–327.

Kaplan, R. S., and R. Cooper. 1997. *Cost & Effect: Using Integrated Cost Systems to Drive Profitability and Performance*. Cambridge, MA: Harvard Business School Press.

Kaufmann, P. J., G. Ortmeyer, and N. C. Smith. 1991. Fairness in consumer pricing. *Journal of Consumer Policy* 14: 117–140.

Kimes, S. E. 1989. The basics of yield management. *Cornell Hotel and Restaurant Administration Quarterly* 30: 14–19.

——— and J. Wirtz. 2003. Perceived fairness of revenue management in the US golf industry. *Journal of Revenue and Pricing Management* 1: 332–344.

Kontzer, T. 2004. Bound for industry upheaval—with a layover in Dallas. *Information Week* (June 7).

Kraft, E. R., B. N. Srikar, and R. L. Phillips. 2000. Revenue Management in railroad applications. *Journal of the Transportation Research Forum* 39: 157–176.

Krueger, A. B. 2004. The economics of rock superstars: The market for rock concerts in the material world. Princeton University working paper.

Kuyumcu, A. 2002. A gaming twist in hotel revenue management. *Journal of Revenue and Pricing Management* 1: 161–167.

Landsburg, S. E. 1989. *Price Theory and Applications*. Orlando, FL: Dryden Press.

Lazear, E. P. 1986. Retail pricing and clearance sales. *American Economics Review* 76: 14–32.

Leibs, S. 2000. Ford heeds the profits. *CFO Magazine* (August): 33–34.

Leslie, P. 2004. Price discrimination in Broadway theater. *Rand Journal of Economics* 35: 520–541.

Levison, M. 2002. Everything must go! *CIO* (May 1): 32.

Levy, M. R., and J. Woo. 1999. Yield management in retail: The application of advanced mathematics to the retail pricing dilemma. *Journal of Professional Pricing* (June): 23–26.

Li, M. Z. F., and T. H. Oum. 2002. A note on the single-leg, multifare seat allocation problem. *Transportation Science* 36: 349–353.

Lieberman, W. H., and T. Dieck. 2002. Expanding the revenue management frontier: Optimal air planning in the cruise industry. *Journal of Revenue and Pricing Management* 1: 7–24.

Lilien, G. L., P. Kotler, and K. S. Murthy. 1992. *Marketing Models*. Saddle River, NJ: Prentice Hall.

Liss, D. 2000. *A Conspiracy of Paper*. New York: Random House.

Littlewood, K. 1972. Forecasting and control of passenger bookings. *AGIFORS Symposium Proceedings* 12: 95–117.

Luenberger, D. 1984. *Linear and Nonlinear Programming*, 2nd ed. Reading, MA: Addison-Wesley.

Mackay, C. 1852 (1980). *Extraordinary Popular Delusions and the Madness of Crowds*, 2nd ed. New York: Three Rivers Press.

Makridakis, S. G., S. C. Wheelwright, and R. J. Hyndman. 1997. *Forecasting: Methods and Applications*, 3rd ed. New York: Wiley.

Margulis, D. L. 2002. Priced to sell . . . you. *InfoWorld* (Feb. 15): 12–14.

Marn, M., and R. Rosiello. 1992. Managing price, gaining profit. *Harvard Business Review* (September/October): 84–93.

Marvel, M. 2004. Trends in hotel distribution. *EHLITE—Institute of Technology and Entrepreneurship Report*. Le Châlet-à-Gobet, Switzerland.

McLaughlin, M. 2002. Highlights from Houston: IMC 2002 National Conference. *Management Consulting News* (September 26): 1.

McPartlin, J. 2004. The price you pay. *CFO-IT* (Spring): 49–51.

Mood, M., F. A. Graybill, and D. C. Boes. 1974. *Introduction to the Theory of Statistics*, 3rd ed. New York: McGraw-Hill.

Moon, S., and G. Russell. 2002. Profiling the reference price consumer. Working paper, University of Iowa. http://www.biz.uiowa.edu/mrktg/pdf/reference_price_consumer .pdf.

Nagle, N. T., and R. K. Holden (contributor). 1994. *The Stategy and Tactics of Pricing: A Guide to Profitable Decision Making*, 2nd ed. Englewood Cliffs, NJ: Prentice Hall.

Narasimhan, C. 1984. A price discrimination theory of coupons. *Marketing Science* 3: 128–147.

National Retail Federation. 1998. *The Combined Financial, Merchandising, & Operating Results of Retail Stores in 1997*.

National Retail Merchants Association. 1968. *Financial and Operating Results of Department and Specialty Stores of 1967*. New York: Author.

———. 1977. *Financial and Operating Results of Department and Specialty Stores of 1976*. New York: Author.

———. 1987. *Financial and Operating Results of Department and Specialty Stores of 1986*. New York: Author.

Nicholson, W. 2002. *Microeconomic Theory: Basic Principles and Extensions*, 8th ed. Mason, OH: South-Western.

Nystrom, P. H. 1915. *The Economics of Retailing*. New York: Ronald Press.

O'Leary, D. E. 2000. *Enterprise Resource Planning Systems: Systems, Life Cycle, Electronic Commerce, and Risk*. Cambridge, UK: Cambridge University Press.

O'Sullivan, O. 1997. Some of your customers are unprofitable. OK, now what? *ABA Journal Online* (August).

Pampel, F. C. 2000. *Logistics Regression: A Primer*. Thousand Oaks, CA: Sage.

Pande, P., and L. Hoppe. 2002. *What Is Six Sigma?* New York: McGraw-Hill.

Pashigian, P. B. 1988. Demand uncertainty and sales: A study of fashion and markdown pricing. *American Economic Review* 78: 936–953.

———— and B. Bowen. 1991. Why are products sold on sale? Explanations of pricing regularities. *Quarterly Journal of Economics* 106: 1015–1038.

Pearce, D. W., ed. 1992. *The MIT Dictionary of Modern Economics*, 4th ed. Cambridge, MA: MIT Press.

Perry, J. 1997. State survey finds women get clipped. *Cape Cod Times* (July 18): 19–20.

Phillips, R. L. 1997. State-contingent revenue management. *Scorecard*. Second quarter.

————. 2003. Teaching pricing and revenue optimization. *INFORMS Transactions on Education* 4.

———— and J. Krakauer. 2002. Pricing and revenue optimization—Driving value from CRM investments. *Journal of the Professional Pricing Society*.

The Pricing Advisor. 2002. Sidebar (May).

Richardson, P. 2002. Manugistics on the new price is right. *AMR Research Alert* (May 10).

Rothstein, M. 1971. An airline overbooking model. *Transportation Science* 5: 180–192.

————. 1985. OR and the airline overbooking problem. *Operations Research* 33: 237–248.

———— and A. W. Stone. 1967. Passenger booking levels. In *Proceedings of the Seventh AGIFORS Symposium*, New York, pp. 130–138.

Shapiro, C., and H. A. Varian. 1992. *Information Rules*. Cambridge, MA: Harvard Business School Press.

Silk, A. J., and S. C. Michael. 1993. *American Airlines Value Pricing (A)*. Harvard Business School Case Study 9-594-001. Cambridge, MA: Harvard Business School Press.

Simon, J. L. 1968. An almost practical solution to airline overbooking. *Journal of Transport Economics and Policy* 2: 201–202.

Simonetto, M., C. Davenport, and R. Olsen. 2004. Focus on price execution: Ways to improve profitability. *Chemical Market Reporter* (October 4): 22–23.

Simpson, R. W. 1989. Using network flow techniques to find shadow prices for market and seat inventory control. *Technical Report Memorandum* M89-1. Cambridge, MA: MIT Flight Transportation Laboratory.

Smith, B. C., J. F. Leimkuhler, J. F., and R. M. Darrow. 1992. Yield management at American Airlines. *Interfaces* 22: 8–31.

Smith, N. C., P. J. Kaufmann, and G. Ortmeyer. 1991. Fairness in consumer pricing. *Journal of Consumer Policy* 14: 117–140.

Streitfeld, D. 2000. On the Web, price tags blur. *Washington Post* (Sept.): 27.

Talluri, K., and G. van Ryzin. 2003. Revenue management. In *Handbook of Transportation Science*. Boston: Kluwer, Chapter 16.

———. 2004. *The Theory and Practice of Revenue Management*. Boston: Kluwer.

Thompson, H. R. 1961. Statistical problems in airline reservation control. *Operations Research Quarterly* 12: 167–185.

Train, K. E. 2003. *Discrete Choice Methods with Simulation*. Cambridge, UK: Cambridge University Press.

Varian, H. R. 1992. *Microeconomic Analysis*, 3rd ed. New York: Norton.

———. 1987. *Intermediate Microeconomics*, 4th ed. New York: Norton.

Vives, X. 2001. *Oligopoly Pricing: Old Ideas and New Tools*. Cambridge, MA: MIT Press.

Wargo, L. G. 2000. Assessing the value in value-based pricing. *Datamation* (January): 11.

Warner, E. J., and R. B. Barski. 1995. The timing and magnitude of retail store markdowns: Evidence from weekends and holidays. *Quarterly Journal of Economics* 110: 321–352.

Welch, M. 2002. Value pricing: A viable software pricing metric. *Saugatuck Technology Strategic Perspectives* (July): 18.

Wild, D. 2002. Tom Petty is pissed. *Rolling Stone Magazine* (Oct.): 23.

Wilde, O. 1892. *Lady Windermere's Fan*. Mineola, NY: Dover.

Wilson, R. 1993. *Nonlinear Pricing*. Oxford, UK: Oxford University Press.

Winer, R. S. 1986. A reference price model of brand choice for frequently purchased products. *Journal of Consumer Research* 13: 250–256.

Wollmer. 1992. An airline seat management model for single leg routes when low-fare classes book first. *Operations Research* 40: 26–37.

INDEX

Italic page numbers indicate material in tables or figures. Page numbers followed by "n" indicate notes.